OPEN CANON

Open Canon

Scriptures of the Latter Day Saint Tradition

Edited by

CHRISTINE ELYSE BLYTHE
CHRISTOPHER JAMES BLYTHE
JAY BURTON

The University of Utah Press | Salt Lake City

The Defiance House Man colophon is a registered trademark
of The University of Utah Press. It is based on a four-foot-tall
Ancient Puebloan pictograph (late PIII) near Glen Canyon, Utah.

LIBRARY OF CONGRESS CATALOGING-IN-PUBLICATION DATA
Names: Blythe, Christine Elyse, editor. | Blythe, Christopher James, editor. | Burton, Jay (Jay
Alan), editor.
Title: Open canon : scriptures of the Latter Day Saint tradition / edited by Christine Blythe,
Christopher Blythe, Jay Burton.
Description: Salt Lake City : University of Utah Press, [2022] | Includes bibliographical
references and index. | Summary: "The publication of the Book of Mormon in 1830 began
a new scriptural tradition. Resisting the long-established closed biblical canon, the Book of
Mormon posited that the Bible was incomplete and corrupted. With a commitment to an open
canon, a variety of Latter Day Saint denominations have emerged to offer their own scriptural
works to accompany the Bible, the Book of Mormon, and other revelations of Joseph Smith.
Open Canon: Scriptures of the Latter Day Saint Tradition's chapters will introduce readers
to scripture dictated by nineteenth century revelators James Strang, William Bickerton, Lucy
Mack Smith, Charles B. Thompson, and Sidney Rigdon and scripture dictated by twentieth
century revelators Matthew Philip Gill, Harry Edgar Baker, Maurice Glendenning, and Denver
Snuffer. Other chapters detail how different Latter Day Saint denominations have responded to
those scriptures introduced during the ministry of Joseph Smith. How have the churches of the
Restoration responded to the Book of Mormon, the Doctrine and Covenants, and the Lectures
on Faith in the nearly two hundred years since they were introduced? Open Canon is the first
volume of its kind asking what we can learn about Latter Day Saint resistance to the closed
canon and the nature of a new American scriptural tradition by bringing in studies across
denominational boundaries"—Provided by publisher.
Identifiers: LCCN 2022012711 | ISBN 9781647690816 (cloth) | ISBN 9781647690823 (paperback) |
ISBN 9781647690830 (ebk)
Subjects: LCSH: Book of Mormon—Criticism, interpretation, etc. | Book of Mormon—Relation to
the Bible. | Church of Jesus Christ of Latter-day Saints—Doctrines.
Classification: LCC BX8627.A3 O64 2022 | DDC 289.3/22—dc23/eng/20220315
LC record available at https://lccn.loc.gov/2022012711

Errata and further information on this and other titles available online at UofUpress.com

Printed and bound in the United States of America.

We dedicate this book to JAN SHIPPS,
whose scholarship has always incorporated
the broader Latter Day Saint tradition.

CONTENTS

ACKNOWLEDGMENTS

We would like to express our thanks to the Neal A. Maxwell Institute for Religious Scholarship at Brigham Young University and the Church History Library of the Church of Jesus Christ of Latter-day Saints for their generous financial support of the project. Others involved directly with this volume include Jared Gillins, who assisted with copyediting, and Anna Allred and Hanna Seariac, who assisted with indexing.

A handful of chapters in this volume are based on articles that were previously published in academic journals. Thus, this volume benefitted from a layer of edits and reviews that took place before our own process. We are grateful to the editors and staff at *Brigham Young University Studies*, *John Whitmer Historical Association Journal*, *Journal of Mormon History*, *Journal of Religion, and Nova Religio*.

We also express our gratitude to those institutions that helped us acquire the images for this volume, including the Community of Christ Library and Archives in Independence, Missouri, the Church History Department in Salt Lake City, Utah, and Brigham Young University in Provo, Utah.

Finally, we are grateful to the John Whitmer Historical Association for providing a venue where we could first promote this project among scholars. *Open Canon* would likely not have come together if not for relationships built from conversations at the annual meeting throughout the years.

CHURCHES AND MOVEMENTS

This short list is included here to help readers identify and distinguish among denominations within the Latter Day Saint tradition. We acknowledge that many of these churches see themselves as a continuation of the original church organized by Joseph Smith in 1830. Describing their formations based on when they were seen as a unique community is not intended as a rebuttal to their internal understandings of continuity. For more information on these and other Latter Day Saint denominations, see Steven Shields's *Divergent Paths of the Restoration: An Encyclopedia of the Smith–Rigdon Movement* (Salt Lake City: Signature Books, 2021).

House of Aaron—Maurice Glendenning (1891–1969)
Also known as the Aaronic Order or the Order of Aaron, the church was founded in 1943 in Utah and remains active today. Its current headquarters are in Eskdale, Utah. While the House of Aaron has historical roots in the Latter Day Saint tradition, it no longer accepts Latter Day Saint scripture or embraces Joseph Smith as a prophetic figure.

Church of Christ—Sidney Rigdon (1793–1876)
One of the three major divisions of the Latter Day Saint tradition that coalesced in the months following Joseph Smith's assassination in 1844. The church's headquarters were in Pittsburgh, Pennsylvania. This was the first of two Latter Day Saint churches founded by Sidney Rigdon. The church collapsed in 1847. Rigdon later organized the Church of Jesus Christ of the Children of Zion, while William Bickerton rallied former Rigdon followers to a new organization, the Church of Jesus Christ. Members of the church have sometimes been called Rigdonites.

Church of Christ—Granville Hedrick (1814–1881)
Organized in 1863 in Illinois, the Church of Christ grew out of a movement of independent Latter Day Saint branches in the Nauvoo area. The church

is now headquartered in Independence, Missouri, where it owns the plot of land designated by Joseph Smith for the building of the temple in Zion. It is typically referred to as Church of Christ (Temple Lot) and its membership sometimes as the Hedrickites.

Church of Christ with the Elijah Message—William Draves (1912–1994)
Organized in 1943 in Independence, Missouri, in response to the revelations of Otto Fetting and William Draves. The original adherents were previously members of the Church of Christ (Temple Lot) but left when these new revelations were not heeded. There are now multiple communities that trace themselves to the original revelations of Otto and Draves.

Church of the Firstborn—Joseph Morris (1822–1862)
Organized in 1861 in Weber, Utah, in response to the revelations of Joseph Morris, who had recently been excommunicated from the Church of Jesus Christ of Latter-day Saints headquartered in Salt Lake City. Morris was killed as part of the "Morrisite War," a standoff between church members and the Utah militia. After this event, many church members gathered in Deer Creek, Montana, where the community continued until the late 1960s. The members of the church are sometimes referred to as Morrisites.

Church of the Firstborn of the Fulness of Times—Joel LeBaron
(1923–1972)
Founded in 1955 in Salt Lake City, Utah, the initial members of the Church of the Firstborn of the Fulness of Times had ties to Mormon fundamentalism. Others converted from the Church of Jesus Christ of Latter-day Saints. The headquarters of the Church of the Firstborn and official gathering place was in Colonia LeBaron, Mexico. After the assassination of Joel LeBaron in 1972 and the death of his successor, Verlan LeBaron in 1981, the church divided into multiple denominations.

Church of Jesus Christ—William Bickerton (1815–1905)
Formally founded in 1862 in Green Oak, Pennsylvania. William Bickerton's church was a reconstitution of many former members of Sidney Rigdon's Church of Christ. The church is today headquartered in Monongahela,

Pennsylvania with a membership worldwide of approximately 24,000. The members of the church are sometimes called Bickertonites.

Church of Jesus Christ of the Children of Zion—Sidney Rigdon (1793–1876)
Founded in 1863 in Philadelphia, Sidney Rigdon's second Latter Day Saint church had centers in Attica, Iowa, and Manitoba, Ontario. Membership estimated to be 200–300 members at its peak. The church disintegrated within a few years of Rigdon's death in 1876.

Congregation of Jehovah's Presbytery of Zion—Charles Thompson (1814–1895)
Founded in 1848 in St. Louis, Missouri. Charles Thompson had been a member of the church in the days of Joseph Smith, briefly aligned with Brigham Young and then James Strang. He began to dictate his own revelations and eventually formed a community. The name of this organization varied. Thompson and his followers founded a commune in Monona County, Iowa, but by 1858 he had been expelled from the community. Thompson continued to publish and spread his teachings into the 1870s.

Church of Jesus Christ of Latter Day Saints—James J. Strang (1813–1856)
One of the three major divisions of the Latter Day Saint tradition that coalesced in the months following Joseph Smith's assassination in 1844. James Strang, who was recognized as Prophet, Seer, and Revelator, initially called for believers to gather to Voree, Wisconsin. At the time of Strang's assassination in 1856, most of the church resided on Beaver Island in Lake Michigan. There are a few small congregations in Voree and elsewhere, as well as independent adherents. Members of the church are sometimes referred to as Strangites.

The Church of Jesus Christ of Latter-day Saints—Brigham Young (1801–1877)
One of the three major divisions of the Latter Day Saint tradition that coalesced in the months following Joseph Smith's assassination in 1844, bringing together the twelve apostles and a majority of the Latter Day Saints

living in and around Nauvoo. Brigham Young led his followers to the Great Basin and set up headquarters in Salt Lake City, Utah. The church currently records its worldwide membership at approximately 16.5 million members. Members of the church are commonly referred to as "LDS" and sometimes as Brighamites.

Latter Day Church of Christ/Restored Branch of Jesus Christ—Matthew P. Gill (1978–)
Founded in 2006 in Derbyshire, England. Matthew P. Gill was previously a member of the Church of Jesus Christ of Latter-day Saints. The Latter Day Church of Christ official website refers to the church as a "young but growing congregation of dedicated members." In 2019, it changed its name to the Restored Branch of Jesus Christ.

Reorganized Church of Jesus Christ of Latter Day Saints/ Community of Christ—(Joseph Smith III) (1832–1914)
Founded in the Midwest in the 1850s when Latter Day Saints who previously aligned with different Latter Day Saint denominations came together with the belief that one of Joseph Smith Jr.'s children would one day succeed his father. In 1860, Joseph Smith III was recognized as the Prophet, Seer, and Revelator of the church. In 2001, the Reorganized Church was renamed Community of Christ. It remains the second largest denomination of the Latter Day Saint tradition following the Church of Jesus Christ of Latter-day Saints with headquarters in Salt Lake City. Historically members were sometimes called Josephites.

Mormon Fundamentalism
Refers to a number of Latter Day Saint denominations, communities, and individuals that have coalesced from members of the Church of Jesus Christ of Latter-day Saints who reject the abandonment of plural marriage and other twentieth-century developments in that church. This term is sometimes used in a limited sense to refer to those communities that emerged from the teachings of Lorin C. Woolley in the 1920s and 1930s.

Remnant Church of Jesus Christ of Latter Day Saints—Frederick Niels Larsen (1932–2019)

Founded in 2000 in Independence, Missouri, the Remnant Church initially consisted of Restorationists who opposed theological developments in the Reorganized Church. In 2002, Frederick Niels Larsen, a great-great-grandson of Joseph Smith Jr. accepted the office of Prophet, Seer, and Revelator of the Church.

Restoration Branches
The Restoration Branches consist of loosely aligned Latter Day Saint congregations that formed in response to changes in the theology and practice of the Reorganized Church of Jesus Christ of Latter Day Saints. While there is not a central organization or headquarters, many of the branches are in Missouri. They first began to appear in the mid-1980s. The movement is held together by joint events, bookstores, and periodicals.

True and Living Church of Jesus Christ of Saints of the Last Days—
James D. Harmston (1940–2013)
Founded in 1994 in Manti, Utah, the True and Living Church of Jesus Christ of Saints of the Last Days initially consisted of members of the Church of Jesus Christ of Latter-day Saints with an affinity toward Mormon Fundamentalist theology and practices, including plural marriage. The church had attracted several hundred members by the late-1990s but met with attrition following a series of scandals and unfulfilled prophecies. Following Harmston's death in 2013, at least two denominations emerged claiming to continue the church as it existed under his leadership.

SELECT CHRONOLOGY

1830—The Book of Mormon, Joseph Smith Jr. (Palmyra, New York)

1833—The Book of Commandments, Joseph Smith Jr. (Independence, Missouri).

1835—The Doctrine and Covenants, Joseph Smith Jr. (Kirtland, Ohio); some revelations altered.

1837—The Book of Mormon, Joseph Smith Jr. (Kirtland, Ohio); second edition.

1840—The Book of Mormon, Joseph Smith Jr. (Nauvoo, Illinois); third edition.

1841—Evidence in Proof of the Book of Mormon, Charles B. Thompson (Batavia, New York); the first book length treatise on the Book of Mormon.

1842—The Words of Righteousness to All Men, James C. Brewster (Springfield, Illinois); first Installment of Book of Esdras.

1843—Revelation on Plural Marriage, Joseph Smith Jr. (Nauvoo, Illinois).

1844—Doctrine and Covenants, Joseph Smith Jr. (Nauvoo, Illinois); second edition with added revelations.

1845—The Voree Plates discovered and translated by James J. Strang (Voree, Wisconsin).

1845—Lucy Mack Smith dictates her history (Nauvoo, Illinois); first published in 1853 as Biographical Sketches of Joseph Smith the Prophet, and His Progenitors for Many Generations by Lucy Mack Smith, Mother of the Prophet.

1849—Revelations Given unto the Messenger of the Covenant, Jacob Syfritt (Philadelphia, Pennsylvania).

1851—The Book of the Law of the Lord, James J. Strang (Beaver Island, Michigan).

1851—Pearl of Great Price, Joseph Smith Jr. (Liverpool, England).

1851—Revelation on the New Organization, Jason Briggs (Beloit, Wisconsin).

1851—Mormons Bog, Joseph Smith Jr. (Copenhagen, Denmark); first published non-English-language translation of the Book of Mormon (Danish). The Church of Jesus Christ of Latter-day Saints has published translations in full or selections in ~120 languages. The Community of Christ and the Church of Jesus Christ (William Bickerton) have also published editions in several languages.

1852—The Book of Enoch the Prophet, Charles B. Thompson (St. Louis, Missouri); published serially in Zion's Harbinger, and Baneemy's Organ.

1852—Plural marriage taught openly by the Church of Jesus Christ of Latter-day Saints. Joseph Smith's 1843 revelation canonized in 1876 as Section 132 of the Doctrine and Covenants.

1855—A proclamation. And a warning voice unto all people . . . , Martin Harris (Cleveland, Ohio).

1856—First revelation by Sidney Rigdon (Friendship, New York); 100 revelations later compiled into Revelation Books A & B.

1856—The Book of the Law of the Lord, James J. Strang (Beaver Island, Michigan); expanded second edition was printed but not bound.

1857—First revelation by Joseph Morris (Provo, Utah); revelations later compiled and published in The Spirit Prevails.

1858—Book of Mormon, Joseph Smith Jr.; published by James O. Wright & Company (New York).

1864—Book of Doctrine and Covenants of The Church of Jesus Christ of Latter-Day Saints, Joseph Smith Jr. (Cincinnati, Ohio); first edition published by the Reorganized Church of Jesus Christ of Latter Day Saints.

1867—The Holy Scriptures, Translated and Corrected by the Spirit of Revelation, by Joseph Smith Jr., The Seer (Plano, Illinois); first edition published by the Reorganized Church of Jesus Christ of Latter Day Saints.

1874—Book of Mormon, Joseph Smith Jr. (Plano, Illinois); first edition published by the Reorganized Church of Jesus Christ of Latter Day Saints.

1878—Reorganized Church of Jesus Christ of Latter Day Saints approves resolution to include Joseph Smith III revelations in the Book of Doctrine and Covenants. Sections 114–118 first appear in the 1882 edition. Precedent set for including revelations of subsequent Prophet-Presidents of the Church in later editions.

1879—Book of Mormon, Joseph Smith Jr. (Salt Lake City, Utah); includes versification of text, edited by Orson Pratt.

1880—Pearl of Great Price canonized by the Church of Jesus Christ of Latter-day Saints.

1890—Manifesto issued; later canonized in 1908 as an Official Declaration in the Doctrine and Covenants of the Church of Jesus Christ of Latter-day Saints.

1897—Reorganized Church of Jesus Christ of Latter Day Saints removes the Lectures on Faith from the Doctrine and Covenants.

1908—Book of Mormon, Joseph Smith Jr. (Lamoni, Iowa). The Reorganized Church of Jesus Christ of Latter Day Saints published what became known as the "authorized version," which included many textual changes based on the printer's manuscript of the Book of Mormon and a new versification of the text.

1917—The Word of the Lord to His Church in the Wilderness, Harry Edgar Baker (Chicago, Illinois).

1920—Book of Mormon, Joseph Smith Jr. (Salt Lake City, Utah); includes double columns, footnotes, and chapter summaries; edited by James Talmage.

1922—The Four Hidden Revelations, John Taylor and Wilford Woodruff (Salt Lake City, Utah); revelations received between 1880 and 1889 on plural marriage.

1921—The Church of Jesus Christ of Latter-day Saints removes the Lectures on Faith from the Doctrine and Covenants.

1927—First revelation by Otto Fetting (Port Huron, Michigan); revelations later compiled and published in The Word of the Lord.

1930—Latter-Day Revelation: Selections from the Book of Doctrine and Covenants (Salt Lake City, Utah).

1937—First revelation by William Draves (Nucla, Colorado); revelations later complied, combined with those of Otto Fetting, and published in The Word of the Lord Brought to Mankind by an Angel.

1955—Revelation given to Rulon C. Allred through the medium of Joel F. LeBaron (Salt Lake City, Utah).

1957—The Book of Mormon (Independence, Missouri); first edition published by the Church of Christ (Temple Lot).

1957—The Record of the Nephites, translated by the gift and power of God, Joseph Smith Jr. being the human instrument (Independence, Missouri); first edition of the Book of Mormon published by the Church of Christ with the Elijah Message.

1966—Book of Mormon, Joseph Smith Jr. (Independence, Missouri); The Reorganized Church of Jesus Christ of Latter Day Saints published the revised authorized version.

1969—The Book of Onias, Robert Crossfield (New York); later published with additional revelations as The Second Book of Commandments.

1978—Levitical Writings, Maurice Glendenning (Eskdale, Utah).

1981—The Church of Jesus Christ of Latter-day Saints published new editions of the King James Bible, Book of Mormon, Doctrine and Covenants, and Pearl of Great Price. The Book of Mormon includes index, topical guide, new chapter summaries and footnotes, and corrections to the text based on the original manuscript and the 1840 edition.

1983—Oracles of Mohonri: An account written by the hand of Mohonri Moriancumer upon gold plates taken from the sealed portion of the Book of Mormon, Davied Israel (Washington, Utah).

1987—Hidden Treasures and Promises: A compilation of sacred scriptures and inspired writings, Antonio Feliz and John Crane (Salt Lake City, Utah).

1990—First revelation by Jim Harmston (Manti, Utah); revelations later compiled in The Manti Revelation Book.

1994—Sacred Scriptures, Mike Rigby (Orem, Utah).

2001—Sealed Portion of the Brother of Jared, Ronald Livingston (Leawood, Kansas).

2002—First revelation by Frederick N. Larsen (Independence, Missouri); revelations compiled into Remnant Church of Jesus Christ of Latter Day Saints Doctrine and Covenants.

2004—The Sealed Portion: The Final Testament of Jesus Christ, Christopher Nemelka (Salt Lake City, Utah).

2006—The Book of Revelations, Fred C. Collier (Hannah, Utah).

2007—The Book of Jeraneck, Matthew Philip Gill (Peterborough, England).

2012—Jesus Christ Message to All Nations, Warren Jeffs (Colorado City, Arizona).

2018—The Restoration Edition of the Scriptures, Denver Snuffer (Boise, Idaho); includes previously uncanonized revelations of Joseph Smith and the revelations of Denver Snuffer.

2019—The Sealed Book of Mormon, Mauricio Berger (Brazil).

SOURCES AND ABBREVIATIONS

Abbreviations for Organizations

CC/CofC   Community of Christ
FARMS   Foundation for Ancient Research and Mormon Studies
LDS   The Church of Jesus Christ of Latter-day Saints
RLDS   Reorganized Church of Jesus Christ of Latter Day Saints

Abbreviations for Repositories

BYU   L. Tom Perry Special Collections, Harold B. Lee Library
           Brigham Young University, Provo, Utah
CCLA   Community of Christ Library-Archives, Independence,
           Missouri
CHL   Church History Library, The Church of Jesus Christ of Latter-
           day Saints, Salt Lake City

Abbreviations for Sources

JSP, A1   Matthew J. Grow, Ronald K. Esplin, Mark Ashurst-McGee,
           Gerrit J. Dirkmaat, and Jeffrey D. Mahas, eds. Council of
           Fifty, Minutes, March 1844–January 1846. First volume of the
           Administrative Records series of the Joseph Smith Papers,
           edited by Ronald K. Esplin, Matthew J. Grow, and Mat-
           thew C. Godfrey. Salt Lake City: Church Historian's Press,
           2016.
JSP, D1   Michael Hubbard MacKay, Gerrit J. Dirkmaat, Grant Under-
           wood, Robert J. Woodford, and William G. Hartley, eds.
           Documents, vol. 1: July 1828–June 1831. Volume 1 of the Doc-
           ument series of the Joseph Smith Papers, edited by Dean C.
           Jessee, Ronald K. Esplin, and Richard Lyman Bushman. Salt
           Lake City: Church Historian's Press, 2013.

JSP, D2   Matthew C. Godfrey, Mark Ashurst-McGee, Grant Underwood, Robert J. Woodford, and William G. Hartley, eds. Documents, vol. 2: July 1831–January 1833. Volume 2 of the Documents series of the Joseph Smith Papers, edited by Dean C.
Jessee, Ronald K. Esplin, Richard Lyman Bushman, and Matthew J. Grow. Salt Lake City: Church Historian's Press, 2013.

JSP, D3   Gerrit J. Dirkmaat, Brent M. Rogers, Grant Underwood, Robert J. Woodford, and William G. Hartley, eds. Documents,
vol. 3: February 1833–March 1834. Volume 3 of the Documents series of the Joseph Smith Papers, edited by Ronald K.
Esplin and Matthew J. Grow. Salt Lake City: Church Historian's Press, 2014.

JSP, D4   Matthew C. Godfrey, Brenden W. Rensink, Alex D. Smith,
Max H. Parkin, and Alexander L. Baugh, eds. Documents,
vol. 4: April 1834–September 1835. Volume 4 of the Documents series of the Joseph Smith Papers, edited by Ronald K.
Esplin and Matthew J. Grow. Salt Lake City: Church Historian's Press, 2016.

JSP, D7   Matthew C. Godfrey, Spencer W. McBride, Alex D. Smith,
and Christopher James Blythe, eds. Documents, vol. 7: September 1839–January 1841. Vol. 7 of the Documents series
of The Joseph Smith Papers, edited by Ronald K. Esplin,
Matthew J. Grow, and Matthew C. Godfrey. Salt Lake City:
Church Historian's Press, 2018.

JSP, D12   David W. Grua, Brent M. Rogers, Matthew C. Godfrey, Robin
Scott Jensen, Christopher James Blythe, and Jessica M. Nelson, eds. Documents, vol. 12: March–July 1843. Volume 12 of
the Documents series of The Joseph Smith Papers, edited by
Matthew C. Godfrey, R. Eric Smith, Matthew J. Grow, and
Ronald K. Esplin. Salt Lake City: Church Historian's Press,
2021.

Citations to the Book of Mormon
Individual chapters cite different versions of the Book of Mormon. For the general reader, the books within the Book of Mormon appear here.

1 Nephi
2 Nephi
Jacob
Enos
Jarom
Omni
Words of Mormon
Mosiah
Alma
Helaman
3 Nephi
4 Nephi
Ether
Mormon
Moroni

Citations to the Pearl of Great Price
Moses
Abraham
Joseph Smith-Matthew
Joseph Smith-History
Articles of Faith

FOREWORD
Philip L. Barlow

"He who is ignorant of foreign languages knows not his own." This once-startling insight, often shortened to, "He who knows but one language knows none," is a bequest of Germany's famous polymath, Johann von Goethe, who penned it around the time of Joseph Smith's first vision. The idea seems simple; its implications are large. There are limits to what we can know of human consciousness, of what it means even to be human, unless we can think about language as such. And we can't do that well unless we can competently contrast with something quite different the deep structures, history, social components, and psychology of our native tongue. We understand heat modestly when we cook or are burnt by the sun, but physicists can tell us more. Similarly, we understand "language" to the extent that we become linguists.

Half a century after Goethe wrote, Max Müller applied his countryman's insight to religion: "He who knows [but] one, knows none."[1] Goethe was a genius and Müller not far behind—a pioneer who made possible the scholarly study of religion in the modern sense. Both men were right about the need for comparison.

The importance of the book you are about to read resides in an extension of Goethe and Müller. We do not understand the complex religion emerging from the life and work of the antebellum American prophet Joseph Smith if we fail to grapple with his relation to scripture. And we understand neither scripture nor Smith's connection to it merely by reading it. We must also ask comparative questions about what defines it, how it came to be, how it evolved, what influenced its formation and achievement of canonical status, what influences its changing and contested interpretation, and what influences it unleashed among its adherents. We cannot comprehend scripture's character unless we grasp its potential for assuming alternate forms.

---

1. Goethe expressed his comparative imperative in multiple places, perhaps first in 1821 in his journal *Kunst und Altertum* (About Art and Antiquity). See F. Max Müller, "Introduction to the Science of Religion," in *Classical Approaches to the Study of Religion*, edited by Jacques Waardenburg, 91. The Hague: Mouton, 1973.

The most obvious path to beginning to appreciate this potential is, of course, to study the alternate forms and processes it has already donned among Joseph Smith's diverse, aspiring heirs. The promise of comparison is keenest when the entities being compared are half-familiar and half-strange in relation to one another. It is then that similarities and contrasts and underlying character are thrown into greatest relief.

The materials for engaging such comparison are precisely what the judicious and imaginative editorial eyes of Christopher Blythe, Christine Blythe, and Jay Burton have afforded us by collecting the disparate work of leading scholars and newer voices in *Open Canon: Scriptures of the Latter Day Saint Tradition*. In this comparative terrain, which does not neglect any of the three centuries in which Mormonism has flourished, we can better ponder what scripture is. We can probe the process by which it was "scripturalized." We can consider the relation of scripture to authority, to coherence or schism, to the coalescence and evolution or devolution of canon, and to rival conceptions of how to be religious and prophetic within this sprouting, dynamic tradition. We can, in short, better understand how an essential dimension of religion functions.

Open Canon warrants study. After all, a person who knows but one canon, knows none.

PART I

Introductory Essays

Opening the Canon
A New Scriptural Tradition
Christopher James Blythe

The late 1820s saw the birth of a new scriptural tradition. During this time, Joseph Smith dictated the first Latter Day Saint scripture to a series of scribes who diligently recorded his words. In March 1830, their efforts appeared in print as the Book of Mormon. The following month, Smith was recognized as "prophet, seer, and revelator," as well as "translator," of the newly organized Church of Christ.[1] While Smith never finished another book-length work, he was a prolific revelator. He revised portions of the King James Bible, revealed texts from the viewpoints of ancient biblical figures, and dictated numerous revelations.

A selection of these revelations was compiled as the Book of Commandments in 1833 and two years later, in an expanded form, as the Doctrine and Covenants. His writings found a receptive audience among the growing church that coupled its devotion to the Bible with a reverence for new scriptures. Some scholars have emphasized the disproportionate use of the Bible compared to the Book of Mormon in early Mormonism, but even if these records were neglected, the Bible was no longer the same once it was read through the lens of new revelation.[2] It was neither Protestant nor Roman Catholic, but over the course of Smith's ministry, Mormons learned to read

1. Joseph Smith, Revelation, April 6, 1830, in *JSP*, D1:129.
2. Terryl L. Givens, *By the Hand of Mormon: The American Scripture That Launched a New World Religion* (New York: Oxford University Press, 2002), 63-64; Janiece Johnson, "Becoming a People of the Books: Toward an Understanding of Early Mormon Converts and the New Word of the Lord," *Journal of Book of Mormon Studies* 27 (2018):1–43; Grant Underwood, "Book of Mormon Usage in Early LDS Theology," *Dialogue: A Journal of Mormon Thought* 17 (1984):35–74.

the Bible in innovative ways, reinterpreting well-known stories to fit their new tradition.

The Latter Day Saint scriptural tradition included a foundational assumption that scripture was perpetually incomplete and corruptible. The Bible was divine, but human transmission had tainted the text. According to the Book of Mormon, the Bible had "many plain and precious things taken away from the book" sometime in the distant past.[3] Other equally significant scriptures had been forgotten or hidden from the modern world. The Book of Mormon promised the return of several of these works.[4] Smith later prophesied the return of others.[5] Perhaps most importantly, God's revelations to the ancients were not his final statements to mankind. Latter Day Saints expected further revelation, which their prophets could provide.

Smith's revelatory works and their corresponding assumptions on scripture soon found an audience that extended beyond the boundaries of a single Christian church. Several notable stalwarts of the faith remained committed to the Book of Mormon and Smith's revelations even when they abandoned the church that it produced and long after they came to consider Joseph Smith a "fallen prophet." For these dissenters, the Latter Day Saint scriptural tradition—the Bible, the Book of Mormon, and often the Doctrine and Covenants—stood on its own merits. Schism would produce additional communities, eventually numbering in the hundreds, that reverenced the scriptural tradition. Viewed in this light, what it meant to be a Latter Day Saint had more to do with the mutual commitment and understanding of scripture than it did with denominational affiliation. This is substantiated by the fact that many Latter Day Saints in the years after Smith's death joined one denomination and then another with only the scriptural tradition providing a continuity of belief.

The early church looked to Joseph Smith as the sole source of new scripture. Indeed, Smith's revelations forbade others from dictating the word of God for the church.[6] Only a few dissidents challenged this prohibition during his lifetime. However, with the splintering of the tradition at Smith's death, several new prophets, seers, and revelators took to scripture-writing.

3. 1 Nephi 13:28 (LDS, CofC).

4. 1 Nephi 5:18 (LDS)/1 Nephi 1:169 (CofC); 2 Nephi 29:13 (LDS)/2 Nephi 12:71–72 (CofC); Ether 4:5–6 (LDS)/ Ether 1:98–100 (CofC).

5. D&C 107:57.

6. Joseph Smith, Revelation, September 1830-B, in *JSP*, D1:186 (D&C 28:11).

FIGURE 1.1. "The Angel Moroni Delivering the Golden Plates to Joseph Smith." Engraving from *Reminiscences of Joseph, the Prophet, and the Coming Forth of the Book of Mormon*, by Edward Stevenson (1893). Courtesy of the Church History Library, the Church of Jesus Christ of Latter-day Saints.

The Book of Mormon, the Doctrine and Covenants, and Smith's smaller scriptural works were now accompanied by the Book of the Law of the Lord, the Book of Enoch, the Book of Esdras, and the Book of Remembrance, as well as numerous dictated revelations and visionary writings. Over the next 175 years, hundreds of texts written and presented as scripture provided the foundation for new prophetic claims. This literature has seldom been the subject of scholarly analysis.[7] *Open Canon: Scriptures of the Latter Day Saint Tradition* seeks to examine these writings as a singular scriptural tradition. Chapters focus on (1) texts considered extracanonical from the perspective of the Church of Jesus Christ of Latter-day Saints, the largest and most well-known segment of the Latter Day Saint tradition, (2) how churches within the Latter Day Saint tradition have responded to the scriptures and revelations introduced by Joseph Smith, and (3) how the process of scripturalization—including revelation, translation, and artifact discovery—played out among later generations of Latter Day Saints.

DEFINING AND CATEGORIZING SCRIPTURE AND CANON

For the purposes of this volume, what makes a text "scripture" is not based on its content but on its presentation and/or reception. "Scripture" only exists where someone has categorized it as such. If the author or revelator of a text understands such writings as scripture belonging to the Latter Day Saint tradition and alone holds such a belief, we study it as "scripture" here.

While we employ a broad understanding of scripture as texts identified by someone as such, it is key to recognize that within religious traditions the category is contested. Institutions leverage formal or informal processes of canonization to construct boundaries around what is and is not scripture and for good reason: a book defined as scripture possesses a special kind of authority for a community of believers. By establishing a canon, they can define orthodoxy. In early Christianity, the New Testament canon was a means to stem the tide of heresies, and it continued to function that way among American Christians in the nineteenth century. The boundaries that

---

7. The only notable exception is George Bartholomew Arbaugh, *Revelation in Mormonism: Its Character and Changing Forms* (Chicago: University of Chicago Press, 1932).

created the accepted Judeo-Christian Bible were likely the greatest impediment for the spread of the Book of Mormon. Even before this objection was leveraged against Mormons, the Book of Mormon predicted that people would respond to new scripture by declaring: "A Bible! A Bible! We have got a Bible, and there cannot be any more Bible!"[8] The argument between a closed and open canon was at the core of Latter Day Saint identity.

The Latter Day Saint tradition has also used canonization to prevent heterodox texts from attaining the status of scripture. While official canonizations of scripture are rare among all Latter Day Saint denominations, the process by which texts can be deemed such was seemingly implied in the canonization of scripture that occurred during Smith's lifetime. New authentic scripture must be revealed by the prophet, seer, and revelator, and it must be ratified by the church's membership. The first of these rules has always been more important than the latter. On one hand, the canon is "open" in the Latter Day Saint tradition so that it allows the addition of new works. On the other, the high level of regulation, by design, precludes most works from attaining an institutionally recognized scriptural status.

THE JOSEPH SMITH CANON

While our definition of scripture would include a vast number of noncanonized works, an awareness of the standard Latter Day Saint canon is crucial to understanding the types of works that Latter Day Saint prophets and adherents might categorize as scripture. The standard canon (or Joseph Smith canon) as it existed in 1844 consisted of only three books. The first was the Bible, which, according to the Articles of Faith, Latter Day Saints accepted "as far as it is translated correctly."[9] Between 1830 and 1833, Smith had undertaken the task of correcting the Old and New Testaments, a project he referred to as the "new translation," but that would also come to be known as the Inspired Version of the Bible. Over 3,410 corrections, deletions, and additions were made to the text of the King James Version.[10] While Latter Day Saints knew about this project, the corrections were not

8. 2 Nephi 29:3 (LDS)/2 Nephi 12:45 (CofC).
9. Articles of Faith 1:8.
10. Philip Barlow, *Mormons and the Bible: The Place of the Latter-day Saints in American Religion* (New York: Oxford University Press, 1991), 50.

available to the average Saint during his lifetime. Thus, church members used the King James Version even as they occasionally listened to sermons in which Joseph Smith, Hyrum Smith, and others theologized on the meaning in the original languages. Philip Barlow was correct in his assessment that there was no official translation of the Bible in the early church, even though the King James Version was the standard translation—as was the case generally among English-speaking Christians who were not Roman Catholics.

The second book in the 1844 standard canon was the Book of Mormon, which by 1840 was on its third edition. Alterations were made to the text in 1837 and 1840. The second edition (1837) incorporated thousands of changes to the text. Most were grammatical, but there were a few significant changes, such as altering references that describe the divinity of Jesus. In four instances, where Christ was referred to as God or the Eternal Father, the text was changed to state "son of God" or "son of the Eternal Father."[11] In 1840, Joseph Smith and Ebenezer Robinson compared the two editions of the Book of Mormon, as well as the original manuscripts. In addition to grammatical changes, they made a handful of significant alterations. For instance, in one place a reference to "white and delightsome people" was altered to "pure and delightsome people."[12]

Finally, the Joseph Smith canon included a collection of Smith's revelations first published as the Book of Commandments in 1833. The collection was expanded and published as the Doctrine and Covenants in 1835. In 1844, it was enlarged by eight sections and concluded with a document memorializing Smith's assassination. The Bible, Book of Mormon, and a collection of revelations—the Book of Commandments/Doctrine and Covenants—were the standard canon during the lifetime of Joseph Smith. With the exception of the Church of Jesus Christ (Cutlerite), one of the very smallest Latter Day Saint denominations, no denominations have tried to maintain the canon exactly as it stood at Smith's death. The canon has either expanded or retracted in each continuation of the Restoration.

11. David J. Whittaker, "'That Most Important of All Books': A Printing History of the Book of Mormon," *Mormon Historical Studies* 6 (Fall 2005):109–110.

12. 2 Nephi 30:6; Kyle R. Walker, "'As Fire Shut Up in My Bones': Ebenezer Robinson, Don Carlos Smith, Joseph Smith, and the 1840 Edition of the Book of Mormon," *Journal of Mormon History* 36, no. 1 (Winter 2010):18.

CATEGORIZING LATTER DAY SAINT SCRIPTURE

There are six broad categories of Latter Day Saint scriptural texts: (1) historical translations, (2) revealed translations, (3) correction literature, (4) dictated revelation, (5) visionary accounts, and (6) contemporary documents from church leaders.

Historical translations denotes scriptures in non-English manuscripts made accessible through scholarly translation and adopted by Latter Day Saint communities. In the church as it existed at Smith's death, the only historical translations were the Old and New Testaments. In the twentieth century, smaller Latter Day Saint denominations have accepted the Dead Sea Scrolls and the Nag Hammadi corpus. Other works, such as the Book of Jasher, the Testaments of the Twelve Patriarchs, and 1 Enoch were widely read and cited among Latter Day Saints.[13]

Many instances of Latter Day Saint scripture fall under the category of *revealed translations*. These texts differ from historical translations in that they are brought about by supernatural means, although they are also believed to originate as ancient writings. Often, revealed translations relate to physical artifacts, which may or may not be available to those not involved in the translation. In the case of the Book of Mormon, Joseph Smith was led by an angel to the original record, interred over a millennium earlier. The record was engraved on gold plates in "Reformed Egyptian," which he was able to translate into English through a revelatory device—the "Urim and Thummim," or a seer stone. Several other Latter Day Saint prophets have also claimed to have had access to the Urim and Thummim by which they brought forth their revealed translations. This was the case with James Strang's Book of the Law of the Lord, and recently Christopher Nemelka's The Sealed Portion and Mauricio Berger's Sealed Book of Mormon.

Revealed translations have also come forward through other revelatory means. In fact, any means of supernaturally transmitting the words of an ancient revelation into modern tongues is a revealed translation, regardless

---

13. Articles on the Book of Jasher and Book of Enoch appeared in Latter-day Saint periodicals. See "The Book of Jasher," *Times and Seasons*, June 1840, Parley P. Pratt; "The Apocryphal Book of Enoch," *Millennial Star*, July 1840. In 1843, a Latter Day Saint, Samuel Downes, printed an edition of *The Testament of the Twelve Patriarchs* in England (*The Testament of the Twelve Patriarchs* [Manchester, 1843]).

of whether it involved a source manuscript or was identified by the revelator as a "translation." This was the case with the Book of Moses and Extract from the Prophecy of Enoch, both of which emerged from Smith's new translation of the Bible.

The third category, *correction literature*, refers to scriptural works that began as a historical translation but that have subsequently undergone revealed alterations. These changes are usually presented to make the translated text conform to an original and unavailable autograph copy of an ancient manuscript subsequently corrupted by scribes or translators. Thus, correction literature comes about as a fusion of historical and revealed translation methods. Smith's only effort to restore a scriptural text through an already translated version occurred with the "new translation" of the Old and New Testaments. Perhaps because of an 1833 revelation instructing Smith not to translate the Apocrypha, correction literature has been rare since.[14] Charles B. Thompson's correction of the Book of Enoch, published in the 1850s, may be the earliest example of correction literature since the "new translation." Only a few have followed. Some of these include works translated by Christopher Nemelka (Book of Malachi based on the book of Malachi in the Hebrew scriptures) and John W. Bryant (Testament of Mary based on the Gospel of Mary).

Dictated revelation refers to texts originating with deity and supernaturally bestowed to a prophet. They are sometimes spoken and recorded by scribes; sometimes they are drafted by the revelator. Usually, in the Latter Day Saint tradition, such texts are examples of what Terryl Givens refers to as dialogic revelations. That is, they come in response to specific questions asked by the prophet.[15] Some churches have added their dictated revelations to new editions of the Doctrine and Covenants, as has been the case with the Utah-based Church of Jesus Christ of Latter-day Saints and the Reorganized Church. Some have added new volumes, such as the Church of the Firstborn (Morrisite)'s The Spirit Prevails, the House of Aaron's Levitical Writings, or the School of the Prophets' Second Book of Commandments.

The fifth category of Latter Day Saint scripture is *visionary accounts*. Visionary texts abounded in early America and were intimately connected to the world of scripture, whether one accepted the Protestant position of

14. Joseph Smith, Revelation, March 9, 1833, in *JSP*, D3:35.
15. Givens, *By the Hand of Mormon*, 217–218.

sola scriptura or not.[16] After all, the Old Testament included several elaborate visions, and the New Testament concluded with the extensive visions of John the Revelator. Early Latter Day Saints were part of that visionary culture and regularly shared their dreams and visions; this was true of Joseph Smith as well. Oddly, only one of Joseph Smith's visions appeared in the established canon during his lifetime—his grand view of the kingdoms of heaven that he shared with Sidney Rigdon.[17] Perhaps because of its novelty as much as its revolutionary teachings, this document was referred to by the Saints as "the vision." Smith spoke of other visions and recorded a number in his personal history. Some of these would be added to future editions of the Doctrine and Covenants published after his death. The visions of other prophets were sometimes added to new volumes. For instance, the visions of Otto Fetting and William A. Draves were collected in the Church of Christ with the Elijah Message's Word of the Lord Brought to Mankind by an Angel.

Finally, *contemporary documents from church leaders* encompasses all scripturalized documents that are not themselves translations or revelations. For example, in 1835, a statement on the church's position on secular governments was added at the close of Doctrine and Covenants with no pretense of a revelatory declaration. A similar statement in favor of monogamous marriage was also included in the 1835 Doctrine and Covenants. When a revelation commanding plural marriage became a part of the Doctrine and Covenants in 1876, the 1835 statement was removed with little controversy. The Pearl of Great Price included two other documents that deserve notice. The first was the Articles of Faith, which included thirteen statements of Latter-day Saint belief and were contained in a letter Smith wrote to a Chicago journalist, John Wentworth. The second was Joseph Smith's personal history, which had been serialized in the church's periodical.

OVERVIEW

Open Canon is divided into four parts with a total of sixteen chapters. Part one features this introduction as well as two additional introductory chapters.

16. For an important discussion on the relationship between vision narratives and the category of scripture, see Seth Perry, *Bible Culture and Authority in the Early United States* (Princeton University Press, 2018), chap. 4.

17. D&C 91 (1835); D&C 76 (LDS and CofC).

The first of these—Laurie Maffly-Kipp's "Anchored by Revelation: Scripture and Schism in the Restoration"—was delivered in 2013 as the Richard P. Howard Lecture at the annual John Whitmer Historical Association conference. Maffly-Kipp argues for the significance of "scriptural logic" in understanding Latter Day Saint schism. Her essay begins by contextualizing Latter Day Saint scripture with other examples of scriptural innovation in early America. She then turns to the earliest instance of an extensive revealed translation dictated by a Saint who was not Joseph Smith—James Brewster's Books of Esdras—and concludes by contrasting the approach toward scripture taken by the Reorganized Church and the Utah-based Church of Jesus Christ of Latter-day Saints.

The second introductory chapter, Richard Saunders's "Revelation, Scripture, and Authority in the Latter Day Saint Diaspora," takes a different approach. While Maffly-Kipp discusses the Latter Day Saint expansion of the biblical canon in the context of the appearance of other nineteenth-century scripture, Saunders sees the Latter Day Saint scriptural tradition as exceptional. He argues that the Book of Mormon and other scripture represented the ultimate rupture with Protestantism and its defining commitment to *sola scriptura*. Saunders documents the proliferation of new scripture throughout the Latter Day Saint diaspora and concludes by showing how eventually the once-scattered movement, now largely coalesced into the Reorganization and Church of Christ (Temple Lot), came to rein in new revelations and condensed its scriptural record to the basics of the canon.

Part II, Reception of Joseph Smith's Revelations, features four chapters that explore how Latter Day Saint denominations responded to the standard Latter Day Saint canon after Smith's death. Chapter 4, "Books of Mormon: Latter-day Saints, Latter Day Saints, and the Book of Mormon," by Joseph Spencer, demonstrates how the Book of Mormon continued to evolve under different sets of readers. Spencer documents the parallel development of the Book of Mormon text and paratext in the Reorganized Church of Jesus Christ of Latter Day Saints/Community of Christ and the Church of Jesus Christ of Latter-day Saints. Chapter five, Chrystal Vanel's "The Church of Christ (Temple Lot): A Solae Scripturae Mormonism," examines how the church founded by Granville Hedrick in 1857 eventually came to limit its canon to the Bible and the Book of Mormon. It even rejected the Doctrine and Covenants but continued to revere Smith's early revelations as published in the Book of Commandments.

Chapters 6 and 7 examine how the Doctrine and Covenants expanded and retracted in subsequent editions published by the Utah-based Church of Jesus Christ of Latter-day Saints. In Chapter 6, "Joseph Smith's Letter from Liberty Jail: A Study in Canonization," Kathleen Flake documents how letters written by Joseph Smith while he was imprisoned were edited to create three sections when Orson Pratt directed the publication of a new edition of the Doctrine and Covenants in 1876. Chapter 7, "The Lectures on Faith in the Latter Day Saint Tradition," by Richard S. Van Wagoner, Steven C. Walker, Allen D. Roberts, and Christine Elyse Blythe, examines the reasons undergirding the removal of the Lectures on Faith from the two largest denominations of the Latter Day Saint tradition in 1897 and 1921 respectively, as well as the Lectures' continued uses and subsequent reactions in the larger tradition.

Part III, Case Studies in New Scripture: Nineteenth Century, covers new scripture in five different denominations of the nineteenth-century Latter Day Saint diaspora. Chapter 8 is Janiece Johnson's "Lucy Mack Smith and Her Sacred Text," which examines Lucy Mack Smith, the mother of Joseph Smith, as a visionary in her own right. Johnson introduces readers both to a small selection of revelations that "Mother Smith" wrote in the year after Joseph and Hyrum's assassination, as well as the production and reception of Mother Smith's History as a scriptural text. In Chapter 9, "Strangite Scripture," Christine Elyse Blythe and Christopher James Blythe examine the variety of scripture produced by James Strang, the most prolific of those prophets to immediately arise in the wake of Smith's death. Chapter 10, Christopher James Blythe's "The Book of Enoch 'Revised, Corrected, and the Missing Parts Restored,'" considers the construction of one of the few nineteenth-century examples of correction literature. Charles B. Thompson presented his followers with his own inspired revision of the Book of Enoch. The original historical translation from the Ethiopian was published in English in 1821 by Richard Laurence. Christopher Blythe shows that the book had already garnered Latter Day Saint attention a decade before Thompson restored what he believed was the original text. Blythe argues that under Thompson, the Book of Enoch became a text condemning plural marriage and the plurality of gods as promoted in The Church of Jesus Christ of Latter-day Saints under Brigham Young.

Chapter 11, Daniel P. Stone's "William Bickerton's Cooperative View on Scripture and Revelation," looks at a movement that coalesced around

William Bickerton in the 1850s. Unlike early Latter Day Saint revelations that placed the role of revelator in the church's leader alone, the Church of Jesus Christ had a singular egalitarian model for revelation. Stone has uncovered a variety of previously unstudied materials from the church, which make this a particularly fascinating contribution. Chapter 12, "Scriptures for the Children of Zion: The Revelations of Sidney and Phebe Rigdon," by Jay Burton, inspects two manuscript books containing over a hundred revelations dictated by Sidney Rigdon beginning in the 1860s. During the lifetime of Joseph Smith, Rigdon was a prominent Latter Day Saint leader, but he moved into relative obscurity after Smith's assassination. He led a short-lived church in Philadelphia until its dissolution in 1847. These revelations were directed to the second church Rigdon founded and that he led via correspondence. The manuscripts were likely intended for eventual publication.

The fourth and final section, Case Studies in New Scripture: Twentieth and Twenty-First Centuries, presents four chapters examining new Latter Day Saint scripture after 1900. Chapter 13, "Harry Edgar Baker and the Word of the Lord," by Thomas J. Evans and Christopher James Blythe, is a fascinating study of a two-part revelation dictated by Harry Edgar Baker in 1916 and 1917 respectively. Evans and Blythe suggest that while Baker may have held sympathies for the burgeoning Mormon fundamentalist movement his revelations are not very enlightening. The Word of the Lord was a cry for the nation to repent, rather than the revealed foundation of a new movement. Instead, Evans and Blythe show how a variety of dissenters from the Utah-based church found meaning in the obscure revelation. In Chapter 14, "The Levitical Writings of the House of Aaron," Casey Paul Griffiths examines another dissenting movement from the Utah-based church. Beginning in the 1930s, Maurice Glendenning revealed a new communal faith based on the idea that he and his followers were descendants of the ancient Levites and would continue their priestly responsibilities. While Glendenning and his followers eventually discarded the Book of Mormon and the Doctrine and Covenants as scriptural texts, Griffith demonstrates how the earliest Levitical revelations were in conversation with the Latter Day Saint tradition from which it emerged.

Chapter 15, Christopher C. Smith's "The Hidden Records of Central Utah and the Struggle for Religious Authority," documents John Brewer's discovery of engraved stone tablets near Manti, Utah. Through this case study, he examines the role artifacts have played in the history of Latter Day Saint scripture. Chapter 16, "Matthew Philip Gill and the Dynamics of Mormon Schism," by Matthew Bowman, examines a twenty-first-century prophet from Great Britain. Gill had revealed the Book of Jeraneck in 2007 after founding the Latter Day Church of Christ. Bowman is particularly interested in the ways that Gill's Book of Jeraneck interacts with the Book of Mormon. The new scripture tells a story much like that of the Book of Mormon, following a group of believers who have left the Middle East to build their own civilization in the British Isles. As with the Book of Mormon, their prophets present a message of warning to the modern world.

DENOMINATIONAL TERMINOLOGY

There is no consensus among scholars as to what term best encompasses the hundreds of institutions with their heritage in the 1830 Church of Christ. Over the past decade, the term "Mormonisms" has perhaps been the most popular in scholarly circles. It nicely recognized the plurality of denominations as well as their shared heritage. It was particularly attractive given the widespread use of "Mormonism" in the academy. Likewise, scholars have been eager to recognize the diversity in other religious traditions by speaking of them in the plural (e.g., Christianities, Buddhisms). The problem is that quite a few denominations reject the term Mormon, so much so that many have come to deploy it exclusively as a disparaging moniker for The Church of Jesus Christ of Latter-day Saints headquartered in Salt Lake City. "Mormonisms" captures the Reorganized Church of Jesus Christ of Latter Day Saints and the Church of Christ (Temple Lot), who reject the label, as a Mormonism. This became even more problematic in 2018 when the Salt Lake City church also officially rejected the name Mormon.

The Restoration Movement may be the most preferable alternative umbrella term. Unfortunately, in academic circles the term is most frequently used for the Campbell-Stone Movement. A third option, "the Latter Day Saint movement," was championed by Newell Bringhurst and John Hamer in their collection, *Scattering of the Saints: Schism within Mormonism.*[18] In this introduction, we have similarly opted for the Latter Day Saint tradition,

18. Newell G. Bringhurst and John C. Hamer, *Scattering of the Saints: Schism within Mormonism* (Independence, MO: John Whitmer Books, 2007).

preferring "tradition" to "movement," since there are many movements within the tradition. Admittedly, this is still problematic. A small portion of the churches in question expressly reject the label of Latter Day Saint as vehemently as they do Mormon. Historically, the church that operated during Joseph Smith's lifetime, originally called the Church of Christ, was renamed the Church of the Latter-day Saints in 1834, and, finally, The Church of Jesus Christ of Latter Day Saints in 1838. Some denominations returned to the earliest name, such as the nineteenth-century Church of Christ led by David Whitmer, the short-lived Church of Christ led by Sidney Rigdon in Pittsburgh, and the late Church of Christ (Temple Lot). Others have organized under the Church of Jesus Christ, such as the followers of Alpheus Cutler in Iowa and the followers of William Bickerton in Pennsylvania. The rejection of Latter Day Saint as a descriptor is important particularly for the smallest expressions of the tradition—an insistence that they have remained pure to the earliest vision of Joseph Smith's restoration. Yet most current practitioners in the tradition would define themselves as Latter Day Saints.

More confusing than how to refer to the full tradition is how to refer to individual denominations of the Latter Day Saint tradition, most of which have very similar names. When there have been schisms from The Church of Jesus Christ of Latter-day Saints, headquartered in Salt Lake City, and from the Reorganized Church of Jesus Christ of Latter Day Saints/Community of Christ with headquarters in Independence, Missouri, new churches often simply add a descriptor before the original name. For example, there are the Fundamentalist Church of Jesus Christ of Latter-day Saints, the Remnant Church of Jesus Christ of Latter Day Saints, and the Restored Church of Jesus Christ of Latter-day Saints. In other cases, the names follow a similar structure—including using a synonym for Jesus Christ and "Latter-day Saints." Two examples: in 1955, the Church of the Firstborn of the Fullness of Times was organized in Salt Lake City; and in 1993, the True and Living Church of Jesus Christ of Saints of the Last Days was founded in Manti, Utah. Here, contributors have chosen their own terminology, which includes the use of historical nicknames based on the names of founding members (e.g., Brighamites, Josephites, Whitmerites) or *shortened* forms such as LDS Church or RLDS Church. This is not meant as a pejorative. In each instance, the full names of the churches are provided in "Churches and Movements" at the front of this book and with their first reference in each chapter.

2

Anchored in Revelation

Scripture and Schism in the Restoration

Laurie F. Maffly-Kipp

The tiny island of Deer Isle hangs off the lower lip of the Maine coastline approximately halfway between Portland to the southwest and the Canadian border to the northeast. Home to two small villages and measuring 124 square miles, the island has a year-round population of fewer than 2,000, which doubles in the warmer months of summer. Lobstering, granite quarrying, small farming, and arts and crafts sustain the locals. Yet this remote corner of the nation is home to at least three congregations that trace their roots to the teachings of Joseph Smith: A Community of Christ church, a Church of Jesus Christ Restoration Branch, and another small gathering of Restorationists that meets in a local home. The LDS meet up the road in Ellsworth.

I begin with this scene, far from Iowa or Independence or Salt Lake, because it speaks to the tenacity of religious identity even in sites distant from formal denominational authorities. It also repeats a pattern characteristic of religious life in the United States since the early nineteenth century: division, schism, and differentiation of belief and practice. Mormonism, as you know, emerged from this era of overwhelming religious energy and a marketplace of novel ideas. We often associate this early variety with the presence of charismatic preachers, itinerant evangelists who could stir up a crowd, debate the fine points of theology, reveal new doctrines, or bring listeners to their knees by raising the specter of divine punishment. These formidable figures, including Charles Finney, Lorenzo Dow, and Joseph Smith Jr., elicited great loyalty, but they also drove wedges between husbands and wives, robbed parents of their children, and introduced dissent into communities, resulting in a dizzying array of churches in small towns across the nation. This is the way historians often narrate the beginnings of Mormonism: a single prophetic individual who offered scripture as a sign of divine presence.

I would like to suggest another crucial element of thinking about religious schism, one linked not only to powerful individuals but also to another kind of authority—the authority of scriptural logic. By this I refer to scripture not just as a sign that points to something transcendent but scripture as having or generating an authority of its own that then shapes—and continues to influence—a religious community, sometimes even in the absence of charismatic leadership. The restoration congregations of Deer Isle demonstrate something beyond the power of religious entrepreneurs. They also highlight a pervasive and deep-seated commitment to sacred texts as the shapers of collective identity. Revelation may have been transmitted through prophets, but once revealed truths are unleashed on the world they can take on a power of their own—a power imbued with both creativity and danger. What I offer here, then, is a slightly different history of Mormonism and its variations that illuminates the central role of scriptural logic, describes how it changes over time, and explains how it can lead (and has led) to sharp and even hostile divisions among believers.

It may seem obvious to state that the history of Christianity has been ineluctably molded by disputes over scriptural authority. In short, Christians have at times fought over the Bible even as, at other moments, they have agreed about it. The battles over canonization in the early years of the church, the skirmishes between Catholics and Protestants beginning in the Reformation with the Protestant insistence on *sola scriptura* (belief that the scriptures were the only and complete authority for the Christian life), and the proliferation of dozens of authoritative translations and formats of the biblical text since the dawn of the industrial revolution, all signal that concerns over the status of the Bible—what it is, what it means, and how it relates to other sacred texts—drive to the heart of Christian identity. Scripture also binds communities together, of course, solidifying relationships and clarifying doctrinal boundaries. Its forces are both centrifugal and centripetal, since every statement or story "authorized" by a community helps to define who is in and who is out. As James Bielo has put it, "Bible Belief is rarely simple and often an object of struggle."[1]

---

1. James S. Bielo, "Introduction," *The Social Life of Scriptures: Cross-Cultural Perspectives on Biblicism* (New Brunswick, NJ: Rutgers University Press, 2009), 2.

The decades following the American Revolution witnessed an unusually fertile and unstable moment for scriptural authority. David Holland has eloquently demonstrated that antebellum believers of all sorts—from orthodox Protestants to Shakers to Seventh-day Adventists—danced around the borders of the biblical canon in many ways, adding to it, cutting out its pages when the necessity arose, and challenging its meanings from all angles. Unleashed by the removal of established church authority, as Holland put it, Americans found in the borderlands of scriptural authority both "breathtaking liberties and a frightening potential for tyranny."[2] He notes astutely that early Americans who renounced allegiance to clerical establishments in the name of religious populism often simply "transferred their deference from ministerial authorities to revelatory ones," those prophets and ancient writers who offered divine records that could then be interpreted by individuals of faith and conscience.[3] Scripture, not the clergy, became the law to which the Christian believer had to answer.

No one traversed canonical borders more exuberantly than did the early followers of Joseph Smith Jr. The Mormon faith was born into American culture in the antebellum era, a period of intense interest in the Bible fueled by the growing dominance of evangelical Protestantism in public life. For most Americans of the day, the Bible shaped the most basic structures of language, social life, habits of mind, and views of the past and the future. Schoolchildren learned to read by poring over its pages, families gathered around a common book for study and guidance, and many churches featured the pulpit—the site from which the words of the book were proclaimed and elaborated—as the center of liturgical practice. Both proslavery and antislavery activists, as well as other political actors of all sorts, pulled from its pages to argue the righteousness of their causes. While English was the young nation's primary language, the words and images of the Bible, especially the King James Version, framed its imaginings.[4]

As with many of the religious movements springing up in the 1820s and 1830s, Mormons understood their new faith not as a departure from the

2. David F. Holland, *Sacred Borders: Continuing Revelation and Canonical Restraint in Early America* (New York: Oxford University Press, 2011), 10.

3. Ibid., 143.

4. See "Introduction," in *The Bible in America: Essays in Cultural History*, eds. Nathan O. Hatch and Mark A. Noll, (New York: Oxford University Press, 1982).

Bible but as the most complete way of enacting its sacred truths. Joseph Smith Jr. claimed to have had his first revelation while contemplating a passage from the New Testament Epistle of James. Thereafter, the Bible became his touchstone for understanding the outpouring of divine instructions that he received. Indeed, Smith and his followers, in a more literal-minded way than most Americans, quickly came to see themselves as living within the world of the biblical story.[5] Guided by visitations from God, Jesus, and prophets and apostles mentioned in the scriptures, Smith took it as his task to restore to the earth the ordinances, rites, and beliefs of God's church, the blueprint for which could be found in a commonsense reading of the Bible.

Few American evangelicals would have taken issue with this approach to the scriptures. For Methodists, Baptists, and members of most other Protestant denominations, the Bible was, indeed, a plain text whose meaning was clear to ordinary believers. They may have argued vociferously over what that meaning called them to do, but all would have conceded that the life of a Christian ought to be shaped by the teachings and precepts of God's revealed word to humanity. And those truths could be found in the text. When Joseph Smith Jr. articulated the foundational principles of his new church in 1842, his eighth article of faith seemed to fit right in with the thinking of many Protestant Americans: "We believe the Bible to be the word of God as far as it is translated correctly."[6]

If pressed to specify, most Protestants would have affirmed that the Bible was the complete and final record of divine intervention in the world. They were taught to believe that the early years of the Christian church, the era of Jesus's life and resurrection and the acts of his apostles, signaled the final age of miraculous healings and direct revelation. Jesus's incarnation was the ultimate sign from God, an action that fulfilled the promises of the Hebrew scriptures and stood as the sole route to human salvation. The task of the Christian church for now—until the future date of Christ's return to reign over the earth—was to live out biblical precepts as spelled out in the books of the Old and New Testaments.

---

5. For more on this theme, see Jan Shipps, *Mormonism: The Story of a New Religious Tradition* (Urbana: University of Illinois Press, 1985), esp. ch. 4.

6. The Articles of Faith, as they came to be known, were first written in a letter written by Joseph Smith Jr. to John Wentworth, editor of the *Chicago Democrat*, and published in the Latter-day Saint newspaper, *Times and Seasons*. They were later included in the canonical text The Pearl of Great Price. See Terryl Givens with Brian M. Hauglid, *The Pearl of Greatest Price: Mormonism's Most Controversial Scripture* (New York: Oxford University Press), ch. 4.

Yet in practice, despite doctrinal commitments to a closed canon, Bible believers of all sorts recognized the unleashed potential of a malleable scripture. Americans sought religious truths that would explain the cosmic significance of the new republic and allow them to communicate their understandings to others. Sacred texts that would both connect them to their (predominantly Christian) past and take them into an uncertain future proved a remarkably potent way of expressing and transforming faith and of wedding the twin imperatives of stability and flexibility. It is no accident, then, that in a society in which the Bible was invested with tremendous cultural power—but also increasingly contested—religious innovators stepped in with new interpretations, commentaries, and even additions to Christian scripture. The earliest scriptural innovator in the new nation was Thomas Jefferson himself, who was known to have kept on his bedstand a copy of the Bible that he had "personalized" by cutting and pasting the passages of the New Testament that he found both believable (as in nonmiraculous) and ethically inspiring.[7] Many others soon followed. Texts as diverse as the Shakers' Holy, Sacred and Divine Roll and Book (1843), James Colin Brewster's A Warning to the Latter Day Saints (1845), Andrew Jackson Davis's Principles of Nature (1847), Ellen White's The Great Controversy (1858), Lorenzo Dow Blackson's The Rise and Progress of the Kingdoms of Light and Darkness (1867), Mary Baker Eddy's Science and Health with Key to the Scriptures (1875), and John Ballou Newbrough's OAHSPE: A Kosmon Bible in the Words of Jehovih and his Angel Embassadors (1882) all claimed to extend or complete the promises of the Bible. Many of these new texts caught the attention of growing numbers of believers willing to commit themselves to the truth of their teachings.

These diverse works, many of which became "scripture" to a variety of American religious communities, asserted authority in divergent ways. Some were presented as ancient texts, newly discovered or revealed. Others came through inspiration, revelation, or channeled communication to authors who declared that they had recovered old truths or revealed new meanings to ancient tales. What connected all these texts is their claimed linkage, either explicit or implicit, to some aspect of the Bible itself. They borrowed cultural

---

7. See Peter Manseau, *The Jefferson Bible: A Biography* (Princeton, NJ: Princeton University Press, 2020).

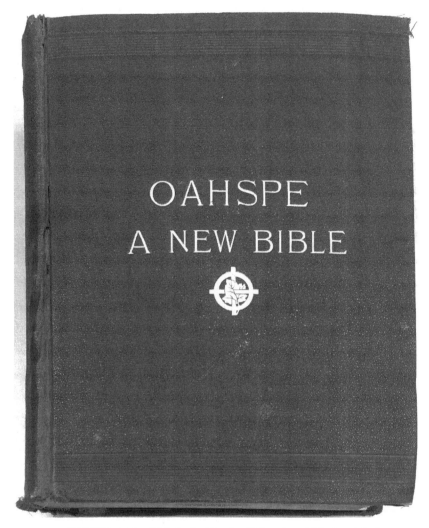

FIGURE 2.1. OAHSPE: A New Bible in the Words of Jehovah and His Angel Embassadors (1891). Church History Library, the Church of Jesus Christ of Latter-day Saints.
Photograph courtesy of Jay Burton (2021).

authority from the Bible—not simply from a charismatic leader—to stake
their own claim to religious value and to convince a biblically literate public
of their importance.

Let me just offer one example from a list that could grow to several dozen:
In 1880, a New York City dentist, John Ballou Newbrough, was gripped

by a strong impression that he must write a book. Sitting before a novel device called a typewriter, Newbrough claimed that a bright light enveloped his hands. He later recounted that he had no conscious knowledge of what he was recording and was told by angels not to read it until it was completed. Newbrough wrote "automatically" for over a year before publishing OAHSPE, his volume of nearly 900 pages. OAHSPE, which, according to Newbrough's glossary, stands for "Sky, earth [corpor] and spirit," related 24,000 years of world history through the voices of father-mother Jehovah the Creator, thousands of gods and goddesses, and a delegation of angel ambassadors.[8] It introduces many new names but also enfolds much familiar biblical and world history, outlining the rise and fall of civilizations and predicting the ultimate defeat of Buddhism, Hinduism, Islam, Christianity, and other world religions and the emergence of a true universal faith. OAHSPE also contains pencil sketches composed by the angels who, according to Newbrough, controlled his hands as he drew.

Within a few years of its publication, the "OAHSPE Lodge of Faithists" formed and made plans to found a community, "Shalam," in New Mexico. Newbrough, a lifelong follower of Spiritualism, a vegetarian, a pacifist, and a social reformer, spearheaded the settlement of several dozen believers along with Andrew Howland, a wealthy Quaker businessman from Massachusetts. Located in the Mesilla Valley along the Rio Grande, the community took into their social experiment orphans and abandoned children in an attempt to live out the ideals related in Newbrough's text. Members ate only two meals a day, children were given names drawn from OAHSPE, and leaders relied on the advice of angels to guide the development of the community. After Newbrough's death in 1891, Howland assumed control of day-to-day operations, but within a decade Shalam was bankrupt and the residents dispersed. Still, Faithists into the late twentieth century remained convinced they saw signs in world events of the fulfillment of the predictions outlined in OAHSPE.[9]

8. "Glossary of Strange Words Used in This Book," OAHSPE: A New Bible in the Words of Jehovih and his Angel Embassadors (1882), viii.

9. Wallace Perry, "The Glorious Land of Shalam," *Southwest Review* 38, no. 1 (Winter 1953):35–43. For more on OAHSPE, see Laurie F. Maffly-Kipp, *American Scriptures: An Anthology of Sacred Writings* (New York: Penguin, 2010), 219ff.

So, in many ways, Joseph Smith Jr. was right in step with many of his fellow religious seekers. Smith claimed that the book he had translated from golden plates buried in a hillside near his upstate New York farm constituted another divine record, a further revelation of God's working in the world that overlapped with the narrative of the Bible itself. Smith and his followers believed he had been called by God to communicate this additional revelation and to begin to restore all the truths of the Bible to human life, many of which they asserted had been lost or misapprehended by generations of Christians. Most important, Mormons believed that Smith himself, as head of this restored Christian church, would inaugurate the return of divine revelation to human beings. Rather than awaiting the return of Christ, God would once again communicate directly with his children.

Nineteenth-century Mormons, by all accounts, took the Bible very seriously. Like the followers of Alexander Campbell and Methodists—religious groups from which many early converts came—Mormons sought Biblical guidance as they set up their church and organized their lives. In the 1830s, Mormon periodicals cited the Bible nearly twenty times as often as they did the Book of Mormon. John Codman, son of a New England Protestant minister and a visitor to the "Mormon country" of Utah in the 1870s, noted that Mormons were "astonishing biblical students" who did not seem to spend nearly as much time reading the Book of Mormon. "They are perpetually flinging texts at your head," he marveled.[10]

Early Mormon scriptural practice, then, was probably not as distinctive as one might imagine, despite the existence of new texts. It is important to acknowledge the many similarities among these disparate biblical communities. Even the often-heard characterization of Mormonism as unique because of its open canon—as opposed to the presumably closed canon of Protestants and Catholics—is often overstated. Other Americans may not have referred to their approach as an "open canon," and in fact some would have adamantly insisted that they were not changing the text of holy writ. But on

---

10. Philip L. Barlow, *Mormons and the Bible: The Place of the Latter-day Saints in American Religion* (New York: Oxford University Press, 1991), 44; John Codman, *The Mormon Country: A Summer with the "Latter-day Saints"* (New York: United States Publishing Company, 1874), 15, 16. For an argument in favor of widespread Book of Mormon literacy among early Latter-day Saints, see Janiece Johnson, "Becoming a People of the Books: Toward an Understanding of Early Mormon Converts and the New Word of the Lord," *Journal of Book of Mormon Studies* 27 (2018):1–43.

close inspection, it would have been difficult, given what they were doing with the text, to tell the difference. As the old saying goes, if it looks like a duck, quacks like a duck, and walks like a duck, then it is probably a duck.

Despite evident continuities, at least two things were amplified in the Mormon approach to scriptures: the intricate interweaving of sacred texts, and a commitment to the restoration of a totality of divine records. The Book of Mormon is a text that elaborates on and refers to the sacred history contained in the Bible. In fact, Joseph Smith's new record even mentions itself in fascinating and complex ways. This demonstrates what literary theorists, in their fancy language, would call a remarkable degree of intertextuality.[11] In this sense, Mormons had something unusual: for all the new scriptures of the Shakers or later the Christian Scientists, no others wove themselves into biblical history through such intricate means.

Mormons also stood out from other Biblicists by virtue of their pronounced commitment to writing and recording as a sacred act. The very existence of another scripture—indeed, a record that mentioned the possibility of still other sacred texts yet to be discovered—opened Mormons to the acts of reading, writing, and preserving as new kinds of religious practices. If God had revealed himself to human beings on many occasions and was now revealing himself once again, there were, in theory, endless numbers of scriptures that had been produced through these ongoing divine-human exchanges (and could continue to be produced). When late-nineteenth-century biblical scholars announced the existence of multiple versions of early Christian manuscripts, their discoveries only confirmed for Mormons that God had called on humans throughout time to create sacred records and to interpret their words through the light of continuing revelation. Whereas for many Protestants the issue of variations in the biblical manuscripts contributed to an intellectual crisis that eventually would result in a split between modernists (who read the Bible more as metaphor and guide) and fundamentalists (who constructed elaborate theories of scriptural

---

11. See Nicholas J. Frederick, "Evaluating the Interaction between the New Testament and the Book of Mormon: A Proposed Methodology," *Journal of Book of Mormon Studies* 24 (2015):1–30; Nicholas J. Frederick, "The Book of Mormon and Its Redaction of the King James New Testament: A Further Evaluation of the Interaction between the New Testament and the Book of Mormon," *Journal of Book of Mormon Studies* 27 (2018):44–87; Grant Hardy, "The Book of Mormon and the Bible," in *Americanist Approaches to* The Book of Mormon, edited by Elizabeth Fenton and Jared Hickman (New York: Oxford University Press, 2019), 107–135.

inerrancy), Mormons in the nineteenth and early twentieth centuries had little trouble with the notion that fallible human beings had written texts that needed to be treated with cautious reverence. Some scholars have attributed the lack of a Mormon controversy over biblical inerrancy to a wariness of literalism. As Terryl Givens has noted, believers, aided by the guidance of latter-day prophets and church leaders—and by the light of their own inspiration—could in theory rely on this world of "scriptural productions" without feeling threatened by textual discrepancies or multiplicity of language.[12]

This commitment to the recovery, conscious reading, and further compilation of sacred records is voiced repeatedly within the Book of Mormon itself. Numerous passages assert that reading brings one to a knowledge of God, and the people who have left their records behind, like the people of Zarahemla referenced in the Book of Omni, can no longer understand the will of their Creator.[13] In several places, Nephi describes how he reads sacred texts and urges his own readers to emulate his study.[14] The purpose of writing, and the purpose of reading, mandated through revelation itself, is to remember how to live in a godly fashion.[15] That directive was carried forward in the religious practice of the early Mormons. Nothing could be clearer than the urgent 1851 revelation of Jason Briggs: "And the Spirit said unto me, 'Write, write, write; write the revelation and send it unto the Saints at Palestine, and at Voree, and at Waukesha, and to all places where this doctrine is taught as my law; and whomsoever will humble themselves before me, and ask of me, shall receive of my Spirit a testimony that these words are of me. Even so, Amen.'"[16] Beyond the requirements of memory or spiritual formation, many of the first Mormons likely viewed the importance of recordkeeping as linked theologically to their salvation. Samuel Brown's work on early Mormon understandings of death suggests that, for Joseph Smith, the recovery of plates buried in the earth by ancient peoples was a

12. Terryl L. Givens, "Joseph Smith's American Bible: Radicalizing the Familiar," *Journal of the Book of Mormon and Other Restoration Scripture* 18, no. 2 (2009):15. See also, Givens, *By the Hand of Mormon: The American Scripture That Launched a New World Religion* (New York: Oxford University Press, 2003), 185–208.

13. Omni 1:17 (LDS)/Omni 1:30–31 (CofC).

14. See, for instance, 2 Nephi 4:15 (LDS)/2 Nephi 3:28–29 (CofC).

15. Matthew J. Haslam, "Mormon Literacy: Reading and Writing in a Religious Context" (PhD diss., University of North Carolina, Greensboro, 2000), 12–13.

16. Jason W. Briggs, Revelation, November 18, 1851, in "History of the Reorganization of the Church of Jesus Christ of Latter Day Saints," *The Messenger*, November 1875.

means of mediating between the living and the dead. Through the record of history and the transformation of familial relationships into an eternal web of affiliation, all human divisions—as well as disjunctions between divinity and humanity—ultimately could be overcome.[17]

Yet, ironically, this dream of human unity was fractured by the very logic of scriptural abundance. With so many scriptures—and more coming along—how was one to prioritize and discern among them? Almost immediately, differences in approach emerged among Mormons over precisely which of the practices described in the Bible should be reinstated in the young church. A significant number of believers, like many Protestants of the day, sought to restore the principles of the early Christian church (those activities described in the New Testament), including foot washing, healing, receiving of the gifts of the spirit (those experienced on the day of Pentecost, such as speaking in tongues), and the calling of elders and apostles. Many early Mormons also believed that they were mandated by God to restore elements of ancient Israelite worship, including the rebuilding of the temple, reinstatement of a priesthood, and the restoration of ordinances such as vicarious baptism for the dead (a rite mentioned in the New Testament book of I Corinthians 15:29 but that had not been practiced by major Christian groups since the fourth century CE).

Using the Israelite Patriarchs as their model, Joseph Smith Jr. and his inner circle also began to practice plural marriage, a controversial rite that led to deep divisions among his followers.[18] At least one important element of this dispute focused on how to interpret the reinstatement of biblical practices and whether God intended for the restored church to include all the ordinances and practices described in the Hebrew Scriptures as well as those in the New Testament. But an underlying question concerned the logic of scriptural interpretation itself: How could one adjudicate among scriptures? Those who became LDS took the option, at least in theory and for the moment, of accepting everything. But others hesitated, questioning whether all the sacred record was equally binding in the same way on God's people. The proliferation of texts thus became a challenge and a burden that sowed divisions among church members.

17. Samuel Morris Brown, *In Heaven as It Is on Earth: Joseph Smith and the Early Mormon Conquest of Death* (New York: Oxford University Press, 2012).

18. See Revelation, July 12, 1843, in *JSP*, D12: 457–478; D&C 132.

After Smith's death and the leadership struggle that ensued, those Mormons who followed Brigham Young from Nauvoo to Utah Territory continued to believe that their church, the Church of Jesus Christ of Latter-day Saints, should model itself after ancient Israel and should include the temple ordinance of plural marriage and the literal rebuilding of Zion. At this point they were, quite literally, interpreting and enacting the Hebrew scriptures through a Christian lens. But initially many others, living in the borderlands of the scriptural canon, were not sure where to turn for leadership or interpretive authority. The significant number who stayed behind in the Midwest, including Smith's widow, Emma, and his extended family, eventually helped pull together a smaller band in what became known as the Reorganization. That community generally modeled biblical restoration on New Testament precedents, rejecting many of the temple rituals that became so central to the Utah Mormons' understanding of salvation.[19] This decision to remain in place did not solve the dilemma of scriptural interpretation. In fact, to say that the early RLDS chose the New Testament over the Old is to read coherence back into a situation that was troubling and deeply vexed. Where was one to turn—not for the records themselves but for the correct way of reading and enacting those records? How was one to live out the fullness of the gospel when the lines of canon were not clearly drawn?

It was also not entirely obvious how one could tell true revelation from the mundane zeal of the enthusiastic believer. Although the LDS Church later related its own history as a relatively straight line of authority and coherence from Joseph Smith Jr. to Brigham Young and beyond, RLDS Church history displays a visceral sense of the messiness of scriptural logic. One of the early histories of the church, penned by President Joseph Smith III and Heman C. Smith, brims with claimants to church authority based on a variety of scriptural calculations. Several of these believers produced scriptures of their own that challenged members seeking a clear path forward after the death of the first prophet.[20]

One of the first and most interesting cases was that of James Colin Brewster (1826–1909), whose family had moved to Kirtland, Ohio, to join the Mormons when he was a young boy. In 1837, the ten-year-old James claimed

---

19. Shipps, *Mormonism*, ch. 5.

20. *The History of the Reorganized Church of Jesus Christ of Latter Day Saints*, vol. 2, *1836–1844* (Independence, MO: Herald House, 1896).

that he had been visited by an angel who had shown him a better way to organize Smith's church. Initially encouraged in his spiritual precocity by church leaders, Brewster's continuing corrections to church teachings eventually caused a rift with Mormon leaders, and his family, while still connected to the faith, moved to Springfield, Illinois.[21] From there, Brewster began to publish pamphlets that he asserted were abridgments of ancient documents furnished by the angel. The first, *The Words of Righteousness to All Men* appeared in 1842.[22] Collectively these writings were called the Book of Esdras, which Brewster claimed was the teaching of an ancient biblical prophet who lived in approximately 160 BCE. The publications contained many predictions related to the fate of the Mormons, criticized the emergence of Mormon temple ceremonies and Mormon economic practices, and prophesied the end of the world in 1878. Brewster and his family were excommunicated in 1842, but this hardly stopped his production of texts.[23]

Several years later, Brewster published *A Warning to the Latter Day Saints, Generally Called Mormons*, alleged to be an abridgment of the Ninth Book of Esdras. In it he included poetry and fragments said to be from other ancient books, as well as a conclusion that detailed the prophecies already fulfilled from his 1842 pamphlet (including the murder of Joseph Smith Jr. in 1844). The bulk of the text is an extended warning of impending doom to the sinful people who have fallen away from God's true teachings—namely, the Mormons in Nauvoo, Illinois. Like a Hebrew prophet, Brewster details the many painful and destructive ways that they will perish for their trespasses, including floods, droughts, pestilence, and earthquakes. The document also predicts the fall of Nauvoo ("Idle City") and ultimately the destruction of the American government that will usher in God's kingdom. That realm, he prophesies, will be established in California ("Bashan"), which will be given to the faithful remnant of saints who keep God's commandments.[24]

In June 1848, after Nauvoo had been destroyed and most Mormons had migrated to Utah or otherwise dispersed, he reorganized his small band

21. "Notice," *Times and Seasons,* December 1, 1842; *Dan* Vogel, "James Colin Brewster: The Boy Prophet Who Challenged Mormon Authority," in *Differing Visions: Dissenters in Mormon History,* edited by Roger D. Launius and Linda Thatcher (Urbana: University of Illinois Press, 1994), 120–122.

22. James Brewster, *The Words of Righteousness to All Men* (1842).

23. Vogel, "James Colin Brewster," 125.

24. James Colin Brewster, *A Warning to the Latter Day Saints, Generally Called Mormons. An Abridgment of the Ninth Book of Esdras* (1845).

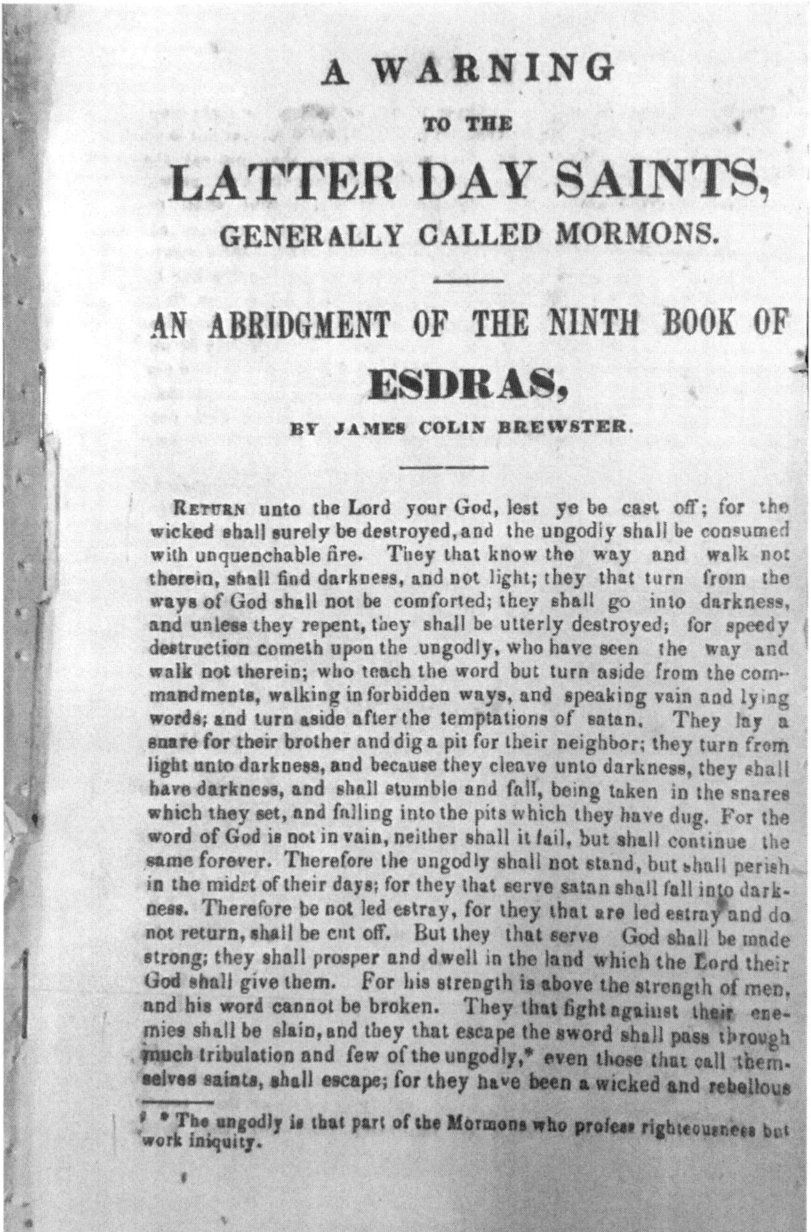

A WARNING

TO THE

LATTER DAY SAINTS,

GENERALLY CALLED MORMONS.

AN ABRIDGMENT OF THE NINTH BOOK OF

ESDRAS,

BY JAMES COLIN BREWSTER.

RETURN unto the Lord your God, lest ye be cast off; for the wicked shall surely be destroyed, and the ungodly shall be consumed with unquenchable fire. They that know the way and walk not therein, shall find darkness, and not light; they that turn from the ways of God shall not be comforted; they shall go into darkness, and unless they repent, they shall be utterly destroyed; for speedy destruction cometh upon the ungodly, who have seen the way and walk not therein; who teach the word but turn aside from the commandments, walking in forbidden ways, and speaking vain and lying words; and turn aside after the temptations of satan. They lay a snare for their brother and dig a pit for their neighbor; they turn from light unto darkness, and because they cleave unto darkness, they shall have darkness, and shall stumble and fall, being taken in the snares which they set, and falling into the pits which they have dug. For the word of God is not in vain, neither shall it fail, but shall continue the same forever. Therefore the ungodly shall not stand, but shall perish in the midst of their days; for they that serve satan shall fall into darkness. Therefore be not led estray, for they that are led estray and do not return, shall be cut off. But they that serve God shall be made strong; they shall prosper and dwell in the land which the Lord their God shall give them. For his strength is above the strength of men, and his word cannot be broken. They that fight against their enemies shall be slain, and they that escape the sword shall pass through much tribulation and few of the ungodly,* even those that call themselves saints, shall escape; for they have been a wicked and rebellous

---

* The ungodly is that part of the Mormons who profess righteousness but work iniquity.

FIGURE 2.2. *A Warning to the Latter Day Saints, generally called Mormons: An Abridgment of the Ninth Book of Esdras,* by James Collin Brewster (1845). Church History Library, the Church of Jesus Christ of Latter-day Saints. Photograph courtesy of Jay Burton (2021).

of perhaps one hundred believers, claiming that, while Joseph Smith had been called to establish the church, Brewster had been anointed to build the kingdom of God on earth. The twenty-four-year-old prophet finally left for California in August 1850 with ninety members, 200 head of cattle, and twenty-seven wagons, even as he continued to translate ancient documents (specifically, Mayan hieroglyphics and New Mexican Indian pictographs from his travels).[25] The group suffered schisms along the way, and Brewster settled briefly in what is now Colonias, New Mexico. By 1853, he had returned to the United States with his family, where he lived a life of apparent obscurity, never to prophesy publicly again. Still, his documents vividly demonstrate the tenor of prophetic religion in antebellum America, the volatility of revelatory power in the early Mormon community, and the ways in which believers were eager to tie biblical history to their new world home. The details of Brewster's story are different, but they repeat the scriptural logic of Joseph Smith himself: Brewster's accounts are intertextual, and they indicate the existence of many more records to come.

Brewster's revelations also point to the delicate balance between scriptural authority and charismatic or institutional authority in the wake of the first prophet's assassination. Even in a religious community that prized individual and continuous revelation, interpretation of those ever-flowing streams required a community to validate and acknowledge the legitimacy of those truths. It needed a leader or group able to sift among scriptures, prioritize them, and decide which truths were binding. Brewster may have received his divine messages, but they were of no use to the larger Mormon community because its leaders invalidated them. As for Brewster's small band of followers, it was hard to garner scriptural authority with ninety members gradually peeling away as they crossed the Southwest. Two hundred cattle alone could not transform the young man's prophetic energy into a religious movement.

Here stood the Mormons, then, after the death of their prophet. Their dilemma was not simply a problem of who would lead them, although that problem was formidable enough. They also puzzled over how to adjudicate among the scriptural stories, injunctions, and myriad revelations that

---

25. See, for instance, James Colin Brewster, "American Antiquities—Translation of Hieroglyphics," *Olive Branch*, January 1849.

had poured from their leader and held them together previously. They also wrestled with new revelations from Brewster, from James Strang, and others, that followed the pattern set by Joseph Smith Jr. but that pulled them in different directions.[26]

The ensuing 160 years witnessed many more iterations of these scriptural dynamics, some of which further divided both the Utah-based church and the communities of the reorganization. The LDS story has been more widely studied, and the fine work of scholars such as Philip Barlow have limned the complexities and changes in the ways Utah-based Mormons have dealt with scripture over time. But the RLDS narrative has been less thoroughly assessed. This history has been fraught with continued and extremely painful disagreements, much as the initial split from the LDS led to deep and long-lasting wounds. But seeing it through the lens of a longer history of struggles over scriptural practice allows us to recognize that religious divisions are not entirely the product of personalities, even though they are made manifest through human interaction. They are also connected to the power we bestow on texts and our readings of those texts. One of the fascinating features of Mormon scriptural logics is that a shared commitment to an open canon has led to dramatically different modes of employing scripture in religious life.

When Joseph Smith III made the decision to take up his father's prophetic mantle in April of 1860, his speech to the assembly in Amboy, Illinois, made two very strategic points about scripture that would characterize his presidency. First, he disavowed the practice of polygamy as taught by Brigham Young. Second, he reaffirmed the importance of canonical texts. "I believe in the doctrines of honesty and truth," Smith asserted. "The Bible contains such doctrines, and so do the Book of Mormon and the Book of Covenants, which are auxiliaries to the Bible." The young man claimed his leadership based on two scriptural principles. The first was the negation of one doctrine. The second was a very carefully worded acceptance of the significance of scripture. We should note that he did not state that sacred texts were entirely composed of sacred truth, and he seemed to give a place of prominence to the Bible over the Book of Mormon and the Book of Covenants. He ended his discourse on scriptures by admitting that he was not

---

26. See Christine Elyse Blythe and Christopher James Blythe, "Strangite Scripture," chapter 9 herein.

terribly well acquainted with all these books and vowed that he would bring himself up to speed on their contents.[27]

Smith's approach set the stage for RLDS wrestling with scriptural precedent throughout the late 1860s and 1870s. Because of their objections to the interpretive lens employed in Nauvoo and the temple practices that arose from that logic, RLDS struggled immediately with questions of which teachings to retain as authoritative and which to remove from their own version of the Doctrine and Covenants. As Richard Howard has demonstrated, this process unfolded contentiously over several decades.[28] The community and its leaders had to devise principles of interpretation, of inclusion and exclusion. One obvious choice was to reject polygamy, a negation that became a prominent feature of the early movement.

Yet, while RLDS could not let their objections to Utah Mormons be their defining feature, providing positive statements of faith meant rethinking the entire canon. The community needed not only a statement of belief but an ordering logic for their textual choices. The caution they exercised in carrying this out is evident in the fact that even the inspired documents delivered by Joseph Smith III in 1863 and 1873 on church leadership, as well as the text permitting the ordination of African Americans of 1865, were not officially added by General Conference Resolution into the Doctrine and Covenants until 1878. They were included in the next publication of the Doctrine and Covenants in 1880.[29] Removing older revelations from the first prophet was even trickier, since it required parsing and choosing among the words of a revered leader, deciding what were mere speculative musings and what were prophetic utterance. Only in 1886 was the ritual of baptism for the dead actively disavowed, a decision that resulted in the withdrawal of several prominent church members. Even then, the original revelations were not removed from the Doctrine and Covenants until the twentieth century, due to the charged nature of these changes.[30]

27. "The Mormon Conference," *True Latter Day Saints' Herald*, May 1860.

28. Richard Howard, *Restoration Scriptures: A Study of Their Textual Developments*, Revised and Enlarged, 2nd ed. (Independence, MO: Herald Publishing House, 1995), chs. 10, 11.

29. General Conference Resolution, No. 216, Adopted on September 13, 1878, in *Compilation of General Conference Resolutions, 1852–1907* (Lamoni, IA: Board of Publication of the Reorganized Church of Jesus Christ of Latter Day Saints, 1908), 48. See also, Howard, *Restoration Scriptures*, 174–175.

30. See Roger D. Launius, "An Ambivalent Rejection: Baptism for the Dead and the Reorganized Church Experience," *Dialogue: A Journal of Mormon Thought* 23 (Summer 1990):61–83.

It is crucial to see this excessive scriptural caution as a sign of the fragile bonds that held together the early RLDS community. Having spent several decades privately nurturing their loyalty to the principles of the restoration, Midwestern Mormons knew they had to tread carefully in knitting together those who remained behind after the westward exodus. Ironically, Utah Saints, self-selected to migrate through their allegiance to Brigham Young, were in a much stronger position to use the flexibility of an open canon to shape their community, although the stability of their leadership meant that they didn't need to wield their scriptural power to the same extent. The RLDS, conversely, had a relatively weak leadership—not because Joseph Smith III himself was weak, but because the initial impetus for gathering the community rested on a considerably less solid foundation. The Book of Abraham, for example, presented all kinds of challenges to a community in which a number of members actively espoused the doctrine of plural gods. How could one keep the community together while steering a road to scriptural orthodoxy? Smith and his leadership knew that to keep the church united, changes to the scriptures would have to be made. But making those changes without thoroughly dividing the community required a cautious, consensual, and very gradual process.[31]

Understanding the precariousness of the young RLDS Church allows us to interpret more clearly the dramatic differences in the current contents of LDS, Restorationist (those who reject the late twentieth-century additions), and Community of Christ versions of the Doctrine and Covenants. Why did the RLDS Doctrine and Covenants end up incorporating so many more sections and changes after 1844 than did the LDS version, especially when the practices of the LDS Church remained far more distinctive? How did the logic of the open canon unfold so differently in these two nascent communities? The RLDS, it seems to me, was strategically cautious, and no one more so than Joseph Smith III, in changing the logic of scripture. By the late nineteenth century, a pattern within the church of cautious movement balanced by decision through consensus had been established.

Another enduring legacy of this era with the RLDS Church echoed Joseph Smith III's statement about where truth resides in sacred texts. Recall his

---

31. A[lma] R. Blair, "Reorganized Church of Jesus Christ of Latter Day Saints: Moderate Mormonism," in *The Restoration Movement: Essays in Mormon History*, edited by F. Mark McKiernan, Alma R. Blair, and Paul M. Edwards (Lawrence, KS: Coronado Press, 1973), 207–230.

words quoted above: "I believe in the doctrines of honesty and truth. The Bible contains such doctrines, and so do the Book of Mormon and the Book of Covenants, which are auxiliaries to the Bible." Primacy is given in this statement to truth as an abstract principle, not truth as set out in specific human formulations. That calculus allowed for the difficult task of deciding that not all the prophet's revelations in the LDS Doctrine and Covenants would be determinative for the church. The thread of this language is woven throughout the later engagement of the RLDS Church and Community of Christ with scripture, in a formula that consistently distinguishes between revelation and the human articulation of that experience. Arthur Oakman explained it this way in the *Saints' Herald* in 1951: "There are, then, strictly speaking, no revealed <u>truths</u>. There are 'truths of revelation'—statements of principles, that is, which stem from the revelatory experience. . . . For revelation is based upon the intercourse between the mind which guides the event and the mind which views it. When appreciation of Divinity in nature and history comes to man, revelation takes place."[32] The First Presidency echoed Oakman's point in 1968: "Scripture of all kinds is not the primary truth itself."[33]

The largest branch of the reorganization, now Community of Christ, has in recent years seen a gradual deauthorization of scripture, as evidenced in the statements above. This tendency was revealed by the leaking of theological papers written and presented as part of internal conversation surrounding an effort to redesign Sunday School curriculum materials for 1967–1968.[34] In those documents, the authors affirmed that no scripture is inerrant or absolute and that cultures develop over time, thus some of the stories of the Bible pertain to earlier stages of human development. In short, the committee fully affirmed modernist biblical criticism of the previous century, readings of the Bible that had riven Protestant churches for decades. They also reasserted the priority given to the Bible in Joseph Smith III's presidential address, arguing for a "strategic caution" in the use of the Book of Mormon as a teaching tool, cautioning readers about its questionable

---

32. Arthur A. Oakman, "Experience, Authority, and Revelation," *Saints' Herald*, January 15, 1951.

33. "Report of the First Presidency," *Saints' Herald*, March 15, 1968.

34. William D. Russell, "The Last Smith Presidents and the Transformation of the RLDS Church," *Journal of Mormon History* 34, no. 3 (Summer 2008):58–59; William J. Knapp, "Professionalizing Religious Education in the Church: The 'New Curriculum Controversy,'" *John Whitmer Historical Association Journal* 2 (1982):47–59.

historical claims, and urging them to use many different versions of the Bible as paths to larger truths. The study papers, in sum, articulated a vision of the scripture as developmental, "illuminating the present age rather than dictating to it."[35]

Reactions to this directive, as well as to the changes in church policy that followed in the 1980s, were dramatic and deeply divisive. After the RLDS leadership approved the ordination of women at the world conference of 1984, approximately one quarter of the membership of the church broke away in protest, splintering into several groups that remain opposed to newer developments.[36] It remains an open question why there were such strong reactions to these more recent changes and not to the shifts of the 1860s and 1870s, which were arguably more dramatic. Such affirmations about the role of scripture had been pronounced for decades—were in fact alluded to by Joseph Smith III—but only in the 1980s did the tethers within the community snap for many Restorationists, who came to see these changes as a violent rejection of timeless truths. One must wonder whether the real rub came over the shift in the process by which the Doctrine and Covenants additions were authorized, not over the content of the changes themselves.

In 1986, the chair of the world conference ruled that only the prophet and president can add or remove text to the Doctrine and Covenants, a power that had previously resided in a vote of the conference itself.[37] This shift of the power to modify sacred texts, more than the specifics of the new additions to the text, did reflect a decisive change of policy. In some respects, the newly bestowed power of the presidency holds out the possibility of a more top-down decision-making process—possibly even, as David Holland put it, the "frightening potential for tyranny" from any direction. Does our foray into the historical logic of scriptural change help us understand these latest schisms in new ways? Or, has the language of the restoration, so much a part

35. The leaked papers were published by the Price Publishing Company as *The Position Papers*. The phrase "strategic caution" appeared in a paper on the Book of Mormon drafted by Wayne Ham. He later published a revised version as "Problems in Interpreting the Book of Mormon as History," *Courage: A Journal of History, Thought, and Action* 1 (September 1970):15–22.

36. William D. Russell, "The Remnant Church: An RLDS Schismatic Group Finds a Remnant of Joseph's Seed," *Dialogue* 38, no. 3 (Fall 2005):76–77.

37. Richard P. Howard, *Church through the Years*, vol. 2, *The Reorganization Comes of Age, 1860–1992* (Independence, MO: Herald Publishing House, 1993), 152–153.

of the nineteenth-century church, become so attenuated that the logic of the open canon no longer holds for many members?

Yet, the compromise language of the recently added Doctrine and Covenants 164, as Community of Christ scholar John Hamer has pointed out, fits well into the mold of late-nineteenth-century cautious change undertaken by the early RLDS Church.[38] In leaving controversial issues such as homosexuality to the discretion of local church bodies rather than legislating across the board, it reflects the same concerns for communal cohesion with measured change reflected in the 1860s decisions. Perhaps in practice the departure from the past has not been radical at all, and we are forced to look for other ways of understanding the latest division in the Mormon family. What is clear is that we miss much of the nuance of history within both the LDS and RLDS wings of Mormonism by resting with the easy platitudes of liberal versus conservative, rationalist versus revelation oriented, or modern versus fundamentalist. Within both movements, there is a decided logic to the use of scripture, a shifting configuration of authority residing in leadership, texts, and institutions that we are well advised to examine.

The story of division within the Mormon tradition is often narrated as an argument over leadership, over strong figures who chose to take church communities in very different directions. But I would suggest that schisms also reflect differing understandings of how scriptural logic functions and where it leads. Within the Mormon fold, an abundance and in some cases continued outpouring of revelation presents a particular challenge, one that has been taken up in very different ways. For the RLDS movement especially, that abundance continues to provoke debates over the authority of scripture and adjudication among scriptural truth.

In the final analysis, Mormon uses of scripture reflect some of the same hybrid influences of charismatic authority, leadership structures, texts, and institutional dynamics that have shaped Christian interpretive strategies for centuries. The scriptural logics of both the LDS and reorganized wings of the movement, far from being anomalous, exhibit tensions between human and textual moorings that have produced schisms among Christians in many eras. Still, the historical particularities are deeply important,

38. John Hamer, "My Response to John-Charles Duffy," *Saints Herald: A Community of Christ Blog*, April 18, 2010, http://saintsherald.com/2010/04/18/dc-164-my-response-to-john-charles-duffy.

since evaluations of personal charisma and scriptural persuasiveness are not ideal types but are instead culturally conditioned judgments, anchored in the lived experiences of distinctive communities. To see Mormon uses of scripture as either utterly exceptional or generically Christian thus misses the point by obscuring the explanatory potential of their histories. In this sense, the possibilities for scriptural discernment are as limitless as human experience itself.

3

Revelation, Scripture, and Authority in the Latter Day Saint Diaspora, 1840–1870

Richard L. Saunders

It is very difficult for us to communicate to the churches all that God has revealed to us [the Latter Day Saints], in consequence of [Christian] tradition; for we are differently situated from any other people that ever existed upon this earth: Consequently those former revelations cannot be suited to our condition, because they were given to other people who were before us; but in the last days, God was to call a remnant, in which was to be deliverance, as well as in Jerusalem, and in Zion. Now, if God should give no more revelations, where will [we] find Zion and this remnant?

Joseph Smith, April 21, 1834[1]

For believers, scripture may be simple. For scholars, scripture is more complex. It is a multidimensional artifact consisting of layers upon layers of comprehension, expectation, experience, supposition, faith, and transmission. Put scripture within a human context, and it becomes a manifestation and invocation of social and intellectual authority. Authority does not merely exist, it is recognized and accepted, challenged and negated. In both social and intellectual terms, *authority* is constructed within society and therefore has a human and a social context. Louis XVI may have been the apex of legal and historical authority as king of France in 1793, but his authority held no sway over the Paris mobs as he went to the guillotine.

---

1. Minutes and Discourse, April 21, 1834, in *JSP*, D4:15.

Because authority is socially constructed, scripture has not only a text but a context. Yet, while history and scholarship are human enterprises lacking the tools to weigh the ultimate, metaphysical truth of scripture, each is well equipped to explore the authors, the history, and the setting in which documents are produced and scripture is created. Scholarship and faith can coexist separately. The conflicts that occasionally arise do so when standards of evidence and interpretation accepted in one sphere are used to measure validity in the other. *Truth* is different than *fact*.

A bit of encouragement by Miriam Levering helps us understand scripture in terms of the period addressed by this collection. She observed that it is profitable to "[examine] all of the ways in which individuals and communities *receive* these words and texts: the ways people respond to the texts, the way they make use of them, the contexts in which they turn to them, their understandings of what it is to read them or to understand them, and the roles they find such words and texts can have in their religious projects."[2] Fulfilling Levering's charge is the purpose of this and other chapters in this volume. This chapter provides an overview of scripture as social authority within the tangled leaves of one slim branch in Restoration history.

Joseph Smith's quote at the head of this chapter is clear: reopened, direct connection to Divinity not only characterizes Mormonism, but it becomes the sole life-giving factor that defined it. Without new revelation and new scripture, the Latter Day Saints were no different from other Christian denominations. Smith and the Latter Day Saints rejected Protestant notions of *sola scriptura*, the idea that scripture alone was a sufficient basis from which to recover saving Christian truth. Latter Day Saints also rejected the idea that the production of scripture ended with the closing of the biblical canon and that one needed only figure out how to properly interpret that text. The very tangible Book of Mormon, nearly 600 pages of dense and complex narrative, provided an important facet of Mormonism's early appeal to converts. Whether one quoted, defended, argued, or dismissed it, the written text and printed book were physically present. The book's claim as new scripture attracted many, its very existence serving as *prima facie* evidence of a reopened revelatory connection to divinity. After its publication, Smith

2. Miriam Levering, "Scripture and Its Reception: A Buddhist Case," in *Rethinking Scripture: Essays from a Comparative Perspective,* edited by Miriam Levering (Albany: SUNY Press, 1989), 59.

continued to restore ancient scripture and reveal modern scripture. Here, I explore how Smith's would-be successors tried to replicate his model. The impulse to produce new scripture led to a proliferation of new texts in the different churches emerging after Smith's death. I also document the stabilization of the canon and a turn toward more traditional, even Protestant, notions of the supremacy of scripture over prophets.

Mormonism under Joseph Smith and the resulting Latter Day Saint heritage was never as coherent as believers would like to perceive—and it has never been monolithic. In 1953, Dale Morgan used the term "churches of the dispersion" to refer to the scattering that followed Joseph Smith's death.[3] Some scholars after Morgan have adopted the term *diaspora* to classify the period of division characterized by the conflicting leadership claims that grew out of the stresses of the 1840s. The Greek term *diaspora* is borrowed from Semitic history; it describes the scattering of the Jews after the Babylonian Exile and again following the destruction of Jerusalem in 70 CE. In Latter Day Saint history, the Mormon diaspora began in Nauvoo before the death of Joseph Smith and lasted until the Reorganized Church of Jesus Christ of Latter Day Saints was firmly established—about 1870. With important exceptions, by this date most of the initial Mormon diaspora followings had evaporated or the members had collected into the Church of Christ (Temple Lot), the Reorganization, the Church of Jesus Christ (Green Oak, Pennsylvania), or simply left the Latter Day Saint tradition entirely for mainstream Christian denominations. Each eventually spawned its own series of schismatic divisions, sometimes over matters first raised in the initial diaspora.

During the first fifteen years of the church's history, the prophet Joseph Smith lived as the very personification of Mormonism. As events progressed and the church expanded, Joseph unwittingly created what would become two competing organizational impulses within the tradition. One was a *charismatic* or *prophetic* tradition, grounded in a "prophetic persona" whose connection to divinity enabled him to speak for God, thereby creating a vehicle

---

3. Dale L. Morgan, "A Bibliography of the Churches of the Dispersion," *Western Humanities Reviews* 7, no. 3 (Summer 1953): suppl. The text is more widely available in *Dale Morgan and the Mormons: Collected Works*, Part 2, *1949–1970*, Kingdom in the West, vol. 15, edited by Richard L. Saunders (Norman, OK: Arthur H. Clark, 2013), 253–337.

for scripture.[4] The other was a *corporate* or *priestly* tradition of ordinances, quorums, priesthood authority, and organization that gave social structure to Mormonism's new message and upon which much of the daily administrative responsibility rested.

The growth of the church under Smith in terms of numbers of converts, social and organizational sophistication, and its doctrinal breadth is a testament to the power of both the message and Smith's personality. There were plenty of challenges to leadership as the church grew but very few premartyrdom schisms in the church, and their impact on the culture of Mormonism was minor compared to postmartyrdom history. As early as 1830, Hiram Page was rebuked for dictating revelations to direct the church as a body.[5] In Kirtland, Ohio, disaffected members accused Smith of being a fallen prophet. Twelve years later in Nauvoo, Oliver Olney and Gladden Bishop were cut off from the church for presenting their own prophetic claims.[6] The 1842 excommunications of Olney and Bishop effectively began the Mormon diaspora. While dissent and disaffection had riven the church repeatedly through its young history, Olney and Bishop were among the earliest to publicly (but ineffectively) advance prophetic claims prior to Smith's death.

During his lifetime, Joseph Smith largely controlled and successfully protected his prophetic role, even as he encouraged others to seek personal instruction from the Divine. Ron Barney makes a convincing case that early experience with the reception of his revelations made the Prophet reticent about discussing revelation too openly.[7] Yet, building on the Book of Mormon, the fact that Smith continued in revelation throughout his life and that it was codified into published and approved scripture, set a standard for the charismatic tradition within Latter Day Saint faith. Revealing new or expanded doctrines and practices was a difficult task for Smith, as demonstrated by the Saints' hot and cold reactions to what he introduced to them.

4. Ronald O. Barney, *Joseph Smith: History Methods, and Memory* (Salt Lake City: University of Utah Press, 2021), 271–291.

5. Revelation, September 1830-B [D&C 28] in *JSP*, D1:183–186.

6. Richard G. Moore, "The Writings of Oliver H. Olney: Early Mormon Dissident; Would-be Reformer," *John Whitmer Historical Association Journal* 33, no. 2 (Fall/Winter 2013):58–78; Richard Saunders, "The Fruit of the Branch: Francis Gladden Bishop and His Culture of Dissent," in *Differing Visions: Dissenters in Mormon History,* edited by Roger D. Launius and Linda Thatcher (Urbana: Univ. of Illinois Press, 1994), 102–119.

7. Barney, *Joseph Smith*, 274–280.

Some wholeheartedly accepted Joseph's doctrinal developments; others rejected them altogether. When personal loyalties to Smith were dissolved by his assassination, these ideological rifts in Mormon Nauvoo became increasingly apparent. Smith's position as "prophet, seer, and revelator," resulting in the creation of scripture, provided a sociocultural benchmark for would-be successors.

It is helpful to see the breakup of the church and of Latter Day Saint society partly as tension over the charismatic/prophetic versus the corporate or priestly traditions within the church. Smith's death in the summer of 1844 created the first general existential and leadership crises in the church's history.[8] A binary competition between Mormonism's broad charismatic and corporate traditions was neither necessary nor inevitable, but the two major figures who stepped onto the stage in the summer of 1844 argued strenuously for one tradition at the expense of the other. A separation and divergence of the two traditions became reality.

The Mormon diaspora in one sense can be regarded as a competition for how Smith's successor was appropriately identified and how that successor's divine authority was demonstrated to other believers. The first challenge was couched in terms of *continuation of authority*. A special conference in Nauvoo followed the Prophet's midsummer death. Sidney Rigdon and Brigham Young essentially argued before this congregation that the church had to choose between Mormonism's charismatic and priestly strains instituted by Smith. Rigdon claimed a position as spokesman for the deceased Smith—a charismatic position. Ridgon's supporters argued that the church "no longer exists, except in connection with him." In other words, there was no church without a prophet.[9] In turn, Young downplayed the role of prophecy not only by claiming *not* to fill Joseph Smith's station but by arguing that the quorums of the church—not individuals—held the rights to lead and govern the kingdom. In Nauvoo, the church, congregations, and

---

8. D. Michael Quinn, "The Mormon Succession Crisis of 1844," *Brigham Young University Studies* 16, no. 2 (Winter 1976):187–233; Edward Leo Lyman, "Succession by Seniority: The Development of Procedural Precedents in the LDS Church," *Journal of Mormon History* 40, no. 2 (Spring 2014):92–158; Benjamin E. Park and Robin Scott Jensen, "Debating Succession, March 1846: John E. Page, Orson Hyde, and the Trajectories of Joseph Smith's Legacy," *Journal of Mormon History* 39, no. 1 (Winter 2013):181–205.

9. *To the Members of the Church of Jesus Christ of Latter-day Saints* (September 8, 1844). The only surviving copy of this broadside is housed in Yale University's Beinecke Library.

individuals stood at a crossroads, forced to choose between priestly/corporate and prophetic/charismatic intellectual traditions that had hitherto grown together. Rigdon's cause attracted defenders from the Nauvoo high council, including its stake president, William Marks.[10] Nevertheless, the conference dismissed Sidney Rigdon's assertion to "guardianship" of the church by a sizable majority. Rigdon's claims were nullified, and his vocal followers were excommunicated.

The Nauvoo membership favored the corporate tradition: Brigham Young and apostolic leadership. Under Young in Nauvoo, the church as a functioning corporate entity began to draw a net around a core of Smith's followers. Beginning with Rigdon, conflicting leadership claims drew off a minority of Saints, a few of whom had been closely involved with Joseph Smith in the operation of the church. The ecclesiastical and social step taken via Rigdon's claim and those that followed clarified the distinction between Mormonism's two organizing traditions. Authority under the corporate tradition was now insulated from potential counterclaims and divisions. Members who recognized corporate authority were provided a basis for judging and dismissing any competing leadership claims that did occur. Nauvoo's Mormon residents did not reject the doctrine or practice of the prophetic call—they rejected the idea of the superiority of that call to the operation of priesthood (i.e., quorum or corporate) authority. The mission of the church was greater than that of its prophet.

But the choice between traditions was not exclusive. Mormonism had fostered both, and believers expected both a church and a prophet. On one hand, followers of Rigdon and other prophetic claimants still had to forge a workable priestly/corporate organization. On the other, even the *Millennial Star* editorial reprinting the Rigdon's excommunication trial commented that though the apostolic quorum appeared to have held the church together, "We want the word of the Lord for such proceedings; our lamented prophet never feared to lay his revelations before the church."[11]

10. Both sides of the discussion are carefully recorded and published in the conference minutes. See *Times & Seasons* 5, no. 17 (15 September):647–655, no. 18 (1 October 1844):660–667; Andrew Ehat, Joseph Smith's Introduction of Temple Ordinances and the 1844 Mormon Succession Question (master's thesis, BYU), especially pp. 189–236.

11. "Editorial," *Millennial Star* 5, no. 7 (December 1844):112.

For the core of Nauvoo believers and European converts heading west under the apostles and Brigham Young after 1846, the Mormon diaspora was an ecclesiastically simple and direct matter of accepting or rejecting a prophetic station or priesthood authority. But those Latter-day Saints who trekked to Upper California were not the only Latter Day Saints. Once the Salt Lake Valley was settled, attention shifted from internal to external issues. Faced with continuing negative public opinion in Illinois and the subsequent logistical nightmare of moving an entire society *en masse* and settling a desert, the apostolic leadership did little else to formally define the new boundaries of the church. Dissenters, schismatics, and laggers were generally left behind to their own devices. For those who went west, the overland trek became a corporate definition of "Mormonism" and was regarded as the measure of faith, in a way; those who would not come to Zion were not considered "faithful."

From the Utah perspective (as stewards of the now-distinct Mormon priestly tradition), the rise of prophetic pretenders created a need to define "the Church" in the face of contradictory claims. Yet, as I've argued elsewhere, the demanding overland experience failed to keep the church as the theologically homogeneous entity it expected to be. In Salt Lake City a decade after the martyrdom, the Gladdenites—the first instance of a heretical group in the Saints' Great Basin retreat—set in motion the forces that would finally isolate the Utah branch of the church as "the Mormons," separating it from the larger scope of Joseph Smith's spiritual legacy.[12] The action with Rigdon set a precedent at least for Brigham Young's branch. Mormons under Young followed the pattern and thereafter simply rejected the validity of rival claims.

Though the question of authority had been settled in the minds of the priesthood leadership in Nauvoo and largely accepted by those in Nauvoo who became the Utah church, a thriving body of dissenting "Mormons," who very much considered themselves orthodox, remained behind. Perhaps as many as 5,000 American Mormons were scattered east of the Mississippi River through the Midwest, Northeast, and South.[13] New challenges to the

12. Richard Saunders, "'More a Movement Than an Organization: Utah's First Encounter with Heresy, the Gladdenites, 1851–1854,'" *John Whitmer Historical Association Journal* 16 (1996):91–106.

13. Richard E. Bennett, *Mormons at the Missouri, 1846–1852* (Norman: University of Oklahoma Press, 1987), 227.

Nauvoo members' decision in favor of the apostles began cropping up almost immediately. Most importantly James J. Strang, a new convert with grand designs of relocating the faith to Wisconsin, made public assertion of leadership in his own newspaper.[14] Strang's campaign attracted attention and new converts to a diverging branch of Mormonism. Despite the popular negation of Rigdon's claim to "guardianship" of the church, the excommunication of apostle Lyman Wight (who had led a colony to Texas), and the summary dismissal of Strang's claim, each was able to establish a following, including some from among those in Nauvoo.[15] This was also true of excommunicated apostle William Smith, the only surviving male of Joseph's immediate family, who would head more than one short-lived church in Kentucky and then Illinois.[16] Alpheus Cutler, a member of the Nauvoo stake high council and Council of Fifty, officially reorganized the church in Iowa in 1853.[17] In the twenty years after Smith's death, a number of other leaders, including Charles B. Thompson, James C. Brewster, Austin Cowles, William McLellin, Gladden Bishop, and David Whitmer, would also lead small movements.[18] Each drew on his own interpretation of Mormonism's prophetic tradition. Together they personified the values of the third stanza of a folksong composed and published in Nauvoo: "A church without a prophet is not the church for me | It has no head to lead it, in it I would not be."[19]

14. *Voree Herald* 1, no. 1 (January 1846):[1–4]. Strang sustained a running attack on virtually every action, decision, and position of the apostles under Young through the entire year of issues, which continued across *Zion's Reveille* (1846–1847) and later *Gospel Herald* (1847–1850).

15. Richard Bennett calculated that between 1848 and 1852 no more than 11.2 percent of the church members (2,132 people) could have left for schismatic followings. Even if an equal number left before 1848, the majority still rested solidly with the Utah faction under Brigham Young. See Bennett, "Lamanism, Lymanism, and Cornfields," *Journal of Mormon History* 13 (1986–87):59. Joseph Smith III testified in the Temple Lot Case that relatively few who had been in the church before the martyrdom ever joined the Reorganization; *Abstract of Evidence in the Temple Lot Case* (Lamoni, Iowa: Herald Publishing, 1893), 83, 90. Most, but not all of those who moved or "returned" from Utah to the Midwest or the Reorganization were converts who had joined the church after 1844.

16. Kyle R. Walker, *William B. Smith: In the Shadow of a Prophet* (Salt Lake City: Greg Kofford Books, 2015).

17. Danny L. Jorgensen, "Conflict in the Camps of Israel: The 1853 Cutlerite Schism," *Journal of Mormon History* 21, no. 1 (Spring 1995):25–64.

18. See Stephen L. Shields, Divergent Paths of the Restoration: A History of the Latter Day Saint Movement, 4th ed. (Restoration Research, 1990), for brief histories of the groups and leaders claiming Smith's legacy.

19. The lyrics (to the tune of "The Rose That All Are Praising") appeared in *Times and Seasons* 6, no. 2 (February 1, 1845):799, and were widely cited and reprinted for more than a decade.

The diaspora was a contest over which prophet would be recognized as the proper head of the church's ecclesiastical and social structures. People voted in conference sessions, but they also voted in print and with their feet. One way to comprehend the social complexity of the Mormon diaspora is to divide its participants into four general classes or groups of people baptized before 1844 who were not divided by time, allegiance, or place, but by circumstance. These four groups can be identified as:

1. the gathered "old Mormons": Nauvoo saints and European converts, the majority of whom moved temporarily into western Iowa Territory and then on to Utah;
2. ungathered "old Mormons": mostly Americans who remained in the eastern and central United States, concentrated in the upper Midwest;
3. new converts to various schismatic diaspora followings (mostly from Europe and the Midwest); and
4. "returned Mormons," old Mormons and converts who may have gone to Utah but rejected the Great Basin experience and moved eastward again.

Those who "gathered to the mountains" but then left Utah commonly did so over doctrinal or social dissatisfaction, which often centered on polygamy or unrealized economic desires. This group of "returned Mormons" has been difficult to identify or trace and has been studied very little, yet the eastward emigrants formed important congregations in Nebraska that the Reorganization drew from heavily.[20] A fifth class—those who left Mormonism to return to mainstream Christian denominations—could be considered, but since

---

20. A few narrow studies touch on returned Mormons. Richard Saunders, "Francis Gladden Bishop and Gladdenism: A Study in the Culture of a Mormon Dissenter and His Movement," (master's thesis, Logan, Utah State University, 1989) chs. 7–8; Richard L. Shipley, "Voices of Dissent: The History of the Reorganized Church of Jesus Christ of Latter Day Saints in Utah" (master's thesis, Logan, Utah State University, 1969); Will Bagley, "One Long Funeral March: A Revisionist's View of the Mormon Handcart Disasters," *Journal of Mormon History* 35, no. 1 (2009):50–116; Polly Aird, *Mormon Convert, Mormon Defector: A Scottish Immigrant in the American West, 1848–1861* (Norman, OK: Arthur H. Clark, 2009). The earliest primary record of "returned Mormons" was made at Fort Bridger, Wyoming, by federal appointee Albert Cumming during the Utah War; Albert Cumming diary, Duke University, Durham, NC.

they did not participate in the diaspora they are not included, having stepped out of the Latter Day Saint tradition for one reason or another. Finally, the European missions remained securely in the hands of the Apostles, meaning that a potential sixth group—foreign converts—entered the diaspora as they chose to emigrate to the Great Basin, then stalled in places such as St. Louis (where they may have been attracted into another schismatic following) or left Utah and its Mormonism for various reasons.

The Utah branch of the diaspora circulated a proclamation in 1852, instructing former Nauvoo residents and new converts who had settled across western Iowa to gather to Utah.[21] Articles and editorials in newspapers associated with the leadership of the twelve apostles such as the *Frontier Guardian* (Kanesville, Iowa), *St. Louis Luminary*, and *The Mormon* (New York) noted and warned of "apostate" activities throughout the 1850s and 1860s. Missionaries contacted, preached, and encouraged gathering when they encountered scattered Mormons. The Utah Mormons made a concerted effort to gather up those who had remained in branches of the church rather than move either to Nauvoo or to Utah, but these branches are unique among diaspora groups in that they rarely sought to claim or reclaim participants in rival schismatic followings, regarding them as unfaithful in the cause. Young's efforts to gather the scattered Saints was capped around 1852 with the call to evacuate Iowa. Individual missionaries encountered the ungathered as they traveled, but by not hunting these branches methodically, the western branch of the diaspora left the door open to other schismatic churches, and later the Reorganization, to actively pursue the scattered flock. Orson Spencer captured the social situation of Mormonism in 1854 as he told his brother, "I found in Cincinnati some dried up fragments of a Church, the best of them only half-hearted, and had been chased down by wolves so often that they feared that every thing that came along was a wolf. There are others, who lack only some shoes, or rather a preparation of the Gospel, after which they will probably join the standard."[22]

21. "To All the Saints in Pottawatamie" [September 15, 1851], Frontier Guardian, November 14, 1851, in *Messages of the First Presidency*, edited by James R. Clark, 6 vols. (Salt Lake City: Bookcraft, 1965–1975), 2:75–76; see also Thirteenth General Epistle, October 29, 1855, Messages of the First Presidency, 2:186.

22. Orson Spencer to Daniel Spencer, November 14, 1854, *Millennial Star* 16, no. 51 (23 December 1854):812–813.

SCRIPTURE IN THE MORMON DIASPORA CONTEXT

For a moment we will leave the historical context to discuss the place of revelation and scripture within the context of the early Mormon diaspora. Here, we should keep in mind three factors. First, the period that saw the rise of new scripture was comparatively short, lasting roughly from 1840 to 1870. Second, the followings of individual claimants were comparatively small and were often limited to specific locales. Many communities rose, flourished, and expired in just a handful of years. Third, most of the schisms of the diaspora, along with their prophetic pronouncements and doctrine, dissolved without directly shaping the groups that eventually coalesced out of the larger movement, chiefly the Reorganization and the Church of Christ (Temple Lot).[23]

To help explain why scripture and revelation were so important in the diaspora, it may be helpful to recall Shlomo Biederman's metacognitive perspective of scripture. Stepping outside both the textual and contextual spheres, Biederman reminds us that, "To understand scripture is to understand the conditions under which a group of texts has gained authority over the lives of people and has been incorporated into human activities of various important kinds."[24] Regardless of how scripture is employed or how its texts are created, Biederman's statement reminds us that we can step back to look at the spaces between them. His observation that texts *gain authority*—authority is given to the text by readers who expect to glean meaning from the document—refers to the creation of a scriptural canon. In other words, the creation and invocation of scripture is essentially a social function, neither strictly theological nor historical. Ultimately, scripture is made not by divine pronouncement but by the people who accept pronouncement as divine. Theologically (i.e., textually), God's word to mankind constitutes scripture, but historically (i.e., contextually) it is believers who create a canon.

Nicholas Wolterstorff's model for scripture clarifies the discursive nature of scripture within the post-Joseph Latter Day Saint traditions because it has

---

23. See Chrystal Vanel, "The Church of Christ (Temple Lot): A *Solae Scripturae* Mormonism," chapter 5 herein. Other communities such as the followings of Alpheus Cutler and James Strang endured well beyond the diaspora years, albeit in small numbers.

24. Shlomo Biederman, *Scripture and Knowledge: An Essay on Religious Epistemology* (New York: Brill, 1995), 50.

social implications. His model involves at least two and perhaps three agents. Considering the element of his model in reverse, Wolterstorff's third agent is the *reader*, a person who approaches scripture for direction (metaphysical or directive truth). The model's second agent is the *recorder* or writer of a text, the one who has set down in human language what he or she understands from the first agent, the *inspirer*, the Holy Ghost or Spirit that prompts or communicates the will or words of God.[25] In faith traditions accepting the Bible as literal or authoritative, the action of the third agent is implicit. Socially, however, Wolterstorff's first agent is the one least important to the formation of scripture. Scripture takes on social authority merely by being recorded and accepted by the second and third agents in his model.

Prior to 1840, Mormons had developed a firm social foundation of scripture, but the diaspora shook things loose again and reopened the challenge of a vital connection to heaven. Multiple claimants argued that they picked up Joseph Smith's mantle and spoke for God as his successor, offering the same kind of evidence of their standing by advancing new revelation intended as scripture. James Brewster attempted a translation of another purportedly ancient record, the Kinderhook plates, and his own new revelation, The Book of Esdras. Gladden Bishop produced and distributed by mail a broadside "flying roll." James Strang recorded The Book of the Law of the Lord in two versions and a translation of an ancient record by "Rajah Manchou of Vorito." Each item was an attempt to establish revelation as a basis for ecclesiastical authority within Mormonism's prophetic tradition.[26] Despite their revelatory claims and activity, the various prophets and believers of the Mormon diaspora did not find their work gaining broad acceptance. All would agree that George Adams's Sword of Truth and Harbinger of Peace, or Gladden Bishop's Ensign, Light of Zion, Shepherd of Israel, and Book of Remembrance, Moses Norris's Ensign to the Nations to Gather Israel, or James Strang's Book of the Law of the Lord, involved Wolterstorff's reader and writer. Each item was an attempt to establish revelation as a basis for asserting ecclesiastical authority within

25. Nicholas Wolterstorff, *Divine Discourse: Philosophical Reflections on the Claim That God Speaks* (Cambridge: Cambridge University Press, 1995), 4–8. This simple model of character involvement is not a comprehensive interpretation. It ignores linguistic and a half dozen other theories and theologies of process, content, and etiology.

26. On Brewster's translation, see Fawn Brodie to Dale Morgan, September 2 19[44], Dale Lowell Morgan papers 10:87; Francis Gladden Bishop, *The Words of Righteousness to All Men* (1851); and James J. Strang, *The Book of the Law of the Lord* (1856).

Mormonism's prophetic tradition. Part of the problem facing diaspora believers, and argued strenuously among them, was the inability to demonstrate or convincingly assert divine inspiration. Almost all of them published, yet few claimants successfully created for their adherents a *canon*, or a generally accepted scripture. The question of competing social authority in the diaspora was both complicated and simplified by texts accepted as recorded revelation.

The Mormon diaspora began in Nauvoo as argument over church (i.e., social) leadership, though understanding its nuances is complicated; some asserted leadership while vigorously denying direct succession to Joseph Smith. Those who aspired to leadership often chose to demonstrate divine authority or inspiration by proposing new revelation and then by attempting to create new scripture. Thus, the creation of scripture became a means of demonstrating social authority in the early years of the Mormon diaspora. The diaspora itself was an amalgam of historical Protestant assumption about the nature of scripture and the expectation that Mormonism's intellectual tradition of revelation and the prophetic station should remain viable. However, where Joseph Smith succeeded in creating new scripture, which established a standard for a prophet providing believers with God's words, his would-be successors largely failed. In fact, the later years of the diaspora are characterized by a *rejection* of new scripture and a social reassertion of Mormonism's basal texts. The diaspora proved that Mormonism's intellectual prophetic/charismatic tradition could not exist independent of a strong institution. The various prophets and believers of the Mormon diaspora did not have the luxury of their work gaining broad, recognized acceptance. Few claimants in the diaspora successfully created for their adherents a *canon*, or a generally accepted scripture.

The production of revelation and creation of scripture became a means of demonstrating social authority in the early years of the Mormon diaspora. Where Smith succeeded in creating new scripture, which established a standard for what a prophet should provide to believers, his would-be successors largely failed. In fact, the later years of the diaspora are characterized by a *rejection* of new scripture and a social reassertion of Mormonism's foundational texts. The diaspora proved that Mormonism's prophetic/charismatic tradition could not thrive independent of a strong institution. Many became disenchanted with new prophets and actively dismissed their theological and ritual innovations after Smith's death. Since those in the diaspora also rejected the existing corporate/priestly tradition in Utah, they needed to reestablish it anew and reincorporate the faith on different grounds.

THE LATE DIASPORA AS A SOCIAL STUDY

In looking at the entire scope of postmartyrdom Mormonism, the distinction between the faithful and apostates is often difficult to make on assertions alone. Everyone claimed to be doing the same thing: faithfully curating the legacy of Joseph Smith. Until the 1860s, those who had once been involved with the Latter Day Saints or became adherents to one or more of its schismatic followings generally considered themselves part of a larger Mormon identity, no matter where they were or who they were following, unless they chose to dissociate with Mormonism entirely and return to mainline Christian sects. Compounding the confusion, many of the diaspora leaders claimed to be the authoritative successor to Joseph Smith and his following to be the "true faith" and heritage of Joseph Smith.[27]

A letter from Isaac Bishop to his sister Anna Maria Brim provides a good example of the complexity of the diaspora experience. Isaac was previously a member of the Springfield, Illinois, stake presidency but was then following Austin Cowles. Anna, on the other hand, was heading west to Salt Lake Valley following Brigham Young. In the letter, which mentioned that their brother Gladden was leading his own following, Isaac explains that Gladden was "as much a Mormon as ever," a sentiment entirely appropriate to the period.[28] Isaac, brother Gladden, and their westering sister—with allegiances as diverse as their geographic movements—were all partakers of a larger albeit divided religious culture. For many, there was no socially clear, mutually acknowledged dividing line between the "faithful" and the "unfaithful" during the diaspora.

Mormonism seems to have maintained a powerful ideological influence in those converted to it. "Verry few, fully apostatize from, or renounce a belief in the principles of what was calld Mormonism," wrote one such individual,

---

27. This generalization is complicated by several who advance their leadership or mission without claiming to be Joseph's prophetic successor. Lyman Wight and James Emmett both asserted that they were fulfilling missions assigned by Joseph Smith, but their claims as prophetic figures are uncertain.

28. I[saac] H. Bishop to Alexander Brim, August 4, 1847, CHL.

"Orthodoxy! is my doxy."[29] Like the Bishop siblings, many of the Mormons who chose to stay in the Midwest in the 1840s became attached to one of the prophetic rivals challenging Brigham Young as steward of Smith's legacy. And they were joined by new converts. An important social characteristic of the diaspora outside of Utah was social cross-fertilization, as individuals and leaders in one organization shifted allegiance to another. This included David Whitmer, one of the three witnesses to the Book of Mormon; Nauvoo stake president William Marks; apostles William E. McLellin and John E. Page; and even the discredited John C. Bennett. Each was sought at different times for the prestige his membership would lend to an organization, and over time each belonged to several different Mormon churches. Both Marks and Page bestowed ordinations on one or more of the diaspora's schismatic figures. Other claimants stood firmly and independently on their claimed prophetic callings, at least for a while. Most prominent were Sidney Rigdon, William Smith, Charles B. Thompson, James Colin Brewster, Oliver Olney, Francis Gladden Bishop, Joseph Morris, and of course James J. Strang. Each left published records documenting attempts to gather the faithful and reclaim the repentant. Even they were challenged by other aspirants whose brief diaspora careers and publications of revelation are barely remembered: Moses Norris, George J. Adams, Jacob Syfritt, Zadoc Brooks, W. A. Minor, "Potter Christ," and John Gaylord.[30] Eventually those who became disenchanted with would-be prophets actively dismissed unique and eyebrow-raising innovation or statements of individual claimants. Since they also rejected the Latter Day Saint corporate/priestly tradition surviving in Utah, they needed to rejoin the intellectual traditions that had been divided by the Rigdon-Young contest in Nauvoo and "re-corporate" the faith on different grounds.

THE DISSOLUTION OF THE MORMON DIASPORA AND EMERGENCE OF NEW DENOMINATIONS

Eventually, the various fires of Mormonism's independent charismatic/prophetic tradition burned out. Expressing revelation and creating a canon had

---

29. Ezra Strong to Solomon Strong, September 30, 1855, Ezra Strong Letters, Washington State University Special Collections.

30. Richard Saunders, ed., *Dale Morgan on the Mormons, Collected Works*, Part 2, *1949–1970* (Norman, OK: University of Oklahoma Press, 2013), 253–337.

become tangled in the central social challenge of the Mormon diaspora: capitalizing on scripture and revelation to establish ecclesiastical authority, and maintaining socially accepted authority sufficiently stable to hold congregations together. Having a prophetic call was one thing; convincing others of that call was quite something else. Often disillusioned by what they found, many drifted out of the diaspora back into mainstream Protestant churches. Others simply disassociated themselves from the diaspora and waited. In 1853, a "New Movement" began to coalesce around the activities of Jason Briggs and Zenas Gurley. Both men had lost faith in one or another diaspora prophet, dismissed the Utah branch of the church, and determined to simply wait for the Lord to move the work of re-corporating Mormonism in His own time. The Reorganization began to take shape around their efforts.

The Reorganization was one group able to transition away from charisma, doing so by continuing the congregational independence of the earliest days and making the church more ecumenical. Still, as new problems presented themselves for revelatory or authoritative resolution, the Reorganization experienced the stresses of adapting to doctrinal change. With change inevitable, the RLDS church drew on the tradition of its earliest history (1853–1859) as a coalition of largely independent groups and began a move toward democratic controls on the position and role of prophet and president of the church—the charismatic role that remained essential to Latter Day Saint theology and social identity.[31]

During its earliest years, the Reorganization concentrated its efforts in the Midwest, gathering those with a Mormon heritage. The movement was able to consolidate a substantial percentage of diaspora Mormonism exactly when earlier followings were beginning to break apart. By 1860, James Strang had been assassinated and Charles B. Thompson chased across the prairie by unhappy followers. Former apostle William McLellin had given up his efforts to reestablish a Kirtland "Church of Christ." Sidney Rigdon had failed to lastingly establish his Pittsburgh following, though a resurrection of his claims came later under Stephen Post.[32] Lyman Wight had died, and Alpheus Cutler would soon pass away. Few Mormon diaspora leaders had focused

---

31. Roger Launius, *Joseph Smith III: Pragmatic Prophet* (Urbana: University of Illinois Press, 1988), 277, 292, 366.

32. See Jay Burton, "Scriptures for the Children of Zion: The Revelations of Sidney and Phebe Rigdon," chapter 12 herein.

on creating a stable ecclesiastical hierarchy. They continued, perhaps unintentionally, the pattern of charismatic leadership instituted by Smith but without generating the kind of priestly tradition that kept the largest part of the church together in 1844. Yet for the most part, the dissolving followings remained geographically close. These groups with a history of Mormonism were thus fertile grounds for the efforts of RLDS missionaries.

Revelatory works such as Bishop's Address to the Sons and Daughters of Zion, Thompson's Book of Enoch, or Brewster's Book of Esdras eventually lost value to former believers.[33] Conversely, the Latter Day Saint canon that existed prior to 1840 took on new significance. Previously canonized scripture became a foundation for taking a stand within the diaspora. As early as the ill-fated single issue of the *Nauvoo Expositor* in 1844, William Law editorialized, "We all verily believe, and many of us know of a surety, that the religion of the Latter Day Saints, as originally taught by Joseph Smith, which is contained in the Old and New Testaments, Book of [Doctrine and] Covenants, and Book of Mormon, is verily true."[34]

In the 1850s, a key theological problem facing the diaspora saints was resolving the position of *human* leadership—those who claimed to be the mouthpiece for God. With Mormonism's intellectual charismatic/prophetic and corporate/priestly traditions effectively divided by the Rigdon-Young contest of August 1844, one historical conclusion is that its charismatic tradition alone was not a sufficiently viable foundation on which to build and sustain a church. If old Mormons and new converts to diaspora Mormonism were to endure in their faith, then believers needed to reestablish the church and control the fires of the charismatic tradition. It remained for the Church of Christ (Temple Lot) and the Reorganization to accomplish that task, employing three different tacks.[35]

First, re-corporating diaspora Mormonism included reining in the presence of spiritual gifts practiced among the laity, such as declarations of prophecy, visions, and speaking in tongues. It seems to have been common

33. For remarks on the Book of Enoch, see Christopher James Blythe, "The Book of Enoch 'Revised, Corrected, and the Missing Parts Restored,'" chapter 10 herein. For remarks on the Book of Esdras, see Laurie Maffly-Kipp, "Anchored in Revelation: Scripture and Schism in the Restoration," chapter 2 herein.

34. *Nauvoo Expositor*, June 7, 1844.

35. I will limit most of my remarks to the Reorganization. For comments on canon in the Church of Christ (Temple Lot), see Vanel, "The Church of Christ (Temple Lot)," chapter 5 herein.

for individual Mormons to look for spiritual gifts as they investigated diaspora congregations. While it would make sense for such communities to promote these gifts, many communities tried to rein in this charismatic tradition. For instance, in 1864, *The Truth Teller*, associated with the Church of Christ (Temple Lot), warned that the presence of spiritual gifts was not sufficient evidence that one division of Mormonism was more correct than another. "It is no evidence that any of these parties are right [merely] because its members enjoy the promised gifts, no matter when they obeyed the gospel. The existence of these very essential and promised gifts prove this and nothing more than this, that those who enjoy them are accepted believers in Christ, no matter to what division they belong."[36] The manifestation of spiritual gifts became increasingly a private rather than congregational matter. Still, it was not the charismatic gifts of the spirit practiced among the laity that caused the most controversy but the unchecked prophetic gift in a leader against which diaspora Mormons reacted.

By the early 1850s, the charismatic fires of the diaspora were beginning to char as well as inflame Restoration believers. A widespread sense of biding time seemed to emerge during the mid and late diaspora. Zenas Gurley, one of the central figures of the New Organization and later the Reorganization, experienced a personal vision in which he was told, "Rise up, cast off all that claim to be prophets, and go forth and preach this gospel, and say that God will raise up a prophet to complete his work."[37] Early Reorganization and Church of Christ (Temple Lot) records are filled with similar accounts of personal inspiration—voices, visions, witnesses, testimonies—in which individual recipients are told specifically not to accept current claimants to Latter Day Saint authority because a prophet would eventually be "raised up" to take his place at the head of the church. By the early 1850s, these communications created an alternative to remaining diaspora congregations, specifically pointing the recipients to something outside the diaspora followings and urging them to look forward to a renewal of the faith. Where new revelation and new scripture was the hallmark of the early diaspora, adherence to a stable canon became key to churchly authority in the late diaspora.

---

36. *Truth Teller* 1, no.4 (October 1864):62.

37. *True Latter Day Saints Herald* 1, no. 1 (1864):22–23, quoted in Pearl Wilcox, *Regathering the Scattered Saints in Wisconsin and Illinois* (Independence, MO: P. G. Wilcox, 1984), 47.

The committee of an 1853 conference of unaffiliated Latter Day Saints at Beloit, Wisconsin—many of whom had been converted to the Restoration in diaspora followings and become disaffected—issued *A Word of Consolation to the Scattered Saints*, bidding them wait for the Lord's "re-establishment of the Church in Zion," naming and explicitly dismissing claimants to the prophetic mantle or priesthood leadership. This conference, which effectively began the move toward the 1860 Reorganization, relied heavily on previously canonized latter-day scripture to frame its message. Importantly, a conference resolution also noted that "the whole law of the Church of Jesus Christ, is contained in the Bible, Book of Mormon, and Book of Doctrine and Covenants."[38] The reemphasis of the fundamental texts of the Restoration is the second element involved in re-corporating the Diaspora saints.

Between about 1852 and 1870, collections of believers coalesced into informal, unaffiliated congregations. Eventually these independent congregations began holding conferences seeking common ground and beliefs. Frustrated with competing prophetic claims, and meeting as equal participants, conference participants instituted a second check on Mormonism's prophetic/charismatic tradition by standing firmly upon a sectarian version of American democratic liberalism. Conferences became constituent assemblies, governed by majority votes. By invoking democracy within the circle of Spirit-moved believers, conferences imposed a check on divine pronouncement that rested both on Book of Mormon scripture and Joseph Smith's modern revelation.[39] Reaching like this into American political culture and adopting the secular strength of American democratic liberalism is the third element in re-corporating a church from the diaspora. With it, believers crafted the foundation for a new administrative structure that controlled the prophetic tradition, one that had previously proved to be socially unstable.[40]

Scorched by the fire of revelation from conflicting prophets, having set aside the reality of spiritual gifts as a sign, and invoking democratic liberalism as a congregational structure, the scattered and unaffiliated congregations

38. Jason W. Briggs, *A Word of Consolation to the Scattered Saints: The Law of Succession, in the First Presidency of the Church of Jesus Christ of Latter-day Saints* (1853), 2.

39. See for example, Mosiah-LDS 29:25–26; Mosiah-CC 13:34–36; D&C-CC 25:1b, 27:4c; D&C-LDS 26:2, 28:13.

40. Representative examples of personal manifestations are cited in Wilcox, *Regathering the Scattered Saints*, and Launius, *Joseph Smith III*, 273–290. Interpretations of the process that constituted "common consent" differ among the denominations.

eventually dealt with an agreed need for new revelation and new scripture by returning to a kind of *sola scriptura*. But there was an important difference: in the case of the Reorganization, the canon was never closed completely. The Reorganization in the late diaspora began as a restoration of the Restoration—a return to first principles, which began in scattered congregations by defining scripture as the Bible, Book of Mormon, and Book of Commandments or Doctrine and Covenants.[41] What Christopher Blythe has called the *standard canon* or *Joseph Smith canon* became an authoritative anchor to groups reacting to flux they perceived within Mormonism's broad tradition. Nor was the move limited to the New Organization groups that eventually coalesced into the Reorganization.

In October 1853, reacting both to news of polygamy in Utah and the emergence of the New Organization, members of the Crow Creek Branch— the northern Illinois congregation that provided a foundation for the Church of Christ (Temple Lot)—decided to hold themselves apart from both groups and specifically stated their canon. "They declared themselves free from all such [diaspora schisms and prophets], and pledged themselves to stand by the Bible, the Book of Mormon, and the Doctrine and Covenants, and to build upon the truths contained in these books."[42] As Chrystal Vanel points out in another chapter of this volume, this group of believers, like others, checked the prophetic fire of new revelation by insisting on a textual foundation. This first step was followed only later with a second step recreating a church structure, or priestly organization, adding a tempering layer of corporate functions grounded firmly in American democratic liberalism to replace the broader priestly tradition headquartered in Utah. Doing so effectively controlled a leader's prophetic or inspired pronouncement without rejecting Mormonism's prophetic tradition. In congregations across the Midwest, once the church had been locally reestablished and the tradition of charisma/prophecy given a firm democratic check, direction of the church by revelation could again become viable.[43]

41. Briggs, *A Word of Consolation*, 2.

42. B. C. Flint, *An Outline History of the Church of Christ (Temple Lot)* (Independence, MO: Board of Publications, 1953), 99.

43. Zenas Gurley eventually clashed with the Reorganization leadership over the centralization of scripture and revelation. Clare D. Vlahos, "The Challenge of Centralized Power: Zenas H. Gurley Jr. and the Prophetic Office," *Courage: A Journal of History, Thought, and Action* 1, no. 3 (March 1971):141–158.

But settling anew a scriptural canon and adopting a democratic check on revelation was abstract when compared to more practical questions of leadership for the emerging social restructuring. By 1860, the New Organization found the figure with the social credentials that they craved and could be confident God had raised up: Joseph Smith III. On April 4, 1860, this "Young Joseph" stood before a conference of believers gathered in Amboy, Illinois, responding to "a will not my own" and agreed to assume the mantle that was offered him. That reluctance contrasted with the self-proclaimed schismatic claimants of ten or twenty years earlier, who pronounced their divine calls and claims in person and in print.[44] For many of those worn out by false promises of prophetic leadership, the Reorganization of the church under Young Joseph offered the last big Latter Day Saint promise.

Despite Joseph III's presence as a figurehead, a leader, and (willingly or reluctantly) the personification of revelatory authority, many believers accepted Mormonism's prophetic/charismatic tradition and its new scripture but still held a skeptical view of a prophet. Building on the practice of conferences that had regathered the scattered saints, the New Organization created a check on prophetic prerogative. The Mormon diaspora coalesced and the Reorganization emerged partly by turning to Protestant views of scripture and inspiration, imposing a layer of social control onto Mormonism's prophetic "living scripture." Conference attendees were not merely individuals but authorized, representative delegates from individual congregations. Resolutions and ratifications of revelatory statements by Joseph III, Frederick M. Smith, and their successors were made by straightforward majority votes.

As the New Organization gained strength and became the Reorganized Church of Jesus Christ of Latter Day Saints, it continued (and continues) to generate and accept revelations, adding them to the Doctrine and Covenants. The edition of the Doctrine and Covenants maintained by the Community of Christ hews directly to the methods established in the Reorganization's early years: recording inspiration by the prophet and president of the church but then relying on discussion and ratification by a constituent assembly for canonization within the scripture.[45] A new democratic tradition

---

44. Launius, *Joseph Smith III*, 115–118.

45. Launius, *Joseph Smith III*, ch. 7; Kyle R. Walker, "William B. Smith and 'The Josephites,'" *Journal of Mormon History* 40, no. 4 (Fall 2014):73–129; Richard D. Howard, "Latter Day Saint Scripture and the Doctrine of Propositional Revelation," *Courage* 1, no. 4 (June 1971):209–225.

FIGURE 3.1. Joseph Smith III. Courtesy of the Church History Library, the Church of Jesus Christ of Latter-day Saints.

successfully checked and stabilized both prophetic/charismatic and priestly/corporate traditions of Mormonism, having emerged from the early Latter Day Saint tradition and been tried in the diaspora.

CONCLUSION

Joseph Smith Jr. changed the religious landscape for converts to his new denomination, reinvoking the status and standing of a Biblical prophet. By inadvertently creating twin expectations of both a charismatic/prophetic expectation of new revelation and a corporate/priestly structure of order and organization, he also crafted deep and long-lasting social traditions. His death in 1844 left open a question about the role of a prophet as the church continued. Though a large proportion of the church accepted the priestly/corporate leadership of the priesthood quorums led by the Twelve Apostles, claimants to prophetic/charismatic station flourished (although often their ministries were comparatively brief). As congregations divided over competing claims or challenges, Mormonism's fiery charismatic tradition proved unstable. Accepting Mormonism but rejecting Utah's branch, new converts to the other branches of Mormonism began seeking ways to maintain but restrain prophetic leadership and to foster both religious and social stability. Looking for alternatives to an independent and unchallengeable prophet, scripture became a common denominator on which believers could agree to re-corporate a socially stable church.

In short, through the Mormon diaspora scripture in the Latter Day Saint tradition became canonical but not fixed, and all the sects claiming Joseph Smith Jr. as a founder have had to come to grips with the place of modern revelation and its relationship to scripture within the church. While each emerging tradition had to settle the question of how an open canon would be supplemented, the Latter Day Saint scriptural canon itself largely endures.

PART II

Reception of Joseph Smith's Revelations

4

Books of Mormon

Latter-day Saints, Latter Day Saints,
and the Book of Mormon

Joseph M. Spencer

Wilfred Cantwell Smith opens his book *What Is Scripture?* with what he calls a basic point: "A number of quite divergent scriptures have been cherished around the world, and have played immensely significant, yet varying, roles in human history because of being treated as scripture."[1] This basic point is, perhaps, relatively obvious when considering world religions. It has been less obvious—or at least has received little attention—in the context of the various branches of the larger Latter Day Saint movement. Happily, the essays making up this volume testify to a growing recognition that often quite divergent scriptures have been cherished among the branches of the movement.

For my own contribution (and in concert with other papers in Part II of this volume), however, I wish to highlight a slightly different point. A crucial feature of scriptural variety is the fact that individual volumes of scripture have (to quote Smith again) "demonstrably been read in a number of divergent ways, ways that have differed from century to century, region to region, village to town, study to palace."[2] Part of what it means to investigate the variety of scriptural traditions among the branches of the Latter Day Saint movement is to look carefully at how works of scripture *common* to different branches have nonetheless operated as functionally *different* texts. It is this aspect of scriptural variety that I mean to address here, focusing specifically on the Book of Mormon.

---

1. Wilfred Cantwell Smith, *What Is Scripture? A Comparative Approach* (Minneapolis: Fortress Press, 2005), 16.
2. Ibid.

Of course, it is not difficult to see that certain passages within the Book of Mormon have been read in drastically distinct ways by different branches of the Latter Day Saint movement—for example, Jacob's discussion of polygamy, long a point of contention among several different churches in the movement. And it would not be difficult either to show—as Chrystal Vanel does in her contribution to this volume—that distinct branches of the movement have dramatically different ways of understanding the import of scripture (over against, say, the authority of ecclesiastical leaders). Yet I intend to make a more radical claim here. I mean to investigate the way in which there have been *at least two Books of Mormon* in circulation since 1860. For a century and a half, the Church of Jesus Christ of Latter-day Saints (LDS) and the Reorganized Church of Jesus Christ of Latter Day Saints (RLDS) or (since 2001) Community of Christ (CofC) have rallied around what should be regarded in the last analysis as distinct texts—despite the fact that the vast majority of the words in the two books are identical.[3] Distinct but intersecting publishing histories help to delineate two strikingly different books that misleadingly look as if they are basically the same. Here, I outline a comparative study of historical LDS and RLDS/CofC editions of the Book of Mormon, aiming to show that the Book of Mormon *itself* should, in certain forms, be numbered among those volumes of scripture prevalent in non-LDS branches of the movement.

I should begin, however, with a quick note about the perspective from which I approach this study. By training, I am a philosopher with a particular interest in scriptural theology.[4] I am not a historian of religions, nor do

3. I refer to the Reorganized Church when speaking of the era before 2001, when the church became Community of Christ, while I refer to Community of Christ when speaking of the era beginning with 2001. I venture here to use the acronyms "LDS," "RLDS," and "CofC" as the simplest way of keeping the two traditions straight during this discussion. The Church of Jesus Christ of Latter-day Saints has recently placed a stronger emphasis on the use of the church's proper name and discouraged the use of "LDS." In a scholarly and comparative context like the present one, it would prove difficult to communicate without using a readily identifiable signifier of which tradition is meant—especially when the slight graphical difference between "Latter-day Saints" and "Latter Day Saints" signals a massive theological and ecclesiological difference. I have therefore, with some regrets, decided it is best here to use the traditional acronyms to ensure clarity and communicability. The signifiers "LDS," "RLDS," and "CofC" are traditional and were used by those involved in much of the history outlined here.

4. For an outline of what "scriptural theology" entails, see James E. Faulconer and Joseph M. Spencer, eds., *Perspectives on Mormon Theology: Scriptural Theology* (Salt Lake City: Greg Kofford Books, 2015), 1–5.

I have training in the discipline of religious studies. I approach this topic as an interpreter invested in the meaning of scriptural texts—particularly the Book of Mormon—who is fully cognizant of the ways in which apparatus and style of presentation inform textual meaning and therefore shape the task of interpretation. As to confession, I am a fully committed, believing member of the Church of Jesus Christ of Latter-day Saints, but I recognize that I stand to learn much about reading my own scriptural texts by considering how the Book of Mormon assumes a distinct shape in another Latter Day Saint tradition. I assume, of course, that my own confessional distance from the storied Community of Christ tradition leaves me with important blind spots, but I nonetheless hope that I have learned much by attempting to consider quite seriously another tradition's wrestle with a sacred text.

BEFORE THE REORGANIZATION

With one remarkable exception to be discussed in the next section, all editions of the Book of Mormon published before 1860 were understood as having been produced by the adherents of a single branch of the Latter Day Saint movement. There were, of course, many branches of the movement already by the time of the Reorganization in 1860—that is, by the time various believers in Joseph Smith's prophetic gifts gathered to create the Reorganized Church of Jesus Christ of Latter Day Saints. To that point, however, only the majoritarian form of this religious tradition, which traced itself back from the Church of Jesus Christ of Latter-day Saints to the first Church of Christ organized by Joseph Smith in 1830, had retained control over printing and distribution of the Book of Mormon. Three editions of the book were issued directly under the supervision of Smith himself: a first edition in Palmyra, New York, 1830; a second edition in Kirtland, Ohio, 1837; and a third edition in Nauvoo, Illinois, 1840.[5] Both the second (1837) and third (1840) editions were products of substantial editorial work. For the second edition, Smith corrected grammatical errors, updated language, eliminated excessive

5. For helpful notes and bibliographical information, see Peter Crawley, *A Descriptive Bibliography of the Mormon Church*, 3 vols. (Provo, UT: BYU Religious Studies Center, 1997), 1:28–32, 66–68, 129–133. For a more popular and somewhat devotional study of these three editions, see Richard E. Turley Jr. and William W. Slaughter, *How We Got the Book of Mormon* (Salt Lake City: Deseret Book, 2011), 26–65.

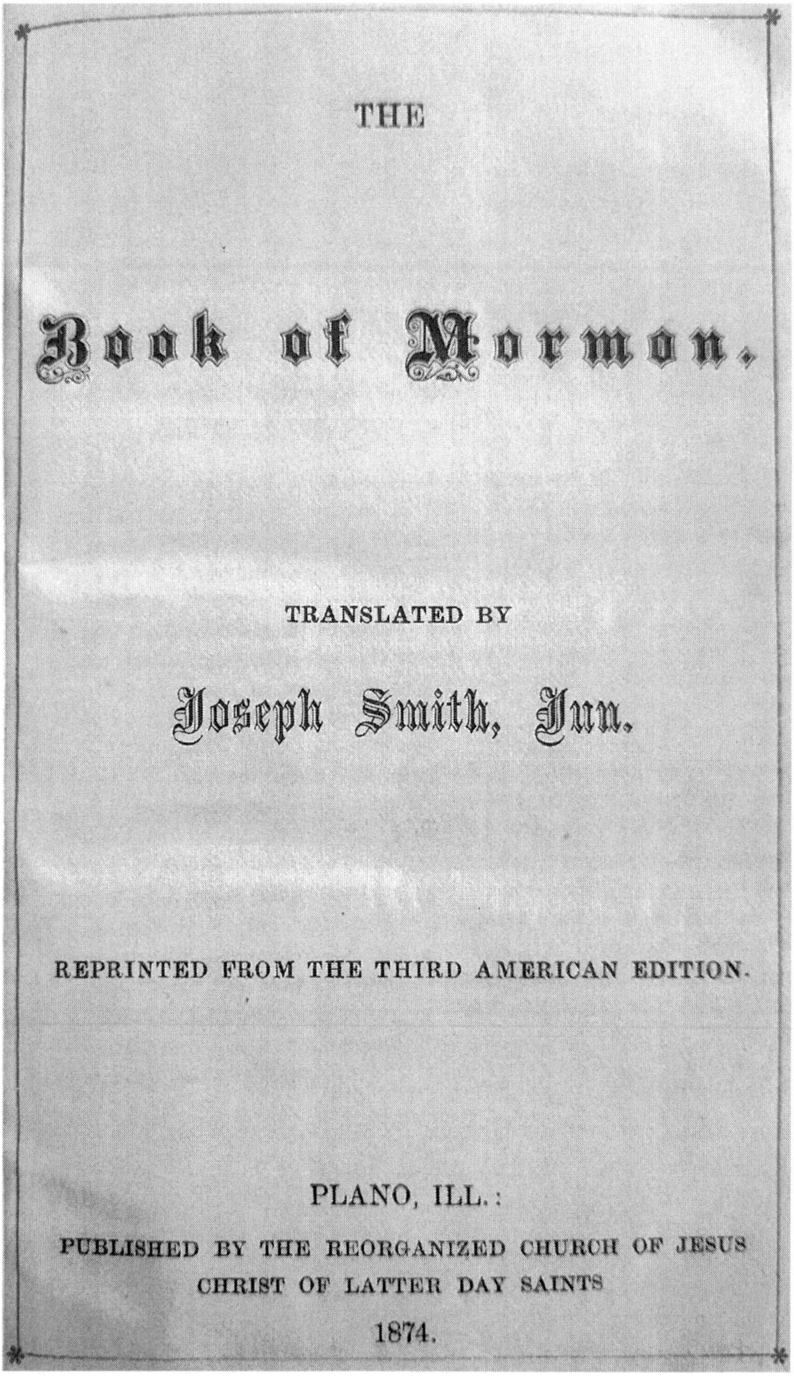

THE

Book of Mormon.

TRANSLATED BY

Joseph Smith, Jun.

REPRINTED FROM THE THIRD AMERICAN EDITION.

PLANO, ILL.:

PUBLISHED BY THE REORGANIZED CHURCH OF JESUS
CHRIST OF LATTER DAY SAINTS

1874.

FIGURE 4.1. Book of Mormon (1874). The first edition of the Book of Mormon published by the Reorganized Church of Jesus Christ of Latter Day Saints.

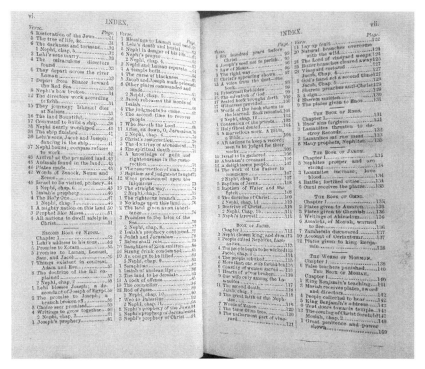

FIGURE 4.2. Index from the Book of Mormon (1874, RLDS).

instances of "it came to pass," and made a few changes in wording. For the third edition, further changes along the same lines were made, and the text was proofed against the original manuscript produced during dictation.[6] (Such attention to minor details of language in the text—however conservatively demonstrated in making alterations to the text—is part of the ongoing process of canonization, as Kathleen Flake's contribution to the present volume makes clear.)

Differences among these first three editions proved to be consequential in subsequent history. Because LDS editions published after 1840 were for

---

6. For a helpful list of the most significant textual changes in the Book of Mormon over its many editions, see Royal Skousen, ed., *The Book of Mormon: The Earliest Text* (New Haven: Yale University Press, 2009), 739–789. Another helpful resource, albeit one limited to the LDS printing tradition, is John S. Dinger, ed., *Significant Textual Changes in the Book of Mormon: The First Printed Edition Compared to the Manuscripts and to the Subsequent Major LDS English Printed Editions* (Salt Lake City: Smith-Pettit Foundation, 2013).

many years produced in England (where it was more affordable to produce books than in Utah), and because those who inaugurated this publishing tradition left the United States for England in 1839, LDS editions were for many years refinements and developments of the 1837 Kirtland edition. For the first fifty years of the RLDS tradition, on the other hand, available editions of the Book of Mormon were derived from the 1840 Nauvoo edition. Significantly, the Reorganized Church deliberately shifted its attention from the 1840 Nauvoo edition to the 1837 Kirtland edition after it came into possession of the printer's manuscript of the Book of Mormon. In parallel, the LDS tradition has since 1981 used an edition produced through careful comparison with the Nauvoo edition and manuscript sources (with some comparison with the Nauvoo edition undertaken already for the 1852 LDS edition). These are details that will be discussed below, but they merit being introduced here.

With the first European edition of 1841, the distinctly LDS publishing tradition took initial shape.[7] A second European edition appeared in 1849 and a third in 1852. The last of these was the most significant for several reasons. Most of the typographical errors of the hurriedly produced first European edition had been corrected by that point. Further, as Royal Skousen notes, the 1852 edition included "a considerable number of changes based on the 1840 [Nauvoo] edition."[8] Still further, for the first time in the book's publishing history, the paragraphs of the text were numbered for ready reference.[9] But perhaps most important of all was the fact that the publisher set this edition from newly created stereotype plates, which "were used for all of the [LDS] Church's subsequent impressions before 1879."[10] Thus, eight years before the Reorganization, the LDS publishing tradition established a relatively stable text and form of presentation for the Book of Mormon, one that would continue in use until after the RLDS tradition published its own first edition.

More needs to be said about the 1852 LDS edition, as well as about the editions available to early adherents to the Reorganization in 1860. But it

---

7. For notes, bibliographical information, and discussion, see Crawley, *A Descriptive Bibliography of the Mormon Church*, 1:148–151; and Turley and Slaughter, *How We Got the Book of Mormon*, 66–79.

8. Royal Skousen, *Analysis of the Textual Variants of the Book of Mormon*, 6 vols. (Provo, UT: FARMS, 2004–2009), 1:15.

9. Turley and Slaughter, *How We Got the Book of Mormon*, 82–84.

10. Crawley, *A Descriptive Bibliography of the Mormon Church*, 2:313.

might be best to group further discussion with an attempt at delineating the initial divergence between the two textual traditions.

ESTABLISHING DIVERGENT TRADITIONS

Because the first RLDS edition of the Book of Mormon appeared only in 1874, one might assume that the beginnings of divergence between the two churches' relationships to the Book of Mormon began in earnest only at that point. As it turns out, however, many adherents of the Reorganization used a deliberately non-LDS edition of the Book of Mormon from the very beginning. In 1858, two years before the Reorganization, James O. Wright and Company published an edition of the Book of Mormon in New York City, presented to the public as a "curious work" about which there was "a general desire for information."[11] It opens with an introduction meant to strike a note of scholarly neutrality, stating that "questions" concerning the Book of Mormon's origins "have never been satisfactorily answered."[12] The introduction then sets side by side the then-standard believing account of the book's divine origins (the story of Joseph Smith and the angel) and the then-standard unbelieving account of the book's entirely human origins (the story of Solomon Spaulding and plagiarism). "The reader" is to "decide for himself from the record."[13] As for the body of the text, the Wright edition is meant to be a faithful reprinting of the 1840 Nauvoo edition, the last prepared during the life of Joseph Smith.[14] It was this Wright edition that many early adherents to the Reorganization used. According to Richard Howard, the Reorganization's "ministers mostly used [this] edition . . . until in 1874 the church was able to publish its first edition."[15]

11. The Book of Mormon, Reprinted from the Third American Edition, Carefully Revised by the Translator, trans. Joseph Smith Jr. (New York: Jas. O. Wright and Company, 1858), iii. See further p. xii: "Considered simply as a literary curiosity, the work is worthy of preservation; but when regarded as the accepted groundwork of the religious faith of a people whose growth has been most extraordinary, and whose fanaticism is an astonishing phenomenon in psychology, the book has more than a mere ephemeral interest."

12. Ibid., v.

13. Ibid., xii.

14. It should be noted that despite the efforts of the publishers there are variants in the Wright edition. These are tracked meticulously in Skousen, *Analysis of the Textual Variants of the Book of Mormon*.

15. Richard P. Howard, *Restoration Scriptures: A Study of Their Textual Development*, 2nd ed. (Independence, MO: Herald House, 1995), 37. It should be noted that the first edition of Howard's

This might seem at first to be a minor detail. Yet the contrast between what RLDS and LDS leaders found as they opened to the first pages of their respective copies of the Book of Mormon was, already in the 1860s, quite substantial. The 1852 LDS edition (like the other two European editions preceding it) begins with the volume's title page and then the testimonies of the Three and Eight Witnesses—affidavit-like documents presenting spiritual and physical evidence for the authenticity of the book.[16] While these testimonies also appear before the body of the text in the Wright edition (unlike the Nauvoo edition it is meant to reproduce and where they appear at the close of the volume), the reader of the Wright edition finds them only after first encountering the intentionally neutral introduction described above.[17] Thus, from the very beginning, RLDS readers of the Book of Mormon often confronted a text whose authenticity was somewhat in question—or at least was presented in the physical product as being in question. They had the testimonies of numerous witnesses to consider but only after they had been asked to consider several reasons to doubt the book's authenticity. During the same period, LDS readers were presented with a text whose provenance was effectively decided: it was introduced only by affirmative witnesses who declared the truth of the book.[18] Where the LDS branch of the movement could cordon itself off from American culture to a remarkable degree, and so had from the outset a stronger sense of control over the meaning of the

---

study suggested more consistent use of the Wright edition. See Richard P. Howard, *Restoration Scriptures: A Study of Their Textual Development*, 1st ed. (Independence, MO: Herald House, 1969), 53–54.

16. The Book of Mormon: An Account Written by the Hand of Mormon, upon Plates Taken from the Plates of Nephi, trans. Joseph Smith Jr. (Liverpool: F. D. Richards, 1852), iii, v. See Crawley, *A Descriptive Bibliography of the Mormon Church*, 1:151, describing the 1841 first European edition: "Unlike its predecessors, it has the testimonies of the three and eight witnesses at the beginning."

17. See The Book of Mormon, Reprinted from the Third American Edition (1858), xiv. By contrast, compare The Book of Mormon, trans. Joseph Smith Jr., 3rd ed. (Nauvoo, IL: Robinson and Smith, 1840), 572–573.

18. Other minor points of consideration might be mentioned. The Wright edition contains the index-like table of contents found in the 1852 LDS edition (as well as in the two preceding European editions), likely because a version of the same index was printed in Nauvoo in 1841 and often tipped in to printed copies of the 1840 Nauvoo edition. See Crawley, *A Descriptive Bibliography of the Mormon Church*, 1:132. Almost certainly, the Wright edition was set from a copy with the index tipped in. Compare The Book of Mormon (LDS 1852), vii–xii, and The Book of Mormon (Wright), xv–xix. By contrast to this point of similarity between the 1852 LDS and the 1858 Wright editions, it might be noted that the Wright edition does not number the paragraphs of the text as the 1852 LDS edition does.

Book of Mormon's text, the RLDS tradition lacked such luxury and was from the outset more directly in conversation with potential critics and criticisms.

Of course, the RLDS tradition soon found the resources to decide how it might present the text of the Book of Mormon to its members and to the world. Their first edition appeared in 1874. Significantly, like the Wright edition of 1858, it takes the body of the text from the 1840 Nauvoo edition (then-current LDS editions took their orientation, as already noted, primarily from the 1837 Kirtland edition).[19] But in every other regard, the 1874 RLDS edition follows the basic format of then-current LDS editions. It of course lacks the Wright edition's intentionally neutral introduction, instead, like the several European LDS editions, opening with a title page and the testimonies of the Three and Eight Witnesses. Perhaps more tellingly, it numbers the paragraphs of the text like the 1852 LDS edition, with paragraph breaks identical to those of the LDS edition. (Thus, between 1874 and 1879, the citation systems for the RLDS and LDS editions were identical—something that would never occur again.) Moreover, like the 1852 LDS edition and the 1858 Wright edition, the 1874 RLDS provides a detailed index (actually called an index in the RLDS edition, rather than a table of contents) at the outset of the volume.[20] For a few years at least, then, the RLDS and LDS editions of the Book of Mormon were remarkably similar, with the RLDS edition in most ways following the format of the LDS edition. Both presented themselves as objects of study and presented the text in largely equivalent formats. The base texts of the two editions slightly differed, but one would have had to do detailed study at the time to note the textual variants in any substantial fashion. Really, the only substantial and apparent difference between the two was their publication information, with the RLDS edition proudly displaying "published by the Reorganized Church of Jesus Christ of Latter Day Saints,"

19. See the discussion in Crawley, *A Descriptive Bibliography of the Mormon Church*, 1:148–151.
20. The "Index to Book of Mormon" that appears early in the 1874 RLDS edition is significantly more detailed than the "Contents" of the 1852 LDS edition. The RLDS "Index," for instance, contains twenty-one entries for what is now 1 Nephi 1–5, the original first chapter of First Nephi, while the LDS "Contents" contains only seven entries for the same stretch of text. See The Book of Mormon (RLDS 1874), v–xii. Further, the RLDS edition's "Index" provides both page numbers and paragraph numbers, while the LDS edition's "Contents" provides only page numbers. These improvements, given the availability of the table of contents from the Wright edition, seem to represent a deliberate effort at producing something stronger than the material in the LDS editions of the time.

whereas the LDS editions of the time do not even mention the name of the church on the title page.[21]

This relative coincidence between the two treatments of the Book of Mormon, however, lasted only a short while. Just five years after the publication of the first RLDS edition, and perhaps in partial response to its publication, a substantial reformatting of the Book of Mormon was undertaken and then made available in Salt Lake City. The work of Orson Pratt, this new 1879 LDS edition rearranged the text into shorter, more Bible-like chapters, as well as into shorter, numbered paragraphs. These are the still-current verses of LDS editions. Further, Pratt provided the text with footnotes containing scriptural cross-references and occasional interpretive glosses.[22] The significance of all these paratextual changes seems to have lain in the need to grant the Book of Mormon equal scriptural status with the Christian Bible. As Paul Gutjahr points out, earlier editions of the Book of Mormon "read much more like a novel or historical work." But with Pratt's edition of 1879, the book "took on the air of a sacred, biblical text"—thanks in large part to format and apparatus.[23] This development in the LDS history of publishing the Book of Mormon therefore put crucial distance again between the two traditions' experiences with the book. For the first time, numerical references used to cite specific passages differed (never to coincide again), and only the LDS edition came with extensive footnoting and interpretive suggestions. Further, the actual content of the interpretive footnotes in the 1879 LDS edition made the Book of Mormon into a more emphatically LDS (and definitively *not* RLDS) book. Pratt "added to the text roughly seventy-five informative geographic footnotes directly linking events in the narrative to specific locations," with one tellingly "noting that the 'pastures . . . in all high places' found in 1 Nephi 21:10 were, in fact, 'the elevated regions of the Rocky Mountains.'"[24] Also, dozens of Pratt's footnotes cross-reference passages to

21. The Book of Mormon (RLDS 1874), i.

22. For a too-brief account of Pratt's work on this edition, see Breck England, *The Life and Thought of Orson Pratt* (Salt Lake City: University of Utah Press, 1985), 255.

23. Paul C. Gutjahr, *The "Book of Mormon": A Biography* (Princeton: Princeton University Press, 2012), 96–97. For a summary discussion of the 1879 Pratt edition, see Turley and Slaughter, *How We Got the Book of Mormon*, 81–85. Still more recently, see also Paul Gutjahr, "Orson Pratt's Enduring Influence on *The Book of Mormon*," in *Americanist Approaches to The Book of Mormon*, edited by Elizabeth Fenton and Jared Hickman (New York: Oxford University Press, 2019), 83–104.

24. Gutjahr, *The "Book of Mormon,"* 95.

those in the 1876 LDS edition of the Doctrine and Covenants.[25] The study apparatus of the 1879 LDS edition in many ways turned its Book of Mormon into a different (because uniquely LDS) book.

Given the above considerations, the publication of the 1874 RLDS edition partially spurred the more explicitly LDS presentation of the Book of Mormon in 1879.[26] But whatever its root motivation, the publication of the new LDS edition reinstated the original contrast between LDS and RLDS experiences with the Book of Mormon. Although the RLDS tradition had in 1874 taken stronger control over the meaning and presentation of the Book of Mormon, the LDS tradition responded by taking still stronger control over the text's meaning and presentation in 1879. For the first time, it could reasonably be said that there were *two* Books of Mormon—with different chapter lengths and paragraphing, rival interpretive traditions marked in crucial ways in the margins of the text, and so on.[27]

INTO THE TWENTIETH CENTURY

Neither the LDS nor the RLDS tradition produced a new edition of the Book of Mormon before the end of the nineteenth century. Yet during the last decades of the nineteenth century, the first efforts at scholarly study of the Book of Mormon emerged in both traditions. In the LDS tradition, these

25. All but one of these references was, nonetheless, to revelations contained in RLDS editions of the Doctrine and Covenants. Yet the one reference to a revelation *not* contained in the RLDS Doctrine and Covenants is especially significant. Pratt cross-references Jacob's preaching against polygamy in the Book of Mormon with the revelation on plural marriage canonized in the LDS tradition as D&C 132. See The Book of Mormon: An Account Written by the Hand of Mormon, upon Plates Taken from the Plates of Nephi, trans. Joseph Smith Jr., ed. Orson Pratt, Sen. (Salt Lake City: Deseret News, 1879), 133. Considering the intense attention the RLDS tradition gave to Jacob's sermon in their polemics against the Utah church's practice of polygamy, Pratt's footnote can only be interpreted as a direct response to RLDS interpretation.

26. Pratt was certainly familiar with RLDS publications. The clearest evidence is the fact that, when assigned to produce a new edition of the Doctrine and Covenants a few years earlier, he borrowed the incorrect dating for LDS D&C 99 from the then-current RLDS edition of the Doctrine and Covenants. Earlier LDS editions had assigned the year of the revelation correctly to 1832, but Pratt changed the year to 1833. The only available source for this "correction" was the RLDS D&C, where the revelation's year was also listed as 1833.

27. It might be noted that the anecdote with which David Howlett opens his discussion of the "splintered saints," one that forcefully illustrates the intensity of the nineteenth-century rivalry between the LDS and RLDS traditions, took place in 1879. See David J. Howlett, *Kirtland Temple: The Biography of a Shared Mormon Sacred Space* (Urbana: University of Illinois Press, 2014), 38.

efforts were spearheaded by two figures in particular: George Reynolds and Janne Sjodahl.[28] In the parallel RLDS tradition, they were led primarily by Henry Stebbins.[29] In both cases, the main effort was to seek intellectually defensible support for the Book of Mormon's claim to antiquity. But these preliminary efforts at serious study of the Book of Mormon did not immediately lead to novel re-presentations of the Book of Mormon text (though it might be noted that a major edition of Stebbins's work was issued the same year as the next new RLDS edition).

Rather different motivations, in fact, seem to have been behind the eventual publication, in 1908, of the next RLDS edition: the "Authorized Version."[30] Richard Howard suggests, "The attractiveness of the shorter verses in the LDS texts must have been a definite encouragement toward a reversification plan," though it should be noted that almost thirty years passed before any serious attempt at reversification was made.[31] Nonetheless, as the preface to the 1908 edition itself states, the motivation for the new edition in part lay in the fact that various available editions of the Book of Mormon—both LDS and RLDS—had different "divisions of chapters and paragraphs, thereby rendering it impossible to prepare concordance and works of reference." The time had come to "prepare a uniform plan for the division of chapters and verses, and, if thought advisable, to prepare or adopt a system of references."[32] Shorter verse lengths were accordingly adopted in the 1908 edition, but significantly without any effort to correlate the referencing system with the 1879 LDS edition. Crucially, the RLDS leadership instructed the committee

28. Their various writings on the Book of Mormon have been compiled into a verse-by-verse commentary. See George Reynolds and Janne M. Sjodahl, *Commentary on the Book of Mormon*, 7 vols., edited by Philip C. Reynolds (Salt Lake City: Deseret Book, 1955).

29. See Henry A. Stebbins, *Book of Mormon Lectures, Being a Series of Nine Sermons Delivered in the Saints' Church, Independence, Missouri, on the Events of February 13–21, 1894*, rev. ed. (Lamoni, IA: Herald Publishing House, 1908). See also Stebbins's account of the research in Henry A. Stebbins, "Autobiography of Henry A. Stebbins," *Journal of History (RLDS)* 18.2 (April 1920):193–195.

30. In addition, there was an 1892 RLDS large-print edition (in two columns), but it was largely a resetting of the 1874 edition. With respect to the 1908 "Authorized Version," the following note from *The History of the Reorganized Church of Jesus Christ of Latter Day Saints*, 8 vols. (Independence, MO: Herald House, 1970), 6:277–278, is of interest: "[The Authorized Version] was authorized in the sense that it was issued by a committee appointed by the General Conference."

31. Howard, *Restoration Scriptures*, 38. It should also be noted that the paragraphing—and hence the citation numbers—of the 1892 RLDS edition was different from that of the 1874 RLDS edition.

32. The Book of Mormon, trans. Joseph Smith Jr. (Lamoni, IA: The Reorganized Church of Jesus Christ of Latter Day Saints, 1908), vi.

in charge of publication "to leave the chapters as in the original Palmyra edition," rather than to utilize the shorter chapters of LDS editions.[33] To this day, LDS and RLDS/CofC editions differ in the length of chapters, though the length of the verses in their respective editions are roughly similar.

Another major spur to produce a new RLDS edition, though, was clearly the 1903 acquisition by the Reorganized Church of the printer's manuscript of the Book of Mormon—a manuscript copy of the dictated manuscript, produced originally for the printer for the 1830 Palmyra (first) edition.[34] In producing the 1908 edition, careful comparison was made among then-extant printed editions from the RLDS tradition, the 1837 Kirtland edition, and the printer's manuscript itself. As Howard has shown, the committee assigned to produce the new edition often ("nearly always") preferred the printer's manuscript over other editions whenever there were textual variants.[35] This may well have been spurred by two particular discoveries the committee made in consulting the printer's manuscript, both relevant to the longstanding LDS-RLDS debate over Joseph Smith's polygamy. The committee determined to publish a notice regarding these discoveries in the preface to the new edition. "Among the more important corrections we note the following," they wrote,

> Concerning the prohibition of polygamy; book of Jacob, chapter 2:6, 7: "I *must* testify unto you concerning the wickedness of your hearts"; *must*, instead of *might*. 2:45: "Behold ye have done greater *iniquity* than the Lamanites, our brethren." *Iniquity*, singular form, specific; instead of *iniquities* in other editions. Ether 1:16: The Palmyra and Kirtland editions both read "thy families," referring to the brother of Jared and the commandment to migrate. The manuscript reads, "thy family"; the singular instead of the plural form of the word.[36]

33. Ibid.

34. A full facsimile edition, along with transcription of the printer's manuscript, has recently been made available by the Joseph Smith Papers. See Royal Skousen and Robin Scott Jensen, eds., *The Joseph Smith Papers, Revelations and Translation*, vol. 3, *Printer's Manuscript of the Book of Mormon*, 2 pts. (Salt Lake City: Church Historian's Press, 2015). For notes on the provenance of the manuscript, see *Printer's Manuscript*, 3–7.

35. See Howard, *Restoration Scriptures*, 38–43. Howard also comments on the fact that this preference shifted the focus of RLDS readers from the Nauvoo to the Kirtland edition as a base text for the Book of Mormon.

36. The Book of Mormon (RLDS 1908), vii.

The committee producing the new edition would naturally have seen these subtle discrepancies between manuscript and editions as reason to elevate the printer's manuscript.[37]

Despite the obviously intense work undertaken in the preparation of the 1908 RLDS edition, the committee did not elect to supply the Book of Mormon with footnotes—interpretive or otherwise—like the 1879 LDS edition. That is, although an LDS edition with uniquely LDS-interpretive notes had been in circulation for almost three decades, the Reorganized Church apparently saw no reason to produce a rival set of interpretive notes. Instead of footnotes, the new RLDS edition offered an extensive index, positioned at the close of the printed volume. Of course, the index is itself interpretive to a certain extent, although it should be said that it focuses principally on proper names and treats theological topics with a relatively light hand.[38] Its occasional interpretive gestures are far less overdetermined than those in Pratt's footnotes for example. The aim of the new RLDS edition thus seems to have been to continue as much as possible to let the text speak for itself—once it had been established critically by comparison with the best available manuscript sources. Thus, although the 1908 RLDS edition *does* follow the 1879 LDS edition in producing shorter verses, in every other regard it seems to keep a deliberate distance from the developing LDS approach to formatting the Book of Mormon for publication. Where the tendency in the LDS tradition was already toward a standardization of the book's interpretation, the tendency in the RLDS tradition was moving in the opposite direction: toward a promotion of study, to be sure, but without any strong determination of what study might look like.

This interpretive minimalism might at first seem not to have influenced the next major LDS edition of the Book of Mormon, which appeared in 1920 as the work of a committee largely led by James E. Talmage. According to

37. It seems that all these textual variants were inadvertent and the work of the compositor of the first (1830) edition—who was not an adherent of the emerging faith tradition—long before the question of polygamy was raised. See the discussions in Skousen, *Analysis of Textual Variants of the Book of Mormon* (Provo, UT: Neal A. Maxwell Institute for Religious Scholarship, 2005), 2:954, 973; 6:3728.

38. Reading through non-nominal entries in the index convinces one that its producers had no theological axe to grind, at least regarding the rivalry between LDS and RLDS traditions. The index nonetheless runs to forty-four pages, providing readers with substantial resources for study. See The Book of Mormon (RLDS 1908), 779–822.

Paul Gutjahr, two formatting changes made by the committee allowed the Book of Mormon's likeness to the Christian Bible to reach "its fullest manifestation," with the text of the book "in two columns" and chronological notes on each page. Both features represent "common formatting practices found in American Bibles since the time of the American Revolution."[39] But the changes to the presentation of the text in the 1920 edition went much further. For the first time in the LDS tradition, individual chapters were introduced with summary headings, which also appear ("with some changes") at the end of the volume in a detailed synopsis of the whole book.[40] Two other study resources appear at the end of the volume as well: a novel "Pronouncing Vocabulary" developed over numerous years,[41] and a detailed index rather clearly developed from that in the RLDS 1908 edition.[42] Further, in addition to the usual testimonies of the Three and Eight Witnesses, the volume opens with a "Brief Analysis of the Book of Mormon," detailing the several textual sources used by its chief editors and outlining the larger structure of the volume. There are also a few pages that describe the "Origin of the Book of Mormon," taken almost entirely from the standard account of Joseph Smith.[43]

All these additional features of the 1920 LDS edition might seem at first as if the LDS tradition were, early in the twentieth century, strengthening its hold on the interpretation of the Book of Mormon. Yet a closer investigation

39. Gutjahr, *The "Book of Mormon,"* 97.

40. Turley and Slaughter, *How We Got the Book of Mormon,* 100. For the synopsis, see The Book of Mormon, trans. Joseph Smith Jr. (Salt Lake City: Church of Jesus Christ of Latter-day Saints, 1920), 523–530.

41. See The Book of Mormon (LDS 1920), 531–534. For a study of the historical production of this guide, see Mary Jane Woodger, "How the Guide to English Pronunciation of Book of Mormon Names Came About," *Journal of Book of Mormon Studies* 9.1 (2000):54–55.

42. See The Book of Mormon (LDS 1920), 535–568. For evidence that the two indexes are related, one might compare just the first four entries in each. Both contain four "Aaron" entries. The similarity between the two entries for "Aaron, king of Lamanites," is telling. The RLDS edition provides two subentries: "defeated by army of Mormon" and "brutality of army of." In parallel, the LDS edition provides the same two subentries but with one slight difference: "defeated by army of Moroni" and "brutality of army of." It seems relatively clear that the LDS edition simply takes over this entry from the RLDS edition while making a slight correction of an error. Other entries, naturally, alter the RLDS index entries more substantially. The entry for "Aaron, son of Mosiah" from the RLDS edition is expanded at several points, while some citations in the RLDS entry are annexed to the LDS entry for "Mosiah, sons of." Other details, however, make clear the derivative status of the LDS edition's index. See The Book of Mormon (RLDS 1908), 779 and The Book of Mormon (LDS 1920), 535, 558.

43. See The Book of Mormon (LDS 1920), iii–vi.

suggests just the opposite, as if the interpretive minimalism of the RLDS tradition had begun to influence those charged with creating the new LDS edition. For instance, while many of Pratt's cross-referencing footnotes are reproduced in the 1920 edition—with some eliminated and other new ones added—all of Pratt's interpretive footnotes quietly disappeared in 1920. The strong interpretive control of the preceding LDS edition was thus loosened to a large extent, as if the new edition were meant somehow to confess that the interpretation of the text was a more complex and less determined affair than previously assumed. Surprisingly similar in spirit are the chapter summaries in the 1920 edition. Although one might guess that the inclusion of summaries would render the new edition *more* interpretive, their actual content is remarkably minimalist. In fact, their presence indicates weakened rather than strengthened control over interpretation.[44] That all these minimalist gestures owed something to the 1908 RLDS edition seems clear when the indexes of the two editions are compared. The 1920 LDS edition's index, unmistakably indebted to the 1908 RLDS edition's index, largely exhibits the same interpretive minimalism as do the other features of the 1920 LDS edition.

At the same time, of course, certain crucial differences between the LDS edition of 1920 and the RLDS edition of 1908 stand out. The LDS edition lacks a certain transparency, providing no preface explicitly detailing the process of production as the RLDS edition does, instead opening with study resources and the story of the Book of Mormon's original coming forth. And while it is true that the removal of interpretive footnotes in the LDS edition suggests the minimalism of the RLDS edition, quasi-interpretive cross-referencing footnotes remain firmly in place.

But the most significant difference between the two editions lay in changes made directly to the text in the 1920 LDS edition, changes over and above those made to the apparatus and general presentation. Of course, the

---

44. Unlike the chapter summaries of more recent LDS editions, then, those of the 1920 edition are interpretively minimalist. Compare, for instance, the heading for 2 Nephi 12, the Book of Mormon's full quotation of Isaiah 2, in the 1920 edition ("Prophecies as recorded on the brass plates") with that of the 1981 edition ("Isaiah sees the latter-day temple, gathering of Israel, and millennial judgment and peace—The proud and wicked shall be brought low at the Second Coming"). The Book of Mormon (LDS 1920), 74; and The Book of Mormon, trans. Joseph Smith Jr. (Salt Lake City: Church of Jesus Christ of Latter-day Saints, 1981), 81. An interesting and relevant exception to the minimalism of the 1920 edition's chapter summaries is that of Jacob 2, where the Book of Mormon touches briefly on polygamy: "Plurality of wives forbidden because of iniquity." This is obviously interpretive in nature. The Book of Mormon (LDS 1920), 109.

1908 RLDS edition contained a good many changes to the text as well, undertaken especially with an eye to the then-recently acquired printer's manuscript. The changes in the 1920 LDS edition, however, were of an entirely different nature. The committee charged with the task of producing the 1920 LDS edition decided to make unprecedented corrections of grammatical errors, as well as transformation of nonstandard English.[45] Of course, such changes were not *entirely* unprecedented. Joseph Smith himself had made corrections to grammar in preparing both the 1837 and the 1840 editions. But no one had since undertaken to substantially improve the grammar of the text—often awkward or simply incorrect in the original.[46]

This last facet of the 1920 LDS edition may be its most striking feature and is certainly what most indelibly points to continued divergence between the two traditions during this time. Only a few years after the Reorganized Church had published an edition seeking to hew as closely as possible to the available manuscript sources, the Latter-day Saints published an edition that incorporated none of the RLDS committee's discoveries while simultaneously introducing *new* differences from the manuscript sources by standardizing the English in many places. A certain RLDS conservatism early in the twentieth century thus contrasted with a certain LDS liberalism at the same time.[47] Or perhaps it would be better to say that a certain RLDS academicism contrasted with a certain LDS populism early in the twentieth century. Certainly, the various features of the 1920 LDS edition together suggest that it was intended to serve primarily as an invitation to familiarity with and close study of the Book of Mormon. It provides as many study resources as possible (an analysis of the text, chapter summaries, cross-referencing footnotes, a pronouncing vocabulary, an extensive index, a running chronology, and so

45. See the comment of Sidney Sperry: "The writer happens to know that Dr. Talmage was a stickler for good English and a close student of the text of the Book of Mormon. He knew as well as anyone the imperfections of the literary dress of the First Edition of the Nephite record and took a prominent part in correcting many of them in a later edition of the work (1920)." Sidney B. Sperry, *Answers to Book of Mormon Questions* (Salt Lake City: Bookcraft, 1967), 190.

46. To develop a sense for the awkwardness of the grammar of the Book of Mormon at first, one should consult either Royal Skousen's *Earliest Text* or the 1830 Palmyra edition. The latter is available in several reprints, perhaps the most useful being Robert A. Rees and Eugene England, eds., *The Reader's Book of Mormon* (Salt Lake City: Signature Books, 2008).

47. As Matthew Bowman has noted, a progressive spirit rather generally inhabited the LDS tradition in the first part of the twentieth century. See the discussion in Matthew Bowman, *The Mormon People: The Making of an American Faith* (New York: Random House, 2012), 152–183.

on), while nonetheless seeking not to overdetermine the reader's interpretive experience.[48] All of this couples with a cleaner—that is, more grammatically accessible—main text, readier for fluid reading.[49]

Of course, the state of things would change rather drastically over the course of the twentieth century. Soon enough, the RLDS tradition responded with far starker liberalism than could be witnessed in the LDS tradition, while the LDS tradition would make an unmistakable conservative turn in its presentation and interpretation of the Book of Mormon. Intellectual interest in the Book of Mormon became ground for a near-about-face in both traditions.

IN THE AGE OF SCHOLARSHIP

Within a year of the appearance of the 1920 LDS edition, as Terryl Givens recounts, "a young member [of the church] wrote a letter to church apostle James E. Talmage that would shake up the world of Mormon apologetics."[50] The letter contained a few largely familiar challenges to the Book of Mormon's claim to ancient historicity, but when it was forwarded to B. H. Roberts, the LDS tradition's most accomplished academic interpreter of Joseph Smith's heritage, the result was a minor crisis of sorts. Roberts developed the short list of questions into "a 141-page report on 'Book of Mormon Difficulties.'"[51] The next few decades witnessed the publication of several high-profile

48. In many ways, it might be appropriate to describe the 1920 LDS edition as a kind of "Study Book of Mormon." As Turley and Slaughter point out, the new edition was described in the church's General Conference as "of such great interest to the Church and its members" that it could be commended to church members and "to all other people for study." Turley and Slaughter, *How We Got the Book of Mormon*, 105. Increased seriousness about study of the Book of Mormon in the LDS tradition was unquestionably on the rise in the first decades of the twentieth century more generally. See, for instance, the discussion in Terryl L. Givens, *By the Hand of Mormon: The American Scripture that Launched a New World Religion* (New York: Oxford University Press, 2002), 106–109.

49. As this volume went to press, an incredibly detailed and unprecedented study of the 1920 LDS edition of the Book of Mormon appeared, unfortunately too late to be incorporated into this study. For astonishing detail on the publication and project of the 1920 edition, see Richard L. Saunders, *The 1920 Edition of the Book of Mormon: A Centennial Adventure in Latter-day Saint Book History* (Salt Lake City, UT: Greg Kofford Books, 2021).

50. Givens, *By the Hand of Mormon*, 109.

51. Ibid., 110. For the text of Roberts's report, see B. H. Roberts, *Studies of the Book of Mormon*, edited by Brigham D. Madsen (Urbana: University of Illinois Press, 1985), 61–148. The original letter spurring Roberts's studies can be found in the same volume on pages 35–37.

critiques of the Book of Mormon's claims to authenticity, most famously in Fawn Brodie's 1946 *No Man Knows My History*, a critical biography of Joseph Smith.[52] With the Book of Mormon in many ways under fire, intellectual Latter-day Saints seemed increasingly to regard the book "as mere allegory, not historical fact"—an attitude that at times "reverberated throughout the [LDS] Church."[53] These developments, however, spurred major efforts at apologetic defense by LDS scholars, primarily by Sidney Sperry, Wells Jakeman, and Hugh Nibley.[54] Many of these defenses apparently quelled the concerns of average Latter-day Saints, but some efforts reinforced the difficulties—especially those aimed at discovering Book of Mormon artifacts in the soil of Mesoamerica.[55]

The volleys over the historicity of the Book of Mormon eventually calmed down, largely because intellectual adherents to both traditions turned their attention to a rather different development: the emergence of a fully professionalized discipline of Mormon history—as much the work of RLDS as LDS scholars. By the mid-1960s, journals and professional organizations were running, and both churches were lending institutional support to the efforts of the historians involved in this movement, the so-called New Mormon History.[56] In the RLDS tradition, one of the earliest products of this new movement was a study of the Book of Mormon's translation, published directly in the church's magazine, the *Saints' Herald*, in 1962.[57] This article was, in many ways, the harbinger of much to come. Within four years, a new RLDS edition of the Book of Mormon appeared, by far the most liberal of editions ever published by either of the two major branches of the movement.

52. Fawn M. Brodie, *No Man Knows My History: The Life of Joseph Smith, the Mormon Prophet*, 2nd ed. (New York: Vintage Books, 1995), 16–82.

53. Gutjahr, *The "Book of Mormon,"* 100. For the relatively standard study of this development—and its subsequent reversal—see Noel B. Reynolds, "The Coming Forth of the Book of Mormon in the Twentieth Century," *BYU Studies* 38.2 (1999):7–47.

54. See especially Sperry, *Answers to Book of Mormon Questions*; and Hugh Nibley, *Lehi in the Desert, The World of the Jaredites, There Were Jaredites*, edited by John W. Welch, Darrell L. Matthews, and Stephen R. Callister (Salt Lake City and Provo, UT: Deseret Book and FARMS, 1988).

55. See Givens, *By the Hand of Mormon*, 112–116.

56. Numerous accounts of the rise (and partial fall) of the New Mormon History can be found. For a nonpolemical treatment, see Davis Bitton and Leonard J. Arrington, *Mormons and Their Historians* (Salt Lake City: University of Utah Press, 1988).

57. See James E. Lancaster Jr., "By the Gift and Power of God," *Saints' Herald* 109 (November 1962):14–18, 22, 33. A fuller version of the article appeared as James E. Lancaster Jr., "The Method of Translation of the Book of Mormon," *Restoration Studies* 3 (1986):220–231.

Thus, in 1966, the Reorganized Church published, not without some controversy, what eventually came to be called the Revised Authorized Version of the Book of Mormon. The new edition was produced explicitly "in response to the need for treating grammatical and language problems" in the text of the Book of Mormon.[58] This is explained by an important foreword to the new edition.

> The corrections made are in the grammatical area of punctuation, ambiguous construction, substitution of synonyms for obsolete and archaic words, revision of out-of-date spellings, and other grammatical changes as needed. Many of the adjustments were in punctuation to solve problems which have persisted from the first edition. Others relate to the translation into English from another language, and still others were made because of the constant changes in a living language during the past 130 years.[59]

Here, the basic spirit of the 1920 LDS edition parallels that of the 1966 RLDS edition, except that the latter goes a great deal farther than the former. Where the 1920 LDS edition focuses almost solely on fixing grammatical errors, the 1966 RLDS edition fully modernizes the text in terms of style and diction. The difference can be seen most easily when the two are placed side by side.

1920 LDS	**1966 RLDS**
And it came to pass that I, Nephi, returned from speaking with the Lord, to the tent of my father. And it came to pass that he spake unto me, saying: Behold I have dreamed a dream, in the which the Lord hath commanded me that thou and thy brethren shall return to Jerusalem. For behold, Laban hath the record of the Jews	And I, Nephi, returned from speaking with the Lord, to the tent of my father. And he spoke to me, saying: "Behold, I have dreamed a dream, in which the Lord has commanded me that you and your brethren should return to Jerusalem. For, behold, Laban has the record of the Jews, and also a genealogy of our fore

---

58. *The Book of Mormon*, trans. Joseph Smith Jr. (Independence, MO: The Reorganized Church of Jesus Christ of Latter Day Saints, 1966), vi.

59. Ibid.

and also a genealogy of thy fore-
fathers, and they are engraven
upon plates of brass." (I Nephi
1:59–61)[60]

fathers, and they are engraved
upon plates of brass." (I Nephi
1:59–61)[61]

The apparent liberalism or populism of the 1920 LDS edition looks relatively conservative by comparison with the liberalism or populism of the 1966 RLDS edition. Although the church in the LDS tradition was willing by 1920 to correct grammar, it apparently drew the line at replacing archaisms and repetitive wording. This further step was only taken by the RLDS Church in 1966.

At the same time, it should be noted that the 1966 Revised Authorized Version *is* nonetheless quite a conservative revision. It retains the sentence structures and wording of the text, except where ambiguities or archaisms intervene. Further, it in no sense proposes a mere paraphrase of the text, nor does it even introduce gender neutral pronouns into the Book of Mormon (as many more recent editions of the Bible have done).[62] The point of the revision was, as the edition's foreword explicitly states, simply to "facilitate [the book's] reading and clarify its meaning, without altering its message."[63] Indeed, the person largely in charge of producing the new edition was Chris Hartshorn, a sustained student of and an unwavering believer in the Book of Mormon.[64] He seems to have had no strong liberalizing motives, and the formatting of his 1966 edition makes the Book of Mormon appear much more Bible-like than previous RLDS editions. Yet it is also clear that those who worked on the 1966 RLDS edition did not adhere to "a plenary or 'verbal

60. The Book of Mormon, trans. Joseph Smith Jr. (LDS 1920), 3.

61. The Book of Mormon (RLDS 1966), 3. A series of helpful comparisons of previous editions with the 1966 edition can be found in Howard, *Restoration Scriptures*, 45–47.

62. Renderings of the Book of Mormon along such lines *are* available in print though none published with the sponsorship of either church here in question. The essential conservatism of the RLDS 1966 edition becomes clear by comparison. The most impressive of reworkings of the Book of Mormon is, without question, Lynn Matthews Anderson, *Easy-to-Read Book of Mormon: A Learning Companion* (St. Cloud, MN: Estes Book, 1995). For an insightful essay on the difficulties involved in producing such a work, see Lynn Matthews Anderson, "Delighting in Plainness: Issues Surrounding a Simple Modern English Book of Mormon," *Sunstone* 90 (March 1993):20–29.

63. The Book of Mormon (RLDS 1966), vii.

64. See, for instance, Hartshorn's unquestioning commentary, published while he was at work on the new edition; Chris B. Hartshorn, *A Commentary on the Book of Mormon* (Independence, MO: Herald House, 1964).

inspiration' approach to the Book of Mormon." They believed that the new edition was marked by real "literary improvement over any previous edition" and saw their work as making the Book of Mormon better than it had been before.[65]

Richard Lancaster has portrayed the dozen years leading up to the publication of the Revised Authorized Version as the key period during which the RLDS tradition transitioned "from sect to denomination." He describes these years as those when "a new generation felt they were led by God to boldness in seeking and speaking the truth."[66] Crucially, many involved in this progressive era did not see the "truth" as including a rejection of the Book of Mormon. (One might thus at first be tempted to use the Book of Mormon as a further case study in decanonization, beyond the Lectures on Faith considered elsewhere in this volume by Richard Van Wagoner, Steven Walker, and Allen Roberts.)

It seems evident, however, that the new edition and the burgeoning attitude toward the Book of Mormon seemed aimed at making the book *more* readily available to average Latter Day Saints. In a study published only three years after the 1966 edition, Richard Howard attempted to show that the kinds of changes in the new edition were directly continuous with those made by Joseph Smith in the 1837 Kirtland edition.[67] Yet average members of the RLDS Church clearly felt the progressive nature of the project. Many viewed the committee's work as being far too liberal with what they regarded as a revealed text, part of a general spirit of reform and progressivism that was characteristic of the RLDS leadership in the 1960s. "A number of the delegates" to the RLDS World Conference of 1966 chose "to reject the 1966 edition as the continuance of the 1908 Authorized Edition."[68] Even so, by the mid-1990s, the Authorized and Revised Authorized Versions appear to have been about equally popular among RLDS readers.[69]

Apart from modernizing alterations made directly to the text (and the inclusion of a related explanatory foreword), other changes in the

65. Howard, *Restoration Scriptures*, 47.

66. Richard B. Lancaster, "The Gathering Storm, Part 1: 1954 to 1966: An Insider's View of the Transition from Sect to Denomination within the Reorganized Church of Jesus Christ of Latter Day Saints," *Restoration Studies* 13 (2014):27.

67. See Howard, *Restoration Scriptures* (1969), 53–63.

68. Howard, *Restoration Scriptures* (1995), 47.

69. See the data in ibid., 48.

presentation of the Book of Mormon in the 1966 RLDS edition might be noted.[70] Significantly, *all* seem to borrow from the 1920 LDS edition. For the first time, the text is divided into two columns, and chronological notes appear at the bottom of each page—making the Book of Mormon appear more Bible-like while its language is modernized. Further, immediately before the index in the backmatter of the volume, there is a pronunciation guide for the Book of Mormon's proper names.[71] These details all suggest influence by the then-current LDS edition. Importantly, the 1966 RLDS edition does not include chapter summaries, as the 1920 LDS edition does, but it does place summary phrases atop each page ("Christ descends" heads the page describing Christ's visit to the New World, or "Alma baptizes believers; priests ordained" heads the page describing the organizing of the Nephite church by Alma).[72] The inclusion of these summary lines seems intended more for reference than for interpretation, much as the chapter summaries in the 1920 LDS edition do. Here too it seems likely that there is some relationship of influence traceable from the LDS to the RLDS edition, although the latter exhibits some ingenuity in formatting. Certainly, both traditions in the early-to-mid-twentieth century wished to align the Book of Mormon more closely with the Bible, and both seemed intent on leaving questions of interpretation largely up to readers—to allow the Book of Mormon to "speak for itself," as a major proponent for change in the RLDS tradition put it.[73]

Significantly, the church in the LDS tradition did not issue a new edition of the Book of Mormon during the most active years of the New Mormon

---

70. There is, of course, much that does not change in the 1966 edition. The 1908 preface appears in the front matter of the volume, as do the title page and the testimonies of the witnesses. And the same index available in previous RLDS editions appears again.

71. The Book of Mormon (RLDS 1966), 375–379.

72. Ibid., 303, 123. The relevant chapter headings in the 1920 LDS edition read: "The Resurrected Christ appears" and "Alma baptizes Helam and others—The church of Christ." The Book of Mormon (LDS 1920), 420–421, 167.

73. See Roy A. Cheville, *The Book of Mormon Speaks for Itself* (Independence, MO: Herald House, 1971). It might be said that the 1966 RLDS edition does slightly less to control interpretation of the text, at least with respect to a major point of contention between the two traditions. Where the 1920 LDS edition supplies a chapter summary for Jacob's sermon on polygamy that guides the reader toward the standard LDS interpretation, the summary lines associated with the same sermon in the 1966 RLDS edition make no interpretive move. They read as follows: "Jacob rebukes the Nephites," "Jacob speaks of grosser crimes," and "A scourge by Lamanites predicted." This interpretive minimalism is quite remarkable, given the history of contention between the two traditions. The Book of Mormon (RLDS 1966), 79–81.

History movement (beginning in the mid-1960s). Instead, it issued a new edition only as those most active years of the movement came to an end—in 1981. By the late 1970s, the New Mormon History was rather clearly entering into a kind of crisis, signaled by sometimes slower and sometimes more rapid withdrawal of support from the institutional church.[74] Simultaneously, a new wave of LDS Book of Mormon scholarship was on the rise, rendered coherent by the centralizing work of the Foundation for Ancient Research and Mormon Studies (FARMS), launched by John Welch in 1979.[75] Within a couple of years, moreover, church President Ezra Taft Benson would issue a call for intense, renewed study of the Book of Mormon, which was met by a remarkable response from the general body of the church.[76]

The 1981 LDS edition was motivated by major institutional developments as well. One was the development of a massive plan called "correlation," an attempt "to restructure the organization of the church, centralizing authority in the priesthood quorums" and reducing discrepancy and unnecessary overlap in published church materials.[77] Because efforts at correlation began taking real shape in the early 1970s, the need was seen to produce a new edition of all Latter-day Saint scripture—the Bible included. Importantly, work on the Bible brought the committee producing the new edition of the Book of Mormon into direct contact with the Reorganized Church, since they wished to draw on insights from the RLDS-owned manuscripts of Joseph Smith's revisions to the King James Bible.[78] The LDS edition of the Bible was issued in 1979, filled with cross-referencing footnotes linking its texts to the Book of Mormon and other LDS scripture. Two years later, the new edition of the Book of Mormon appeared, identically formatted, and cross-referenced in turn to the Bible and other LDS scripture.

---

74. Davis Bitton lays out the narrative of these years; Bitton, "Ten Years in Camelot: A Personal Memoir," *Dialogue: A Journal of Mormon Thought* 16.3 (Autumn 1983):9–33. But see also the astute analysis of the crisis in Martin E. Marty, "Two Integrities: An Address to the Crisis in Mormon Historiography," *Journal of Mormon History* 10 (1983):3–19.

75. See the summary history of the rise of FARMS in Givens, *By the Hand of Mormon*, 124–132.

76. See his several sermons on the topic, gathered in Ezra Taft Benson, *A Witness and a Warning: A Modern-day Prophet Testifies of the Book of Mormon* (Salt Lake City: Deseret Book, 1988).

77. Bowman, *The Mormon People*, 195.

78. These are now available in full. See *Joseph Smith's New Translation of the Bible: Original Manuscripts*, edited by Scott H. Faulring, Kent P. Jackson, and Robert J. Matthews (Provo, UT: BYU Religious Studies Center, 2004).

The 1981 LDS edition in certain ways participates in the spirit of the 1908 RLDS edition. The actual text was altered at various points after careful study of extant portions of the original manuscript, as well as—quite significantly— the RLDS-owned printer's manuscript. (As Turley and Slaughter note, "By the mid-1970s, excellent relations between scholars in the [LDS] Church Historical Department and the historical staff of the Reorganized Church resulted in exchanging copies of important documents, including the printer's manuscript.")[79] Historical printed editions were also considered, with particular weight being given to the 1840 Nauvoo edition, the last in which Joseph Smith had an editorial hand.[80] The aim, however, was neither to establish a critical text (by reverting to the earliest possible readings) nor to develop further the 1920 LDS edition's corrections (by smoothing out overlooked grammatical errors or otherwise modernizing the language). The purpose of the new edition was to retain as much as possible the base text of the 1920 edition (grammatical corrections included) while correcting inadvertent errors and privileging the 1840 Nauvoo text over the 1837 Kirtland text. The result is a rather unique edition of the Book of Mormon. (Importantly, for the first time in LDS publishing history, this edition provides a note in the frontmatter about correcting typographical errors, grammatical infelicities, and other issues.)[81]

In certain ways, of course, the 1981 LDS edition follows the 1920 LDS edition, although most of the 1920 elements were reworked substantially. It contains the "Brief Analysis," the excerpts from Joseph Smith's history, the testimonies of the Witnesses, a two-column presentation of the text, chapter summaries, chronological notes, the pronunciation guide, and a full index. The only major element of the 1920 edition that disappears is the synopsis of chapters, eliminated because it was considered "redundant."[82] To all this it adds only an introduction for the whole book and the already-mentioned brief note regarding corrections to the text.[83]

79. Turley and Slaughter, *How We Got the Book of Mormon*, 112.
80. This is evident from Skousen, *Analysis of Textual Variants of the Book of Mormon.*
81. The Book of Mormon (LDS 1981), xiv. The full note reads: "Some minor errors in the text have been perpetuated in past editions of the Book of Mormon. This edition contains corrections that seem appropriate to bring the material into conformity with prepublication manuscripts and early editions by the Prophet Joseph Smith."
82. Turley and Slaughter, *How We Got the Book of Mormon*, 109.
83. The Book of Mormon (LDS 1981), ix, xiv.

Of course, neither of these additions is minor in nature. The introduction—only a page long—has already familiarized two generations of LDS readers with Joseph Smith's statement that the Book of Mormon is "the most correct of any book on earth, and the keystone of our religion."[84] Further, this introduction for the first time in the history of the Book of Mormon's publication lays emphasis from the very first pages of the book on the "promise" found at the volume's conclusion: "We invite all men everywhere to read the Book of Mormon, to ponder in their hearts the message it contains, and then to ask God, the Eternal Father, in the name of Christ if the book is true. Those who pursue this course and ask in faith will gain a testimony of its truth and divinity by the power of the Holy Ghost. (See Moroni 10:3–5.)"[85] The 1981 LDS edition's introduction has profoundly shaped the use of the book in proselytizing efforts. In addition, the note regarding typographical errors has served to alert LDS readers more readily to the complicated publishing history of the Book of Mormon.

As noted, almost all the apparatus carried over into the 1981 LDS edition from the 1920 LDS edition was drastically reworked. The "Brief Analysis" of the various sources described within the Book of Mormon was expanded and developed, supplied with textual references, and retitled "Brief Explanation."[86] What in 1920 was presented as an account of the "Origin of the Book of Mormon" became in 1981 the "Testimony of the Prophet Joseph Smith," largely identical in content (lengthy quotations from Smith's history) but significantly coupled by its new title with the testimonies of the Three and Eight Witnesses that follow immediately.[87] The most substantial changes concern the footnotes and chapter summaries, however. The footnotes are drastically expanded.[88] In addition, *many* of them refer not to other scriptural passages

---

84. Ibid., ix.
85. Ibid.
86. Ibid., xiv.
87. Ibid., xi–xiii.
88. To take a random example, compare the footnotes for Jacob 2:1–7 in the two editions (Jacob 2:1–3 in the RLDS citation system). There are only two footnotes in the 1920 LDS edition, one for "rid my garments of your sins" in verse 2 and one for "feelings [which] are exceedingly tender and chaste and delicate" in verse 7. The former notes the connection with the final verse of Jacob 1, where a passage from 2 Nephi 9:44 (RLDS II Nephi 6:86–87) is also cited. The latter cross-references a few passages: verses 9, 28, 33, and 35 within Jacob 2 itself (RLDS verses 9, 36, 42, and 45–47), but then also Jacob 3:7 (RLDS Jacob 2:57–58) and Moroni 9:9, 10 (RLDS Moroni 9:11). By contrast, the 1981 LDS edition contains nine footnotes for the same verses. Verse 1's reference to "the words which

but to the then–newly minted LDS Topical Guide (still in use today). The latter appeared for the first time in the 1979 LDS edition of the Bible, a massive study guide providing lists of scripture references for a wide variety of topics—many of them unique to LDS interests. The Topical Guide effectively serves as an interpretive key for many LDS readers of the Book of Mormon.[89] The chapter summaries of the 1981 LDS edition are similarly interpretive, far more than those of the 1920 edition. These occasionally enshrine traditional LDS interpretations of texts that more recently have been called into question by scholarly interpreters of the text.[90]

Jacob ... spake unto the people of Nephi" is cross-referenced to a similar note before the quotation of Jacob's sermon in 2 Nephi 6–10 (RLDS II Nephi 5–7). Verse 2's reference to the magnification of one's office is cross-referenced to passages in the New Testament (Romans 11:13) and the LDS Doctrine and Covenants (D&C 24:3), as well as to a passage in Jacob 1 (verse 19). The same reference in verse 2 to ridding garments of sins is cross-referenced here to Mosiah 2:28 (RLDS Mosiah 1:65), where King Benjamin uses the same image. A reference in verse 3 to Jacob's previous preaching to the Nephites is helpfully cross-referenced to his earlier sermon but also to the use of the word "welfare" in Mosiah 25:11 (RLDS Mosiah 11:87). A claim in verse 5 that Jacob can know his people's thoughts is cross-referenced to similar passages in Amos 4:13, Alma 12:3 (RLDS Alma 9:3–4), and LDS D&C 6:16. Finally, verse 7's talk of boldness is linked to Leviticus 19:17 ("Thou shalt not hate thy brother in thine heart: thou shalt in any wise rebuke thy neighbour, and not suffer sin upon him") and LDS D&C 121:43. See The Book of Mormon (LDS 1920), 109; and The Book of Mormon (LDS 1981), 119.

89. References to the Topical Guide throughout all the 1979–1981 editions of the LDS scriptures effectively made the guide a kind of map of sanctioned LDS themes and doctrines. It has often been used in precisely this way, with footnote references to the Topical Guide interpreted as clarifications of the meaning of the text they accompany. Thus, for example, references to the Topical Guide's entries for "Election," "Foreordination," and "Man, Antemortal Existence of" in connection with Alma's discourse on high priests "being called and prepared from the foundation of the world" are often taken to provide the official interpretation of the passage. See The Book of Mormon (LDS 1981), 241.

90. A good example can be found in the chapter summary for 2 Nephi 15 (RLDS II Nephi 8:71–100), a reproduction of Isaiah 5. Where the 1920 LDS edition simply reads, "Scriptures from the brass plates continued—Compare Isaiah 5," the 1981 LDS edition reads, "The Lord's vineyard (Israel) shall become desolate and his people shall be scattered—Woes shall come upon them in their apostate and scattered state—The Lord shall lift an ensign and gather Israel—Compare Isaiah 5." The last element of the 1981 chapter summary interprets Isaiah 5:26–30 as a positive description of proselytizing missionaries, gathering Israel, but the text is a relatively straightforward description of a divinely orchestrated battle against Israel. This inscribes in the text a traditional LDS interpretation of the passage, found, for example, in LeGrand Richards, *A Marvelous Work and a Wonder* (Salt Lake City: Deseret Book, 1976), 230. Contrast this interpretation with that offered in a recent popular LDS book on Isaiah: "The chapter ends with a prophecy of the Lord lifting up an ensign to those he calls to punish his wicked people. They will speedily come, without weariness.... Many scholars see this as a prophecy of the Assyrian conquest and deportation of Israel that occurred around 727 B.C." Terry Ball and Nathan Winn, *Making Sense of Isaiah: Insights and Modern Applications* (Salt Lake City: Deseret Book, 2009), 23. For an interesting attempt at harmonizing the two interpretations, see Victor L. Ludlow, *Unlocking Isaiah in the Book of Mormon* (Salt Lake City: Deseret

These expansions and reworkings in the 1981 LDS edition of elements already present in the 1920 LDS edition in certain ways reverse the basic spirit of the latter. Where the 1920 LDS edition followed then-current RLDS editions in pursuing a certain interpretive minimalism, largely leaving to readers the task of interpreting the text, the 1981 LDS edition moves rather far in the direction of interpretive control. The drastically expanded use of footnotes, especially with quasi-interpretive references to the Topical Guide, coupled with far more interpretively robust chapter summaries and a more strongly interpretive introduction, makes the 1981 LDS edition a more institutionally centralized work, mirroring the increasing centralization associated with the Correlation program. It is perhaps significant that two of the three LDS apostles who oversaw production of the edition were important and vocal defenders of doctrinal orthodoxy: Boyd K. Packer and Bruce R. McConkie.[91] One further feature of the 1981 edition, also strongly interpretive, was only added to printings beginning in 1982: a *subtitle* for the whole volume, "Another Testament of Jesus Christ."[92] This subtitle alone has done much to direct interpretation.[93] All these elements suggest a general tightening of control over interpretation by the LDS tradition, presumably in part in response to complexities raised by the emerging field of critical study of the tradition.

As the history of Book of Mormon publication approached the end of the twentieth century, the two major traditions within the movement again diverged in crucial ways. In the spirit of emerging scholarship, the RLDS tradition, formerly relatively conservative, produced a reader's edition of the Book of Mormon. The aim was apparently to continue in the already-established RLDS tradition of interpretive minimalism, but now putting this at the service of an attempt to give the Book of Mormon new life in

Book, 2003), 110–112. For the chapter summaries themselves, see *The Book of Mormon* (LDS 1920), 77; and The Book of Mormon (LDS 1981), 84.

91. They, along with later church President Thomas S. Monson, were "appointed to oversee production." Turley and Slaughter, *How We Got the Book of Mormon*, 108. McConkie was, of course, the author of the widely influential *Mormon Doctrine*, a not uncontroversial compendium of LDS beliefs, presented as normative. See Bruce R. McConkie, *Mormon Doctrine*, 2nd ed. (Salt Lake City: Bookcraft, 1966).

92. Gutjahr, *The "Book of Mormon,"* 110.

93. See, for instance, the almost systematic interpretation of the whole book in light of this subtitle in Jeffrey R. Holland, *Christ and the New Covenant: The Messianic Message of the Book of Mormon* (Salt Lake City: Deseret Book, 1997).

a tradition where its antiquity and often its divinity were beginning to be called into question. The tradition's former conservatism was thus replaced with a relative liberalism. By contrast, the LDS tradition, formerly relatively liberal, conservatively produced a new edition of the Book of Mormon only when emerging scholarship had made the basic stakes of its project clear. The relative freedom used with the text in its previous edition of 1920 disappeared in 1981 as a stronger commitment to textual continuity (especially with manuscripts and early printed editions) emerged. Moreover, the tradition's early-twentieth-century interpretive minimalism gave way to a more centralized sense of control over the meaning of the text. Thus, somewhere about mid-century, the two traditions seem almost to have exchanged places. Interestingly, at no point in the twentieth century did the two traditions really coincide with respect to the Book of Mormon. Each had its own sacred text throughout.

THE CURRENT DIVERGENCE

In the years during which the LDS tradition began anew to exercise stronger control over the interpretation of the Book of Mormon—and especially to insist all the more strongly on the book's antiquity and divinity—the RLDS tradition began shifting its attention away from the Book of Mormon entirely. William Russell notes that, when in the mid-1960s he "joined the Graceland faculty, teaching religion" at an RLDS institution of higher learning, he "felt guilty for not having read the Book of Mormon." Yet what he found upon arrival was that his "two colleagues in the Religion Department ... had not read the Book of Mormon either."[94] In 1979, the RLDS First Presidency officially stated that the Reorganized Church had "no position" on the Book of Mormon's historicity, while nonetheless continuing to embrace it as scripture.[95] By 2003, shortly after the church was renamed Community of Christ, Russell could say that "most of the RLDS leaders, and many of the rank-and-file members" had "come to doubt the Book of Mormon's historicity as well as some of its doctrinal affirmations"—tracing these

---

94. William D. Russell, "History and the Mormon Scriptures," *Journal of Mormon History* 10 (1983):59.

95. Richard D. Moore, *Know Your Religions*, vol. 2, *A Comparative Look at Mormonism and the Community of Christ* (Orem, UT: Millennial Press, 2009), 113.

difficulties all the way back to the late 1960s.[96] He went on: "Today it seems that although the Book of Mormon is still part of our canon of scriptures, it is not revered as highly as it used to be."[97]

Crucially, the same years that witnessed a retreat of the Book of Mormon within the RLDS tradition saw the exact reverse in the LDS context. In the wake of the publication of the 1981 LDS edition, and especially of President Ezra Taft Benson's strong emphasis on the Book of Mormon, a resurgence of interest in the Book of Mormon occurred in the LDS tradition. "By 1988," Terryl Givens writes, "it was clear that Benson had launched the [LDS] church into a new era in which the Book of Mormon received unprecedented attention and respect."[98] Thus, writing only a year before Russell, cited above, Givens could describe the status of the Book of Mormon at the outset of the twenty-first century in the LDS context.

> The Book of Mormon is now the focus of vigorous scholarly research by Mormon academics that is unprecedented in scope, professionalism, and church support.... An army of over 60,000 missionaries continues to use the Book of Mormon as the centerpiece of a proselytizing effort that was bringing in over a quarter of a million converts a year by the new century. In LDS worship services and Sunday schools, the Book of Mormon is now absolutely central rather than peripheral. Hundreds of thousands of young Mormons daily attend early morning seminary, a four-year program of gospel study, through their high school years. Every participant spends one full year immersed in the keystone of their religion, the Book of Mormon. And perhaps most tellingly, Benson's prophetic promises keyed specifically to Book of Mormon attentiveness mean that in countless LDS homes throughout the world, devout families meet together every day for a devotional in which they read together from the Book of Mormon.[99]

96. William D. Russell, "The LDS Church and Community of Christ: Clearer Differences, Closer Friends," *Dialogue: A Journal of Mormon Thought* 36.4 (Winter 2003):186.

97. Ibid.

98. Givens, *By the Hand of Mormon*, 241.

99. Ibid., 242.

The result of the rise of scholarship has been in one tradition to assist a shift of attention away from the Book of Mormon but in the other to help turn attention directly to the Book of Mormon. Divergence between the two traditions, regarding the Book of Mormon, continues.

Right into the first part of the twenty-first century, it can be said that the LDS and RLDS/CofC traditions have read rather different things that each nonetheless called the Book of Mormon. Of course, what each tradition regarded as the Book of Mormon was itself dynamic rather than stable, the basic text itself being in flux, along with a whole set of interpretive apparatuses. But at no point between 1860 and the present have the two traditions regarded the Book of Mormon in basically the same way. Their understandings of the text, their approaches to its publication, and their ways of introducing it to the world have diverged consistently.

One might well wonder, however, whether the possibility of something more like convergence might be on the horizon. In 2013, Dale Luffman noted "a growing interest in the Book of Mormon in Community of Christ over the past several years,"[100] marking a resurgence somewhat parallel to increased attention to and study of the book in the LDS tradition.[101] Additionally, LDS scholars have made efforts—albeit unofficially—to make interpretively minimalist reader's editions of the Book of Mormon available to average readers,[102] as well as to call for a more nuanced (but still believing) understanding of the Book of Mormon's claims to ancient historicity.[103] With these

---

100. Dale E. Luffman, *The Book of Mormon's Witness to Its First Readers* (Independence, MO: Community of Christ Seminary Press, 2013), 10.

101. For another recent CofC study of the Book of Mormon exhibiting this resurgent interest, see Alan D. Tyree, *Millions Call It Scripture: The Book of Mormon in the 21st Century* (Independence, MO: Community of Christ Seminary Press, 2013).

102. See especially Grant Hardy, ed., *The Book of Mormon: A Reader's Edition* (Urbana: University of Illinois Press, 2003); and, more recently, Grant Hardy, ed., *The Book of Mormon, Another Testament of Jesus Christ: Maxwell Institute Study Edition* (Salt Lake City and Provo, UT: Deseret Book, Neal A. Maxwell Institute for Religious Scholarship, and Brigham Young University Religious Studies Center, 2018).

103. This has been undertaken most systematically by Brant A. Gardner, *Second Witness: Analytical and Contextual Commentary on the Book of Mormon*, 6 vols. (Salt Lake City: Greg Kofford Books, 2007). Arguably, at least one such gesture can be found in the *most* recent LDS edition of the Book of Mormon, published in 2013. There, former claims about the identification of the Book of Mormon's peoples with all ancient Americans was nuanced to suggest only that they were "among the ancestors of the American Indians." See The Book of Mormon, trans. Joseph Smith Jr. (Salt Lake City: Church of Jesus Christ of Latter-day Saints, 2013), ix.

movements within both traditions, there are perhaps some indications that after having effectively canonized different books with the same title and much of the same content, both are approaching each other in significant ways. It may yet be that a singular Book of Mormon will emerge—a something more like a singular Book of Mormon than has yet existed.

Whatever *may* emerge, however, it should be said that the past century and a half has witnessed the parallel existence of *two* Books of Mormon, ultimately irreducible to each other. Each has taken its basic text from rather different original sources; each has utilized profoundly distinct paratextual apparatuses to present the Book of Mormon to its adherents and to the world. Each tradition has borrowed from the other, of course, but always in dissymmetrical ways, such that every borrowing complicates the relationship between the two, rather than bringing them closer to one another.

In the end, then, it must be said that at least *one* Book of Mormon ranks among the scriptural volumes uniquely held sacred by non-LDS branches of the movement. Latter-day Saints might well benefit from coming to know the Book of Mormon they have *not* known, at the very least because it might help them to see with much greater clarity the Book of Mormon they *do* know. And of course, it may be that their own Book of Mormon, always in flux, may yet appear more strikingly like the Book of Mormon they mostly do not know.

5

The Church of Christ (Temple Lot)
A Solae Scripturae *Mormonism*
Chrystal Vanel

Most scholars of Mormonism focus on the Church of Jesus Christ of Latter-day Saints headquartered in Salt Lake City, Utah. In his classic work on denominations emerging from the 1830 Restoration, first published in 1975, Steven L. Shields wrote that "six movements" developed following the death of the founding prophet Joseph Smith in 1844.[1] Massimo Introvigne, a specialist in new religious movements, referred to them as the "six historical branches"[2]: the Church of Jesus Christ of Latter-day Saints; the Community of Christ; the Church of Christ (Temple Lot); the Church of Jesus Christ organized around William Bickerton's (1815–1905) leadership; the Church of Jesus Christ of Latter Day Saints that accepted James J. Strang (1813–1856) as prophet and king; and the Church of Jesus Christ that followed the leadership of Alpheus Cutler (1784–1864).

I use the term "Mormonisms" when referring to the movements that came out of Joseph Smith's religious tradition after the publication of the Book of Mormon, as the terms "Mormons" and "Mormonism" originally referred to believers in the Book of Mormon,[3] and even though many of those movements

---

1. Steven L. Shields, *Divergent Paths of the Restoration* (Independence: Herald Publishing House, 2001 [1975]), 11.

2. Massimo Introvigne, *Les Mormons* (Maredsous, BE: Éditions Brepols, 1991), 21.

3. Mark Lyman Staker, *Hearken, O Ye People: The Historical Setting of Joseph Smith's Ohio Revelation* (Salt Lake City: Greg Kofford Books, 2009), 72–73, 87. The plural term "Mormonisms" may have been used for the first time by Grant Underwood, "Re-Visioning Mormon History," *Pacific Historical Review* 55, no. 3 (1986):420, and since then by Danny Jorgensen, "Conflict in the Camps of Israel: The 1853 Cutlerite Schism," *Journal of Mormon History* 21, no. 1 (1995):64; David Howlett, *Kirtland Temple: The Biography of a Shared Mormon Sacred Space* (Urbana: University of Illinois Press, 2014).

do not use—or even reject—the terms "Mormon" and "Mormonism" when referring to themselves, preferring other designations.[4] The Church of Christ (Temple Lot) does not consider itself "Mormon," as is the case for the Church of Jesus Christ (Bickertonite) and the Community of Christ. Those three Restoration traditions rejected the category in the nineteenth century to distance themselves from the Utah Mormons then on the margins of U.S. society and Christianity. Each of these Mormonisms had a unique historical trajectory and theological evolution. The LDS Church is today by far the "Majority Mormonism"[5] with more than 16 million members worldwide. Community of Christ, the second largest movement with fewer than 200,000 members (most of them in North America),[6] was organized around the leadership of Joseph Smith III (1832–1914) in 1860. First referred to as the New Organization, then as the Reorganized Church of Jesus Christ of Latter Day Saints, it adopted its current name in 2001. It evolved from a "moderate Mormonism"[7] to an "American Progressive Christianity, with Mormonism as an Option."[8]

This chapter focuses on another of the six historical Mormonisms: the Church of Christ (Temple Lot). Organized in the 1850s around the leadership of Granville Hedrick (1814–1881), the Church of Christ and its members are traditionally referred to as "Hedrickites." I argue that the Church of Christ (Temple Lot) could be defined from its creation in the 1850s as a *solae scripturae* Mormonism. *Sola scriptura* is one of the founding principles of Protestantism, according to which the "ecclesiastical institution, not being

4. In 2018, under the direction of its president Russell M. Nelson, the Church of Jesus Christ of Latter-day Saints insisted that neither the institution nor its members are "Mormons" but should be referred to as members of the Church of Jesus Christ of Latter-day Saints.

5. Introvigne, *Les Mormons*, 22.

6. According to sociologist Danny Jorgensen, there were 128,689 CofC members in North America, and 70,236 outside of North America. Danny Jorgensen, "Community of Christ and the Decline of American Religion: A Study of the Sociology of Secularization," *John Whitmer Historical Association Journal* 39, 1 (Spring/Summer 2019):50n76. According to the Community of Christ December 2020 Financial Update, in 2018, 7,600 USA households supported Worldwide Mission Tithes, whereas 10,700 supported Local Mission Tithes (Financial Update, December 2020, p. 4, https://www.cofchrist.org/common/cms/resources/Documents/Financial-Update-Dec2020.pdf. The Financial Update doesn't communicate data about Mission Tithes given by contributors outside of the USA.

7. Alma Blair, "Reorganized Church of Jesus Christ of Latter Day Saints: Moderate Mormonism," in Alma Blair, Paul Edwards, and Mark McKierman, eds., *The Restoration Movement: Essays in Mormon History* (Lawrence, KS: Coronado Press, 1973), 207–231.

8. Chrystal Vanel, "Community of Christ: An American Progressive Christianity, with Mormonism as an Option," *Dialogue: A Journal of Mormon Thought* 50, no. 3 (Fall 2017):89–114.

holy of itself, can fail, and its faithfulness must be evaluated according to the Scripture."[9] The church is not bound by its traditions—embodied by a priestly institutional authority—but by scripture alone. The Church of Christ fits two characteristics of a *solae scripturae* Mormonism. First, it bases its doctrines and practices solely—or at least primarily—on the two founding scriptures of early Mormonism, the Bible and the Book of Mormon (the "Independence edition," first published by the Church of Christ in 1990[10]) and thus rejects Joseph Smith's late theological innovations such as plural marriage and baptism for the dead. Second, it is willing to evaluate and reform itself according to those two scriptures (thus the pluralization of the term: "sola*e* scripturae").

First, I will briefly summarize the origins of the Church of Christ (Temple Lot). Then I will show that, from its beginning, Hedrickite Mormonism claimed to be solely founded on Mormonism's two foundational scriptures. I will then argue that another foundational principle of Mormonism—continuing revelation—expressed itself in Hedrickitism. Drawing mainly upon a survey administered to a Hedrickite congregation, I will show that Hedrickites recognize scriptures as the primary source of authority, above church leadership and tradition, a characteristic that encourages individualism. In conclusion, I will share some thoughts on Mormon fissiparousness.

THE ORGANIZATION OF HEDRICKITE MORMONISM

Granville Hedrick, a farmer in Crow Creek, Illinois, joined Mormonism between 1841 and 1843.[11] Three Illinois Mormon congregations gathered

---

9. Jean-Paul Willaime, *Sociologie du protestantisme* (Paris: Presses Universitaires de France, 2005), 10.

10. The preface of the Independence edition of the Book of Mormon explains that "The 1984 General Conference of the Church of Christ on the Temple Lot determined that initial steps be taken to publish the Book of Mormon. A committee of three—William A. Sheldon, Harvey E. Seibel and Amy Schrader—was recommended by the Council of Apostles to the Board of Publications to undertake this work. Initially, it was planned to use the text as found in the 1908 authorized edition, published by Herald Publishing House [RLDS], but to thoroughly review the scriptural references and to include more reference matter from the Bible [...] Since the printer's manuscript prepared by Oliver Cowdery for the 1830 Palmyra edition is available at the RLDS Church library in Independence, Missouri, it was also determined to use this material to obtain an even more accurate version of the book." "Preface," The Book of Mormon (Independence, MO: Board of Publications, Church of Christ [Headquarters, Temple Lot], 1990), xi.

11. Unless otherwise specified, I have relied here on R. Jean Addams, *Upon the Temple Lot: The Church of Christ's Quest to Build the House of the Lord* (Independence: John Whitmer Books, 2010), 6–13.

for the first time in his house during the winter of 1852. They were deeply concerned by developments in Utah Mormonism, especially polygamy. In March 1857, this group declared their "independence and separation from all those apostate and polluted characters who teach or practice polygamy," stating that they "have no fellowship in union or association with any such person or persons who teach or practice the doctrine of polygamy."[12] In April, Hedrick was chosen as presiding elder.

During a conference on November 8, 1862, John E. Page (1799–1867) joined the group. Converted to Mormonism in 1833, Page had been ordained as an apostle in 1838, after a successful mission in Canada. Following Joseph Smith's death, he briefly accepted Brigham Young's leadership but in 1846 affiliated with James J. Strang, whose claims were bolder than Young's. While Young first considered himself to be church president, Strang declared himself a prophet. However, disappointed with Strang's authoritarianism, Page joined James Brewster (1826–1909), whose Mormonism was solely based on the Bible and Book of Mormon. In 1850, Brewster and his followers moved to California where his movement gradually dissolved. Page stayed in the Midwest, joined the Hedrickite congregations that declared their independence in March 1857, and used his own apostolic ordination during Joseph Smith's lifetime as authority to ordain Hedrick an apostle on May 17, 1863.[13] Two months later, during a conference on July 9, Page ordained Hedrick as president, prophet, seer, and revelator. Still, given his skepticism about James Strang and Brigham Young, Page refused to show deference to Hedrick and even cautioned against the danger of corrupt prophets. Quoting a leader of the New Movement who scoffed at Page's ordination of Hedrick as possibly producing a flood of "spurious revelations," Page warned: "Well, that may be the case if he becomes as corrupt as his predecessor did the latter part of life; but we hope and pray for better things."[14] Indeed, it turned out that Hedrick was not an autocrat; his branch of Mormonism seemed to revere only the scriptures.

12. A Declaration of Independence and Separation, March 5, 1857 (Independence: Church of Christ [Temple Lot], 1857).

13. John Quist, "John E. Page: Apostle of Uncertainty," in *Mormon Mavericks: Essays on Dissenters*, edited by John Sillito and Susan Staker (Salt Lake City, UT: Signature Books, 2002), 19–33.

14. Ibid., 33–34; John E. Page, "Ordaining Bro. G. Hedrick," *The Truth Teller* 1, no. 3 (September 1864):41.

THE SCRIPTURES AS PRIMARY HEDRICKITE AUTHORITY

From its beginning, the Hedrickite movement characterized itself as insisting on earliest Mormonism's two sacred texts: the Bible and the Book of Mormon. As Granville Hedrick himself noted in the first issue of the *Truth Teller*: "The principles of the faith and doctrines which were given for the foundation of this church are recorded in the Bible and Book of Mormon, which is the rock and pillar of the foundation of this church of Christ, which was organized on the 6th day of April, 1830, for the last time."[15] In October 1864, the *Truth Teller* editorialized that it "will not endorse any doctrine that cannot be sustained by the Bible or the Book of Mormon."[16]

Relying on these two canonical books, the Church of Christ condemned the doctrines and practices of other Mormonisms, especially those of the Church of Jesus Christ of Latter-day Saints and the Reorganized Church of Jesus Christ of Latter Day Saints. Concerning the Reorganized Church, the Church of Christ denounced the doctrine of hereditary succession to the church presidency. John Page wrote in the November 1864 *Truth Teller*, "There is not one word in the Book of Mormon nor Bible to sustain it."[17] Apostle Adna Haldeman compared hereditary succession to a monarchy, which was repellent to Americans, and argued that the church president must be elected democratically, as was Joseph Smith in January 1831.[18] From 1856 to 1861, leaders of the RLDS Church and of the Hedrickite Church, united by a common loathing of polygamy, sought a possible union, but the project failed, partly due to the Hedrickite rejection of hereditary succession.[19]

Both Mormonisms together condemned plural marriage, as taught by the "Brighamites." The *Truth Teller* editorialized: "There is no book in the world that furnishes stronger evidence against polygamy than the Book of Mormon." This article concluded, "All who are called Mormons whose faith

15. Granville Hedrick, "An Address," *The Truth Teller* 1, no. 1 (July 1864):8. This periodical was published 1864–1868.

16. "Contrast of Doctrines," *The Truth Teller* 1, no. 4 (October 1864):49.

17. John Page, Letter to Brother Fairchild, *The Truth Teller* 1, no. 5 (November 1864):79.

18. Adna Haldeman, "The Governed Elect Their Governors," *The Truth Teller* 1, no. 2 (August 1864):27–28.

19. R. Jean Addams, "The Church of Christ (Temple Lot) and the Reorganized Church of Jesus Christ of Latter Day Saints: 130 Years of Crossroads and Controversies," *Journal of Mormon History* 36, no. 2 (2010):11–12.

and practice are contrary to the teachings of the Book of Mormon, are not Mormons. Therefore, there never was a Mormon who practiced polygamy, nor never can be, for that moment such a lewd practice is conceived in his heart, he ceases to be a Mormon."[20]

The official position of the RLDS Church was that plural marriage was Brigham Young's innovation,[21] but the Church of Christ attributed it to Joseph Smith. Granville Hedrick wrote, "It is a well-known fact that cannot be successfully controverted that the doctrine of polygamy . . . was taught by many of the elders in the church before Joseph preached his blasphemous sermon at the April conference, in 1844. Where did those elders get such abominable doctrines? It was not from Brigham Young, he was not yet in power. Joseph and Hyrum were still living and acting as the two great leaders of the church."[22] Polygamy was evidence of a "fallen" prophet: "And let it also be remembered that it is the design of this work to maintain the position that Joseph Smith was at one period of his life a true prophet of the most high God, and that he did fall from that standing and relation that he once held as a prophet, and afterwards gave false counsel to the church, though it may sound grating to the ears of some."[23]

Because the Hedrickite church concluded that some of Joseph Smith's late teachings contradicted the Bible and the Book of Mormon, it ceased using the Doctrine and Covenants, reverting to the Book of Commandments (1833), the first collection of Joseph Smith's revelations. Even though the Book of Commandments is not part of the Hedrickite scriptural canon, it is still published today by the Church of Christ (Temple Lot).[24]

A second Joseph Smith doctrine espoused by the Brighamites but denounced by the Hedrickites was baptism for the dead: "The Bible and the Book of Mormon contain the fullness of the everlasting gospel, which is the rock and pillar of the church. The doctrine of baptism for the dead by proxy is not found in it."[25]

20. Untitled article, *The Truth Teller* 1, no. 8 (February 1865):115.

21. Mark H. Scherer, *The Journey of a People: The Era of Reorganization*, vol. 2, *1844 to 1946* (Independence, MO: Community of Christ Seminary Press, 2013), 265–266.

22. Granville Hedrick, "The Second Address," *The Truth Teller* 1, no. 4 (October 1864):53.

23. Untitled article, *The Truth Teller* 1, no. 2 (August 1864):19.

24. Book of Commandments (Independence, MO: Board of Publication, Church of Christ, 2007).

25. Untitled article, *The Truth Teller* 1, no. 2 (August 1864):20.

In founding itself solely on the Bible and Book of Mormon, the Church of Christ claimed to be faithful to Mormonism as founded in 1830. The *Truth Teller* mission statement stated from its second issue, "The Truth Teller—Will advocate the Primitive Organization of the Church of Jesus Christ (of Latter Day Saints) which was organized on the 6th day of April, 1830, and maintain her Doctrines in all Truth: Also, an exposition of all the False Doctrines that have been imposed upon the Church."[26] This return to the Mormonism of 1830 could also explain why Hedrickite Mormonism stopped calling itself the "Church of Jesus Christ of Latter Day Saints" in the 1860s, instead reverting to the original 1830 "Church of Christ."[27]

Hedrickite Mormonism not only justified its practices and beliefs according to the Bible and Book of Mormon, but it also reformed itself according to them. In 1925, it gave up the office of "presiding elder," held by Granville Hedrick and his successors, and reverted to a Council of Twelve Apostles, judging this type of organization to be more in accordance with the Bible and Book of Mormon.[28] In "A Latter Day Apostasy," a booklet dealing with Hedrickite beliefs of apostasy during Joseph Smith's life, Hedrickite Apostle William Sheldon argues that "structural innovations in the church restored through Joseph Smith and others began at a much earlier time than is generally supposed."[29] Among other things, the creation of the First Presidency contradicts the Bible and Book of Mormon. Hedrickite Apostle Clarence Wheaton explains three reasons for this position.

> First, that God promised to establish his church in the last days "like unto the church in days of old"; Second, that ten months before the church was organized, the Lord gave two revelations directing that the church should be organized after the apostolic plan set forth in the New Testament and the Book of Mormon; Third, that the pattern furnished by the church "in days of old," as set forth in the New

---

26. Untitled article, *The Truth Teller* 1, no. 2 (August 1864):17.

27. R. Jean Addams, "The Church of Christ (Temple Lot) and Their Quest to Build a Temple in Zion," *John Whitmer Historical Association Journal* 28 (2008):90.

28. B. C. Flint, *An Outline History of the Church of Christ* (Temple Lot), 1953. (Reprint, Independence, MO: Board of Publications, The Church of Christ [Headquarters-Temple Lot], 2005), 139–140.

29. William Sheldon, *A Latter Day Apostasy* (Independence, MO: Board of Publications, Church of Christ, 2008), 5.

Testament and the Book of Mormon, the pattern pointed to and commanded in two revelations given preparatory to the organization of the church, make the twelve apostles the highest quorum in the church.[30]

In short, the Bible and Book of Mormon are the primary source of authority defining truth in Hedrickite Mormonism. Based on these scriptures, the Church of Christ condemned other Mormonisms and even reformed itself. Many scripturally based Hedrickite reforms were made in the 1920s, a period of emergent Protestant fundamentalism in the U.S. An orthodox reaction against the liberalization of Protestant theology, Protestant fundamentalism defended biblical inerrancy.[31]

CONTINUING REVELATION, 1864 AND 1929

However, even though the Bible and Book of Mormon have been foundational since Hedrickitism's beginnings, still the Church of Christ believes in an open scriptural canon, as their tenth "Article of Faith and Practice," which states, "We believe in the principle of continuous revelation; that the canon of scripture is not full, that God inspires men in every age and among all people, and that He speaks when, where, and through whom He may choose. (Amos 3:7; Acts 2:17–18; 2 Pet. 1:21; 1 Ne. 1:82–83)"[32]

The *solae scripturae* Church of Christ here justifies its belief in continuous revelation and the open canon of scripture with verses from its two books of scripture, the Bible (Amos 3:7, Acts 2:17–18, 2 Peter 1:21) and the Book of Mormon (1 Nephi 1:82–83). While early Mormonism was founded on those two scriptural books, the Book of Mormon stands on the founding epistemological and theological principle of continuing revelation. Because the canon of scriptures is not closed, Joseph Smith could add revelations to the Bible. In fact, the Book of Mormon mocks Christians believing in a

---

30. Clarence Wheaton, *First Apostles Not a First Presidency* (Independence, MO: Board of Publications, Church of Christ, 2004), 10.

31. Sébastien Fath, *Dieu bénisse l'Amérique: la religion de la Maison-Blanche* (Paris: Seuil, 2004), 88; Sébastien Fath, *Militants de la Bible aux États-Unis: évangéliques et fondamentalistes du Sud* (Paris: Autrement, 2004), 202.

32. "Articles of Faith and Practice," https://www.churchofchrist1830.org/basic-beliefs. The "Articles of Faith and Practice" were first published in 1927. Addams, *Upon the Temple Lot*, 62.

closed canon: "Thou fool, that shall say, A Bible, we have got a Bible, and we need no more Bible."[33]

Whereas some argue that the Book of Mormon greatly reflected American evangelical populist Christianity,[34] Joseph Smith's later revelations departed radically from orthodox traditional Christianity. Citing the authority of the Bible and Book of Mormon, Hedrickitism criticized those theological innovations yet perpetuated a belief in continuing revelation. A resolution from the October 6, 1925, conference, "adopted by unanimous vote,"[35] states: "Resolved, that this Church of Christ accept nothing purporting to be a revelation from God, past, present, or future, as a revelation from God, save that which is in harmony with both the Bible and the Book of Mormon. Be it further resolved, that if there be any ruling, understanding, or resolution conflicting herewith, that it be hereby rescinded."[36]

Granville Hedrick announced revelation as a guide, including a commandment on April 24, 1864, to gather in Jackson County, Missouri: "Prepare, O ye people, yourselves in all things, that you may be ready to gather together upon the consecrated land which I have appointed and dedicated by My servant, Joseph Smith and the first Elders of My church, in Jackson County, State of Missouri, for the gathering together of my Saints.... [P]repare yourselves and be ready against the appointed time which I have set and prepared for you, that you may return in the year A.D. 1867."[37]

Joseph Smith, also by revelation, had designated this locale as the "New Jerusalem" in July 1831.[38] The first Hedrickite families arrived in Independence in 1865–66. Granville Hedrick did not follow until late in 1868 or early 1869.[39] Even before his arrival, Hedrickites began purchasing parts of the land Joseph Smith had dedicated for the temple that would see Christ's

---

33. The Book of Mormon, "Second Book of Nephi (12:53)," (Independence, MO: Board of Publications, Church of Christ [Headquarters, Temple Lot], 1990), 157.

34. Nathan Hatch, *The Democratization of American Christianity* (New Haven, CT: Yale University Press, 1991), 113–122.

35. Flint, *An Outline History*, 139.

36. Record no. 5, p. 85, quoted in Flint, *An Outline History*, 139.

37. "Revelation," *The Truth Teller* 1, no. 1 (July 1864):4.

38. "Section 57:1," Doctrine et Alliances (Independence, MO: Herald Publishing House, 2004), 104.

39. R. Jean Addams, "The Church of Christ (Temple Lot)," in *Scattering of the Saints: Schism within Mormonism*, edited by Newell Bringhurst and John Hamer (Independence, MO: John Whitmer Books: 2007), 209–210.

second coming. Between August and December 1867, Hedrick's brother John bought three lots. By 1906, the Church of Christ had nine contiguous lots from the original site.[40] To this day, Hedrickites prize their possession of this land, which appears in the name often used to differentiate it from other similarly named denominations: "Church of Christ (Temple Lot)." The Articles of Faith and Practice of the Church of Christ state, "We believe a temple will be built in this generation, in Independence, Missouri, wherein Christ will reveal himself and endow his servants whom he chooses with power to preach the gospel in all the world to every kindred, tongue and people, that the promises of God to Israel may be fulfilled (Micah 4:1–2; Malachi 3:1–4; 3 Nephi 10:4; Ether 6:8)."[41] This belief in the gathering in Independence is not justified with the revelations received by Joseph Smith (1831) and Granville Hedrick (1927) but through verses from the two scriptural books, the Book of Mormon and the Bible. The following Article of Faith and Practice nevertheless states, "We believe that a New Jerusalem shall be built upon this land unto the remnant of the seed of Joseph ... which city shall be built, beginning at the Temple Lot (3 Nephi 9:57–59, 10:1–4; Ether 6:6–8; Revelation to Joseph Smith given Sept., 22 & 23, 1832)."[42] The article thus finds its justification first in scripture (the Book of Mormon) but secondly in a revelation received by Joseph Smith. The revelation received by Granville Hedrick is not mentioned.

Beginning on February 4, 1927, "continuing revelation" was once again expressed in the Church of Christ (Temple Lot) through messages delivered by the Angel Elijah—John the Baptist resurrected—to Apostle Otto Fetting (1871–1933). Fetting joined the Church of Christ after leaving the RLDS Church due to an internal controversy. Frederick M. Smith, the RLDS Church president, argued for a theocratic democracy under which "there would be a lasting centralization of church government in the office of the Presidency" or "supreme directional control." The Presidents of the Seventy, the Presiding Bishopric, and several apostles opposed this form of church governance, arguing that supreme authority rested in the general conference and that, according to F. Henry Edwards, a member of the First Presidency, the

---

40. Ibid., 213. Jackson County old settlers forced the Mormons out in 1833, putting an end to their plans to build this temple.

41. "Articles of Faith and Practice," https://www.churchofchrist1830.org/basic-beliefs.

42. Ibid.

"Three Standard Scriptures are the primary source of constitutional law in the church."[43] The April 1925 RLDS conference sided with the First Presidency. "Almost overnight, Church of Christ membership soared," as dissident RLDS members joined a Mormonism without an autocratic prophet.[44] Among them was Daniel McGregor, "a highly respected RLDS missionary and writer,"[45] who became editor of the Church of Christ's publication *Zion's Advocate*. Fetting also found clout in his new church and was ordained an apostle in 1926.

In 1927, he delivered the first message from Elijah, reminding Hedrickites of the temple's importance: "The revelation that was given for the building of the Temple was true and the Temple soon will be started."[46] During his fifth visit to Fetting, Elijah instructed: "You men, with others, shall assist in the building of The Temple, the House of the Lord, which shall be started in 1929. The Lord will give you seven years in which to complete the work. While it may be slow in the beginning, the Lord will open the way and many will help."[47] The Church of Christ (Temple Lot) endorsed these messages by Elijah/John the Baptist to Fetting through its official institutional publication *Zion's Advocate*. An article in August 1927 quoted the Bible and the Book of Mormon prophesying these visits, concluding, "The visitation therefore to Bro. Fetting agrees with the prophetic word."[48] On April 6, 1929, the Church of Christ broke ground for the temple's construction.[49]

But Hedrickites became divided on the fourth verse of Fetting's twelfth message from Elijah dated July 18, 1929: "Behold, the Lord has rejected all creeds and factions of men, who have gone away from the Word of the Lord and have become an abomination in His sight. Therefore, let those that come to The Church of Christ be baptized."[50] This verse challenged the 1918 "Agreements of Working Harmony" signed by the RLDS and Hedrickite Mormons recognizing the other's priesthood as valid. Thus, RLDS members had been

---

43. Steven Shields, "The Temple of the Church of Christ (Temple Lot)," *John Whitmer Historical Association Journal* 28 (2008):117; Scherer, *The Journey of a People*, 2:481, Edwards quoted p. 467.

44. Addams, *Upon the Temple Lot*, 54

45. Ibid.

46. Otto Fetting and W. A. Draves, *The Word of The Lord: Brought to Mankind by an Angel* (Independence, MO: The Church of Christ with the Elijah Message, the Assured Way of the Lord, Inc., 2008), 11.

47. Ibid., 14.

48. "John The Baptist," *Zion's Advocate*, August 1927, 114.

49. Jason Smith, "Scattering of the Hedrickites," in *Scattering of the Saints*, 234.

50. Fetting and Draves, *The Word of the Lord*, 17.

able to join the Church of Christ without rebaptism, as Otto Fetting himself and more than 3,000 Josephites did after the supreme directional control controversy.[51] Now, according to Fetting's interpretation of the twelfth message, all should be baptized anew, including himself. The Church of Christ rejected his twelfth message and, in October 1929, "voted . . . to silence Fetting, effectively ending his ministry."[52] The membership divided with nearly one third of the 4,000-member Church of Christ (Temple Lot) following Fetting.[53]

Fetting's revelations up to his death in 1933 were compiled in a volume titled The Word of the Lord. In 1944, further schism occurred when another visionary, William Draves, began to receive messages from Elijah. Draves had belonged to the RLDS Church and LDS Church in his youth but eventually joined the Church of Christ (Temple Lot) after becoming familiar with Fetting's revelations. He followed Fetting's schismatic move.[54] In 1937, four years after Fetting's death, Draves claimed to have been visited by Elijah. While initially supportive, the church eventually divided over his new messages. Draves and his supporters organized the "Church of Christ with the Elijah Message," which then became "The Church of Christ With the Elijah Message, established Anew in 1929." An expanded version of The Word of the Lord, retitled The Word of the Lord with the Elijah Message contains both the thirty messages delivered to Otto Fetting and the ninety messages delivered to Draves. Decades passed without visits from Elijah, but in 2018 apostle Norman D. Lyles began to present messages. The current online version of The Word of the Lord with the Elijah Message includes 131 sections, the last message being received on December 28, 2020.[55]

THE CHURCH OF CHRIST TODAY: SURVEY RESULTS

As part of my PhD dissertation on "Mormonisms," I conducted a survey questionnaire in one congregation of each of the six historical Mormonisms.

51. R. Jean Addams, "The Church of Christ (Temple Lot), Its Emergence, Struggles and Early Schisms, 218–219," in Smith, Scattering of the Saints, 218–219.

52. Smith, "Scattering of the Hedrickites," 235.

53. Flint, An Outline History, 142; Smith, "Scattering of the Hedrickites," 236–237.

54. "Brief History in W. A. Draves' Life," https://johnthebaptist.info/Brief_History_WA_Draves .pdf.

55. "One-hundred Thirty First Message," The Word of the Lord (Brought to mankind by an Angel), https://www.elijahmessage.net/files/message131.html.

Although membership numbers vary from the LDS Church's 16 million members to the dozen in the Church of Jesus Christ (Cutlerite), the survey was a good methodological tool for analyzing whether members follow the official institutional discourse. The questionnaire, prepared under the supervision of my advisor, sociologist Jean-Paul Willaime (EPHE-Sorbonne), was confidential and anonymous, allowing respondents to express themselves beyond the official institutional discourse and the researcher's personal biases. Furthermore, my questionnaire moved beyond surveys of LDS Church members in the U.S. and France by including other Mormonisms.[56] One could argue that in a conservative church, respondents might reflect institutional discourse, rather than their personal convictions (if the two differed). However, from my personal interactions with Hedrickite members, I have concluded that they openly differ on matters of faith, as long as these beliefs do not contradict the "Articles of Faith and Practice" rooted in scriptures.

I administered my questionnaire in the Church of Christ local (congregation) in Independence, Missouri (known as the Temple Lot [Independence] local). The meeting hall also houses the church's general headquarters. The congregation meets twice a week. The Sunday worship service, following the Sunday School, consists of sermons based on the Bible and the Book of Mormon and hymns. A communion service is held monthly. The Wednesday evening service meeting, like the Sunday worship service, has hymns and sermons.

Before the service on Wednesday, April 28, 2010, I introduced myself to the pastor as a PhD student from France, described the questionnaire, and asked whether it would be possible to conduct the survey. I positioned myself in the lobby of the main worship room at the end of the service. The pastor made the announcement at the end of the worship, and twenty-five individuals accepted the questionnaire and pencils.

The full questionnaire was divided into six question sets. The first section had five yes/no questions dealing with beliefs about the church: (1) do you

56. Pew Research Center, "Mormons in America: Certain in Their Beliefs, Uncertain of Their Place in Society," January 12, 2012, http://www.pewforum.org/2012/01/12/mormons-in-america-executive-summary. In France, 1,431 LDS members answered Christian Euvrard's questionnaire as part of his PhD dissertation: Socio-Histoire du mormonisme en France (PhD diss., École Pratique des Hautes Études, Paris-Sorbonne, 2008).

believe that the Church is essential for salvation? (2) that its sacraments (ordinances) are essential for salvation? (3) that it is the "only true and living Church upon the face of the whole earth"? (4) that other religions have truth? and (5) do you support interfaith dialogue?

The second set of three questions dealt with authority. Do you believe that authority in the church lies mostly in (check 2 answers): the Bible, Book of Mormon, Church leaders, and/or your own personal revelations or those of other individuals (not necessarily leaders)? The other two questions were yes/no. Do you always agree with Church leaders and Church policies? Do you believe that complete obedience to Church leaders is important?

Section 3 contained nine yes/no questions. (1) Do you believe in the Bible literally? (2) Should the Bible be interpreted through scientific research? (3) Do you believe in the Book of Mormon? Literally? (4) In the Doctrine and Covenants? Literally? (5) In the virgin birth of Jesus? (6) In the resurrection of Jesus Christ? (7) in The Trinity? (8) Do you believe the USA to be a special place, a promised land? (9) Do you think the Church's beliefs and practices should be adapted to different cultures?

The fourth section queried five areas of ethics and politics. (1) Should abortion be legal? (2) Should gay marriage be legal? (3) Do you support the death penalty? (4) Do you believe sexual relationships should be practiced outside of marriage? (5) You vote mostly: Republican? Democrat? Independent? Other?

Four religious practices were the focus of the fifth section. (1) Do you attend church weekly? Monthly? Other? (2) Are you a priesthood member? (3) Do you consume tea? Coffee? Alcohol? Tobacco? (4) Do you give regular financial contributions to the Church? [If yes], less (or more) than a tenth of your monthly salary/pension?

Standard demographics constituted the sixth section—age, sex, occupation (or previous occupation). I also asked: (1) Are you a member of the Church? (2) Why are you a member of the Church? (3) If you are not a member, why do you attend this Church?

Because this chapter focuses on the importance of the scriptures to modern Hedrickites, I analyze only the questions pertaining to "the Church" and "authority" (Sections 1 and 2). The first section shows the importance that respondents attribute to the institution; the second set probes what has the most authority for respondents: the scriptures, church leaders, or personal revelation. In this analysis, I sometimes compare Hedrickites' responses to those of members of other Mormonisms. I also administered the survey to thirty-six *LDS* respondents at Independence Second Ward, on April 18, 2010. In answering the question about whether the church is essential for salvation, 64 percent (16/25) of the Hedrickites said that it was, while 92 percent (33/36) of LDS respondents agreed.

First, one must admit that despite the importance of scriptures that even reformed the institution itself, the latter is still more important to 64 percent of Hedrickite respondents. Yet, it is less important than among 36 LDS respondents. One of the five Hedrickites who did not answer the question, wrote an explanation instead: "Belief in Christ not Church is essential to Salvation."

In responding to the question of whether the sacraments are essential for salvation, 76 percent (19/25) of Hedrickites and 91.5 percent (33/36) of Latter-day Saints agreed. This belief reflects the Church of Christ (Temple Lot) fifth Article of Faith and Practice: "We believe that through the atonement of Christ all men may be saved by obedience to the laws and ordinances of the Gospel; viz.: Faith in God and in the Lord Jesus Christ; Repentance and Baptism by immersion for the remission of sins; Laying on of Hands for: (a) Ordination; (b) Blessing of Children; (c) Confirmation and the Gift of the Holy Ghost; (d) Healing of the Sick. (John 3:16–17; Hel. 5:69–72, 6:1–2; 2 Ne 13:12–17; Mi. 8:29; (a) Acts 13:1–3; Mi. 3:1–3; (b) Mark 10:13–16; 3 Ne 8:20–27; (c) Acts 8:14–17; Mi. 2:1–3; (d) Mark 16:17–18; James 5:14–16)."[57]

Seventy-two percent (18/25) of Hedrickites agreed that the Church is the "only true and living Church upon the face of the whole earth" while 94 percent (34/36) of the LDS respondents agreed. Even though they believe in an exclusivist ecclesiology, most Hedrickite respondents also believe that "other religions have truth" (72 percent, 18/25), and they support interfaith dialogue (68 percent, 17/25).

But although they showed some variation on beliefs about the church, all Hedrickite respondents checked the two same options in the second set of questions concerning the primary sources of authority: the Bible and the Book of Mormon. This belief accords with the Church of Christ's ninth Article of Faith and Practice: "We believe that in the Bible is contained the

57. "Articles of Faith and Practice," https://www.churchofchrist1830.org/basic-beliefs.

word of God, that the Book of Mormon is an added witness for Christ, and that these contain the fullness of the gospel. (Book of Commandments 44:13) (Ezekiel 37:15–20; 1 Nephi 3:157–166, 191–196)."[58]

On the final question, "Why are you a member of the Church?" many Hedrickites expressed the value of a church founded on the Bible and the Book of Mormon, stating, for example, "Because I am convinced that the Lord restored His authority to the earth and that it is contained in the Bible and Book of Mormon"; "I grew up without a church but was converted by the message of the Book of Mormon after my grandmother married an apostle of the Church of Christ"; "Based on the 2 scriptures it is the near duplication of the church Jesus established 2 000 years ago"; "Because I believe the Church of Christ TL [Temple Lot] adheres most closely to the principles of the Gospel of Christ and the New Testament Church"; "Because I believe words, commandments and blessings of God and that Gospel is contained in Bible and Book of Mormon"; "Because in accordance to the Bible + Book of Mormon"; "I believe this church follows and practices the teachings of Christ as contained in Scripture."

In contrast, when LDS members responded to this survey, they often focused on the institution: "Because I know it is the only true Church of Jesus"; "Because I know this Church is the True Church of Jesus Christ"; "Because I know that out of all churches on this Earth that this one (LDS) is the true one"; "A personal testimony that it is the Lords Church"; "I have faith and belief that this is the true church"; "I received personal revelation from the spirit that this church belongs to Jesus Christ."

Even though Hedrickitism still accepts an open scriptural canon, the authority of the Bible and the Book of Mormon serve as safeguards against "prophets" who could appear as authoritative charismatic leaders. However, members also express individual freedom as a core value. Eighty-eight percent of Hedrickite respondents (22/25 "no," 3 "yes") say that they do not always agree with church leaders and policies; and 92 percent (23/25 "no," 2 did not answer) claim that total obedience to church leaders is not important. Here is also expressed a Midwestern identity attached to individual liberties. A woman who had converted to the Church of Christ (Temple Lot) from the RLDS Church, explained, "We have freedom to question, express

58. Ibid.

opinion." In contrast, half of the thirty-six LDS respondents said they "always agree" with church leaders, and 89 percent (32/36) replied that "complete obedience to church leaders" is "important." Even more striking, 100 percent of Community of Christ respondents answered "no" to the question about "always agree[ing]" with leaders and policies, and 88 percent (43/49) did not believe that "complete obedience to church leaders" is important.[59] However, the Community of Christ is not a *solae scripturae* Mormonism. The Book of Mormon is seldom mentioned in official institutional discourse, which relies mainly on a progressive American Christian (thus mostly Protestant) cultural trend.[60]

Hedrickite individualism, like the orthodox Protestant sola scriptura, accepts that the believer has direct access to the truth through unmediated access to the scripture(s). Consequently, this theology produces a "privatization" of religion.[61] Indeed, Hedrickite beliefs foster democracy and individual freedom, rather than charismatic authoritative leadership. As an example, in 1930, following Otto Fetting's message on rebaptism, the church instructed each congregation to organize a referendum on the issue and communicate the results to headquarters using a coupon printed in the February 15 issue of *Zion's Advocate*.[62] According to Apostle Samuel Wood,

> "Re-baptism" is not the real issue that the church has been called upon to decide by referendum at this time. As I see it, underlying the whole matter is a question of far greater importance. And it is of an astonishing and dreadful nature. It is the question of church government. Can the church as established by Christ, with Twelve Apostles at the head, survive? If this "Twelfth Message" in its entirety is accepted, together with the attempt of the brethren to force it upon the church; if their attitude in ignoring the Twelve, and their rebellion

59. I administered this survey to forty-nine members at the Colonial Hills Community of Christ congregation near Independence on September 12, 2010.

60. Chrystal Vanel, "Community of Christ: An American Progressive Christianity, with Mormonism as an Option," *Dialogue: A Journal of Mormon Thought* 50, no. 3 (Fall 2017):102–109.

61. Jean-Paul Willaime, *La Précarité protestante: sociologie du protestantisme contemporain* (Geneva, CH: Labor et Fidès, 1992), 107.

62. "Proposal for Referendum in the Acceptance of Members from Other Factions," *Zion's Advocate* 7, no. 4 (February 15, 1930):35.

against the action of the conference in referring the whole matter to the people for decision, finds support in the referendum, then the order of church government as we now have it will go down to defeat, and one man will emerge as PROPHET SUPREME.[63]

Wood, a former member of the RLDS Church who had been ordained a Hedrickite apostle at the same time as Fetting,[64] may have been alluding to RLDS President Frederick M. Smith's insistence on supreme directional control. But no "prophet supreme" emerged from the rebaptism referendum, as Hedrickite congregations from twenty states, Canada, England, and Wales returned a total of 369 "no" votes and 71 "yes" votes.[65]

CONCLUSION: MORMON FISSIPAROUSNESS

Max Weber's analysis of charisma helps clarify why Mormonism splintered following the founder's death. That result is common following the death of a charismatic religious leader.[66] Ron Graves observed that the death of Muhammad was the catalyst for the first large-scale schism in Islam.[67] Alan Cole argues, "The history of Buddhism, in the twenty-five centuries since the Buddha's death, could be told as a series of schismatic developments."[68] And when William Miller died in 1849, Adventism, yet another American denomination, splintered into many movements, with the Seventh-day Adventist Church comprising the largest number.[69] The Mormon propensity to schism could also be explained like Protestant fissiparousness, about which sociologist Steve Bruce writes,

63. Samuel Wood, "Re-Baptism: Not the Real Issue," *Zion's Advocate* 7, no. 2 (January 15, 1930):17.

64. Flint, *An Outline History*, 138, 140.

65. "The Proposal of the Twelve, Submitted to the Referendum of All Churches Is Approved," *Zion's Advocate* 7, no. 4 (April 1, 1930):58; "Additional Referendum Votes," ibid., 59.

66. Max Weber, *Économie et société*, vol. 2, *L'organisation et les puissances de la société dans leur rapport à l'économie*, French translation by Julien Freund, Pierre Kamnitzer, Pierre Bertrand, Éric de Dampierre, Jean Maillard, and Jacques Chavy (Paris: Pocket, 1995), 326; Gordon Melton, "Introduction," in *When Prophets Die: The Postcharismatic Fate of New Religious Movements*, edited by Timothy Miller (New York: State University of New York Press, 1991), 8–10.

67. Ron Graves, "Charismatic Authority in Islam," in *Sacred Schisms: How Religions Divide*, edited by James Lewis and Sarah Lewis (Cambridge, UK: Cambridge University Press, 2009), 43.

68. Alan Cole, "Schisms in Buddhism," ibid., 61.

69. Richard Lehmann, *Les Adventistes du septième jour* (Maredsous, BE: Brespol, 1987), 15.

For Protestants, schism is easy. The Bible, the sole legitimate source of authority, is accessible to all believers and hence it is always open for one group to challenge the dominant orthodoxy by showing that its new revelation accords better with scripture than the doctrine of the establishment. While committed Protestants believe that the Bible is in some sense self-interpreting, the history of conflict among those who claim no source of authority other than the Bible makes it clear that such a belief does not solve the problem of divergent interpretation.[70]

Mormonism's many scriptures are the objects of multiple interpretations, a role played by the Bible in Protestantism. Furthermore, Mormonism's high propensity to schism is due to and multiplied by its characteristic of continuing revelation. Thus, continuing revelation leads to continuing fissiparousness. Mormon denominations have tried to control continuing revelation, thus limiting fissiparousness. In the Church of Jesus Christ of Latter-day Saints (headquartered in Salt Lake City, Utah) and Community of Christ, only the church president can receive revelations. In the *solae scripturae* Mormonism of the Church of Christ (Temple Lot), continuing revelation is highly limited by its primary sources of authority: the Bible and Book of Mormon. Hedrickite fissiparousness is thus somewhat limited—or at least less important—than LDS and Community of Christ schisms.[71]

Hedrickitism emerged following the 1844 succession crisis. As of 2013, 8,000 Hedrickites[72] still rely primarily on the Bible and Book of Mormon for matters of faith and beliefs. As the Hedrickites, the Bickertonites (members of the Church of Jesus Christ headquartered in Monongahela, Pennsylvania) could also be defined as a *solae scripturae* Restoration tradition.[73] In Chapter 11 of the present book, "William Bickerton's Cooperative Views on Scripture

70. Steve Bruce, *A House Divided: Protestantism, Schism, and Secularization* (London: Routledge, 1990), 45.

71. As of 2001, specialist Steven L. Shields identified ninety-four breakoffs from the LDS Church; twenty from the RLDS Church, to which we can add the Remnant Church of Jesus Christ of Latter Day Saints; and twenty from the Church of Christ (Temple Lot). Shields, *Divergent Paths of the Restoration* (Independence, MO: Herald Publishing House, 2001).

72. R. Jean Addams, email to Chrystal Vanel, August 6, 2013, printout in my possession.

73. Chrystal Vanel, Des mormonismes: une étude historique et sociologique d'une fissiparité religieuse américaine (1830–2013), PhD diss., Ecole Pratique des Hautes Etudes-Sorbonne, 2013, pp. 219–236.

and Revelation," scholar Daniel P. Stone shows that Bickerton preached the Restoration Gospel "using mainly the Book of Mormon and the Bible," and, even though continuing revelation was available to all Bickertonites, "it had to correlate with the Bible and the Book of Mormon. Otherwise, the revelation could be considered false and could be disregarded." One could argue that the Bickertonite tradition is a purest form of *solae scripturae* Restoration tradition: it did not promote the gathering in Independence (Missouri), since there is no explicit justification for it in the Bible or the Book of Mormon. In both the Hedrickite and the Bickertonite traditions, those scriptures composed of two books are interpreted mostly literally, like the Bible in fundamentalist American Protestantism—as the de facto absence of continuing revelation neither facilitates nor allows for a changing hermeneutic worldview.

6

Joseph Smith's Letter from Liberty Jail

A Study in Canonization

Kathleen Flake

Once canonized, it can be forgotten that all scripture originates as human thought or experience represented in human terms. More than origin, however, is obscured by a canonization process that hides or ignores scripture's human elements. Meaning can also be elided. One of the more interesting and illuminating aspects of Mormonism is its retention of historical context and the role of human actors in the production of its scriptures, especially in its Book of Doctrine and Covenants.

This analysis of one of the Book of Doctrine and Covenants' several revelatory sections argues for the value of remembering the temporal, even human qualities of canon or "the role of writing . . . in the shaping of a religious community's sense of its boundaries, history, and identity."[1] My wager is that doing so illuminates the process of canon construction and the doctrinal or normative force of the resulting scripture itself. I ask what about writing—whether ancient or contemporary—makes it susceptible to designation as divinely inspired utterance and, more, religious law? Or, more specific to this exercise, how has a modern account of human misery and longing held sway with the lamentations of Jeremiah and the epistles of first-century Christian witnesses?

---

1. W. Clark Gilpin, letter of invitation to participate in a conference commemorating his retirement from the University of Chicago Divinity School held on May 19, 2011. The conference proceedings were published as a special issue of the *Journal of Religion*. See *Journal of Religion* 92, no. 4 (October 2012).

During the winter of 1838–1839, Joseph Smith wrote a two-part letter to the church while incarcerated in Missouri.[2] Like virtually all letters from prison, this one reveals the human soul in the grasp of dehumanized authority, or that abstraction we call "the state" and its disciplinary technologies. The technology applied to Smith and his five cohorts was very rudimentary: a below-ground, dungeon-like jail, with a ceiling too low to allow its prisoners to stand upright, and open slits too high in the wall to allow sight but always open to the cold. Smith spent four winter months in the inaptly named Liberty Jail, sleeping on stone, choking on a draftless fire in the dark, and fed tainted and sometimes poisoned food. Possibly most burdensome were the tales his jailers told of their participation in the mayhem that was driving the Latter-day Saints from Missouri.[3] For Smith, the jail was "hell surrounded with demonds," where he was "compeled to hear nothing but blasphemo[u]s oaths and witness a seen of blasphemy and drunkeness and hypocracy and debaucheries of evry description."[4]

In late winter, after hearing word of his family's escape to Illinois, Smith wrote the first part of a letter addressed "To the church of Latter-day saints at Quincy Illinois and scattered abroad." The letter was to be delivered first to his wife Emma and then to Mormonism's ordained priesthood of all believers, who were aggregating in a small town on the other side of the Missouri border, two hundred miles east of his jail cell. A few days later, he wrote the second part of the letter beginning simply, "Continued to the church of Latter-day-saints." Together, both parts filled nearly twenty-six pages. The letter displays the typical elements of prison letters that achieve literary significance: a famous writer in a complex historical situation, forceful

2. All quotations from the letter are from "Letter to the Church and Edward Partridge, 20 March 1839," *JSP*, D7:356–372, and "Letter to Edward Partridge and the Church, circa 22 March 1839," *JSP*, D7:388–401. For a discussion of the variety of Smith's correspondence from confinement in Missouri, see David W. Grua, "Joseph Smith's Missouri Prison Letters and the Mormon Textual Community," in *Foundational Texts of Mormonism: Examining Major Early Sources*, edited by Mark Ashurst-McGee, Robin Scott Jensen, and Sharalyn D. Howcroft (New York: Oxford University Press, 2018), 124–153.

3. Smith was incarcerated on charges of treason and other crimes following an armed conflict between Latter-day Saints (LDS) and non-LDS settlers. For an analysis of the charges against Smith, see Stephen C. LeSueur, "'High Treason and Murder': The Examination of Mormon Prisoners at Richmond, Missouri, in November 1838," *Brigham Young University Studies* 26, no. 2 (Spring 1986):3–30.

4. *JSP*, D7:361.

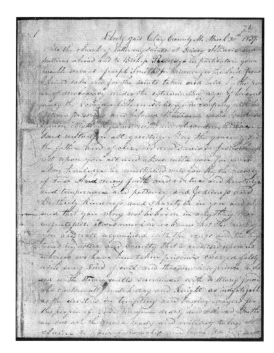

FIGURE 6.1. Joseph Smith, Letter to Edward Partridge and the Church, March 20, 1839. Courtesy of the Church History Library, the Church of Jesus Christ of Latter-day Saints. ©Intellectual Reserve Inc.

eloquence driven by intense personal suffering, and richly philosophical expressions of social protest and existential insight. I do not choose it for these attributes only, however, but also for its distinction, at least in the modern era, of achieving canonical status—not in the literary but in the strictly religious sense.

I will argue, first, that Smith's letter shows the role of writing in making sense of religious disappointment and suffering. Second, the letter illustrates the way personal writing can, through poetic function, transcend its time and place and sustain corporate religious identity, thus showing the power of writing to turn event into history. Third, the letter reveals the way writing legislates a preventive boundary, a rule of praxis capable of directing subsequent believers away from past defeat and ever-present danger.

FROM LETTER TO SCRIPTURE

In 1876, Smith's successor as church president, Brigham Young, assigned Mormonism's resident intellectual and ecclesiastical hierarch, Orson Pratt, the task of editing and presenting to the body of the church an updated version of its canonical texts. Pratt's proposed revision added several of Smith's writings—including the 1839 Liberty Jail letter—to Mormonism's already distinctively large corpus of scripture.[5] In its canonized form, the letter constituted three new chapters or sections of the church's book of order, the Doctrine and Covenants (D&C). The longest and most philosophical chapter—denominated Section 121—was a composite of noncontiguous portions of the letter and is the focus of this analysis. The other canonized portions, Sections 122 and 123, were composed of contiguous paragraphs. Section 122 was set apart in its own chapter because it was deemed a reflection by Smith on his death, which would occur five years later. Section 123 instructed the Saints to create a record of their losses in support of a petition for redress from, inter alia, the federal government, as discussed below.

It is tempting to assume that the scriptural authority granted Smith's letter arose necessarily from his already-established status among the Latter-day Saints as prophet and president of the church. This was, no doubt, a significant and even necessary factor but of itself was an insufficient cause. Smith wrote other letters, many from jail—even this jail—that were not granted scriptural status. Thus, while the prophetic identity of the author may have been necessary as a threshold matter, it did not ensure the letter's canonization. Neither did canonization require acceptance of every word he wrote. Only 40 percent of the letter's contents were deemed scriptural, thus providing an opportunity for this analysis of the judgment at work in turning a letter into canonical rule.

Of course, nothing necessitates canon. Its formation is multidetermined and the result of a complex interplay of interests and authorities, both authorial and communal. It is, however, generally agreed that while prophets may write scripture, only believing communities can construct canon.[6] For its redactors and the church community at large, there was no question that a prophet had produced the letter. Although Smith had dictated it to two fellow prisoners who served as scribes, the original manuscript showed corrections

---

5. Brian Passantino, "Orson Pratt and the Expansion of the Doctrine and Covenants," master's thesis, Utah State University, 2020.

6. See, e.g., Lieven Boeve, "Tradition, (De)Canonization, and the Challenge of Plurality," in *Canonization and Decanonization*, edited by Arie van der Kooij and Karel van der Toorn (Leiden, NL: Brill, 1998), 371–80.

in his own hand as well as his signature. Readers were thus assured of the authoritative source for the letter's sentiments and ideas. Of course, even in 1876, many, including Young and Pratt, were knowledgeable of the events described in the letter, having lived through them or having heard survivors' stories firsthand. Many more would have been familiar with the letter's contents and would have assumed its significance from its having been printed three times in church newspapers between 1840 and 1854.[7]

Missouri was a watershed experience for Mormonism's first generation, and Smith's reflections on it had always been a chief means of rationalizing their suffering. It was not the only means, however. Smith's letter from Liberty Jail had encouraged the refugees from Missouri to write their own accounts. He "suggest[ed]" they record "the whole concatenation of diabolical rascality and nefarious and murderous impositions ... practised upon this people that we may not only publish to all the world but present them to the heads of the government in all there dark and hellish hugh." Making such a record was, he urged them, "an imperious duty that we owe to God to angels ... and also to ourselves to our wives and our children who have been made to bow down with grief sorrow and care."[8]

CALCULATING LOSSES

Wives, too, took up this "imperious duty." Newly widowed Philindia Myrick wrote her petition within a year of escaping: "The mob came a ponus in the after part of the day with Mr Cumstock at thare hed and commens fireing on helpless men womens and children and thare was fifteen killed and was burried in one hole the next day and others wounded sum mortally and amung whom was my husband Levi N. Myrick instantly killed and also a child of mine mortaly wounded who died about 4 weeks after."[9] With license from

7. For the letter's publication history, see Dean C. Jessee and John W. Welch, "Revelations in Context: Joseph Smith's Letter from Liberty Jail, March 20, 1839," *Brigham Young University Studies* 39, no. 3 (2000):130.

8. *JSP*, D7:397; cf. D&C 123:1, 5–7.

9. Affidavit of Philindia Myrick, in *Mormon Redress Petitions: Documents of the 1833–1838 Missouri Conflict*, edited by Clark V. Johnson (Provo, UT: Religious Studies Center, Brigham Young University, 1992), xvii. These petitions were met with sympathy but nothing more. "Your cause is just," President Van Buren is reputed to have said to Smith, "but I can do nothing for you. . . . If I take up for you, I shall lose the Vote of Missouri." History, 1838–1856, vol. C-1 [November 2, 1838–1831, July 1842], p. 1016, CHL.

the governor and the assistance of state arms, posses composed of recognizable neighbors such as "Mr Cumstock" freely commandeered land, looted and demolished homes, torched crops, and stole or destroyed domestic animals. Some atrocities were impossible to redress: men hunted like animals, women raped, and children shot at point-blank range. All lost something, many lost everything, and some lost their faith. Even their prophet was compelled to ask his god, "Where is the pavilion that covereth thy hiding place[?]" Pratt chose this question from the Liberty Jail letter as the opening line for Section 121.[10]

As Talcott Parsons observes, "Good fortune and suffering must always . . . be endowed with meaning. They cannot, except in limiting cases, be accepted as something that 'just happens.'"[11] However much this overstates the case generally, especially with respect to good fortune, it is very true with respect to bad fortune and most true of religious bad fortune. If God is, as the hymn says, "our help in ages past and hope for years to come," his failure to help in the present sunders the necessary sense of continuity of past and future that constitutes the identity of a chosen people. Here, I argue that those parts of Smith's letter preserved and canonized in Section 121 removed the "just happens" from Mormonism's greatest tragedy: the eight-year Mormon War in Missouri and the resultant Latter-day Saint failure to build a temple there, a temple in which God had promised to reveal himself.

The Latter-day Saints came to Missouri in 1831 to build a heavenly city but soon found themselves in hell. Beginning in 1833, attacks on Mormon settlers drove them from Independence, a small settlement on the edge of tribal lands and the Missouri-Kansas border. Most Americans thought of it as the far frontier, even a marshland devoid of civilization and sparsely settled, if at all, by southerners whose slaves constituted a third of the population.[12] To the Mormons, however, it was chosen land, site for a millennial Zion. While others spoke of Missouri's rich soil and plentiful water in figurative terms as a new Eden, the Mormons believed that through their temple-building

---

10. *JSP*, 7:362; D&C 121:1.

11. Talcott Parsons, quoted by Martin Marty, "America's Iconic Book," in *Humanizing America's Iconic Book*, edited by Gene M. Tucker and Douglas A. Knight (Chico, CA: Scholars Press, 1982), 6. I am indebted to Marty not only for the quotation but the application of it to religious text. In his case, to the Bible as having the capacity to "remove the 'just happening' dimension from human existence."

12. Craig S. Campbell, *Images of the New Jerusalem: Latter Day Saint Faction Interpretations of Independence, Missouri* (Knoxville: University of Tennessee Press, 2004), 26.

aspirations, the state was to become literally the paradisiac habitation of God. By revelation they had been told "the city New Jerusalem . . . shall be built beginning at the Temple lot which is appointed by the finger of the Lord" in Independence, Missouri. They had also been promised, "This generation shall not all pass away untill an house shall be built unto the Lord and . . . the glory of the Lord . . . shall fill the house."[13] But less than a year later, approximately 1,200 Mormon residents were forcibly evicted and would never return.

Removal of the Mormons from Independence did not bring peace, however. Violence continued to mount in the counties to which the Saints were successively reassigned, either by mob action or legislative intervention. In their new locales too, the Latter-day Saints gathered in even larger numbers and broke ground for a second temple. Some fought back in not-so-saintly fashion. A few zealots earned the church a reputation for violence that it would never shake.[14] In addition, the Saints began to contend with one another. Even within the leadership, dissent led to threats of violence on both sides. Most foolishly, some made boastful, warmongering threats to the Missourians. One Fourth of July orator announced, "We take God, and all the holy Angels to witness this day, that we warn all men, in the name of Jesus Christ, to come on us no more forever, for from this hour . . . that mob that comes on us to disturb us, it shall be between us and them a war of extermination, for we will follow them till the last drop of their blood is spilled, or else they will have to exterminate us."[15] Three months later, he got what he asked for. Missouri's governor issued an order that unleashed local militias and opportunistic neighbors against the Mormon settlements. "The Mormons," it proclaimed, "must be treated as enemies, and must be exterminated or driven from the State."[16]

By the spring of 1839, the Mormons were routed and their leadership in disarray: some dead, others in jail, and many others in apostasy. Former

13. Joseph Smith, "Revelation, September 22–23, 1832," in *JSP*, R1:274–275; D&C 84:3–5.

14. For an important historiographic analysis of the source of the Danite critique in Mormon studies, see Dean C. Jessee and David J. Whittaker, eds., "The Last Months of Mormonism in Missouri: The Albert Perry Rockwood Journal," *Brigham Young University Studies* 28, no. 1 (Winter 1988):36n19.

15. Jedediah M. Grant, *A Collection of Facts Relative to the Course Taken by Elder Sidney Rigdon. In the States of Ohio, Missouri, Illinois and Pennsylvania* (Philadelphia: Brown, Bicking, & Guilbert, 1844), 11.

16. Greene, *Facts Relative to the Expulsion*, 26.

bishop John Corrill broadcast his disillusionment in print: "Calculation after calculation has failed, and plan after plan has been overthrown, and our Prophet seemed not to know the event till too late." Joseph Smith was an especial disappointment: "If he said go up and prosper, still we did not prosper; but have labored and toiled, and waded through trials, difficulties, and temptations, of various kinds, in hope of deliverance. But no deliverance came. The promises failed."[17] Meanwhile, those who still believed were scattered throughout the Midwest in search of shelter from winter and mob violence. While Smith was held as leverage on charges of treason to guarantee their exodus, at least 8,000 of his followers—including his own family—were fleeing Missouri at gunpoint and little more than what they had on their backs. Many died in the violence or from exposure. Elizabeth Barlow's letter to her cousin in the East admitted: "To look at our situation at this present time it would seem that Zion is all destroyed."[18]

MAKING SENSE OF SUFFERING

Joseph Smith knew the state of his followers and, in his own letter, described it less calmly than Barlow. "Oh! . . . the inhumanity and murderous disposition of this people," he exclaimed of the Missourians. "It shocks all nature it beggers and defies all discription. it is a tail [tale] of wo a lamentable tail yea a sorrifull tail too much to tell too much for contemplation too much to think of for a moment too much for human beings . . . that a man should be mangled for sport women be . . . ~~violated~~ rob[b]ed of all that they have their last morsel for subsistance and then be violated to gratify the ~~hells~~ hellish desires of the mob and finally left to perish with their helpless of[f]spring clinging around their necks."[19] This emotional indictment of the Missourians did not, however, make the canonical cut. It and similar outbursts of pity and exasperation were excluded from Section 121.

---

17. John Corrill, *A Brief History of the Church of Christ of Latter Day Saints (Commonly Called Mormons) . . . with Reasons of the Author for Leaving the Church* (St. Louis, MO: John Corrill, 1839), 49.

18. Elizabeth Haven Barlow, Quincy, IL, to Elizabeth Howe Bullard, Holliston, MA (February 25,1839), in *Women's Voices: An Untold History of the Latter-day Saints 1830–1900*, by Kenneth W. Godfrey, Audrey M. Godfrey, and Jill Mulvay Derr (Salt Lake City, UT: Deseret Book, 1982), 108. Elizabeth was not among the discouraged, however. The letter assures her cousin that "it is not so; the work of the Lord is on the march."

19. *JSP*, D7:361–362.

Neither did Smith's unqualified assertion of the Saints' innocence qualify for inclusion.[20] Rather, Section 121 omits the first two pages of the letter and begins, as mentioned, with Smith's lament: "O God, where art thou? And where is the pavilion that covereth thy hiding place?" This is joined to a petition: "Let thy hiding place no longer be covered; let thine ear be inclined; let thine heart be softened, and thy bowels moved with compassion toward us. Let thine anger be kindled against our enemies; and ... remember thy suffering saints."[21] The redactor's choice of these sentences in preference to others that preceded them had two primary effects. It both elevated the tone from invective to petition and removed the limits of historical particularity. This allowed readers who did not share the event to nevertheless identify with the canonical message. It did so, however, without losing the sentiment of grief and indignation so central to Smith's original text. In addition, Pratt's chosen first sentences framed the text as a prophet's invocation of divine manifestation and report of God's response.

After six introductory sentences, the canonical text does not return to the original for another five pages. The point of reentry is a section of the letter marked by a dramatic shift in voice: "My son, peace be unto thy soul; thine adversity and thine afflictions shall be but a small moment."[22] In the original letter, this shift was preceded by Smith's description of the softening effects on him of correspondence from his wife, his brother, and a close friend and church leader responsible for aiding the Mormon refugees in Quincy. These letters were, he said, "to our ~~soles~~ souls as the gentle air ... call[ing] into action evry simpathetick feeling ... [which] sesses [seizes] the presant with a vivasity of lightning [and] ... grasps after the future with the fearsness [fierceness] of a tiger ... untill finally all enmity ... lie slain victoms at the feet of hope and when the hart is sufficiently contrite ~~and~~ then the voice of inspiration steals along and whispers my son pease be unto thy soul."[23] Although the scriptural redactor's omission truncated the emotional journey described in these words and lost the poetry in Smith's revelatory process,

20. The Liberty Jail letter contained the following assertion, not included in the canonized version: "If the inhabitance [*sic*] of the state of Missouri had let the saints alone and had been as deserable of peace as they ware there would have been nothing but peace and quiatude [*sic*] in this State unto this day we should not have been in this hell surrounded with demons." *JSP*, D7:361.

21. D&C 121:1, 4–6; cf. *JSP*, D7:362–363.

22. D&C 121:7; cf. *JSP*, D7:366.

23. *JSP*, D7:365–366.

the canonized version remained true to Smith's petition and reassured the scriptural reader of the letter's claim to a divine response.

That response was twofold. Neither aspect is surprising to those who study religious disappointment. First came assurances that, God's absence notwithstanding, the refugees were still his people. Though predictable to us, this assurance was made in terms particularly definitive of the Latter-day Saints: the promise of further revelation. Specifically, former promises of theophany, with its attendant knowledge and power, were generously restated. "How long can rowling watters reamin [remain] impure what power shall stay the heavens," wrote Smith, "as well might man streach forth his puny arm to stop the Missouri River ... as to hinder the Almighty from *pooring down knoledge from heaven* upon the heads of the Latter day saints."[24] This sentence, which the redactor included, carried good and bad news. On one hand, the breach between present and past was healed by reinstitution of the feared lost promise of theophany. But with the assurance came the judgment that the church, like "rowling watter," had been thrashed in Missouri because of its impurities. This is the second unsurprising aspect of the answer to Smith's petition: God had absented himself because of the sins of the Latter-day Saints.[25] The kind of sin they were accused of, however, is surprising. The Saints were guilty of abusing power.

Usually, when abuses of power are noted in this particular moment in American religious history, they concern the governor's extermination order or the mobs that harassed the Mormons until the militia succeeded in driving them from the state. But Smith was not inclined to give the mobocrats full credit for the mayhem, if only because it would also give these civil servants of the devil all the power. Neither were the Saints "sinners in the hands of an angry God."[26] Rather, they had fallen out of God's hands; they

24. *JSP*, D7:370 (emphasis added); cf. D&C 121:33.

25. Certainly, those who caused the Saints' afflictions were given their due in Smith's letter and the redactor's edit of it. "Cursed are all those that shall lift up the heal against mine anointed. ... [W]o unto all those that discomfort my people and drive and murder and testify against them ... a generation of viper[s] shall not escape the damnation of hell" (*JSP*, D7:367; cf. D&C 121:16, 23) But, again, the historical detail in Smith's letter is lost in the scripture. Instead, the retaliatory sentiment of the original is elevated and authorized by the redactor's preferring those portions of the letter that rely on biblical, not personal, invective.

26. Jonathan Edwards, "Sinners in the Hands of an Angry God (1741)," in *The Sermons of Jonathan Edwards: A Reader*, edited by Wilson H. Kimnach, Kenneth P. Minkema, and Douglas A. Sweeney, (New Haven, CT: Yale University Press, 2008), 49–65.

had lost their connection to saving power by abusing it. This was not merely a convenient fiction to rationalize bad fortune. As indicated above, the historical record shows the Mormon experience in Missouri was fraught with internal contention, coercive excommunications, and threats of retaliation among their leadership. Moreover, some had attempted to recover property lost to mobs in the same manner in which it had been taken from them: forcibly and violently.

Most dramatically, Sidney Rigdon's aforementioned Fourth of July threat of "a war of extermination" against any "mob that comes on us" proved to be an invitation.[27] His speech, wrote a contemporary, "fanned into a flame the burning wrath of the mobocratic portion of the Missourians. . . . Death and carnage, marched through the land, in their most terrific forms."[28] Left in a dungeon to reflect on these events, Smith concluded, "We have learned by sad experiance that it is the nature and disposition of almost all men as soon as they get a little authority as they suppose they will imediately begin to [e]xercise unritious dominion. hence ma[n]y are called but few are ch[osen]."[29] Smith's reflection on chosenness and dominion is the longest single canonized excerpt from the Liberty Jail letter. It turns Section 121 into a discourse on the abuse of ecclesial authority or "priesthood," the effect of such abuse, and a prescription for priesthood's proper exercise.

The original text shows Smith working his way tentatively toward a definition of what went wrong in Missouri—what caused the Saints, particularly their leadership, to fail at their calling: "I beg leave to say unto you Brethren that ignorance supe[r]stition and bigotry placing itself where it ought not is often times in the way of the prosperity of this church."[30] The next day, when finishing the letter, his voice assumed the more authoritative tone noted above, and here the redactor takes up the letter again for canonization. The scriptural note is struck with an imperative assertion.

> The rights of priesthood are inseperably connected with the powers of heaven and ... may be confered upon us it is true but when we undertake to cover our sins or to gratify our pride or vain ambition

27. Grant, *Collection of Facts*, 11.
28. Ibid., 11–12.
29. *JSP*, D7:393–394; cf. D&C 121:39–40.
30. *JSP*, D6:370.

or to exercise controle or dominion or compulsion ... in any degree
of unritiousness behold the heavens withdraw themselves the spirit of
the Lord is grieved and when it has withdrawn <u>Amen</u> to the <u>priest-
hood</u> or the authority of that man.[31]

This was, for Smith, the "amen" heard in Missouri when God withdrew
himself, entered that "pavilion" that covered his "hiding place," and left the
now-disconnected Saints without power to defend themselves "against
the whole concatination of diabolicalil rascality and nefarious and murderous impositions." In other words, according to the letter from Liberty Jail,
the Saints not only bore the brunt of the mayhem in Missouri, they also
bore some responsibility for it. Still, naming the Saints' sin was not the only
significance of Smith's letter. It also introduced a rule of faith.

CANONICAL LEGISLATION

Canonization denotes legislation, not just memorialization or even explanation. Smith's redactor chose to make his promulgation of law the turning point in the letter's narrative of suffering, sin, and redemption. Here
we see the final shift in the letter's function as scriptural canon. Having
made sense of suffering and rewoven the Saints' narrative of chosenness
with the renewed promise of theophany, Smith's next words stated a rule
of praxis. They stipulated the standard by which power was to be judged as
good or evil and established the rule of future practice by the community.
First, the standard was stated, as we have seen, in negative terms: covering
sin, gratifying ambition, and exercising coercive dominion. Ideally, however,
religious lawmaking results in more than a proscription. A positive rule of
faith, a prescriptive aspiration if you will, is also provided.

At least that is the case with Smith's letter, the canonized version of
which climaxes in a description of righteous dominion that leverages biblical phrases to legislate boundaries of ecclesial power. "No power or in
fluence can or ought to be maintained by virtue of the priesthood, only
by persuasion, by long-suffering, by gentleness and meekness, and by love
unfeigned; By kindness, and pure knowledge, which shall greatly enlarge

31. *JSP*, D6:393; cf. D&C 121:36–37.

the soul without hypocrisy, and without guile." Admitting that it may be necessary to "reprov[e] betimes with sharpness," the letter limits reproof to such occasions "when moved upon by the Holy Ghost" and requires the demonstration "afterwards [of] an increase of love toward him whom thou hast reproved, lest he esteem thee to be his enemy." If obeyed, this rule would ensure "that he may know that thy faithfulness is stronger than the cords of death." Thus, it would also ensure the proper exercise of authority between Saints requiring "reproof" and those holding them accountable, but not between them only: "Let thy bowels also be full of charity towards all men, and to the household of faith."[32] In sum, all priestly action was to be prompted by revelation as "moved" by the Spirit, guided by and productive of love. Any other exercise of authority was a self-executing nullity—it was the "amen to the authority of that man." Worse, on a collective level, it threatened a reprise of the Missouri experience, forever afterward the object lesson of powerlessness for a church whose raison d'être was the mediation of divine power.

From his earliest sense of prophetic mission, Smith had unapologetically claimed that the religions of his day "teach for doctrines the commandments of men, having a form of Godliness but they deny the power thereof."[33] Thus, while other antebellum restorationists were intent on replicating the primitive Christian church, Smith was intent on reception of divine power, "that every man might Speak in the name of God the Lord."[34] If Mormonism was, as Emerson quipped, the "after clap of Puritanism," its particular sound was John Winthrop's worst, antinomian nightmare.[35] In Missouri, it became a nightmare for Joseph Smith as well. The Liberty Jail letter was an attempt to wake up, to rationalize how the power had failed him and his followers and to find a way back to their originating vision. The answer found there enunciated the way back. Because their powerlessness was caused by their abuse of power, the solution was within reach, even comfortable reach through the familiar processes of repentance. Thus, to the refugees who waited in Quincy, Illinois, for the release of their prophet, his letter offered the possibility of a

---

32. D&C 121:41–45; cf. *JSP*, D6:394.

33. "History of Joseph Smith," *Times and Seasons,* April 1, 1842. For the canonized text of these words, see, the Pearl of Great Price, Joseph Smith—History 1:19; cf. 2 Tim. 3:5.

34. *JSP*, R1:224–225; D&C 1:20.

35. Ralph Waldo Emerson, as quoted in James Bradley Thayer, *A Western Journey with Mr. Emerson* (Boston: Little, Brown, 1884), 39.

restored sense of continuity with their origins and its claim of divine power. It provided the rule of praxis whereby they could imagine a future out of the disappointments of the present. Finally, it described the path to a future characterized by divine presence and sanctifying power: "Then shall thy confidence wax strong in the presants of God and the doctrins of the Priesthood shall destill upon thy soul as the dews from heaven the Holy Ghost shall be thy constant companion and thy septer an unchanging septer of ritiousness and truth and thy dominion shall be an everlasting dominion and without compulsory means it shall flow [un]to thee for ever and ever."[36] With this prescription and promise, the canonized version of Smith's letter ends.

So, what does this tell us about how and why personal writings become religiously authoritative? Why, forty years later, did the now-established community of Utah Saints canonize Smith's letter from Liberty Jail? As stated above, the letter honored in its day and memorialized for future generations a watershed experience of personal suffering and collective loss, made sense of a colossal failure related to core aspects of the church's mission, and authoritatively legislated a rule of faith that gave hope of overcoming that failure.

In addition, however, contemporary historical circumstances invited canonization of Smith's emotion-laden, sense-making, and hope-giving letter. In 1876, the Utah Saints were in another power struggle, internally and externally. Federal antipolygamy legislation was wrenching the fabric of their self-government, destabilizing their family structure, and infringing upon their personal and civil liberties. Dissenting movements were causing internal friction, including on questions of ecclesial authority.[37] Mormonism's first generation was passing. Brigham Young would die in 1877, a year after the lessons of Missouri were canonized, and redactor Orson Pratt died three years later. Why did they submit this letter in this form to the church for canonization, an act that would bind generations to come? Ultimately,

---

36. *JSP*, D6:394; cf. D&C 121:45–46.
37. For the history of federal antipolygamy legislation, see, e.g., Sarah Barringer Gordon, *The Mormon Question: Polygamy and Constitutional Conflict in Nineteenth-Century America* (Chapel Hill: University of North Carolina Press, 2002). For an example of dissent, see Ronald W. Walker, *Wayward Saints: The Social and Religious Protests of the Godbeites against Brigham Young* (Provo, UT: Brigham Young University Studies/Brigham Young University Press, 2009).

because in it the community recognized itself—both what it was and what it wished to become. The Liberty Jail letter was canonized because it succeeded in reweaving and forwarding a "grand narrative, enfolding individuals and congregations within larger historical structures of inclusion and exclusion and charting the path of 'the pilgrim's progress.'"[38]

38. Gilpin, letter of invitation.

7

Lectures on Faith
in the Latter Day Saint Tradition

Richard S. Van Wagoner, Steven C. Walker,
Allen D. Roberts, and Christine Elyse Blythe

The Lectures on Faith, seven 1834–1835 lessons on theology and doctrine prepared for the "School of the Elders" in Kirtland, Ohio, were canonized in the 1835 edition of the Doctrine and Covenants by official vote of the church. In the preface of that volume, Joseph Smith, Oliver Cowdery, Sidney Rigdon, and Frederick G. Williams—then the First Presidency—specifically justified the inclusion of the Lectures.

> We deem it to be unnecessary to entertain you with a lengthy preface to the following volume, but merely to say, that it contains in short, the leading items of the religion which we have professed to believe.
>
> The first part of the book will be found to contain a series of Lectures as delivered before a theological class in this place, and in consequence of their embracing the important doctrine of salvation, we have arranged them into the following work....
>
> We do not present this little volume with any other expectation than that we are to be called to answer to every principle advanced.[1]

Eighty-six years later, upon recommendation of a committee of apostles, the Lectures were deleted from the 1921 edition of the Doctrine and Covenants. This action, though neither controversial nor particularly public, highlighted the problematic procedure of decanonization in a church characterized by

---

1. Joseph Smith Jr., Oliver Cowdery, Sidney Rigdon, and F. G. Williams, "Preface," Doctrine and Covenants (1835).

an open canon.[2] This chapter examines this process of institutional decanonization in the Church of Jesus Christ of Latter-day Saints and then how the decanonization in both the LDS and RLDS Churches led to a revival of the Lectures on Faith among smaller denominations of the Restoration.

The purpose of the Lectures on Faith, as noted in the first lesson, is "to unfold to the understanding the doctrine of Jesus Christ."[3] The Lectures contain extensive discourse and scriptural references not only on faith, miracles, and sacrifice, but on the character and attributes of God as well. They are systematically arranged with accompanying catechisms designed for missionaries to memorize and teach.

The authorship of the Lectures has long been debated. Sidney Rigdon, a member of the 1835 First Presidency and a respected theologian and orator in the church at that time, has traditionally been identified as the person who delivered them. Some assume that Rigdon also wrote the Lectures.[4] Alan J. Phipps statistically compared the Lectures with verified works of Joseph Smith and Sidney Rigdon and concluded that Rigdon authored Lectures 1 and 7; Smith was responsible for Lecture 5. He concluded that the remaining Lectures were collaborations.[5] But a computerized study of stylistic wordprints by Wayne A. Larsen, Alvin C. Rencher, and Tim Layton indicates that Rigdon wrote Lectures 1, 3, 4, 6, and 7; Smith wrote Lecture 2;

2. The only other case of removing a canonized section in the Church of Jesus Christ of Latter-day Saints involved the "Article on Marriage," Section 101 in the 1835 Doctrine and Covenants. This section explained the church position on marriage as "one man should have one wife, and one woman, but one husband, except in case of death, when either is at liberty to marry again." Many have felt that because W. W. Phelps, Joseph Smith's scribe, read this declaration for inclusion into the Doctrine and Covenants during Joseph Smith's absence from Kirtland, that neither the document nor its inclusion met with Joseph's approval (see T. B. H. Stenhouse, *Rocky Mountain Saints* (New York: D. Appleton, 1873), 193; and Bruce R. McConkie, *Mormon Doctrine* (Salt Lake City: Bookcraft, 1966), 52–53. But if this were true, the prophet would have had ample opportunity to modify or delete the statement before publication. A "Notes To The Reader" addendum, p. xxv, in the 1835 edition details changes in the statement after it had been canonized but prior to publication. The section detailing the opposition to fornication and polygamy was unchanged. Moreover, the prophet later authorized the second printing of the edition after proofreading the text. This "Article on Marriage" was deleted from the 1876 edition of the Doctrine and Covenants without a vote of the general church membership and was replaced by Section 132, an 1843 revelation declaring the principle of celestial marriage and the plurality of wives. See Richard S. Van Wagoner, *Mormon Polygamy: A History* (Salt Lake City: Signature Books, 1986), 6–7.

3. Lectures on Faith 1:1. The Lectures on Faith are quoted as found in the Doctrine and Covenants (1835).

4. Leland H. Gentry, "What of the Lectures on Faith?" *BYU Studies* 19, Fall (1978):5–19.

5. Alan J. Phipps, "The Lectures on Faith: An Authorship Study" (master's thesis, Brigham Young University, 1977).

and W. W. Phelps wrote Lecture 5.[6] Editors for the Joseph Smith Papers have noted that while "Rigdon likely had a large role in producing the lectures, JS was apparently involved as well," although they also acknowledged that the extent of his participation "cannot be clearly determined."[7]

The question of authorship remains speculative. Whatever Joseph Smith's original position, he was involved in preparing the Lectures for publication in the Doctrine and Covenants.[8] He underscored his personal support of the Lectures by noting in the introduction to the 1835 edition that he accepted responsibility for "every principle advanced." Furthermore, the First Presidency's introduction makes no distinction between the inspirational quality of the Lectures and the second part of the book, which contained the Covenants and Commandments.[9]

Apostle Orson Pratt may have been the first to suggest removing the Lectures on Faith when he was undertaking a new edition of the Doctrine and Covenants. On March 1, 1879, Pratt wrote then-Quorum of the Twelve President John Taylor for permission to "incorporate in the edition the Book of Abraham, and also, that portion of the New translation of the Bible which is in the 'Pearl of Great Price.'" He suggested that if Taylor thought the volume would be too large with this addition, then they could remove the Lectures on Faith. Clearly not too concerned with the future of the Lectures, Pratt assured Taylor, "If it were deemed necessary, at any future time to republish the 'Lectures on Faith,' it could be done in pamphlet form."[10] In response, Taylor reaffirmed, "The Lectures on Faith were published with the sanction and approval of the Prophet Joseph Smith and we do not feel that it is desirable to make any alteration in that regard."[11]

In 1921, a scripture committee broached the topic again. On March 18, 1920, the First Presidency selected Elder George F. Richards to chair a committee that would prepare a new edition of the Book of Mormon. Other committee members included Anthony W. Ivins, Melvin J. Ballard, and James E. Talmage.

---

6. Wayne A. Larsen, Alvin C. Rencher, and Tim Layton, "Who Wrote the Book of Mormon? An Analysis of Wordprints," *BYU Studies* 20, Spring (1980):249.

7. *JSP*, D4:4:459.

8. *History, 1838–1856*, vol. B-1 [1 September 1834–2 November 1838], 538.

9. Joseph Smith Jr. et al., "Preface," D&C (1835).

10. Orson Pratt, Letter to John Taylor, March 1, 1879, CHL.

11. John Taylor letter to Orson Pratt, April 1, 1879, First Presidency Letterpress Copybooks, vol. 2, 1877–1949, CHL, Salt Lake City, UT.

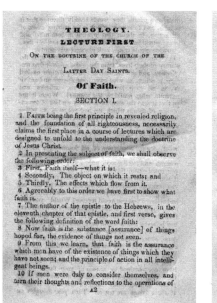

FIGURES 7.1 AND 7.2. The 1835 Doctrine and Covenants included both a "Theology" section containing the Lectures of Faith and "Covenants and Commandments" section containing various revelations. Courtesy of the Church History Library, the Church of Jesus Christ of Latter-day Saints. ©Intellectual Reserve Inc.

By June, the group had expanded to include John A. Widtsoe and Joseph Fielding Smith. After the work on the Book of Mormon was completed, the committee turned its attention to the Doctrine and Covenants. Elder Talmage reported in a February 23, 1921, letter to Apostle George Albert Smith,

> Preliminary steps have already been taken toward a thorough revision of the Doctrine and Covenants, and we all know that the current editions, as printed in this country and in Liverpool, contains [*sic*] many errors by way of omission. Moreover there are certain improvements by way of Section Headings, amplification of notes, and rearrangement of text in the double column style to be made, if the present tentative plans are carried into execution.[12]

12. James E. Talmage letter to George Albert Smith, February 23, 1921, George Albert Smith Letter Collection, Special Collections, Marriott Library, University of Utah.

Deletion of the Lectures on Faith was one of the changes. The committee's introductory explanation in the 1921 Doctrine and Covenants states, "Certain lessons, entitled 'Lectures on Faith,' which were bound with the Doctrine and Covenants in some of its former issues, are not included in this edition. Those lessons were prepared for use in the School of Elders ... but they were never presented nor accepted by the Church as being otherwise than theological lectures or lessons."[13]

Canonization procedures in the church have never been officially specified. And not all revelations given to church presidents have been presented to the church for sustaining. The 1835 Doctrine and Covenants title page notes that the contents were "Carefully Selected From The Revelations of God" and compiled by a committee of four presiding elders, including Joseph Smith. Elder George F. Richards, original chairman of the 1921 Doctrine and Covenants committee, wrote in his journal on July 29, 1921, regarding other noncanonized revelations, "We read the revelations which do not appear in the present edition of the Doctrine and Covenants, about twenty in number, with the view of recommending to the First Presidency certain of them to be included in the edition we are just now preparing."[14] The First Presidency apparently did not approve these suggested additions, for no new revelations were included in the 1921 edition.

This would seem to suggest that while all scripture is revelation, not all revelation is scripture. Smith's revelations in the Doctrine and Covenants seem contradictory regarding what constitutes scripture. A revelation he dictated in November 1831 affirmed, "Whatsoever they shall speak when moved upon by the Holy Ghost shall be scripture, shall be the will of the Lord, shall be the mind of the Lord, shall be the word of the Lord, shall be the voice of the Lord, and the power of God unto salvation."[15] But another revelation dictated a year earlier implied that revelations must be accepted by a church vote prior to canonization: "For all things must be done in order, and by common consent in the church by the prayer of faith."[16]

---

13. Doctrine and Covenants of the Church of Jesus Christ of Latter-Day Saints (Salt Lake City, UT: Church of Jesus Christ of Latter-day Saints, 1921), v.

14. George F. Richards, Journal, 1921–1934, George F. Richards papers, CHL, Salt Lake City, UT.

15. D&C 68:4.

16. D&C 28:13.

Statements by General Authorities on this issue also seem to conflict. First Presidency member George Q. Cannon responded to this very issue in an 1891 question,

> It seems nonsensical that the Prophet of God should submit to such a test as this [common consent], and not deem the revelations he received authentic until they had the approval of the different quorums of the Church. They were authentic and divinely inspired, whether any man or body of men received them or not. Their reception or non-reception of them would not affect in the least their divine authenticity. But it would be for the people to accept them after God had revealed them. In this way they have been submitted to the Church, to see whether the members would accept them as binding upon them or not. Joseph [Smith] himself had too high a sense of his prophetic office and the authority he had received from the Lord to ever submit the revelations which he received to any individual or to any body, however numerous, to have them pronounce upon their validity.[17]

Elder Bruce R. McConkie, writing in 1966, several years before he was called to the Twelve, supported Cannon's thinking.

> Revelations given of God through his prophets ... are not subject to an approving or sustaining vote of the people in order to establish their validity. Members of the Church may vote to publish a particular revelation along with the other scriptures, or the people may bind themselves by covenant to follow the instructions found in the revealed word. But there is no provision in the Lord's plan for the members of the Church to pass upon the validity of revelations themselves by a vote of the Church; there is nothing permitting the Church to choose which of the revelations will be binding upon it, either by a vote of people or by other means.[18]

17. George Q. Cannon, "On Revelation," *Juvenile Instructor*, January 1, 1891, 13–14.
18. Bruce R. McConkie, *Mormon Doctrine* (Salt Lake City, UT: Bookcraft, 1966), 150.

These two statements contradict statements from two presidents of the church. Wilford Woodruff declared the following in 1892, while giving a legal deposition before the Western District of the Missouri U.S. Circuit Court:

> The church has a right to reject or approve of revelations and any man independent of the action of the church has a right to accept it or reject it as he sees fit and the church has a right to say whether they will accept it or reject it as a revelation, and before a revelation can be accepted by the church, as a law, it must in some form or other be presented to the church and accepted by the church, and that has been true since the time I first became connected with the church.[19]

President Joseph F. Smith stated similarly in his 1904 testimony before the U.S. Senate committee investigating the seating of recently elected senator and apostle Reed Smoot. "I will say this, Mr. Chairman, that no revelation given through the head of the church ever becomes binding and authoritative upon the members of the church until it has been presented to the church and accepted by them." Questioned whether "the church in conference may say to you, Joseph F. Smith, the first president [sic] of the church, 'We deny that God has told you to tell us this?'" President Smith replied, "They can say that if they choose. . . . And it is not binding upon them as members of the church until they accept it."[20] It thus appears that at least two church presidents have verified the principle of common consent in canonizing revelation into the standard works of LDS scripture. There is no mention, however, of a procedure for decanonizing scriptural items such as the Lectures on Faith.

While writing a master's thesis at Brigham Young University in 1940, John W. Fitzgerald wrote to Elder Joseph Fielding Smith, a member of the 1921 committee that had deleted the Lectures on Faith from the Doctrine and Covenants, to ask him why items published under Joseph Smith's direction were removed. Smith listed four reasons.

19. Wilford Woodruff, "Testimony of 16 March 1892 before the Circuit Court of the United States, Western District of Missouri, Western Division at Kansas City. Complainant's Abstract of Pleading and Evidence" (Lamoni, IA: Herald Publishing House and Bindery, 1893), 206.

20. Joseph F. Smith "Testimony of March 1904, Proceedings before the Committee on Privileges and Elections of the United States Senate in the Matter of the Protests against the Right of Hon. Reed Smoot, a Senator from the State of Utah, to Hold His Seat" (Washington, D.C.: Government Printing Office, 1906), 59th Cong., 1st sess. Senate. Doc. 486.

1. They were not received as revelations by the Prophet Joseph Smith.
2. They are instructions relative to the general subject of faith. They are explanations of this principle but are not doctrine.
3. They are not complete as to their teachings regarding the Godhead....
4. It was thought by Elder James E. Talmage, chairman, and other members of the committee who were responsible for their omission that to avoid confusion and contention on this vital point of belief [i.e., on the Godhead], it would be better not to have them bound in the same volume as the commandments or revelations which make up *The Doctrine and Covenants*.[21]

This reply poses several historical difficulties. While it is true that Joseph Smith never identified the Lectures as revelations, Section 102 (present Section 134) is similarly not termed a revelation in the 1835 Doctrine and Covenants but declared the church position on "Governments and Laws in general." Probably written by Joseph Smith and Oliver Cowdery and later declared by the Prophet to be the belief of the church, the statement has never purported to be a revelation, though it has been included in all editions of the Doctrine and Covenants.

The Wilford Woodruff Manifesto, first placed in the Doctrine and Covenants in 1908 as an "Official Declaration" and now Official Declaration 1, was not presented to the church as a revelation either. It was first issued on September 25, 1890, as a press release through the office of Utah's delegate in Congress, John T. Caine. Addressed "To Whom It May Concern," the document encouraged Mormon support of recent laws "enacted by Congress forbidding plural marriages."[22] Moreover, though the Manifesto in essence negates the last half of the 1843 revelation dealing with plural marriage (Section 132), that part of the revelation has not been removed—even though those who enter polygamy are excommunicated. Furthermore, a glance through the Doctrine and Covenants shows that a sizable portion of it includes documents described in the book itself as "declarations of belief," "reports of visions," "historical narratives," "admonishments," "answers to

---

21. John William Fitzgerald, "A Study of the Doctrine and Covenants" (master's thesis, Brigham Young University, 1940), 343–345.
22. "Official Declaration," *Deseret Evening News*, September 25, 1890.

questions," "explanations of scripture," "minutes of instruction meetings," "prayers," "letters," and "items of instruction."

Joseph Fielding Smith's assertion that the Lectures are "instructions," not "the doctrine of the Church," is historically erroneous. The 1835 Doctrine and Covenants specifically titles them "the Doctrine of the Church of the Latter Day Saints." The second part of the 1835 edition was labeled "PART SECOND Covenants and Commandments."[23] Furthermore, the Articles of Faith, written by Joseph Smith and later canonized in 1880 as part of the Pearl of Great Price, directly paralleled the Lectures as instructions on the general subject of faith.[24] Moreover, the 1835 First Presidency declared in the preface to the first edition of the Doctrine and Covenants that the Lectures on Faith contain "the important doctrine of salvation."[25] The Lectures were expressly given to teach church leaders and missionaries doctrines considered truthful and binding upon present and future church members. To hold that such materials did not contain authoritative doctrine puts the missionaries in a curious position.

Smith's third and fourth points, which question the Lectures' Godhead teachings, touch on their main difficulty. Simply put, the Lectures present Joseph Smith's 1835 understanding of the Godhead, which was modified by the time of his death in 1844. For example, Lecture 5 explains, "There are two personages who constitute the great, matchless, governing and supreme power over all things, by whom all things were created, and made.... They are the Father and the Son—the Father being a personage of spirit, glory, and power ... the Son ... a personage of tabernacle, made or fashioned like unto man."[26] The catechism for this lecture also queries, "How many personages are there in the Godhead? Two: the Father and Son." The Father "is a personage of glory and power" and the Son is a "personage of tabernacle." It also explained the doctrine of the Holy Spirit: "The Only Begotten of the Father possess[es] the same mind with the Father, which mind is the Holy Spirit."[27]

23. See Robert J. Woodford, "The Historical Development of the Doctrine and Covenants" (PhD diss., Brigham Young University, 1974), 41–42.

24. Terryl Givens with Brian Hauglid, *The Pearl of Greatest Price: Mormonism's Most Controversial Scriptures* (New York: Oxford University Press, 2019), ch. 4.

25. Joseph Smith Jr. et. al. "Preface," D&C (1835).

26. Lectures on Faith, 5:2

27. Lectures on Faith, 5:55.

It was not until 1841, twenty-one years after the First Vision, that the Prophet taught that "there is no other God in heaven but that God who has flesh and bones."[28] That idea was further developed when Joseph Smith declared two years later in Ramus, Illinois, "The Father has a body of flesh and bones as tangible as man's; the Son also; but the Holy Ghost has not a body of flesh and bones, but is a personage of Spirit. Were it not so, the Holy Ghost could not dwell in us."[29]

Near the end of Joseph Smith's life, his 1844 King Follett funeral sermon enunciated such key Mormon concepts as "God, who sits enthroned in yonder heavens is a man like unto one of yourselves"; "God came to be God"; "God himself, the father of us all dwelt on an earth the same as Jesus Christ"; and, "You have got to learn how to be Gods yourself."[30] Present-day Mormon theology parallels Joseph Smith's Nauvoo teachings, though most Latter-day Saints are unaware that the Prophet's understanding of the Godhead evolved. The Lectures on Faith provide a window through which to view his 1835 perceptions.

Since the Lectures on Faith have not been included in the Doctrine and Covenants for more than sixty years, most Latter-day Saints are not familiar with their content and historical importance. Joseph Fielding Smith recognized this when he wrote in 1966, "I suppose that the rising generation knows little about the Lectures. . . . In my own judgement, these Lectures are of great value and should be studied. . . . I consider them to be of extreme value in the study of the gospel of Jesus Christ."[31] Despite the 1921 Doctrine and Covenants committee's concern over the Godhead confusion, Elder Bruce R. McConkie remarked about one of the lectures in a January 4, 1972, address at BYU: "In my judgment, it is the most comprehensive, intelligent, inspired utterance that now exists in the English language—that exists in one place defining, interpreting, expounding, announcing, and testifying what kind of being God is." He continued, "It was written by the power of the Holy Ghost, by the spirit of inspiration. It is, in effect, eternal scripture; it is true."[32] Over

28. "Accounts of Meeting and Discourse, 5 January 1841," *JSP*, D7:494.

29. D&C 130:22.

30. "Conference Minutes," *Times and Seasons* (Nauvoo, IL), August 15, 1844, 612–617.

31. Joseph Fielding Smith, *Seek Ye Earnestly* (Salt Lake City, UT: Bookcraft, 1966), 194.

32. Bruce R. McConkie "The Lord God of Joseph Smith," BYU Devotional Speech, January 4, 1972, https://speeches.byu.edu/talks/bruce-r-mcconkie/the-lord-god-of-joseph-smith/.

the hundred years since the Lectures on Faith were decanonized, church leaders continued to cite and study the Lectures on Faith even as it grew into obscurity among the general membership.

THE LECTURES ON FAITH IN THE BROADER
LATTER DAY SAINT TRADITION

Throughout the nineteenth century, most Latter Day Saint denominations accepted the Lectures on Faith. This included not only the church led by Brigham Young, as discussed above, but also those led by Joseph Smith III, Alpheus Cutler, James Strang, Sidney Rigdon, and Charles B. Thompson. In time, the inclusion or exclusion of the Lectures on Faith in scripture became a point of difference and thus identity for many of these movements.

Because neither the Church of Christ (Temple Lot) nor The Church of Jesus Christ (Bickertonite) accepted the Doctrine and Covenants as part of their canons, in effect they were the earliest churches to decanonize the lectures.[33] While the Church of Christ (Temple Lot) rejected the Doctrine and Covenants in preference for the Book of Commandments, the Reorganized Church of Jesus Christ of Latter Day Saints defended it as an essential aspect of faith, refuting the claim that the Book of Commandments was "a more sacred and infallible character than the Doctrine and Covenants" by pointing to the significance of the Lectures in the minds of early Saints.[34]

And yet, during Joseph Smith III's presidency of the RLDS Church, in 1897, the Lectures were decanonized—twenty-four years before the LDS Church followed suit. While the RLDS Church offered no official justification for its decision, historian Richard Howard has speculated that it had something to do with the Lecture's biblical quotations from the "unfinished manuscripts" of Joseph Smith. These quotations did not match the canonized version of the new translation that appeared in the Holy Scriptures of the RLDS Church.[35] In 1952, the RLDS Church's Herald Publishing House printed the Lectures in pamphlet form with the quotations updated to the

33. See Vanel, "The Church of Christ (Temple Lot)," chapter 5, and Stone, William Bickerton's Cooperative Views on Scripture and Revelation, chapter 11 both herein.

34. Joseph Smith III, Book of Commandments and Book of Doctrine and Covenants, 6.

35. Richard Howard, *Restoration Scriptures*, 144, 176.

canonized versions. While this made them more accessible, they were no longer presented as scripture.

Many smaller Latter Day Saint churches viewed the the decision by both LDS and RLDS Churches to decanonize the Lectures as proof of apostasy. In 1978, Julian Whiting, President of the Church of Jesus Christ (Cutlerite), referred to the removal as a great "disservice" to the RLDS and LDS people as perpetrated by their respective leaders. . . .

> When we read and study these lectures we can begin to understand why they were omitted and no longer printed. They teach a road that is far too close for anyone but those with the spirit of God and a desire to learn. . . . Man at best does a pretty sorry job of serving their God, and with the obstacles placed in their path by the powers of Evil, only by the acceptance of the truths contained in these lectures can this be thwarted. What spirit would you say actuated those leaders in these two factions when they voted the lectures were no longer of value as doctrine and omitted them from that book?[36]

For the Cutlerites, the Lectures validated their beliefs by aligning their teachings with those of Joseph Smith and the early restoration. "Who was right," Whiting continued, "the early officers who voted they should be in there and were profitable for doctrine, or those who voted later that they were not[?]"[37]

RLDS and LDS schisms have often reincorporated the Lectures on Faith into their scriptural canons. Three examples are the those established by the Restoration Church of Jesus Christ, Jim Harmston's True and Living Church of Jesus Christ of Saints of the Last Days, and the Remnant movement affiliated with Denver Snuffer. In 1987, the Restoration Church, founded in Los Angeles, California, two years earlier, sustained the Lectures on Faith as "the Word and Will of the Lord for the Church." When the Restoration Church republished the Lectures, it argued that in addition to Joseph Smith's original intention of including them as scripture, "the doctrines presented herein are true principles designed to build faith in the minds and hearts of men

36. Julian Whiting, "The Lectures on Faith," (1978). BYU Special Collections, Provo, UT.
37. Julian Whiting, "The Lectures on Faith," (1978). BYU Special Collections, Provo, UT.

and women who apply them."[38] The True and Living Church, founded in Manti, Utah, in 1993, published the Lectures on Faith on its website in the late 1990s. Introductory remarks noted that the Lectures "are replete with concepts expressed in the ancient Hebrew tradition, as is the Book of Mormon, which is a foot print of truly inspired writings—which indeed these Lectures on Faith are."[39] Members also put together a digital version of the Doctrine and Covenants that removed sections from the LDS version they considered uninspired and added previously uncanonized revelations for a total of 188 sections. There was also a plan to print copies with the Lectures on Faith restored to its original place in the beginning of the volume.[40]

The Remnant movement, likewise, restructured its scripture to include the Lectures on Faith, placed as section 110 of Teachings and Commandments. Denver Snuffer had long included the lectures within his own sermons, even criticizing the LDS Church's documentary history project, the Joseph Smith Papers, in 2016 for being "unwilling to be accountable for what is a rebellious departure from a law binding on the institution."[41]

Those movements that separated from the Reorganized Church/Community of Christ have also recanonized the Lectures on Faith in scripture. While the Restoration branches are independent congregations with loose ties to one another, the Restoration Bookstore emerged to provide them with older RLDS literature and new publications. The Bookstore issued a version of the Doctrine and Covenants based on the 1950 RLDS edition but with the addition of the Lectures on Faith.[42] The Remnant Church of Jesus Christ of Latter Day Saints also accepts the Lectures on Faith as part of the canon and includes them on its denominational website.[43]

Over time, the two dominant factions of the Latter Day Saint tradition came to view the Lectures on Faith as a liability. Yet, for many denominations, their inclusion in the canon—or their reincorporation in the

38. Lectures on Faith, from the School of the Prophets, as Prepared and Delivered by the Prophet Joseph Smith Jr. (published by John R. Crane), available at https://john144restoration.files.wordpress.com/2017/12/faith.pd.

39. Tlcmanti.net. Available on the Internet Archive.

40. "Introduction and Explanation," Doctrine and Covenants, Manti, Utah Edition, Sections 131–188. Digital copy in the possession of the author.

41. October 2, 2016, https://denversnuffer.com/tag/lectures-on-faith/.

42. Restorationbookstore.org.

43. Theremnantchurch.com/index.php/lectures-on-faith.

canon—functioned as a sign of adherence to an original tradition in practice before Joseph Smith's death. While it is true that the memberships of the LDS and RLDS Churches make up the vast majority of Latter Day Saint adherents, more denominations seem to accept the Lectures on Faith than to reject them.

PART III

Case Studies in New Scripture
Nineteenth Century

8

Lucy Mack Smith and Her Sacred Text

Janiece Johnson

*I feel it a privilege as well as my duty to all ... to give (as my last
testimony to a world from whence I must soon take my departure) an account exclusively of my own manner.*[1]

Mother Smith

In October 1845, a weary, seventy-year-old woman rose to her feet in Nauvoo,
Illinois, as the first woman to speak in Latter-day Saint general conference.
Lucy Mack Smith, mother of the slain Prophet Joseph Smith Jr., strained to
speak to the large congregation.

> There is maybe 2,000 people here that never were acquainted with
> Mr. Smith or my family. I raised up 11 children, 7 boys. I raised them
> in the fear of God. When they were two or three years old I told them,
> I wanted them to love God with all their hearts. I told them to do good.
> I want all you to do the same.
> I call you brothers and sisters and children. If you consider me a
> Mother in Israel I want you to say so.[2]

---

1. Lucy Mack Smith, History, 1844–1845, p. [1], bk. [1]. This manuscript has been digitized on
the Joseph Smith Papers website, https://www.josephsmithpapers.org/paper-summary/lucy-mack
-smith-history-1844-1845/1. Note: All citations to the Book of Mormon use the versification of the
current LDS edition.

2. Lucy Mack Smith, General Conference, October 8, 1845, Nauvoo, Illinois, Historian's Office,
General Church Minutes, 1839–1877, October 6–8, 1845, 7–13, CHL, in *At the Pulpit: 185 Years of
Discourses by Latter-day Saint Women*, edited by Jennifer Reeder and Kate Holbrook (Salt Lake City:
Church Historian's Press, 2018), 1.5.

Brigham Young then rose and declared, "All who consider Mother Smith as a Mother in Israel signify it by saying yes." With this, the crowd erupted into "loud shouts of 'Yes!'"[3] For Mother Smith, the title Mother in Israel was never just a statement of respect; it was her calling, the source of her authority, and a duty for which she felt a keen sense of responsibility.

At the time of the conference, Smith had just finished dictating her history. It would not be published for another eight years, yet her work to unfold the sacred history of the first family of the Restoration had already begun. In this chapter, I argue that Lucy—Mother of the Prophet—and those who helped midwife the account into existence continued the work of ancient prophets: they created a new sacred history of a modern prophet and his family. Doing so cemented her place as the Mother of the Church and a Mother in Israel. These titles were not just honorific; they played related but distinctive roles in Smith's vision of her own mission.

Never seen as canonically binding, Lucy Mack Smith's history gained unofficial authority through wide acknowledgement and repeated use. First published in 1853 with at least ten different major editions since then, the public life of Lucy Mack Smith's history continues. Lucy's narrative, arguably the most often-read Mormon woman's writing, remains a consistent source shaping the narrative of early church history.[4] Claudia Bushman even argued for its inclusion in the LDS canon, alongside a number of other women's writings.[5] Here, I examine Smith's role and intention in crafting what in practice became informal scripture.

In one sense, thinking of Lucy's history as "scripture" should not be a radical exercise, especially considering the context and tradition in which it was derived. Mormons are knee-deep in scripture. In 1831, Joseph Smith dictated a broad definition of scripture: "Whatsoever they shall speak when moved upon by the Holy Ghost shall be scripture" (Doctrine and Covenants 68:4).

3. Lucy Mack Smith, General Conference, 1845.

4. It is cited more than one hundred times in the first volume of *Saints* published by the Church History Department of the Latter-day Saint church in 2018. *Saints: The Story of the Church of Jesus Christ of Latter-day Saints*, vol. 1, *The Standard of Truth, 1815–1846* (Salt Lake City, UT: Church of Jesus Christ of Latter-day Saints, 2018). In 2021, amazon.com sells fourteen different book editions and dozens more digital and used editions.

5. Claudia Bushman, "Reading Women Back into the Scriptures," in *The Expanded Canon: Perspectives on Mormonism and Sacred Texts*, edited by Blair G. Van Dyke et al. (Salt Lake City: Kofford Books, 2018), 62–63.

Thus, the classification of scripture treads substantial ground in Mormon traditions, from those books officially accepted by the body of the church as canon to anything inspired. The continued reception of Lucy Smith's history signals its informal acceptance as a sacred narrative of those who count themselves followers of her son Joseph Smith.

Academic definitions of scripture have expanded as religious studies scholars broadened their areas of interest beyond the Judeo-Christian canon. Wilfred Cantwell Smith argued that scripture can be an oral tradition or written, but it becomes scripture when it is received and interpreted, and when an individual and a community develop a relationship with the text. Scripture will never be static: as the relationship with a text expands over time, it endures as scripture. Communities "make a text into scripture, or keep it scripture by treating it a certain way."[6] Mormons exist as a group because of the production of the Book of Mormon and their relationship with it. If history is theology for Mormons, as Richard Bushman argues, it is fitting that the narrative of the origins of the Church of Christ has become sacred history.[7]

Smith's history also shares multiple markers of similarity with canonical scripture, though none of the Mormon schisms has ever included it in their official canon. Like New Testament writers weaving the Hebrew Bible through their own writings, Smith wove old scripture (the Bible) and new scripture (the Book of Mormon) throughout her own history. Her authorship was always clear, yet her history is not simply a single-author memoir, as one might assume. Like the biblical text, it passed through a variety of different hands and editors who molded and then published this new holy writ.[8] And, like scripture, this effort was never without controversy.

The metamorphosis of the title and presentation of Smith's history over time constructs a tale of the competing claims on this history.[9] In tug-of-war

6. Wilfred Cantwell Smith, *What Is Scripture? A Comparative Approach* (Minneapolis, MN: Fortress Press, 1993), 1–20.

7. Richard Bushman, *A Very Short Introduction to Mormonism* (New York: Oxford University Press, 2008), 15.

8. Sharalyn Howcroft, "A Textual and Archival Reexamination of Lucy Mack Smith's History" in *Foundational Mormon Documents: Examining Major Early Sources*, edited by Mark Ashurst-McGee, Robin Jensen, and Sharalyn Howcroft (New York: Oxford University Press, 2018).

9. *Biographical Sketches of Joseph Smith the Prophet, and His Progenitors for many Generations by Lucy Mack Smith, Mother of the Prophet*, edited by Orson Pratt (Liverpool: S.W. Richards, 1853); "History of the Prophet Joseph By His Mother Lucy Smith as revised by George A. Smith and Elias Smith," *Improvement Era* (Salt Lake City, UT: 1902); Lucy Smith, Mother of the Prophet, *Biographical*

FIGURE 8.1. Lucy Mack Smith. Courtesy of the Church History Library, the Church of Jesus Christ of Latter-day Saints.

fashion, both the publication saga and much of the scholarly work done on Smith's history strains between two poles: focusing on Lucy Mack Smith's own contribution at one end and those working to control her narrative for their own purposes at the other end. In 2001, Lavina Fielding Anderson's critical edition of *Lucy's Book* enabled extensive side-by side comparison of the different versions of the text for the first time. Sharalyn Howcroft offered a corrective to some of Anderson's assumptions about the text in 2018, arguing that the dictated history was significantly edited and later supplemented by other sources.[10] Considering these source limitations, this essay will trace Smith's voice through patterns established in her writings before her history project began, enabling us to better understand her creation of a new holy narrative and to further reclaim her voice.

LUCY'S HISTORY

Born in New Hampshire just prior to the American Revolution, Lucy grew immersed in the Bible. Her mother and her New England heritage infused it into her soul. Literal reading of the biblical text centered Smith on the need for baptism. She searched until a local Presbyterian minister offered to baptize her without requiring specific church membership in his congregation.[11]

Sketches of Joseph Smith the Prophet and His Progenitors for Many Generations (Lamoni, IA: Reorganized Church of Jesus Christ of Latter Day Saints, 1912); Preston Nibley, *History of Joseph Smith by His Mother, Lucy Mack Smith* (Salt Lake City, UT: Deseret Book, 1954); Scot Proctor and Maurine Proctor, eds., *The Revised and Enhanced History of Joseph Smith by His Mother* (Salt Lake City, UT: Deseret Book, 1996); Dan Vogel, *Early Mormon Documents*, vol. 1 (Salt Lake City, UT: Signature Books, 1996); Lavina Fielding Anderson, ed., *Lucy's Book: A Critical Edition of Lucy Mack Smith's Family Memoir* (Salt Lake City, UT: Signature Books, 2001); Susan Easton Black, annotation, and Liz Lemon Swindle, illustrator, *The History of Joseph Smith by His Mother Lucy Mack Smith* (Salt Lake City, UT: Deseret Book, 2016).

10. Sharalyn Howcroft, "A Textual and Archival Reexamination of Lucy Mack Smith's History," in *Foundational Texts of Mormonism: Examining Major Early Sources*, edited by Mark Ashurst-McGee, Robin Jensen, and Sharalyn Howcroft (New York: Oxford University Press, 2018), 298–335. Though most have assumed that Lucy's history fits the conception of a "solitary author and the author-controlled text," the creation and publication of her history exemplifies social authorship. It represents the work and contributions of many. Though ultimately a social production, we should not assume that this negates her voice. Social authorship did not mean that the additional contributors didn't care about accuracy or authenticity. David D. Hall, *Ways of Writing: The Practice and Politics of Text-Making in Seventeenth-Century New England* (Philadelphia: University of Pennsylvania Press, 2008), 82–83.

11. Richard L. Bushman, *Joseph Smith and the Beginnings of Mormonism* (Urbana, IL: University of Illinois Press, 1984), 205n32.

While her husband, Joseph Smith Sr., leaned toward Universalism, the Bible held a sacred place for all in the Smith family home. As Lavina Fielding Anderson argued, the Smith family's mother tongue originated in the King James text.[12] Their writing and speech patterns manifest an immersion in the biblical text, and, like many Americans, they saw their lives through a lens provided by the Bible. The intonations, rhythms, and phraseology of the King James narrated their lives. Lucy Mack Smith ardently studied scripture, employed its language, and inhabited the text, as she saw models for herself and her family in its narratives. Adopting the first Book of Mormon prophet Nephi's philosophy, she "likened" scripture unto herself for "profit and learning" long before she ever read those words in the Book of Mormon (1 Nephi 19:23).

When Joseph Smith Jr. introduced the Book of Mormon to his family, they became his first converts. Lucy Smith's earliest extant writing, a letter to her brother and sister-in-law, demonstrates her burgeoning relationship with the Book of Mormon. Written in her own hand just nine months after the publication of the new scripture, it shows that Lucy had already immersed herself in the Book of Mormon, as evidenced by her detailed synopsis of its first two books. Lucy's letter is awash in scripture and offers a glimpse of her conversion and commitment. She expanded her Bible-based mother tongue to include this new book she now deemed scripture, as she shared its content with others.

Historian David Hall calls this practice "patchwork quoting," though the term's simplicity may obscure the dynamism of the process. Both preachers and careful hearers of the word would weave echoes, paraphrases, and allusions from the biblical text into their patterns of speech and writing without reference.[13] Those who were likewise immersed in the Bible would recognize the claimed authority as they recognized the familiar words. This is not haphazard work; Lucy Smith precisely gathered, plotted, and intricately sewed together biblical echoes and allusions with those from the Book of Mormon in her speaking and writing as she quilted an original patchwork of

12. Lavina Fielding Anderson, "Mother Tongue: KJV Language in Smith Family Discourse" (paper, 44th Annual Mormon History Association Conference, Springfield, IL, May 22, 2009), manuscript in author's possession.

13. David Hall, *Worlds of Wonder, Days of Judgment* (Cambridge, MA: Harvard University Press, 1989), 23–31.

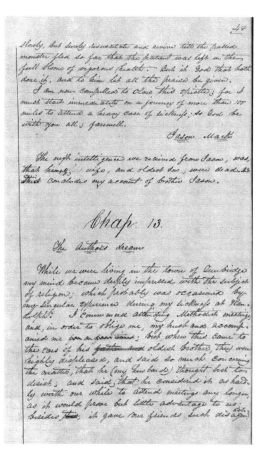

FIGURE 8.2. Manuscript of Lucy Mack Smith, History, 1844–1845. Courtesy of the Church History Library, the Church of Jesus Christ of Latter-day Saints. Intellectual Reserve Inc.

scripture. Though meticulous, this process became second nature because of her immersion in sacred texts. Moreover, it establishes a point of stability for the reader to recognize a voice that we can follow in her history.

Like the biblical text, Smith's earliest extant manuscripts are limited. However, her history is not the only source we have from her. Her history follows specific patterns established in earlier sources, and these textual markers demonstrate specific patterns of voice. The earliest manuscript—the rough manuscript—maintains most completely the scriptural intertextuality inherent to Lucy's speech and writing patterns demonstrated elsewhere.[14]

14. Lucy Mack Smith, History, 1844–1845. I have cited from Anderson's critical edition for ease of use.

A VISIONARY CALL

In the winter of 1844, Lucy Smith began to dictate her history, "relying chiefly upon her memory," to Martha Jane Knowlton Coray.[15] Though each subsequent editor shaped the text in specific ways, each edition's title page continued to mark its authorship "by Lucy Mack Smith" and acknowledge her biological position as "Mother of the Prophet." In July 1845, Smith applied for and secured a copyright establishing both authorship and ownership.[16] In the 1840s, most women's writings were still generally published under pseudonyms. However, opportunities began to open for some female writers. Antislavery tracts and female preachers' writings were exceptions to increasing strictures placed on upper- and middle-class women, as moral or spiritual obligation could lead a woman to go beyond societal constraints to publish in her own name.[17] Sensing a spiritual duty, Lucy Smith went beyond cultural expectations and used her narrative to highlight her role as the Mother of the Prophet—matriarch of the Restoration's first family. Moreover, she would extend her own prominent place in the Restoration as Mother of the Church and a Mother in Israel.

Lucy continued to work on her history in the summer of 1845. Amid succession tensions on the anniversary of the deaths of Joseph and Hyrum and feeling "troubled," Lucy detailed to others the following day how she had "called on the Lord" that night "to show me what was wrong, and if it was me. I called upon him until I slept." Later that evening, she woke to "a voice calling"—"awake, awake, awake." The first call of the voice drew an explicit parallel to Deborah's melodic call as a Mother in Israel in Judges 5—"awake, awake, Deborah: awake, awake, utter a song." Lucy certainly didn't miss the visionary allusion: a decade earlier her son Joseph Smith called her as "a Mother in Israel" in a blessing.[18] Without any reference to

15. Martha Jane Knowlton Coray, Provo, UT, to Brigham Young, June 13, 1865, Brigham Young Office Files, CHL.

16. Lucy Mack Smith, "The History of Lucy Smith," July 18, 1845, Robert Wright Harris, Copyright Registry Records for Works Concerning the Mormons to 1870, CHL.

17. Joanne Dobson and Sandra A. Zagarell, "Writing Women in the Early Republic," in *A History of the Book in America*, vol. 2, *An Extensive Republic: Print, Culture, and Society in the New Nation, 1790–1840*, edited by Mary Kelley and Robert A. Gross (Chapel Hill: University of North Carolina Press, 2010), 364–381.

18. "Blessing to Joseph Smith Sr. and Lucy Mack Smith, between circa 15 and 28 September 1835," *JSP*, D4:488.

children, the visionary prophetess and judge Deborah led Israel as the first specifically called a Mother in Israel. While a significant portion of the record of the vision focuses on Lucy's son William and his uneasy relationship with the church's Quorum of the Twelve Apostles, for Lucy the vision cemented her calling as the Mother of the Church and a Mother in Israel.[19] The vision reiterated the central role of her family—her husband and sons— as the "first founders, fathers, and heads of this Church, raised up in these last days." However, not just the men in her family had responsibilities. The voice told her three times: "Thou art the Mother in Israel." Again echoing Deborah's narrative, it commanded, "Arise, Arise, Arise, and take thy place." The last call as the Mother in Israel likewise established Lucy as a type of Mary, mother of Jesus, and emphasized the singularity of her call in the Restoration and elevated her role as Mother of the Prophet. "Thy spirit arose and said in eternity, that it would take a body to be a mother of [the] Prophet who should be raised up to save the last dispensation." Beyond mere reproductive function, she was chosen for her ability. The symbiotic relationship between her two roles thus pulled Lucy from cloistered domestic existence in the Smith family and out into the church. The following day she detailed her vision to sixteen others, making the personal call public.

While Lucy's role as mother to Joseph Smith, Prophet of the Restoration, was biologically established, her vision further delineated two other roles— Mother of the Church and Mother in Israel. "Mother of the Church" was a title for Mary as early as the fourth century, though not officially decreed until Vatican II.[20] Mary was both *Mater Christi* and *Mater Ecclesia*. In the nineteenth century, other American denominations—such as Shakers and

---

19. The extant copies of the vision—included in John Taylor's Nauvoo Journal and Brigham Young's office file—are considerably focused on William Smith as Patriarch and President of the church. According to John Taylor, three days later Mother Smith requested that the Twelve come to her house "to settle some misunderstanding and difficulty that existed in her mind in relation to a vision that she had." Concerned, Lucy told the Twelve that they did not have a "a correct copy of her vision"—perhaps implying that William had altered the text of the transcription. Certain that it was correct, John Taylor suggested that perhaps the "old lady was feeble and excited." Whatever the content regarding William in the original vision, "she did not profess to be a revelator only for herself and family." The negative construction is ambiguous at best. However, according to Taylor they ended the visit with a united wish for "peace, union, and harmony." Despite his frustrations with William, Brigham Young continued to support Lucy as a Mother in Israel. Dean Jessee, ed., "The John Taylor Nauvoo Journal," *BYU Studies* 23:3 (1983):56–60; and Mother Smith's Visions, June 27, 1845, Brigham Young Office Files, 1832–1878, CHL.

20. Hugo Rahner, *Our Lady and the Church* (New York: Pantheon, 1961), 1–14.

Methodists—also used the label of Mother to denote a position of female leadership.[21] But for Lucy the title was never merely honorific. As she contemplated the weight of responsibility she felt as Mother of the Prophet in her history, she queried and then rejoiced,

> Am I indeed the mother of a prophet of the God of Heaven[?]—The honored instrument in performing so great work[?] [cf. Alma 26:3, 15]—I felt I was in the purview of angels and my [soul?] bounded [cf. Numbers 30] at the thought of the great condescension of the A[l]mighty [cf. Jacob 4:7]—thus I spent the night surrounded by enemies and yet in an extacy [*sic*] of happiness and truly I can say that "My soul did magnify and my spirit rejoiced in God my savior" [Luke 1:46].[22]

Stitching together Book of Mormon language with Mary's Magnificat from the King James Version of Luke's first chapter, Lucy rejoiced at her call and worked to fulfill the responsibility she felt. The role of Mother in Israel worked in a related but distinct manner, further emphasizing her authority.

Scholar Irene Bates argues that Smith met the ideal of republican motherhood as the "first Mormon mother."[23] Republican motherhood refers to economically advantaged women who searched for a way to contribute to the new nation after the Revolutionary War. They developed a new ideology that validated women's contribution to civic life by highlighting their responsibility to raise children as noble and virtuous citizens.[24] Although Mother Smith certainly would have appreciated the middle-class respectability inherent to republican motherhood, focusing solely on the example of a "moral mother" limits her work. Certainly women were considered essential to shape the nation's virtue, but republican motherhood was always carefully circumscribed and did not venture into public participation. Bates and Anderson both emphasize Lucy Smith's power in the domestic sphere, but again, this

21. Stephen Stein, *The Shaker Experience in America* (New Haven: Yale University Press, 1992), 18–25, 123–124 and Wigger *Taking Heaven by Storm: Methodism and the Rise of Popular Christianity in America* (Oxford and New York: Oxford University Press, 1998), 151–172.

22. Lucy Mack Smith, History, 1844–1845, p. [7], bk. [9]; Anderson, *Lucy's Book*, 465–466.

23. Irene M. Bates, "Lucy Mack Smith—First Mormon Mother," in Anderson, *Lucy's Book*, 2–10.

24. Linda Kerber, *Women of the Republic: Intellect and Ideology in Revolutionary America* (Chapel Hill: University of North Carolina Press, 1980), 265–288.

obscures Smith's outgoing interaction with the Latter-day Saints and the public role that she repeatedly accentuated through her history.

As Catherine Brekus points out, in eighteenth- and nineteenth-century America, many female preachers claimed the title of "Mother in Israel" as a mantle with expansive potential well beyond a designation that still confined women's power and example to the home. In fact, the biblical text offers just two examples of Mothers in Israel, and "both were powerful women who took on leadership roles outside of the patriarchal household."[25] Deborah was not given the label of "Mother in Israel" for her work to instill civic virtue in her children. Lucy Mack Smith thus fits with the female preachers whom Catherine Brekus examined—women speaking with authority who went beyond their prescribed sphere because the Holy Spirit compelled them to fulfill a sacred mission. The Saints offered these titles to Mother Smith: Mother in Israel and Mother of the Church. And Lucy Mack consistently professed them for herself.[26]

Later that year when Smith spoke in conference, she demonstrated what had by then become second nature to her. Heartbroken at the loss of her sons, her feelings were also hurt when some dismissed her as "old Mother Smith." However, despite her pain, she delivered her message like a prophet in the wilderness. She wanted to extend hope to the forlorn Saints. Speaking to them, Mother Smith reviewed a condensed narrative of her family's history and the publication of the Book of Mormon. She saw a replication of scriptural patterns in her family's lives and employed a Book of Mormon pattern. When Nephi and his brothers were frustrated in their efforts to get the brass plates, Nephi recounted the story of Moses and the Red Sea to offer them hope (1 Nephi 4:2–3). Lucy related her family's own sacred history to rally the Saints and promised, "My family could go to work and get means to print the Book of Mormon. Do not be discouraged and say that you can't get wagons and things; as Brigham says you must be all honest or you will not get there."[27] Standing as a Mother in Israel, she expanded the narrative to include the Saints, offered them hope in their immediate predicament, and reinforced the authority of the Book of Mormon as scripture.

25. Catherine Brekus, *Strangers and Pilgrims: Female Preaching in America, 1740–1845* (Chapel Hill: University of North Carolina Press, 1998), 152.

26. See, for instance, Lucy Mack Smith, History, 1845, p. 289–290.

27. Lucy Mack Smith, General Conference, October 8, 1845.

As noted, that same year Lucy applied for a copyright to claim ownership over her history still in manuscript form. Her spectacularly commonplace nineteenth-century title deposited in the county recorder's office read

> The History of Lucy Smith wife of Joseph Smith the first Patriarch of Jesus Christ of Latter Day Saints, who was the father of Joseph Smith, Prophet, Seer & Revelator; containing an account of the many persecutions, trials and afflictions which I and my family have endured in bringing forth the Book of Mormon, and establishing the church of Jesus Christ of Latter Day Saints, and also an account of many remarkable dreams and visions never before published a genealogy of our family for many generations and the history of the murder of my sons Joseph and Hyrum Smith in Carthage Jail.[28]

The verbose title operates as a synopsis and reveals to us her primary aims in writing her history. Appeals to the patriarchal authority of her husband and son both temper and support her bold naming of herself, implying her position as the matriarch. Her family, the Book of Mormon, and church organization are her central concerns, though she likewise appeals to charismatic authority and affliction as a justification for writing. All these aims had earlier precedence in her life and practice. Sharing her history was now a fulfillment of her public spiritual roles as the Mother of the Church and a Mother in Israel.

QUILTING A NEW SACRED SCRIPTURE

Lucy Smith's history did not originate when first dictated to her amanuensis. Prior to its publication, Mother Smith's family narrative began as a story told orally. She dictated her history for transcription out of a perceived responsibility to expand her audience but orally transmitted it long before the deaths of her sons. The Saints yearned for her witness. She told her son William of their frequent petitions to hear "the particulars of Joseph's getting the plates seeing the angels at first."[29] This was not an easy task. In 1843 at the age of

28. Lucy Mack Smith, "The History of Lucy Smith," July 18, 1845, Robert Wright Harris, Copyright Registry Records for Works Concerning the Mormons to 1870, CHL.

29. Lucy Mack Smith, Nauvoo, IL, to William Smith, January 23, 1845, CHL.

sixty-eight she felt herself in the "decline of life" and "requested the prayers of the [Relief] Society ... that she might yet be ennabled [*sic*] to prove a Blessing to those who may enquire of the things of the Kingdom."[30] Over the next few years, she worked to "gratify [the Saints'] curiosity." After Joseph Smith's death, church members also solicited "many other thing[s] which Joseph never wrote or published."[31] Though willing, she could not physically sustain it. She felt that the consistent recitals had "almost destroyed [her] lungs." Between her physical limitations and a possible request from the Twelve to undertake "a history of the family," Lucy "concluded to write down every particular as far as possible and if those who wish to read them will help me a little they can have it all in one piece to read at their leasure [*sic*]." Writing down the sacred narrative could expand the influence of her history. Moreover, she hoped that it would also be a benefit to her family.[32] Her body failing, she could not do this on her own. An oral tradition—an oral text—can be considered scripture, but some scripture is later written down to produce a new text.

This text did not become scripture the moment it was written; it was already scripture. Much of scripture is founded in an oral tradition, and Mother Smith's record is no different. As people listened to her tell the sacred narrative of the origins of the Book of Mormon and her family's call, their reception made the narrative stand apart. Vincent Wimbush has coined the term *scripturalizing* to describe the process through which some texts, employing an expansive definition of text, become different from other texts—how they become special and set apart. This applies to those words that have been accepted as scriptural canon as well as other sacred books that signify their specialness by incorporating scripture. The canonical text is located in the middle of the process. Others then take the text and produce new sacred works as they incorporate other scripture into their own writing and replicate the effort of the original scriptural narrators.[33] The way Lucy

30. Meeting of the Third Ward July 21, 1843, "Nauvoo Relief Society Minute Book," p. 99. The minute book is accessible on the Joseph Smith Papers website.

31. Lucy Mack Smith, Nauvoo, IL, to William Smith, January 23, 1845, CHL.

32. Ibid.

33. Vincent Wimbush, "Introduction," *Theorizing Scriptures: New Critical Orientations to a Cultural Phenomenon* (New Brunswick, NJ: Rutgers University Press, 2008), 3–4. See also Seth Perry, *Bible Culture and Authority in the Early United States* (Princeton, NJ: Princeton University Press, 2018), 5–7.

incorporates the Bible and Book of Mormon into her own text—written and oral—has the dual effect of both certifying the Book of Mormon text as scripture and quilting her own new scripture. The act of writing it down further expanded the audience of those who could receive the new holy record of the Restoration.

Lucy also saw a pattern in the Book of Mormon for her own creation of scripture. Its first book begins as its prophet Nephi names himself—"I, Nephi." Despite the later additions by others, Mother Smith likewise named herself in her history. Nephi then proceeds with his rationale for writing: "Having seen many afflictions in the course of my days, nevertheless, having been highly favored of the Lord in all my days; yea, having had a great knowledge of the goodness and the mysteries of God, therefore I make a record of my proceedings in my days" (1 Nephi 1:1). Reviewing his life, Nephi sees affliction consistently juxtaposed with God's blessings and it propels him to keep a special record. Perhaps recording her history was also a way for Lucy to see the hand of God amid her own great affliction after the death of her sons. However, beyond the immediate, Lucy desires that, like other Book of Mormon prophets, her words—her family's history—might speak after they all lay in the dust.

Mother Smith was never the only one to scripturalize. As I have written elsewhere, many Latter-day Saints channeled Nephi as they started their own sacred records—they were "born of goodly parents."[34] The first time Joseph Smith sat down to write his history in 1832 he, too, was "born . . . of goodly parents."[35] All put into practice Nephi's pattern of sacralizing the personal. Lucy's history builds on and then expands the same allusive practice, though she skips this most common echo of the Book of Mormon's first book.[36] Despite that specific absence, she more completely channels this Book of Mormon pattern: "Having attained my 69 year, and being afflicted

---

34. 1 Nephi 1:1, Book of Mormon. See also Erastus Snow, Autobiography, 1818–1837, CHL; Archibald Gardner, Autobiography, 1857, L. Tom Perry Special Collections, Harold B. Lee Library, BYU, 3; Solomon Chamberlain, Autobiography of Solomon Chamberlain, L. Tom Perry Special Collections, BYU, 1. Also, Janiece Johnson, "Becoming a People of the Books: Toward an Understanding of Early Mormon Converts and the New Word of the Lord," *Journal of Book of Mormon Studies* 27 (2018):1–43.

35. "History, circa Summer 1832," *JSP*, D2:280.

36. While she is effusive about the influence of her mother, Lucy Smith's father is more absent than present in her narrative. Similarly, Louisa Barnes Pratt begins her personal history mirroring Nephi's words, minus "goodly parents." S. George Ellsworth, ed., *The History of Louisa Barnes Pratt:*

with a complication of diseases and infirmities [cf. 1 Nephi 1:1] ... [I] give as my last testimony to a world from whence I must soon take my departure" [cf. 2 Nephi 1:14].[37] Echoing words and content, she sewed together Nephi's first words with Lehi's last teachings and claimed ownership over the scripture. Like Nephi, she evaluated her life, and like Lehi—Nephi's father—she wanted to share things of importance before she took her "departure." Unlike other early Latter-day Saints who consciously inscribed their histories for their direct posterity, Lucy Mack Smith dictated her history with a broader view of her intended audience—she was the Mother of the Church and a Mother in Israel for all those who would accept her. She not only directly and pervasively alluded to the Book of Mormon and biblical text but also organized the structure of her record after the Book of Mormon. Again mimicking Nephi as the prophetic narrator, she detailed divisions within her words denoting a shift "from spiritual to temporal things" (cf. 1 Nephi 9:4).[38] Her history related the spiritual preparation of the Smith family, the divine origin of the Book of Mormon, and the family's temporal geographical moves and economic fluctuations. Lucy's incorporation of both biblical and Book of Mormon scripture functioned to reify the importance and the sacred nature of her family history and the Book of Mormon alike.

As laid out in her verbose title, Mother Smith wrote her history to establish the place of her family at the head of the Restoration. In addition to her immediate family, she also included the Smith family "progenitors for many generations."[39] Mirroring the work of Mormon, the Book of Mormon's prophet/editor, Lucy's history brings together several different sources to outline her family history. Like the biblical text the history lays out the narratives of individual family members, family genealogies, and then moves on to the spiritual witnesses. Biblical scholars argue that the function of biblical genealogies is primarily theological, providing credentials for the character and spiritual pedigree of an individual, rather than being a clear-cut historical record. In Lucy's history, the genealogies and Mack family narratives function much the same way: they established providential credentials for

Being the Autobiography of a Mormon Missionary Widow and Pioneer (Logan: Utah State University Press, 1998), 220.

37. Lucy Mack Smith, History, 1844–1845, p. [1], bk. [1]; Anderson, *Lucy's Book*, 220.
38. Lucy Mack Smith, History, 1844–1845, p. [6], bk. 2; Anderson, *Lucy's Book*, 281.
39. Pratt, *Biographical Sketches*, title page.

the Smiths and Macks.[40] Furthermore, Lucy uses Book of Mormon and biblical allusions to expand the Restoration narrative to include her family of origin—the Macks—some of whom died before Joseph's call. When describing her sisters Lovisa and Lovina, she echoes Mosiah. "They were one in faith, in love, in action, and in hope of eternal life" (cf. Mosiah 18:21).[41] She characterizes Lovina as "a true follower of Christ" (Moroni 7:48), again employing Book of Mormon language: one who "lived as she died contemplating her final change with that peaceful serenity which characterizes those who fear God and walk uprightly."[42] Through her history, Lucy Smith presented her family as not only the biological forbears of Joseph Smith, but the spiritual forbearers of the Restoration and the Book of Mormon's first converts.[43]

Lucy's original title pointed to the charismatic authority of "many remarkable dreams and visions" as partial rationale for her to write her history. Adding to her vision received in the summer of 1845, dreams, visions, and prophecies are consistent elements.[44] She presents a series of seven dreams received by her husband, Joseph Smith Sr., with remarkable Book of Mormon parallels—the second including a tree and a spacious building, duplicating Lehi's vision of the Tree of Life (1 Nephi 8). She saw her husband as a specific fulfillment of Joel's biblical prophecy "your old men shall dream dreams" (Joel 2:28). Nor was her husband the only one to fulfill such prophecies. In her history, Smith and Mack daughters prophesy (likely including Lucy herself), and young men have visions. Mother Smith herself has a series of visions—one a vision of a sparkling stream running through two trees. One of the trees is "lively and animated," seeming to

40. Nicholas Perrin, Jeannine K. Brown, and Joel B. Green, *Dictionary of Jesus and the Gospels* (Downers Grove, IL: IVP Academic, 2013), 299–301.

41. This phrase is not in the rough manuscript but appears in the 1853 edition and follows what has become a standard allusive practice for Lucy. Pratt, *Biographical Sketches*, 23; Anderson, *Lucy's Book*, 236.

42. Lucy Mack Smith, History, 1844–1845, p. [12], bk. [1]; Anderson, *Lucy's Book*, 240. "Fear God" and "walk uprightly" are both common biblical phrases.

43. Many early converts saw their spiritual lives prior to conversion leading to their conversion as Latter-day Saints. Christopher C. Jones and Stephen J. Fleming, "'Except among this Portion of Mankind': Early Mormon Conceptions of the Apostasy" in Miranda Wilcox and John D. Young, eds. *Standing Apart: Mormon Historical Consciousness and the Concept of Apostasy* (Oxford and New York: Oxford University Press, 2014), 66–72.

44. Anderson, *Lucy's Book*, 28, 42–43, 49, 51, 168, 292–294, 323, 697, 699, 781.

express "the utmost joy and happiness," likewise alluding to Lehi's dream.[45] In the spring of 1839, as she thought her sons Joseph and Hyrum languished in Liberty Jail, she received a heavenly "assurance" that they would arrive home the following night.[46] That evening, she had a vision of her "very tired and hungry" sons "upon the prairie travelling" with "but one horse" and then sleeping on the ground. When they actually returned the following day, she "then asked brother Partridge"—who had been particularly upset at Joseph's continued absence—"if . . . he would forever after that time acknowledge me a true prophet."[47] Her charismatic gifts and visionary leadership moved from centering on her family to offering consolation to the broader church. Enumerating these gifts fortified her role as matriarch to the Restoration's first family as well as her responsibility to lead as the Mother of the Church and a Mother in Israel.

When the Smith family and most of the New York Saints moved to Kirtland in early 1831, Lucy led one of the groups. She recalled gathering "them all round me" and promising them, "Brothers and Sisters we have set out just as father Lehigh [Lehi] did to travel by the commandment of the Lord to a land that the Lord will show unto us if we are faithful and I want you all to be solemn and lift your hearts to God in prayer continually that we may be prospered."[48] Lucy's Book of Mormon allusion not only offered comfort and confidence to the people as they embarked on their own journey but placed them in a continuation of the new scripture's sacred narrative into the present. And, like Lehi, she led and talked as prophet.

Earlier, Lucy commented, "Wherefore we did all things according to the pattern that was given" [cf. Hebrews 8:5].[49] As with her immediate family, she understood scriptural narrative as patterns and models that applied to the lives of Saints in the present and further empowered by explicit parallels among her family's life, the lives of the modern Saints, and the lives of ancient holy ones. Lehi's journey with his family in the Book of Mormon and the wanderings of the children of Israel are patterns for their own journey.

---

45. Pratt, *Biographical Sketches*, 55.
46. Lucy Mack Smith, History, 1844–1845, p. [3], bk. [17]; Anderson, *Lucy's Book*, 292–293.
47. Lucy Mack Smith, History, 1844–1845, p. [4], bk. 17; Anderson, *Lucy's Book*, 699.
48. Lucy Mack Smith, History, 1844–1845, p. [3], bk. [11]; Anderson, *Lucy's Book*, 514.
49. Lucy Mack Smith, History, 1844–1845, p. [3], bk. [9]; Anderson, *Lucy's Book*, 460.

As their trip continues, so does conflict. Though not as prolific in her use of "murmur" as was Nephi, murmuring is likewise a consistent theme.[50] Like Nephi's bow, the canal lock "broke," and the Saints worry that they will starve. As Lucy collapses moments of crisis in the record of Nephi's family and moves on to his efforts to build a ship for the promised land, she further reinforces the parallel. At this point, the sisters among the modern pilgrims voice their opposition: "We would have done better to have remained at home for there we might set in our rocking chairs and take as much comfort as we were mind to," just as the brethren of Nephi worried that "it would have been better" had their wives died in Jerusalem than experience the afflictions of the desert.[51] In Lucy's narrative, the language of scripture appears most prolifically in moments of crisis or great emotion.

When the Saints again began to snip and chafe at each other, she chastises them: "Brethren and sisters you who were with me do you recollect this circumstances which I am relating [I] know you remmember [sic] this journey well for I am not now speaking of that which took place in a former century but what your eyes have seen and your ears have heard."[52] Echoing the King James text, she again pulls their group into a holy narrative in the present. Perhaps most like Nephi in her consistent rebukes, Lucy again chastises the Saints with whom she travels. "We call ourselves latter day saints and profess to have come out from among the world [cf. 1 Corinthians 5:10] for the purpose of serving God with determination to serve him [cf. Doctrine and Covenants 20:37] with our whole might mind and strength [cf. 2 Nephi 25:29] at the expense of all earthly things [cf. John 3:12] and will you suffer yourselves to being at the very first sacrifice of comfort to complain and Murmur like the children of Israel [cf. Numbers 14:27] and even worse."[53] As she recounts this history for wider audiences, she continues the work of scripture and expands her role as prophetess, engraving her own sacred history.

A narrative of persecution also weaves throughout the book, culminating in the murders of her sons. After detailing their deaths, Mother Smith

50. "Murmur" occurs at least a dozen times in a single chapter. Anderson, *Lucy's Book*, 517–518, 522, 527–530.

51. Lucy Mack Smith, History, 1844–1845, p. [5], bk. [11]; Anderson, *Lucy's Book*, 517–518; 1 Nephi 16:18, 17:20.

52. Lucy Mack Smith, History, 1844–1845, p. [4], bk. [11]; Anderson, *Lucy's Book*, 519; cf. Deuteronomy 29:4, 1 Corinthians 2:9, 3 Nephi 17:16.

53. Lucy Mack Smith, History, 1844–1845, p. [12], bk. [11]; Anderson, *Lucy's Book*, 529.

ends her history in its most raw form with her witness shaped by scripture. Her rough manuscript ends with a dense amalgamation of the concluding words of Nephi, Mormon, and Moroni in addition to other echoes and allusions from the Bible, the Book of Mormon, and the new revelations. References mark the nature of her scripture patchwork and her intense allusive practice. An early draft of her conclusion reads,

> I have now given a history of My life as far as I intend carrying at this time. I leave the world at liberty to pass judgment upon what I have written as seemeth them good [cf. 2 Nephi 33:3, 11; 3 Nephi 26:4; Moroni 10:1] but this much I will say that all that I have written is true [1 Nephi 1:3] and will stand forever yes it will stand before God at that hour when it shall [end] and great I shall appear to answer at his bar [cf. 2 Nephi 33:11; Moroni 10:27] for the deeds done in the body [Alma 5:15] whether they be good or evil [Alma 40:11; Mormon 3:20]—then and there will I Meet the persecutors of . . . my family who are the enemies of the church and declare with a voice that shall penetrate the ear s [cf. D&C 1:2] of every intelligence [D&C 93:29] which shall be present on that momentous occasion. . . . let me leave the bones of my fathers and brothers and the bones of my Martyrd children and go to a land where never man dwelt fare well my country thou that killest the prophets [Matthew 23:27] and hath exiled them that were sent unto thee once thou wert fair once thou wert pure and lovely [cf. Mormon 6:17].[54]

Mother Smith had become her own prophetic narrator proffering new scripture to the Saints. The Saints aided in the fulfillment of these roles as they received her offering—those who requested and listened to her oral tradition and ultimately received her published history.

Orson Pratt was the first to continue Lucy's work to present her patchwork of new sacred history to the Saints, with its first publication in 1853. Unable to do so herself but happy it was going to be published, Lucy allowed Pratt to purchase the copyright from her.[55] At least ten subsequent major

---

54. Lucy Mack Smith, History, 1844–1845, pp. [13, 16], bk. [19]; Johnson, "Becoming a People of the Books," 36.

55. Orson Pratt to Lucy Mack Smith, February 4, 1854, CHL.

editions with proliferating reprints mark the continued reception of Mother Smith's history into the present. First as an oral tradition and then published, Lucy Mack Smith's history cemented her authority as the Mother of the Church and a Mother in Israel not just for her contemporaries who knew and respected her as Mother Smith but for all those believers who would follow and listen to her words.

9

Strangite Scripture

Christine Elyse Blythe and Christopher James Blythe

At the very moment of Joseph Smith's death, an angel appeared to James J. Strang and set him on a path to become a Prophet, Seer, Revelator, and Translator. Strang was the least experienced of those men claiming to succeed Smith in the wake of his assassination, having only converted six months previously and having met his predecessor only once. Yet even as a novice in the tradition, he would quickly become its most prolific revelator. Over the course of his twelve-year ministry, Strang produced several revelations in the voice of deity, two translations, and a particularly significant revelation allegedly dictated by Joseph Smith before his death. Strang's supporters touted his ability to bring forward the words of God as evidence that he was the proper head of the Church of Jesus Christ of Latter-day Saints.

The new scriptures established Strang as Smith's rightful successor, condemned the twelve apostles led by Brigham Young, and legitimated a call for the Saints to gather in Voree, Wisconsin. While these early revelations did little else theologically and practically, they did promise more to come: the Restoration was continuing now under Strang, and his flock expected new mysteries. This was achieved in 1851 with the publication of the Book of the Law of the Lord, which would pave the way for a radical reimagining of Latter Day Saint practice and ecclesiology. This new book was the most ambitious scriptural work in the Latter Day Saint tradition after the Book of Mormon. It masterfully scripturalized ideas and practices introduced in Nauvoo and Voree that had yet to become part of the tradition's sacred writ.

THE

BOOK OF THE LAW

OF

THE LORD,

CONSISTING OF AN INSPIRED TRANSLATION OF
SOME OF THE MOST IMPORTANT PARTS OF
THE LAW GIVEN TO MOSES, AND A VERY
FEW ADDITIONAL COMMANDMENTS,
WITH BRIEF NOTES AND
REFERENCES.

PRINTED BY COMMAND OF THE KING,

AT THE ROYAL PRESS,

SAINT JAMES,

A. R. I.

FIGURE 9.1. The Book of the Law of the Lord (1851). Courtesy of the
Church History Library, the Church of Jesus Christ of Latter-day Saints.

THE LETTER OF APPOINTMENT

The first item of scripture associated with James Strang was "the letter of appointment," a letter ostensibly written by Joseph Smith on June 18, 1844, and sent the following day to Strang in Burlington, Wisconsin, where it arrived on July 9.[56] The authenticity of this document is contested. Many scholars have dismissed it as a forgery, but we will describe it as Smith's work since that was how it was understood by the Latter Day Saints who accepted it as scripture. The letter was a response to Strang's petition for establishing a Latter Day Saint community in Wisconsin. Smith began his reply by acknowledging that he had intended to reject the plan after meeting in council with some of Nauvoo's leaders. However, in the aftermath of this decision, he had received a revelation forcing him to reconsider his initial skepticism. Smith confided that he had "long felt" that his martyrdom was impending, and while reflecting on how the church would survive his death, he had gone to the "hill of the temple" to pray. As he prayed, he saw "a light in the heavens," which he recognized as God descending from his throne. "[The Almighty] appeared, and moon and stars went out. The earth dissolved in space. I trod on air and was borne on wings of Cherubims. The sweetest strains of heavenly music thrilled in my ear, but the notes were low and sad as though they sounded the requiem of martyred prophets."[57]

Smith continued, "I bowed my head to the earth and asked only wisdom and strength for the church." What followed was a revelation foreseeing Smith's martyrdom and appointing Strang the head over a "stake of Zion in Wisconsin" in a city "called Voree, which is, being interpreted, Garden of Peace, for there shall my people have peace and rest and wax fat and pleasant in the presence of their enemies." This future city would offer the persecuted Saints refuge and prosperity. And it would have a temple just like earlier Latter-day Saint sites. While scholars have noted that the letter does not directly appoint Strang as Smith's successor, the implications seemed clear: "To him [Strang] shall the gathering of the people be."[58] Whatever

---

56. *The Diamond: Being the Law of Prophetic Succession* (1848), 5.

57. "Letter from Joseph Smith to James Strang," *Voree Herald*, January 1846. The original letter is housed in the Beinecke Library, Yale University.

58. Ibid.

the intentions of the original author, Strang never considered more modest interpretations.

Strang was cautious at first, sharing the letter with only a few individuals living near his home. He formally presented it to a small group of supporters during a conference held in Florence, Wisconsin, on August 5, 1844. Strang was accompanied by Aaron Smith, who had been appointed his counselor in Smith's letter of appointment. The response from the conference was less welcoming than the two would have hoped. The president of the conference, Crandell Dunn, condemned the letter as a forgery and ordered Strang and Smith to not speak of it until they reported to Nauvoo and received the approval of the twelve apostles.[59] Those at the conference did not challenge Strang on the improbability that Smith would have appointed a new convert as his successor, but they questioned the document itself. Norton Jacob thought it "carried upon its face the marks of a base forgery, being written throughout in printed characters. The postmark was black while that issued from the [Nauvoo post] office was uniformly red. But above all the contents of the thing was altogether bombastic, unlike the work of God, and dishonorable to the name of Joseph Smith whose signature it bore in a hand he never wrote."[60]

The letter of appointment was not the only revelation allegedly dictated by Joseph Smith but dismissed by many as a forgery. John C. Bennett claimed Smith had asked him to safeguard a revelation dated April 7, 1841, intended for the church after Smith's death.[61] The July 12, 1843, revelation concerning plural marriage, although accepted as authentic by scholars, was often declared a forgery by those who did not support the leadership of the twelve apostles.[62] Each of these documents, including the letter of appointment, garnered controversy because they ostensibly settled questions at the core of the succession crisis by appealing to Smith's revelatory voice.

The letter of appointment signaled that Strang and his community were a continuity of the original church. Strang pointed to a February 1831 revelation that acknowledged Smith's right to "appoint another in his stead" and

59. Crandell Dunn Papers, CHL.
60. Norton Jacob Journal, CHL.
61. John Cook Bennett, Revelation given to Joseph Smith, April 7, 1841 [1844], CHL.
62. Joseph Smith, Revelation, July 12, 1843, *JSP*, D12:453–478.

the fact that he (Strang) was the only one to have claimed such an appointment.[63] He took this approach when answering a query from a Latter Day Saint who asked his views on succession. "[T]o dispute my prophetic calling, is to say that Joseph Smith is an impostor, and Mormonism a lie. Probably you are not now prepared to take my word for this. I only ask you to take Joseph's."[64]

TRANSLATION OF THE VOREE PLATES

In 1845, Strang introduced an item of scripture that not only served to validate his succession claims but also allowed him to personally reenact the beginning of Smith's prophetic career by discovering and translating metal plates also deposited by an ancient American people. On September 1, 1845, an angel came to Strang "and he showed unto me the plate of the sealed record and he gave into my hands the Urim and Thummim."[65] To those familiar with the Book of Mormon, the phrase "sealed record" would have brought to mind the "sealed portion" of the Book of Mormon that Smith had been forbidden to translate but that the very text promised would be translated sometime in the future.[66] In the the angel's presence, Strang heard the voice of the Lord.

> A work shall come forth and the secrets of the past shalt thou reveal. Yea by little and little shalt thou reveal it, according to the ability and faithfulness of my Church and of my servant whom I have placed above them. Behold the record which was sealed from my servant Joseph. Unto thee it is reserved.[67]

This was a prophecy. Strang would complete Smith's work and eventually bring forth the rest of the Book of Mormon. However, the Saints' faithfulness would be required before this promise could be fulfilled. "Yea, as my servants

63. D&C 43:4.

64. James Strang, A Letter from James J. Strang to Mrs. Corey, September 26, 1854, in *The Prophetic Controversy: A Letter from James J. Strang to Mrs. Corey* (Saint James [Beaver Island], MI: 1878).

65. "Revelation given to James J. Strang, September 1, 1845," *Voree Herald,* January 1846.

66. Ether 3:27; Joseph Smith History 1:65.

67. "Revelation given to James J. Strang, September 1, 1845," *Voree Herald,* January 1846.

serve me, so shalt thou translate unto them." In the meantime, Strang would
be led to a previously unknown set of plates.

> And while I was yet in the Spirit the Angel of the Lord took me away
> to the hill in the East of Walworth against White River in Voree, and
> there he shewed unto me the record buried under an oak tree as large
> as the body of a large man; it was enclosed in an earthen casement
> and buried in the ground as deep as to a man's waist, and I beheld
> it as a man can see a light stone in clear water, for I saw it by Urim
> and Thummim, and I returned the Urim and Thummim to the Angel
> of the Lord and he departed out of sight.[68]

The revelation had instructed Strang to "take with thee faithful witnesses,"
and on September 13 he invited four church members to accompany him
to the location of the plates. These men—Aaron Smith, Jirah B. Wheelan,
James M. Van Nostrand, and Edward Whitcomb—wrote an affidavit describing how Strang brought them to the hill and oak tree where he told them to
dig for the plates. Their account emphasized just how impossible it would
have been for someone to have planted the records in the recent past. Strang
had urged them to be suspicious "and charged us to examine the ground
that we should know we were not imposed upon, and that it had not been
buried there since the tree grew." They testified that the grass near the tree
had been undisturbed. They likewise found "no sign or indication that [the
earth] had been moved or disturbed at any time previous." In fact, the tree's
roots seemed to have grown around "the case of slightly baked clay containing three plates of brass."[69] Just like the testimonies of witnesses in the
Book of Mormon, the affidavit was designed to compel individuals to take
the record's claims of antiquity seriously.

The act of bringing witnesses as part of an excavation team to uncover
the plates distinguishes the Voree plates' history from the Book of Mormon's origin account. Joseph Smith made a lone journey—accompanied only
partway by Emma Hale Smith—to retrieve the gold plates in upstate New
York. Instead, the discovery of the Voree plates more closely resembled the

---

68. "Revelation given to James J. Strang, September 1, 1845," *Voree Herald,* January 1846.
69. *Voree Herald*, January 1846.

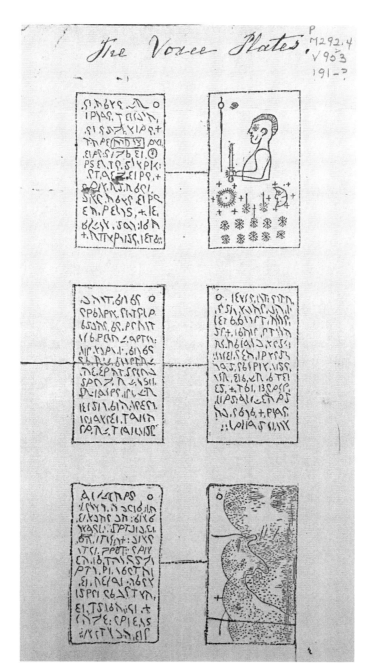

FIGURE 9.2. "The Voree Plates," broadside (circa 1911). Church History Library, the Church of Jesus Christ of Latter-day Saints. Photograph courtesy of Jay Burton(2021).

unearthing of the so-called "Kinderhook plates." In April 1843, men from Kinderhook, Illinois, presented Smith with six bell-shaped plates "covered with ancient characters of language containing from 30 to 40 on each side of the plates."[70] The men had allegedly located the plates while excavating an Indian burial mound and turned to Smith for his ability to translate unknown languages. Smith did so by comparing the hieroglyphics to the Grammar and Alphabet of the Egyptian Language that Latter-day Saints had created as part of an effort to translate an Egyptian papyrus in 1835.[71]

The three small brass plates found in Voree were estimated at one and a half inches by two and a half inches. Four sides included an otherwise unknown script and two sides featured engraved images.[72] One image depicted the hill where the plates were buried; the other was of a figure holding a scepter above the sun, moon, and stars. Like the finders of the Kinderhook plates, Strang was amiable to publicly displaying the Voree plates, which he did throughout his ministry.

Strang translated the writings on September 18 and presented them publicly three days later. The short text was written from the perspective of Rajah Manchou of Vorito, then the lone survivor of the ancient inhabitants of the region. His people had died in combat after "hav[ing] fallen in transgression." Rajah Manchou foresaw the future gathering of God's people in Voree. While there was no compelling theology to emerge from the translation, it tied Voree to a sacred American past already established in the Book of Mormon. The text even named the hill where the plates were recovered as the Hill of Promise, paralleling the significance paid to the "Hill Cumorah" where Smith obtained the gold plates.[73]

The translation concluded with a reference to the significance of Strang's ministry. "The forerunner men shall kill, but a mighty prophet there shall dwell. I will be his strength, and he shall bring forth thy record." The

70. William Clayton, Journal, May 1, 1843, in *An Intimate Chronicle: The Journals of William Clayton*, edited by George D. Smith (Salt Lake City, UT: Signature Books, 1995), 100.

71. Don Bradley and Mark Ashurst-McGee, "'President Joseph has Translated a Portion': Joseph Smith and the Mistranslation of the Kinderhook Plates," in *Producing Ancient Scripture: Joseph Smith's Translation Projects and the Making of Mormon Christianity*, edited by Michael Hubbard MacKay, Mark Ashurst-McGee, and Brian M. Hauglid (Salt Lake City: University of Utah Press, 2020), 507–513.

72. For a study of the script and its translation, see John Hamer, "The Miraculous Plates of Voree Examined," *By Common Consent*, June 23, 2008.

73. Unnamed article, *Voree Herald*, January 1846.

"forerunner" was an unmistakable reference to the martyred Joseph Smith. At this point, it was not clear why Strang was the "mighty prophet" or—as the text seemed to imply—the mightier prophet.[74] Yet, Strang's role as the architect of God's kingdom in the last days would be revealed in further revelations.

THE BOOK OF THE LAW OF THE LORD: STICK OF JUDAH

Now that Strang had proven his ability to bring forth ancient records, his supporters looked forward to more revelations. For instance, one adherent alluded to the September 1845 revelation when closing a letter to Strang with the petition: "May the God of heaven sustain you and prepare the church for the reception of the sealed records that are reserved for a day of righteousness."[75] Strang continued to hold out the promise of additional scripture. On July 1, 1846, he dictated a revelation designating a room in his home (then under construction) for translating "ancient records [and] hidden truths."[76] Strang had every intention of continually adding to the Latter Day Saint canon.

Recall that the September 1845 revelation had seemingly promised the sealed portion of the Book of Mormon. This sealed part of the Book of Mormon was, like the rest of the book, the product of the fifth-century prophet Mormon's editing of various other records. The Strangites seem to have been even more interested in the restoration of what the Book of Mormon referred to as the brass plates, a set of ancient records Mormon possessed and cited in the Book of Mormon. The brass plates were the ancient collection of Hebrew scripture passed down in Book of Mormon civilization, containing "the five books of Moses ... a record of the Jews from beginning ... also the prophecies of the holy prophets, from the beginning, even down to the commencement of the reign of Zedekiah; and also many prophecies which have been spoken by the mouth of Jeremiah."[77] When the Book of Mormon quoted from Isaiah and other Hebrew scriptures, it was from a variant of these texts kept on the brass plates. It was also from these plates that the Book

74. Ibid.
75. J. W. Nichols, Letter to James J. Strang, July 4, 1848.
76. "Revelation," *Voree Herald*, July 1846.
77. 1 Nephi 5:11–13.

of Mormon editors accessed writings from previously unknown prophets Zenos, Zenock, and Neum.[78] According to the Book of Mormon prophet Lehi, the brass plates "should go forth unto all nations, kindreds, tongues, and people who were of his seed."[79]

In 1846, Strangite Lewis Van Buren expressed his hopes to see this record. He recalled that years before, he possessed "an old-book printed in Germany some hundreds of years ago, containing many curious historical facts, which I considered worthy of notice." The book described ancient records "engraved upon plates of copper or brass" that had been passed down through the biblical patriarchs and dated to "[a]s early as in the days of Enoch." Van Buren believed these were the brass plates mentioned in the Book of Mormon.

> Doubtless these records must contain many mysteries which have not been revealed to the world, and were kept secret among those who were in possession of the holy priesthood. What has become of these precious, original, patriarchal records, the book of Mormon seems to reveal, and are they not the very plates of brass that Lehi brought with him from Jerusalem, when he emigrated to the land of Joseph [i.e., the Americas], which plates were preserved until that time by the Elders of that tribe after Joseph's death, and containing the revelation of God from the beginning, to come forth in the latter days, in order to be united with the record or Stik [*sic*] of Judah.[80]

Van Buren curiously believed this record would come forth to fulfill a passage in Ezekiel 37 that Latter Day Saints had often cited as a prophecy of last days scripture. "Take thee one stick, and write upon it, For Judah ... then take another stick, and write upon it, For Joseph, the stick of Ephraim.... And join them one to another into one stick; and they shall become one in thine hand."[81] Van Buren's interpretation was unusual in that he identified the future translation of the brass plates with the stick of Ephraim and the Bible with the stick of Judah. In contrast, Smith's revelations had already identified

78. See, for instance, 1 Nephi 19:10; Alma 33:10, 34:7; and Helaman 8:20.
79. 1 Nephi 5:18.
80. Lewis Van Buren, unnamed, *Voree Herald*, June 1846.
81. Ezekiel 37:16–17.

the Book of Mormon as the stick of Ephraim.[82] When Strang produced a translation of the plates, he also saw it as a fulfillment of Ezekiel 37 but took a different interpretation of the prophecy than either Smith or Van Buren. We will return to this point below.

By 1849, Strang had come to possess the brass plates. Curiously we know very little about how Strang acquired the plates or the way he translated them, especially when we compare the coming forth of the brass plates to the wide publicity given to the discovery and translation of the Voree plates four years before. The new emphasis on confidentiality may have come because of Strang's July 1, 1846, revelation that commanded him to translate in the privacy of his home "and not in the field as thou hast, nor in the houses of unbelievers, that they may look upon sacred things."[83] The brass plates were not to serve the same sort of ongoing sign of Strang's legitimacy that the Voree plates had.

According to Dale L. Morgan, Strang largely drafted the translation in the winter of 1849–1850 while in Baltimore and Philadelphia.[84] Historian Vickie Cleverly Speek realized that Strang's correspondence discusses this translation cryptically as the "Swedish work," thus safeguarding knowledge of it from the uninitiated.[85] The only direct reference to the plates was a letter from George J. Adams congratulating Strang on the progress of the translation.[86] It would appear that Samuel Graham, who acted as an assistant of some sort during the translation, possessed the plates for a time.[87]

The product of Strang's translation was published in 1851 as the Book of the Law of the Lord, an ancient Jewish text mentioned in Deuteronomy and 2 Chronicles. According to the Book of the Law's preface, this was the "most important" of the "lost books" of the Bible. After the original was revealed to Moses, it was "kept in the ark of the covenant and was held too sacred to go into the hands of strangers." Because it was so closely guarded, future

---

82. D&C 27:5.

83. "Revelation," *Voree Herald,* July 1846.

84. Dale L. Morgan, "A Bibliography of the Church of Jesus Christ of Latter Day Saints [Strangite]," *Western Humanities Review* 5 (Winter 1950):69.

85. Vickie C. Speek, *"God Has Made Us a Kingdom": James Strang and the Midwest Mormons* (Salt Lake City, UT: Signature Books, 2006), 147–148.

86. George J. Adams, Letter to James Strang, February 18, 1850, quoted in Morgan, "A Bibliography," 69.

87. Speek, "God Has Made Us a Kingdom."

generations read the Pentateuch, "containing abstracts from some of the laws," as a substitute.[88] The biblical story of the Book of the Law, as it appears in 2 Kings, is that the Israelites had lost the book and rediscovered it during the reign of King Josiah.[89]

Strang never possessed the autograph copy of Moses's Book of the Law but depended on "an authorized copy" kept on the brass plates.[90] Strangites initially followed the typical Latter Day Saint interpretation of Ezekiel 37, identifying the stick of Ephraim as the Book of Mormon and the stick of Judah as the Bible. However, by July 1849, Strangites looked forward to "the day not far distant when the stick of Judah shall come forth in its purity, and be united with the stick of Ephraim."[91] After the Book of the Law was published, Strang spoke of the translation of the brass plates as the stick of Judah. He believed its name came from the fact that he as a descendant of Judah had translated it.[92]

The book opens with a testimony of seven men addressed to "all nations, kindreds, tongues and people, to whom this Book of the Law of the Lord shall come."[93] The testimony parallels the testimonies of three and eight witnesses in the Book of Mormon. In fact, the testimony in the Book of the Law of the Lord was very similar to the format of the affidavit of the eight witnesses. While the three witnesses had a visionary experience that included the appearance of the angel Moroni, the eight witnesses simply observed and handled the plates as presented by Joseph Smith. The eight described their "curious workmanship."[94] The Book of the Law of the Lord's witnesses likewise declared that Strang had shown them the plates. "We examined them with our eyes, and handled them with our hands." The seven also provided more details than the eight witnesses in the Book of Mormon.

> The engravings are beautiful antique workmanship, bearing a striking resemblance to the ancient oriental languages; and those from which the laws in this book were translated are eighteen in number, about

88. The Book of the Law (1851), 3.
89. 2 Kings 22–23.
90. The Book of the Law (1851), 6.
91. "The Lamanites," *Gospel Herald*, July 26, 1849.
92. *Prophetic Controversy*; The Book of the Law, 2nd ed; 2 Nephi 3:12.
93. "Testimony," The Book of the Law (1851), 2.
94. Testimony of the Eight Witnesses, Book of Mormon.

seven inches and three-eights wide, by nine inches long, occasionally embellished with beautiful pictures.[95]

The seven witnesses closed their testimony declaring, "The everlasting kingdom of God is established, in which this law shall be kept, till it brings in rest and everlasting righteousness to all the faithful."[96]

Consistent with the secrecy surrounding the translation of the plates, Strang did not intend wide distribution for the Book of the Law when it was first published in 1851. It had a limited run of only 200 copies.[97] Five years later, when the second edition was published, the community anticipated it would reach a much larger audience. The initial goal was to have the new edition ready for purchase in the spring of 1856; however, 1,500 copies still awaited binding at the time of Strang's death in July. Copies were eventually bound and used by the dwindling church membership over the succeeding decades.[98] In the second edition, Strang added nine additional chapters to the original thirty-eight.

Strang's translation held several connections to Smith's scriptural projects. Its relationship with the Book of Mormon was obvious: it was translated from the brass plates mentioned and cited there. It was also related to Smith's new translation of the Bible and the larger concept of restoring a corrupted biblical text. This was, after all, the original scripture from which the Pentateuch served "as a convenient substitute."[99] The Book of the Law's preface even began by noting that "the necessity of a new translation of the Sacred Oracles into the English language has long been felt by all biblical students."[100] A key example to how the Book of the Law restored ancient texts appearing in a corrupted form in the King James Bible was in the first chapter, titled "The Decalogue." It contained ten numbered commandments that were vastly more extensive than those that appear in Exodus 20 or Deuteronomy 5.

The restored decalogue included Jesus's two great commandments from the Gospel of Matthew: "Thou shalt love the Lord thy God with all thy heart,

---

95. "Testimony," The Book of the Law (1851), 2.
96. "Testimony," The Book of the Law (1851), 2.
97. "Our Publications," *The Northern Islander*, January 26, 1856.
98. Morgan, "A Bibliography," 75.
99. The Book of the Law, 44.
100. The Book of the Law, 3.

and with all thy soul, and with all thy mind" and "Thou shalt love thy neighbor as thyself" as part of the ten.[101] As with many of Smith's revisions of the
Old Testament, by integrating New Testament verses Strang's decalogue was
a Christianizing move. The first of Jesus's great commandments was integrated into the first of the ten commandments, which included the imperatives to have no other gods and to make no graven images. Thus, the first
commandment in the Book of the Law reads

> Thou shalt love the Lord thy God with all thy heart, and with all thy
> might, and with all thy strength: thou shalt adore him, and serve
> him, and obey him: thou shalt have no other gods before thee: thou
> shalt not make unto thee any image or likeness of anything that is
> in the heaven above, or in the earth beneath, or in the waters of
> the earth, to bow thyself unto it, or to worship it: thou shalt not
> bow down thyself unto, nor adore anything that thine eye beholdeth,
> or thy imagination conceiveth of; but the Lord thy God only; for the
> Lord thy God is a jealous God, visiting the iniquity of the fathers
> upon the children, from generation to generation, even upon all that
> hate him, and showing a multitude of mercies unto them that keep
> his commandments.[102]

Interestingly, the text did not follow the wording in Matthew but borrowed
from a revelation dictated by Joseph Smith on August 7, 1831. Thus, following the wording in Smith's revelation, it read, "Thou shalt love the Lord thy
God *with all thy heart, with all thy might, mind, and strength*," rather than
"Thou shalt love the Lord with all thy heart, and with all thy soul, and with
all thy mind."[103]

Jesus's second great commandment served as the basis of the fourth commandment in Strang's decalogue, which had no precedent in the traditional
decalogue. The space for an additional commandment was based on a unique
numbering scheme. Strang was aware that Protestant, Roman Catholic, and
Jewish commentators had divided the verses differently to come to the total

101. Matthew 22:37–40. The first of these great commandments initially appears in Deuteronomy 6:5.

102. The Book of the Law, 1:1.

103. D&C 59:5.

of ten commandments. His solution for this discrepancy was to assert that there were only nine commandments that had survived in the available manuscripts. From a note published alongside the decalogue in the Book of the Law's second edition we find: "The wisdom of men never made the discovery. It was left till the translation of the plates of Laban, by the gift and power of God. But the discovery once made, the Bible of all the sects is our witness."[104]

The Book of the Law, as it was published in 1851 and 1856, also bore a relationship to the Doctrine and Covenants, a collection of Smith's revelations. While the majority of the Book of the Law was presented as a revealed translation of an ancient text, it also contained "a very few additional commandments," as stated in the subtitle of the 1851 edition. That edition included six instances of Strang's contemporary dictations in the text. The first was Chapter 5, entitled "Baptism for the Dead," a revelation Strang dictated on August 9, 1849. Chapter 13, "The Calling of a King" included six verses "written by the prophet James, by inspiration of God, and the nine following are the words of the angel of God when he conferred upon James J. Strang the prophetic authority, and made him the chief shepard of the flock of God on earth."[105] There are two other instances of Strang's revelations appearing alongside ancient translation, updating its original content: Chapter 26, "Law of Inheritances" (with revelation dictated on July 8, 1850) and Chapter 30, "The Feasts" (with revelation dictated in February 1851). Like the first verses of Chapter 13, Chapter 2, "The True God," "was written by the prophet James, by inspiration of God," differentiating it from his dictated revelations.[106] Chapter 38, the concluding chapter of the 1851 edition, was titled "Establishment of the Law," a revelation Strang dictated in February 1851. When the 1856 edition was published, Chapter 5 was altered to read as part of the flow of the book, removing specific references to Voree, Wisconsin. The revisions were intended to allow for future readers to apply the teachings to temples built elsewhere.

In 1854, Strang differentiated the Book of the Law from the Bible and Book of Mormon. For context, Joseph Smith had once touted the Book of Mormon as "the most correct of any Book on earth & the keystone of our religion & a man would get neared to God by abiding by its precepts than any

104. The Book of the Law, 43.
105. The Book of the Law, 8.
106. The Book of the Law, 8.

other Book."[107] Strang had come to have a more modest understanding of the original Latter Day Saint scripture. "The Book of Mormon is not a text book among the Saints of the last days. . . . The Book of Mormon is not a book of doctrine, but a book of history." The Bible, on the other hand, was used to settle "public controversies." The Book of the Law was superior when considering "their domestic affairs" and in this regard was "the end of controversy."[108] The Book of the Law included regulations governing the household, marriage, inheritances, adoption, and other "domestic affairs," but it also contained discussions of ecclesiastical structure, ceremony, responsibilities of royal officers, and items on personal conduct. Domestic affairs did not relate to the household alone; "domestic" was understood more broadly to pertain "to a nation considered as a family, or to one's own country."[109] The key here was that the Book of the Law was an internal document for the collective people of the church.

The Book of the Law was published at the time it was to reorganize Latter Day Saint society. The church had relocated its headquarters to Beaver Island in Lake Michigan, where Strang would reimagine the church as a kingdom. While Strang had known very little about the esoteric teachings of Joseph Smith in 1844, by 1850 he had embraced what he had learned about Smith's ideas of theocratic government, sacred fraternal rituals, and plural marriage. In 1846, with the aid of former Nauvoo insider John C. Bennett, Strang initiated individuals into a secret society known as the Order of the Illuminati.[110] In 1849, Strang secretly married Elvira Eliza Field while still married to his first wife, Mary Perce.[111] On July 8, 1850, he was crowned "King in Zion" before an assembly of Saints on Beaver Island. It was also at this time that the community recognized the king's privy council, which would meet to deliberate on the kingdom's laws.[112]

Beaver Island Mormonism was a unique version of the Latter Day Saint tradition. It was based on a rudimentary knowledge of Smith's esotericism, interpreted through a lens of Judeo-Christian primitivism. Smith had

107. Wilford Woodruff, Journal, November 28, 1841, CHL.

108. *The Northern Islander*, September 7, 1854.

109. "Domestic," Webster's Dictionary, 1828.

110. Christopher James Blythe, "The Coronation of James J. Strang and the Making of Beaver Island Mormonism," *Communal Societies* 34, no. 1 (2014):11–13.

111. Roger Van Noord, *King of Beaver Island*, 82.

112. Stephen Post, Journal July 8, 1850, CHL.

declared scriptural precedents for his innovations in Nauvoo, but his own revelations had yet to integrate many of his innovations. This was the genius of the Book of the Law.

Neither Strang nor the Book of the Law mentioned Smith's vision of a theocracy in Nauvoo. In 1844, Smith had even been recognized as a king in what he called the Council of Fifty or the Kingdom of God.[113] Strang learned of these developments from a handful of Strangite converts who had been members of this Nauvoo council. His coronation was thus in part based on this precedent; in turn, the Book of the Law systematized the theocracy that Strang began then. While Smith saw his own efforts to found a royal government as distinct from the church he founded, the distinction led to confusion even from those directly involved.[114] The Book of the Law remedied this problem of two organizations by recasting church officers with royal dimensions. The first presidency became the King's Council. The High Council became the King's Court. The twelve apostles and others became princes. Beaver Island itself was recognized as the Lord's dominion where the laws of the kingdom were established.[115]

The Book of the Law's treatment of plural marriage likewise paved the groundwork for a public acknowledgement of the Strangite practice. Strang had initially been an opponent of plural marriage until some Nauvoo insiders, including the openly polygamous George Miller, joined his church and relocated to Wisconsin.[116] There was sufficient concern about plural marriage—even if its current practice was not widely known—that it became a discussion in July 1850 at the first meeting of the privy council. The council ruled that "from this time forth no man shall have but one wife."[117] When the Book of the Law appeared the following year, it did not directly reverse this prohibition but included various marital regulations that implied the possibility of plural marriage.

This included a rule in Chapter 15, "Abstinence of the King," that declared, "He [the king] shall not multiply to himself wives; lest he forget the law, and

113. *JSP*, A1:95–96.

114. Christopher James Blythe, "The Church and the Kingdom of God: Ecclesiastical Interpretations of the Council of Fifty," *Journal of Mormon History* 43, no. 2 (2017):103–105.

115. Blythe, "The Coronation of James J. Strang," 23–27.

116. Speek, *"God Has Made Us a Kingdom,"* 151.

117. Stephen Post, Journal, July 9, 1850, CHL.

avenge not his people; and lest his heart turn from them to strange women."[118] Chapter 36, "Household Relations" similarly forbids all men from marrying "a multitude of wives disproportioned to their inheritance" but also added the command "nor shalt thou take wives to vex those thou hast."[119] Historian Roger Van Noord described these proscriptions as a means to "cleverly back into an authorization of polygamy."[120] The Old Testament setting for the Book of the Law also meant that readers might assume that the instruction applied to the past and was not necessarily a modern endorsement of plural marriage. Joseph Smith had used a similar strategy of setting revelation intended for a modern audience in an ancient scriptural setting by using biblical code-names when referring to living individuals to conceal the church's financial dealings.[121]

When the 1856 edition was published, additional commentary clarified that the Strangites had come to embrace plural marriage in the present as well. The commentary defended the practice with rhetoric not unlike that used by Brighamite advocates of plural marriage.[122] Monogamy had afflicted society with sin and sickness. It had resulted in "unrestrained indiscriminate intercourse of the sexes," which in turn "greatly aggravate the diseases and the miseries of life."[123] Monogamy deprived women of their choice in husbands. In turn, plural marriage "elevates woman, by making her man's companion, instead of a piece of furniture in the house as some, or a domestick drudge, as others are; by bringing marriage and suitable companionship to all."[124] The commentary argued for the divine approval of plural marriage based on the biblical record that "God has in many ways sanctioned Polygamy by bestowing great blessings on the parties to such marriages, and upon their posterity."[125] If the patriarch Abraham did not face God's disapproval for his multiple wives, then it stood to reason that there was no inherent

---

118. The Book of the Law 15:2.

119. The Book of the Law 36:5.

120. Roger Van Noord, *King of Beaver Island: The Life and Assassination of James J. Strang* (Urbana: University of Illinois Press, 1988) 108.

121. Christopher C. Smith, "The Inspired Fictionalization of the 1835 United Firm Revelations," *Claremont Journal of Mormon Studies* 1, no. 1 (April 2011):15–31.

122. See Christopher James Blythe, "The Book of Enoch 'Revised, Corrected, and the Missing Parts Restored,'" chapter 10 herein.

123. The Book of the Law, 310–311.

124. The Book of the Law, 327.

125. The Book of the Law, 320.

sinfulness in the practice. Finally, because the Book of the Law also instituted the concept of eternal marriage, it was argued, "If it be yielded that marriage concerns the everlasting life, quite as much as this mortal, then it follows that every one who is truly married to several successive wives, will, in the immortal life, be a Polygamist."[126]

Although Joseph Smith's 1843 revelation was widely known after its Brighamite publication in 1852, Strang's 1856 commentary did not so much as acknowledge Nauvoo polygamy. Still, a comment on the prohibition against "tak[ing] wives to vex those thou hast" seemed to implicitly address and oppose the so-called "law of Sarah," a rule that a man must only marry a plural wife after obtaining the permission of his first wife.[127] Strang's comment reads: "Every man having a wife, and seeking another, ought to consult the wishes of the former. But she cannot interpose an absolute veto." The text seems to suggest that a woman could oppose a husband's attempts to marry a second wife by presenting her objection to the judges. Nevertheless, "It is better not to press an objection which her husband is not satisfied with, unless it is a really strong one, founded in a legal obstacle, or a positive unfitness." On the other hand, "Any objection from a good wife should weigh greatly with her husband."[128]

The Book of the Law systematized and publicized Nauvoo esotericism, but it also scripturalized new innovations. We will consider two instances: the institution of a seventh-day (i.e., Saturday) sabbath and animal sacrifice. Joseph Smith had not enacted a seventh-day sabbath during his ministry, but such a change was in keeping with his project of restoring both New Testament and Old Testament practices.[129] In fact, some Latter Day Saints, such as Wilford Woodruff, had kept a seventh-day sabbath before their conversions and still held sympathy to the practice afterward.[130] Strangites waited until they settled on Beaver Island in 1850 to institute a seventh-day sabbath. Strangite periodicals explained that the "saints have been compelled, partly by law, but more by that public opinion or prejudice, which is above all

---

126. The Book of the Law, 321.

127. D&C 132.

128. The Book of the Law, 314.

129. Jan Shipps, *Mormonism: The Story of a New Religious Tradition* (Urbana: University of Illinois Press, 1985), 74–75.

130. Devery S. Anderson, ed., *School of the Prophets: 1867–1883* (Salt Lake City, UT: Signature Books, 2018), 167–168.

law, to observe" the sabbath on Sunday, having done so with God's blessing "while under the Gentile power." However, "The Saints at Beaver keep this law. They sanctify the SEVENTH DAY and KEEP IT HOLY, and there is none to make them afraid."[131] The Book of the Law provided additional instructions on how the sabbath should be kept—including rest for beasts and children—in both notes published alongside the decalogue and a chapter on feasts. The seventh-day sabbath continues to be a major component of Strangite identity and practice.

While the seventh-day sabbath may have originated with Strang without an earlier precedent, in Nauvoo, Joseph Smith had predicted the eventual restoration of animal sacrifice. On October 5, 1840, Smith taught, "All the ordinances and duties that ever have been required by the Priesthood, under the direction and commandment of the Almighty in any of the dispensations, shall all be had in the last dispensation ... those things which existed prior to Moses' day, namely, sacrifice, will be continued." In his oration, he drew on Malachi 3:3—a prophecy that the sons of Levi would "offer unto he the Lord an offering in righteousness," declaring that in the temple this revelation would be fulfilled.[132] However, only three months later, on January 19, 1841, Smith seemed to retract this literalist interpretation and in a revelation regarding the Nauvoo temple adopted a more metaphorical slant. The revelation did not state that sacrifices would be performed in the temple but instead referred to the "memorials for your sacrifices" that would be performed there.[133]

But the first edition of the Book of the Law instituted animal sacrifice as an integral part of the newly instituted King's Day feast celebrated each July 8 in memory of Strang's coronation. It commanded each man "to offer a clean beast, or a clean fowl, according to his household."[134] There would be a specially selected male priesthood to perform these rites. Women could serve as priests in the roles of "singers, and musicians, and assistants in the ceremonies, but they shall not kill sacrifices."[135] The 1856 second edition

131. "The True Sabbath," *Gospel Herald,* May 23, 1850. See also, *Northern Islander*, December 12, 1850.
132. Joseph Smith, Instruction on Priesthood, ca. October 5, 1840, *JSP*, D7:440.
133. D&C 124:39.
134. The Book of the Law 40:6.
135. The Book of the Law 32:7.

added a chapter on sacrifices that seemed to expand on passages concerning sacrifices in Deuteronomy 15, including a classification of offering types— "a sacrifice for sinofferings, and for tresspassofferings, and for memorials, and for peaceofferings, and for thanksofferings"—as well as directives on the quality of the offering: "firstling of male or female, without deformity or blemish" and "of the choice of thy fields."[136] The Book of the Law also allowed for other sacrifices—"whatsoever is used for bread for man."[137]

Strang's assassination in 1856, and the Saints' subsequent exodus from Beaver Island, put an end to much of these innovations. There was no longer a need for animal sacrifices or King's Days. There was no king nor other royal officers. And at least for a time, there was no dominion for the Kingdom. But other ideas and practices introduced or scripturalized in the Book of the Law—such as sealing, seventh-day sabbaths, and the particulars around various ceremonies—still seem to have kept the scripture relevant. Just as the Book of Mormon as a new work of scripture separated Latter Day Saints from other Christians, the Book of the Law of the Lord continued to distinguish the faithful Strangite from other restoration believers.

In 1977, three Strangites wrote an extensive overview of their faith, entitled *James J. Strang: Teachings of a Mormon Prophet*. They presented the Book of the Law as a text with the potential to bring about the millennium.

> [I]t will be only the successful establishment of divine law every where over it; which often in the past has been sought, but as often failed through the rebellion and corruptions of man. We are able to conceive how perfect peace, and universal happiness, can *ever* be arrived at only in obedience to a perfect law, or rule of action.... These rules that could help people to establish this perfect peace is contained in a little book entitled "The Book of the Law of the Lord." It is a sad fact, though, that this book that has so much to offer has been appreciated by only a few.[138]

136. The Book of the Law 8:1.
137. The Book of the Law 8:4.
138. William Shepard, Donna Falk, and Thelma Lewis, *James J. Strang: Teachings of a Mormon Prophet* (n.p.: Church of Jesus Christ of Latter Day Saints, 1977), 184.

QUESTIONS OF FORGERY

Each instance of Strangite scripture discussed here would be subject to accusations of forgery and fraud. Strang may have naively believed in August 1844 that the Florence, Wisconsin, conference would gratefully acknowledge his leadership when he appeared to showcase the letter of appointment. Yet by the time he organized the excavation of the Voree plates the following year, he was fully aware that skepticism was unavoidable. He hoped to preempt these objections. Not only had he enlisted independent witnesses, but his refusal to participate in the dig seemingly made it impossible for him to have orchestrated the find.

Yet, although the plates might have served to compel conversion for some, the audacity of providing material evidence of one's prophethood provoked suspicion and accusations of fraud among others. This had been the case with the Book of Mormon gold plates as well. As Richard Bushman has written, "The plates cast doubt on everything. They move the Book of Mormon into the realms of the fantastic. Without the plates story, the Book of Mormon would have seemed like a simple literary fiction dreamed up by a talented folk writer. . . . Add the angel and the gold plates, and the Book of Mormon became an insidious fraud."[139] Strang, in contrast to Smith, had kept the plates available to be examined by interested parties. There could be no question that there were actual plates. His willingness to display them publicly brought unparalleled attention. In 1854, he recalled that in the wake of their discovery, "several thousand persons came to examine the ground and the plates, and inquire after the occurrence."[140] Indeed, the plates drew both believers and skeptics to Voree for several years. When Stephen Post asked Strang to see them on Beaver Island in July 1850, Strang "handed them to me from his pocket."[141] Strang was used to the request, and this was enough to convince some that he was indeed a seer.

Those who sought to expose him also focused on the nature of the plates. Stories circulated of how Strang constructed the plates and then orchestrated

---

139. Richard Bushman, "The Gold Plates as Foundational Text," in *Foundational Texts of Mormonism: Examining Major Early Sources*, edited by Mark Ashurst-McGee, Robin Scott Jensen, and Sharalyn D. Howcroft (New York: Oxford University Press, 2018), 14–15.

140. James Strang, Letter to Mrs. Corey, September 26, 1854, in *Prophetic Controversy*.

141. Stephen Post, Journal, CHL.

the scene of their discovery. In the 1840s, there were already claims that he had forged them from a brass kettle.[142] The most complete accusation was published in 1888. I. F. Scott recounted that he had met a man from Burlington, Wisconsin, named C. P. Barnes, who claimed to have helped to fabricate the plates with Strang and two others in order "to sell lands which they owned where they intended to build Voree." Now that the others involved in the plot had died, Barnes was eager to reveal their scheme.

> He said they made their "plates" out of Ben Pierce's old kettle and engraved them with an old saw file and made the characters similar to those on the plates found near Kinderhook, Pike Co., Illinois, but mixed up the engravings so they could not be easily detected; that when completed they put acid on them to corrode them and give them an ancient appearance; and that to deposit them under the tree, where they were found, they took a large auger, used for rafting purposes, which Ben Pierce owned, put a fork handle on the auger and with it bored a long, slanting hold under a tree on "The Hill of Promise," as they called it, laying the earth in a trail on a cloth as taken out, then put the "plates" in, tamping in all the earth again, leaving no trace of their work visible.[143]

The brass plates that became the Book of the Law of the Lord were likewise legitimated with witnesses, although the details of their discovery were not publicized. In 1888, former Strangite Chauncy Loomis claimed that Samuel Graham, one of the witnesses, had "declared that he and Strang made those plates that Strang claimed to translate the Book of The Law from." He explained how he and Strang had "prepared the plates and coated them with beeswax and then formed the letters and cut them with a pen knife."[144] Loomis also claimed that Samuel Bacon, another witness of the plates, had while "repairing Strang's house ... found hid behind the ceiling the fragments of those plates" and left the church and community as a result.[145]

---

142. Peter Hess, Letter to James Strang, November 30, 1848, *Gospel Herald*, December 28, 1848.

143. I. F. Scott, "James J. Strang in Voree," *Saints' Herald*, December 29, 1888.

144. Chauncy Loomis, "Experience on Beaver Island with James J. Strang," *Saints' Herald*, November 10, 1888.

145. Ibid.

CONCLUSION

Strangite scripture continued the Latter Day Saint scriptural tradition closer than any other nineteenth-century examples. At the same time, it continued the debate over authenticity and fraud that has plagued the tradition's introduction of new scripture. While most would come to dismiss Strang's writings as an effort to manipulate an uncertain church following Smith's death, for several dozen living Strangites (and thousands in the 1840s and 1850s) these works are fully embraced as part of the Latter Day Saint canon.

10

The Book of Enoch "Revised, Corrected, and the Missing Parts Restored"

Christopher James Blythe

Joseph Smith's genius was not in his ideas alone but also in the way he posed those ideas. Instead of presenting "creedal statement and dogmatic restatement," he wrote scripture set in a biblical past. As Kathleen Flake has noted, these new narratives "challenge[d] the Christian tradition in ways not possible through discursive debate or speculative theology."[1] With Smith's death, new scriptures and revelations again emerged—this time in response to competing visions of the Latter Day Saint tradition. Whether it was James Strang's Book of the Law of the Lord or James Brewster's Books of Esdras, these new writings rivaled competing interpretations of the faith, legitimating the authority of one prophet-leader over another and reinforcing a movement's claims to a scriptural heritage. This chapter examines the Book of Enoch, "Revised, corrected, and the missing parts restored by Divine inspiration," a Latter-day Saint revision of the nineteenth-century English translation of the Book of Enoch, otherwise known as 1 Enoch or the Ethiopic Enoch. Its modern reviser, Charles B. Thompson, was an early Latter-day Saint convert known for having written the first full-length treatise on the Book of Mormon, entitled *Evidences in Proof of the Book of Mormon* (1841).

Thompson's Enoch was a rare example of correction literature, which I have defined as the product of "a fusion of historical and revealed translation methods."[2] It was to Richard Laurence's translation of the Book of Enoch

---

1. Kathleen Flake, "Translating Time: The Nature and Function of Joseph Smith's Narrative Canon," *Journal of Religion* 87, no. 4 (October 2007):497, 500.

2. See Blythe, "Opening the Canon: A New Scriptural Tradition," chapter 1 herein.

what Joseph Smith's new translation of the Bible was to the King James Version. And, it was a thoroughly Mormon scripture, capturing both in content and concept key elements of the Latter Day Saint scriptural tradition. Published in 1852–1853, Thompson's Enoch responded to the most controversial elements of mid-century Mormon theology: plural marriage and the plurality of gods. The Church of Jesus Christ of Latter-day Saints headquartered in Utah defended these doctrines, pointing to their introduction by Smith during the Nauvoo period and documenting the scriptural precedence for plural marriage in the lives of the patriarchs recounted in Genesis. Rather than simply debate the apostles' exegesis, Charles B. Thompson returned to the ancient patriarchs, specifically the revered figure of Enoch, to establish monogamy and monotheism as ideals of the ancient faith. While an obscure work, Thompson's Enoch demonstrated the key position of scriptural narrative as a strategy of contest between rival Mormon bodies.

THE BOOK OF ENOCH AND
THE LATTER DAY SAINT TRADITION

Modern readers of the Bible have often been curious about otherwise unknown books mentioned in the Old and New Testaments. Parley P. Pratt, an early Latter-day Saint apostle, counted "something like fourteen books actually quoted by the prophets, which are not found in our English Bible."[3] Among these "lost books" was a prophecy attributed to Enoch, the patriarch who, according to Genesis, "walked with God and . . . was not; for God took him."[4] This ancient text was explicitly quoted in the New Testament Epistle of Jude.[5] In the Middle Ages, references to Enoch appeared in a variety of texts, including forgeries designed to appear as the source for Jude's quotation.[6] While most of the Bible's "lost books" have not been discovered in the modern world, the Book of Enoch was located in 1773 by James Bruce, a Scottish explorer, who journeyed through Abyssinia (modern-day Ethiopia) to locate

---

3. Parley P. Pratt, *A Voice of Warning* (New York, 1837), 127.
4. Genesis 5:24.
5. Jude 1:14–15.
6. Annette Yoshiko Reed, *Fallen Angels and the History of Judaism and Christianity* (New York: Cambridge University Press, 2005), 2–3; Colby Townsend, "Revisiting Joseph Smith and the Availability of the Book of Enoch," *Dialogue: A Journal of Mormon Thought* 53, no. 3 (Fall 2020):41–72.

the source of the Nile River.[7] In Abyssinia, Bruce became familiar with the Abyssinian Christian larger canon of scripture, which included the Book of Enoch.[8]

For nearly fifty years, Bruce's discovery was housed at the Bodleian Library at Oxford University, until 1821, when professor of Hebrew Richard Laurence translated the Ge'ez script into English.[9] His translation was published in four editions over the next several decades.[10] Despite wide interest in Enoch, no Christian denominations seem to have considered recommending it as an inspired work. This is not surprising—the canon was closed after all. There was acceptance—or perhaps an open-minded curiosity—among individual believers and some literati, but commentaries on Enoch warned readers not to confuse it with legitimate scripture.[11] In contrast, at various moments, Mormon leaders encouraged a serious look at Enoch. Naturally, they were sympathetic to the idea that an authentic book of scripture might be lost and later rediscovered. I will return to the reception of the Book of Enoch by Latter-day Saints, but first it is important to consider that by the time Latter Day Saints knew of Laurence's translation, Smith had already revealed an Enoch text, soon published as "Extract from the Prophecy of Enoch," and had predicted the entirety of Enoch's writings would again be revealed.[12]

Smith's Enoch text was part of the new translation project that he began in the summer of 1830. He had expanded the traditional five verses on Enoch

7. James Bruce, *Travels to Discover the Source of the Nile, In the Years 1768, 1769, 1770, 1771, 1772, and 1773*, 2nd ed. (Edinburgh, 1804), 2:421–426.

8. As Leslie Baynes has noted, while "traditionally the Ethiopian Orthodox Church has numbered eighty-one books in its biblical canon … the primary readers of 1 Enoch and Jubilees traditionally have been the scholarly elite, as is true of their readers today." Leslie Baynes, "*Enoch* and *Jubilees* in the Canon of the Ethiopian Orthodox Church," in *A Teacher for All Generations: Essays in Honor of James C. VanderKam*, edited by Eric F. Mason, Kelley Coblentz Bautch, Angela Kim Harkins, and Daniel A. Machiela (Boston: Brill, 2012), 2:799.

9. For a concise history and commentary of the Book of Enoch, see Margaret Barker, *The Lost Prophet: The Book of Enoch and Its Influence on Christianity* (Sheffield, UK: Sheffield Phoenix Press, 2005).

10. *The Book of Enoch, the Prophet: An Apocryphal Production, Supposed for Ages to Have Been Lost…*, trans. Richard Laurence (Oxford: J. H. Parker, 1821, 1833, 1838, 1883).

11. "The Book of Enoch," *London Times*, April 9, 1841; "Theological Controversies, No. 17," *Universalist Watchman*, April 25, 1846.

12. "Extract from the Prophecy of Enoch," *The Evening and Morning Star*, August 1832; Doctrine and Covenants [1835] 3:29.

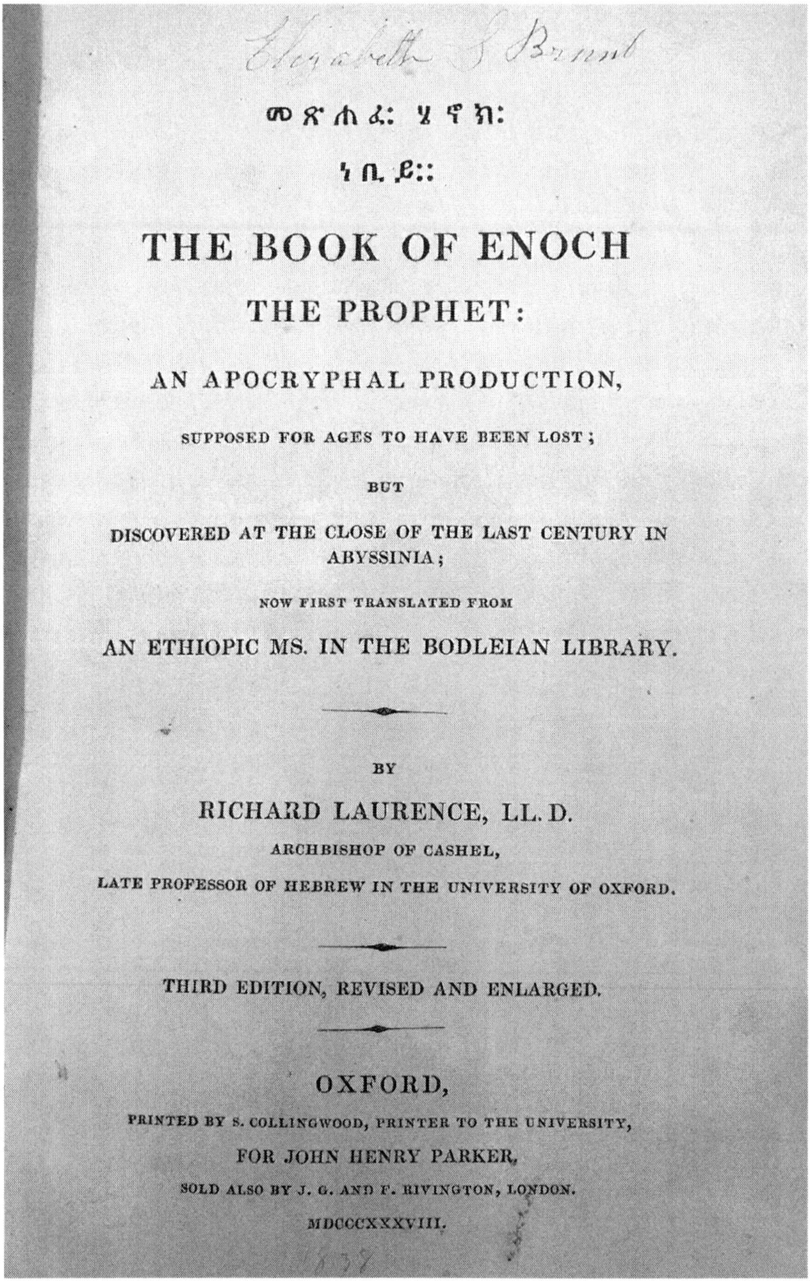

መጽሐፈ: ሄኖክ:

ነቢ ይ::

THE BOOK OF ENOCH

THE PROPHET:

AN APOCRYPHAL PRODUCTION,

SUPPOSED FOR AGES TO HAVE BEEN LOST;

BUT

DISCOVERED AT THE CLOSE OF THE LAST CENTURY IN
ABYSSINIA;

NOW FIRST TRANSLATED FROM

AN ETHIOPIC MS. IN THE BODLEIAN LIBRARY.

———◆———

BY

RICHARD LAURENCE, LL. D.

ARCHBISHOP OF CASHEL,

LATE PROFESSOR OF HEBREW IN THE UNIVERSITY OF OXFORD.

———◆———

THIRD EDITION, REVISED AND ENLARGED.

———◆———

OXFORD,

PRINTED BY S. COLLINGWOOD, PRINTER TO THE UNIVERSITY,

FOR JOHN HENRY PARKER,

SOLD ALSO BY J. G. AND F. RIVINGTON, LONDON.

MDCCCXXXVIII.

FIGURE 10.1. Title page, Laurence's translation of The Book of Enoch (1838). Church History Library, the Church of Jesus Christ of Latter-day Saints. Photograph courtesy of Jay Burton (2021).

in Genesis 5 into 110 verses.[13] The passage included details concerning Enoch's prophetic call, a vision foreseeing the coming of the flood, an account of his ministry, and an explanation of the enigmatic culmination of his life. In a major departure from other Enoch material, Enoch was not taken to heaven alone but had established a holy city, Zion, which God removed from the earth because of its righteousness and to preserve it from the impending destruction of the flood. The newly restored prophecies described the millennium when the City of Enoch would return to meet a last-days Zion established by the Saints. According to Philip Barlow, in this expanded Enoch narrative, "The sacred past merged with the Mormon present and future."[14] Terryl Givens has called it "a comprehensive blueprint for the church and its people."[15] This is to say that in the story of the City of Enoch, the Saints had a myth to drive their utopian endeavors, thereafter referred to as the Order of Enoch.

Scholars have debated whether Smith was familiar with the 1821 edition of the *Book of Enoch* and whether he used it as a source text for his own Enoch material.[16] To be sure, Charles Thompson was not the first Mormon to discover Laurence's translation. The earliest definite reference to the "lost book" appeared in the *Millennial Star*, the church's newspaper in Great Britain, in July 1840.[17] Apostle Parley P. Pratt was ecstatic when he discovered the Book of Enoch. He believed its prophecies addressed the experience of contemporary Latter-day Saints. Enoch had predicted

> the coming forth of the Book of Mormon, and the mission of our Elders, which they are now performing among the nations, together with the late persecution which has befallen our people in America, with the conduct of the rulers of that Republic, in refusing to give

13. Richard Lyman Bushman, *Joseph Smith: Rough Stone Rolling* (New York: Knopf, 2005), 138.

14. Philip Barlow, *Mormons and the Bible: The Place of the Latter-day Saints in American Religion* (New York: Oxford University Press, 1991), 49.

15. Terryl Givens, with Brian M. Hauglid, *The Pearl of Greatest Price: Mormonism's Most Controversial Scripture* (New York: Oxford University Press, 2019), 42.

16. See D. Michael Quinn, *Early Mormonism and the Magic World View*, rev. ed. (Salt Lake City: Signature Books, 1998), 190–192; Hugh Nibley, *Enoch the Prophet* (Salt Lake City, UT: Deseret Book, 1986), 105–106; Richard Bushman, *Joseph Smith: Rough Stone Rolling*, 138; Colby Townsend, "Revisiting Joseph Smith and the Availability of the Book of Enoch," *Dialogue: A Journal of Mormon Thought* 53, no. 3 (Fall 2020):41–71.

17. Parley P. Pratt, "The Apocryphal Book of Enoch," *Millennial Star*, July 1840.

us redress; yes, in fact, it predicts the final result of that matter, and the complete triumph of the saints.[18]

Following an enthusiastic introduction, he reproduced Book of Enoch chapters 103 through 105 "without further comment, [leaving] our readers to form their own judgment in regard to this remarkable book."[19] In 1841, Charles B. Thompson's *Evidences in Proof of the Book of Mormon* reprinted this material with additional comments as another evidence of the Book of Mormon.[20]

Over the next several decades, Saints across denominational boundaries also discovered the Book of Enoch. The journal of Warren Post, an early Strangite, included notes from his reading of Laurence's translation. He recorded the names of four archangels and their associated responsibilities.[21] In the late 1860s, the RLDS *Saints' Herald* serialized Laurence's translation. In the mid-1900s, Mormon Fundamentalists discovered the text. Numerous authors published excerpts with particular emphasis on Enoch's "prophecy of the ten weeks," an apocalyptic timeline.[22] Later in the century, LDS scholars from Brigham Young University, including Hugh Nibley, sought to demonstrate the ancient nature of Joseph Smith's narratives of Enoch by appealing to similarities in ancient Enoch literature.[23]

CHARLES B. THOMPSON AND JEHOVAH'S PRESBYTERY OF ZION

Like many who united with the fledgling church, Thompson was engrossed in newly restored scripture and the promise of more to come. In 1841, he published the first book-length defense of the Book of Mormon, *Evidences in Proof of the Book of Mormon*.[24] In 1843, in a meeting held at Ramus, Illinois, he even publicly argued with Joseph Smith over his interpretation of passages

---

18. Pratt, "The Apocryphal Book of Enoch."
19. Ibid.
20. Charles B. Thompson, *Evidences in Proof of the Book of Mormon* (1841), 125–132.
21. Warren Post, Warren Post Diaries, June 20, 1847, CHL.
22. See for example, Francis M. Darter, *Michael Adam God* (Salt Lake City, UT: self-pub., 1949); and Ross Wesley LeBaron, *Proclamation* ... (Salt Lake City, UT: self-pub., 1964.)
23. Nibley, *Enoch the Prophet*.
24. Thompson, *Evidences* ...

in the Book of Revelation.[25] Thompson's passion for scripture likely played a role in his attraction to James Strang. In 1846, he wrote a poem that extolled the new prophet for his revelatory gifts as demonstrated by the discovery and translation of the Voree plates.[26]

Thompson considered the Church of Jesus Christ of Latter Day Saints based in Voree, Wisconsin, the rightful continuation of the church founded by Joseph Smith. But he left Strang's movement in 1847 and would soon conclude that God had already rejected the church when the Saints failed to complete the temple in Nauvoo by a divine deadline.[27] According to Smith's January 1841 revelation, the Saints were commanded to construct the temple and were cautioned that, following a "sufficient time" to complete the work, if they delayed, they would "be rejected as a church."[28] If there was no church, Thompson reasoned, there was no need for a president of the church, no matter how closely he had once believed Strang's leadership paralleled Smith's.[29]

In January 1848, Thompson dictated his first revelation intended for public attention. According to his account, he heard a voice, which identified itself as Baneemy, the true successor of Joseph Smith.[30] Thompson, not unlike a Spiritualist medium of the time, recorded the utterances of this unseen messenger who was in turn the conduit of divine revelation. Thompson presented himself as a scribe analogous to the role of Oliver Cowdery, who recorded much of Smith's recital of the Book of Mormon translation. The prophet-acting-as-medium organized his movement the same year. It was initially referred to as Jehovah's Presbytery of Zion.[31] Previous to his revision of the Book of Enoch, Thompson produced several revelations through Baneemy's voice, in addition to what he termed "true translations" of biblical excerpts. He quickly became one of the most prolific

25. History, 1838–1856, vol. D-1 [August 1, 1842–July 1, 1843], p. 1523.

26. *Voree Herald,* August 1846.

27. See Bill Shepard, "The Concept of a 'Rejected Gospel' in Mormon History, Part 1," *Journal of Mormon History* 34, no. 2 (Spring 2008):130–181; "The Concept of a 'Rejected Gospel' in Mormon History, Part 2," *Journal of Mormon History* 34, no. 3 (Summer 2008):142–186.

28. D&C [LDS Edition] 124:32–33.

29. Charles B. Thompson to James J. Strang, April 29, 1848 in *Zion's Harbinger and Baneemy's Organ,* March 1852.

30. *Zion's Harbinger and Baneemy's Organ,* August 1852.

31. For a history of Thompson's community, see Junia Braby, "Charles B. Thompson: Harbinger of Zion or Master of Humbuggery?" *John Whitmer Historical Association Journal* 23 (2003):149–163.

Mormon revelators. Importantly, he credited the otherworldly Baneemy for revising the Book of Enoch.

The Book of Enoch "Revised, corrected, and the missing parts restored" appeared in *Zion's Harbinger and Baneemy's Organ*, the Presbytery's official periodical in fourteen installments from October 1852 to December 1853. Because this newspaper included the only known references to Thompson's Enoch, we do not know whether the new scripture ever obtained substantial use among the Presbytery's adherents. However, we can be assured that this was the text's intended purpose. It was presented as authentic as any other book of scripture. On multiple occasions, Thompson and other theologians cited the text of Enoch in published treatises.

THE MORMONIZATION OF AN ANCIENT SCRIPTURE

Through Thompson's revisions, the Book of Enoch took on a number of features associated with the Latter Day Saint scriptural tradition. First, it was a rare instance of correction literature. While we know that ancient Christians altered texts for theological reasons, Smith had presented this form of textual editing as the work of a prophet. Despite the importance ascribed to the "new translation" of the Bible, Smith did not revise other ancient texts. On March 9, 1833, Smith prayed whether he should translate the Apocrypha, which, following the Protestant tradition, was published in a third intertestamental section in his Bible. His petition resulted in a revelation that would establish Latter Day Saint thought on apocryphal works thereafter.

> There are many things contained therein that are true, and it is mostly translated correct: there are many things contained therein that are not true, which are the interpolations by the hands of men. . . . Therefore, whoso readeth it let him understand, for the Spirit manifesteth truth; and whoso is enlightened by the Spirit shall obtain benefit therefrom.[32]

This revelation was a major force in the future development of Mormon scripture. Although it addressed only the fourteen apocryphal books

32. D&C (1835), Section 92; also D&C (LDS), Section 91; D&C (CofC) Section 88.

published in the King James Bible, Latter Day Saints of various denominations would go on to draw from its message when considering whether to include new historical records to the canon or whether to prophetically correct a historical translation. Thus, with very few exceptions, Latter Day Saint denominations have not added revisions of ancient scripture to their canons. Instead, leaders typically echo the council of Smith's revelation, assuring individuals that they might gain personal benefit from such records in a private setting if they are truly "enlightened by the spirit." Usually, this counsel is coupled with encouragement to focus one's study within the confines of the trusted canon.

Correction literature was an indictment of the initial uncorrected translation. Joseph Smith's history proposed three possibilities for who was to blame for the corruption of biblical texts, namely, "ignorant translators, careless transcribers, or designing and corrupt priests."[33] Thompson, on the other hand, posited only one scenario for how the Book of Enoch had been corrupted. Rather than place the blame ambiguously on apostate or well-meaning scribes in the distant past, he indicted the translator, Richard Laurence, himself. "The English translator has labored hard to cover up the most important, and consequently to this generation the most objectionable truths contained in it." Thompson assumed a sincere motive for Laurence's subterfuge, however, stating, that "undoubtedly ... [h]e was conscientious in doing so, thinking thereby to bring the book in better repute among the Christians of the present day."[34]

Thompson's contribution to the text varied. In some installments, an initial, albeit brief, excerpt from the Book of Enoch began a several-page treatise with little semblance to the original. For instance, the first installment of Thompson's Enoch consisted of a slightly corrected version of the first two chapters of Laurence's translation, before leading into a five-page Creation and Garden of Eden narrative.[35] At other times, an installment was almost entirely a reproduction of Laurence's translation. This is the case with the sixth installment, which included Book of Enoch chapters 96 through 103 with only minor emendations.[36] Finally, there were occasions in which short

---

33. History, 1838–1856, vol. E-1 [July 1, 1843–April 30, 1844], 1755, CHL.
34. *Zion's Harbinger and Baneemy's Organ*, October 1852.
35. Ibid.
36. *Zion's Harbinger and Baneemy's Organ*, March 1853.

phrases from the Book of Enoch were dispersed through passages with only a minor relationship to their original placement.

Thompson also acted in the role of prophet-compiler, restoring "missing parts" of the Book of Enoch by adding portions that had been extracted from other texts. This had been modeled in the Book of Mormon. Scholar Philip Barlow identified "a forthright and dramatic instance of the 'documentary hypothesis' at work: the Book of Mormon portrayed the fifth-century prophet-historian Mormon freely abridging, editing, and appropriating the records of many earlier writers in his account of the rise and fall of the ancient Nephite civilization."[37] Thompson's Enoch was put together by this same method of inspired editorial work. It was a composite text consisting of the Book of Enoch, revelations of Joseph Smith, the published excerpts of the Joseph Smith Translation (i.e., the Book of Moses and the Prophecies of Enoch), and the Book of Jasher. The Book of Jasher, a midrashic volume documenting the history of the patriarchs, represented a large portion of the text.[38]

Thompson altered the compiled revelations of Joseph Smith and the Book of Jasher, as he did Laurence's translation of the Book of Enoch. This might provide a clue to the text's construction, suggesting that he first compiled his sources together and then treated each of his pieces as ancient parts of "the original book written by Enoch."[39] Like other examples of revealed translations in early Mormonism, the text of Enoch was written from the perspective of Enoch himself. This motif of the first-person prophet is present, though not as pronounced, in the Bible. Smith sought to remedy this. For example, tradition holds that Moses wrote the first five books of the Old Testament; yet the text does not make this claim, featuring Moses's own death. The first restoration Joseph Smith made to the biblical canon was a prologue to ensure that the reader understood that Moses was, in fact, the book's true author. The creation narrative that followed in the first three chapters of Genesis was now presented as Moses's own personal record of a cosmic vision.[40]

---

37. Barlow, *Mormons and the Bible*, 110.

38. The *Book of Jasher* was embraced with great interest by segments of both the LDS and RLDS Church. For example, *Jasher* was republished in Utah by George Q. Cannon & Sons in 1883. The RLDS Church distributed copies of the 1840 publication, as advertised in the *Saints Herald*.

39. *Zion's Harbinger and Baneemy's Organ*, October 1852.

40. David Bokovoy, "'The Book Which Thou Shalt Write': The Book of Moses as Prophetic Midrash," in *The Expanded Canon: Perspectives on Mormonism and Sacred Texts*, edited by Blair G.

The Book of Enoch claimed to be a record of the ancient patriarch himself but does not employ the first-person when narrating Enoch's story. Likewise, the Book of Jasher and the revelations of Joseph Smith did not use the first-person for Enoch. Thus, one way that Thompson united these texts was by inserting the first-person voice of Enoch throughout. Like the Book of Mormon's opening, "I, Nephi, having been born of goodly parents," or the Book of Abraham's, "I, Abraham, saw that it was needful for me to obtain another place of residence," Thompson altered the Book of Enoch from its initial phrase, "The word of the blessing of Enoch," to "I, Enoch, the son of Jared ... having been instructed in the mysteries of those things that were before the foundation of the world."[41]

Another detail important to Mormon scripture is setting. Latter Day Saint scripture, based on Joseph Smith's precedents, took place in familiar locations. Smith not only believed the Book of Mormon occurred in the Americas, he had been to the hill where the ancient Nephite prophet Moroni deposited the records. He would later speak of his trek as part of Zion's Camp as a journey through the "plains of the Nephites."[42] James Strang likewise translated a short record from a former inhabitant of Wisconsin who decried the slaughter of his people.[43] Thompson believed the Book of Enoch had also occurred in the Americas. This may have been problematic since the Book of Enoch was an Old World text. However, Joseph Smith had already identified modern-day Missouri as the location where Adam and Eve lived and died. Because he had specifically revealed the location of Adam-ondi-Ahman in northern Missouri, and Enoch had attended this council, it was predetermined that his record would be set in America. A fascinating news item published in *Zion's Harbinger and Baneemy's Organ* following the thirteenth installment of Thompson's Enoch referred to the physical remains of Leviathan and Behemoth, two monsters from the Hebrew scriptures that also appeared in the Ethiopic Enoch: "A part of the jaw bone of one of those monsters Enoch speaks of, has been found near Peru, Illinois. The teeth measured

---

Van Dyke, Brian D. Birch, and Boyd J. Petersen (Salt Lake City, UT: Greg Kofford Books, 2018), 122–123.

    41. *Zion's Harbinger and Baneemy's Organ*, October 1852.

    42. Joseph Smith, Letter to Emma Smith, June 4, 1834, *JSP*, D4:57.

    43. See Christine Elyse Blythe and Christopher James Blythe, "Strangite Scripture," chapter 9 herein.

across three and five inches."[44] Thus, Thompson even pointed to archaeological discoveries to reinforce the literal history and setting of Enoch.

Beyond these traits of style and genre, Thompson's Enoch was, also, Mormon in its content. This was after all the design of correction literature: to bridge the gap between ancient scripture and modern traditions. It was crafted to address the most pressing theological issues facing Latter Day Saints in the mid-nineteenth century. Specifically, the narrative of Enoch would differentiate Thompson's movement from the heretical teachings he believed were being propagated by the largest segment of Latter Day Saints based in the Rocky Mountains.[45] Thompson was particularly disturbed by plural marriage and multiple deities. In an 1853 letter addressed to the followers of Brigham Young, he described their religion "Mormonism" as "nothing more nor less than a new edition of heathen mythology, corrected and revised, and cloaked under the guise of revelation." Continuing, he wrote,

> Polygamy—upon which rests their salvation, and exaltation in the eternal worlds, is nothing more than a heathen and uncivilized custom.... The doctrine of plurality of Gods, is likewise a heathen and idolatrous doctrine of Brahmins, Chinese, Hindoos, and all heathen nations.[46]

Thompson's Enoch was a narrative condemnation of this new strain of revised Heathenism.

THOMPSON'S ENOCH'S CREATION NARRATIVE AS A CRITIQUE OF THE PLURALITY OF GODS

On multiple occasions, Joseph Smith revised the story of creation. He did so as part of the new translation of the first chapters of Genesis, the May 6,

---

44. *Zion's Harbinger and Baneemy's Organ*, November 1853.

45. Other works considering Thompson's theology include Newell G. Bringhurst, "Forgotten Mormon Perspectives: Slavery, Race, and the Black Man as Issues among Non-Utah Latter-day Saints, 1844–1873," *Michigan History* 61 (Winter 1977):352–370; Newell G. Bringhurst, "Charles B. Thompson and the Issues of Slavery and Race," *Journal of Mormon History* 8 (1981):37–47; and George Bartholomew Arbaugh, *Revelation in Mormonism: Its Character and Changing Forms* (Chicago: University of Chicago Press, 1932):159–171.

46. George Hickenlooper, "To the Council of the St. Louis Conference of the Church of Jesus Christ of Latter Day Saints, February 18, 1853." *Zion's Harbinger and Baneemy's Organ*, March 1853.

1833, revelation (D&C 93 LDS), the new translation of the first chapter of the Gospel of John, the Book of Abraham, the King Follett Discourse, and the Nauvoo Endowment drama. Each time Joseph Smith re-presented the story of the creation, he introduced new understandings of man's relationship with deity. If his goal was a radical reformulation of the faith, what better place to begin than humanity's origins—helping the Saints to reconceive the universe and their place in it. As Smith stated when he publicly introduced the idea of deification, "If we start right, it is easy to go right all the time; but if we start wrong, it is a hard matter to get right."[47]

Joseph Smith's understanding of creation was in stark contrast to creation ex nihilo, a central tenant of mainstream Christianity. His May 6, 1833, revelation stated that "the elements are eternal."[48] It was through this preexisting matter that creation was organized. In turn, creation, rather than being carried out by one God, or a God and his son, was performed by a quorum of gods subservient to a supreme deity. In 1842, the Book of Abraham synthesized concepts in Smith's thought—which had been brewing for the past decade—into a coherent, Genesis-like, seven-day creation account. Abraham witnessed the events of creation beginning with a vision of the "intelligences that were organized before the world was."[49] Among them were "many of the noble and great ones" who were destined to be significant rulers on the earth. "One like unto God"—usually interpreted as Jesus Christ[50]—appeared as a separate being from God the Father. The future Savior declared, "We will go down, for there is space there, and we will take of these materials, and we will make an earth whereon these [spirits] may dwell."[51] Following the traditional division between the righteous and wicked angels, these noble and great ones led by Jesus begin the creation. This collective body is, thereafter, referred to as "the gods."

The Book of Abraham revolutionized the Saints' cosmology. In particular, Smith was affected by the book's claim of an eternal hierarchy of intelligences. According to the Book of Abraham, "These two facts do exist, that there are

---

47. "Conference Minutes," *Times and Seasons*, August 15, 1844.

48. D&C (LDS) 93:33.

49. Abraham 3:22.

50. An alternative interpretation suggests that this is a reference to Archangel Michael, whose name in Hebrew means one like unto God.

51. Abraham 3:24.

two spirits, one being more intelligent than the other; [then] there shall be another more intelligent than they."[52] From this passage, Smith concluded that even God himself must have a father through an endless lineage of deities.[53] In his well-known King Follett Discourse, he explained "how God came to be God and what sort of a being he is." God, according to Smith, had once been "a man like one of us and that God himself, the father of us all, once dwelled on an earth." Continuing, he explained the implications to his audience.

> You have got to learn how to be Gods yourselves; to be kings and priests to God, the same as all Gods have done; by going from a small degree to another, from grace to grace, from exaltation to exaltation, until you are able to sit in glory as doth those who sit enthroned in everlasting power.[54]

Smith then revealed a similarly controversial insight, although it had been contained in the revelations since 1833, that there was a part of mankind—his intelligence—that was eternal and uncreated.[55]

> We say that God himself is a self existing God; who told you so? it is correct enough but how did it get into your heads? Who told you that man did not exist in like manner upon the same principles? ... The mind of man is as immortal as God himself.[56]

There was no first god and no absolute beginning. Both matter and spirit were self-existent, not the creation of a supreme deity.

This radical departure from orthodox Christian teachings on the nature of God met with controversy, even among Latter Day Saints. Dissenters, such as the founders of the "Reformed Mormon Church," William Law and Robert Foster, saw this apparent polytheism as heretical. A statement in the Reformed Church's newspaper, the *Nauvoo Expositor*, declared the plurality of gods

52. Abraham 3:19.
53. Joseph Smith, *Teachings of the Prophet Joseph Smith*, 373; Joseph Smith, Discourse, June 16, 1844-A, as Reported by Thomas Bullock, josephsmithpapers.org.
54. "Conference Minutes," *Times and Seasons*, August 15, 1844.
55. D&C 93:29.
56. "Conference Minutes," *Times and Seasons*, August 15, 1844.

one of the most direful [doctrines] in its effects that has characterized the world for many centuries. We know not what to call it other
than blasphemy, for it is most unquestionably, speaking of God in an
impious and irreverent manner.[57]

Even those Saints who remained dedicated to the LDS Church's leadership
under Brigham Young questioned these theological innovations. Smith's
rejection of the traditional "first cause" was particularly unsatisfying to the
apostle and theologian Orson Pratt. In contrast, Pratt held that the personal
deity of this world had an origin as Smith suggested but that this being
is subservient to a higher self-existent divinity. Pratt called this first deity
the "Great God," who governed all things and was the "sum of intelligent
matter."[58] Because these ideas contradicted Smith's theology, Pratt's writings
eventually attracted the disapproval of Brighamite church leaders.[59]

    Charles Thompson shared Pratt's and Law's concerns with deification.
The Book of Enoch echoed the theology laid out in Pratt's 1851 pamphlet,
The Great First Cause, or the Self-Moving Forces of the Universe. As with Pratt,
the question was whether there was an endless progression of deities or a
supreme deity of the first cause. Siding with the latter, Thompson's Enoch
named this first intelligence Iame.[60] According to the text,

> In the beginning, before any of the creations had taken place, Iame,
> (which signified the embodiment of all intelligence,) by his wisdom
> constructed Iada, (which signifies the place of light,) out of Zebo,
> (which signified unorganized matter,) and clothed himself there-
> with. In Iada were constructed many wombs; and Iame quickened
> Iada, so that Iada became a living being, and principle of power with
> Iame; and Iame impregnated Iada with the seed of intelligence. Iada,
> therefore brought forth from her variously constructed wombs many

57. *Nauvoo Expositor*, June 7, 1844.

58. Jordan T. Watkins, "The Great God, the Divine Mind, and the Ideal Absolute: Orson Pratt's
Intelligent-Matter Theory, and the Gods of Emerson and James," Claremont Journal of Mormon
Studies 1, no. 1 (April 2011):33–52.

59. Breck England, *The Life and Thought of Orson Pratt* (Salt Lake City: University of Utah
Press, 1985), 228.

60. Iame may be borrowed from the name "I Am" in Exodus 3:14.

Intelligences of various forms, clothed with semile (which signifies very refined matter.)[61]

Like Pratt's Great God, Iame was the equivalent of all intelligence, and an entity present in all things. This consciousness organized "Iada, the place of light," as well as his own material body through self-existent matter and then, in turn, "quickened" Iada as a female divinity, who would aid in the organization of the universe. The cosmic union of Iame and Iada brought forth individual intelligences or spirits. Then, Iame,

> finding these Spirits imperfect as to the quantity of intelligence they possessed, by his wisdom concerted a plan to increase their intelligences and thereby make them perfect; and having completed the plan, he called them together to consult them in reference to their willingness to enter into his plan; and when he had made known his plan to them they were glad, and he organized them that they might accomplish his will and be made perfect.[62]

Thompson's Enoch followed the creation accounts of the Book of Abraham and the King Follett Discourse. As in Abraham, deity discovered that the spirits varied in intelligence; as in the King Follett Discourse, "God himself finds himself in the midst of spirits and glory, because he was greater, and because he saw proper to institute laws, whereby the rest could have a privilege to advance like himself."[63] The next step for Iame was to organize a celestial hierarchy—another element present in Abraham.

> And he chose seven Chief Ones and placed them over the rest of the Spirits, and he Ordained them, and he Ordained three of these, Chiefs over the seven and he Ordained one of the three, who was elected over all, to be over the three, and he was called the Elect One; and one of his fellows was anointed to represent him in the flesh, and he was called the Anointed, his other fellow was to remain concealed under the appellation of the Father, until the consummation of righteousness;

61. *Zion's Harbinger and Baneemy's Organ*, October 1852.
62. Ibid.
63. "Conference Minutes," *Times and Seasons*, August 15, 1844.

therefore he was called the Concealed One. And Iame chose twenty-four of the most noble remaining Spirits, and he Ordained them to minister for the seven; (and he called them Arch-Angels;) and he chose, Ordained and Organized four grand Quorums of Angels of different grades of authority; and their number is written down in the Heavens, and their names are all there recorded. And when Iame had completed their Organization, they rose up with one accord and called Him the Lord of Spirits; and prostrating themselves before him, they worshipped him, calling Him God Almighty. And Iame blessed those he had Ordained, calling them the Sons of God, then the Morning Stars sang together, and all the Sons of God shouted for joy.[64]

This angelic organization paralleled John the Revelator's vision of seven "spirits of God" and twenty-four elders surrounding the throne of deity. Thompson's seven spirits, identified by Enoch as archangels, are the heads of the twenty-four elders. Specifically, three of the seven took on roles equivalent to the Christian godhead: the Father, referred to as the *Elect One* in Thompson's Enoch and identified as Adam or the Archangel Michael; the Son, referred to as the *Anointed One* and identified as Jesus Christ; and the Holy Spirit, referred to as the *Concealed One* and identified as Baneemy, the invisible being who communicated with Thompson.

Throughout the text, Iame is referred to as the Lord of Spirits or God Almighty. He alone is God, serving above the "sons of God," including the three equivalents of the Christian godhead. Although in this model Adam or Michael preside over Jesus, this was not the Adam-God doctrine proposed by Brigham Young.[65] It was, however, a clear example of the elevation of Adam in Latter Day Saint thought.[66]

Unlike the Book of Abraham, which re-couched the Genesis creation to speak of Gods (plural) forging the world on each respective day, Thompson's Enoch softened the blow of plural creators by referring to them as Sons of God. In Abraham, these same Gods command the creation of the world and wait

---

64. *Zion's Harbinger and Baneemy's Organ*, October 1852.

65. Terryl L. Givens, *Wrestling the Angel: The Foundations of Mormon Thought: Cosmos, God, Humanity* (New York: Oxford University Press, 2014), 112–116.

66. Samuel Brown, "William Phelps's 'Paracletes': an Early Witness to Joseph Smith's Divine Anthropology," *International Journal of Mormon Studies* 2, no. 1 (Spring 2009):62–81.

for the earth to obey. Thompson's Enoch, instead, depicted the Sons of God praying to Iame, beckoning him to perform the desired tasks of organization. Thus, God Almighty created the world in response to his children's petition.

Enoch's new creation story was a compromise between Nauvoo theology and more traditional understandings of deity. God Almighty is the self-existent "first cause." Thompson's Enoch recast the Christian trinity in a subservient role to the one true God. The text concurred with the radical idea of human deification brought about through the test of mortality, only that the scenario did not apply to the supreme deity. Individuals progressed to a type of subdivinity operating under the reign of the Lord of Spirits.

THE ANGELIC FALL NARRATIVE
AS A CRITIQUE OF PLURAL MARRIAGE

It is probably no coincidence that Thompson's Enoch was published in the immediate wake of the apostles' announcement of plural marriage. On August 29, 1852, Orson Pratt issued a statement defending plural marriage on multiple counts. First, he explained that there were many spirits who still waited to be embodied before the Second Coming of Christ. If the righteous Latter-day Saints could have more children through plural marriage, then "many spirits that are more noble . . . [could be born] through a just and righteous parentage."[67] Second, Pratt posited that, cross-culturally, polygamy was the preferred form of marriage. He claimed 80 percent of the world's cultures practiced polygamy. Third, Pratt drew on the example of the biblical Abraham to legitimate the newly restored system of marriage. Finally, alongside this announcement, the Brighamites publicly issued the 1843 revelation of Joseph Smith that commanded the practice of plural marriage as "a law of the holy priesthood."[68] Thompson would address each of these arguments through the narrative of Enoch.

Thompson's Enoch paid particular attention to the subjects of premortality and embodiment. This was Iame's plan to advance his offspring. As with other accounts of disembodied spirits in the cosmic past, Enoch alluded to the war in heaven mentioned in Revelation 12, John the Revelator's vision of

67. *Deseret News Extra*, September 18, 1852.
68. Ibid.

a "great red dragon" whose "tail drew the third part of the stars of heaven, and did cast them to the earth." John revealed that the dragon was Satan and the stars were angels thrust from heaven by the archangel "Michael and his angels" during the "war in heaven."[69] The earliest Mormon text that bears on this scene was a revelation received by Moses in Smith's new translation.

> That Satan . . . is the same which was from the beginning, and he came before me, saying—Behold, here am I, send me, I will be thy son, and I will redeem all mankind, that one soul shall not be lost, and surely I will do it; wherefore give me thine honor. But, behold, my Beloved Son, which was Beloved and Chosen from the beginning, said unto me—Father, thy will be done, and the glory be thine forever. Wherefore, because that Satan rebelled against me, and sought to destroy the agency of man, which I, the Lord God, had given him, and also, that I should give unto him mine own power; by the power of mine Only Begotten, I caused that he should be cast down.[70]

This passage introduced the idea that Lucifer's rebellion pertained to the coming mortal experience and the need for there to be a redeemer. From God's perspective, the angel sought to provide universal salvation through depriving mankind of agency. Another revelation dictated just before this account also describes the loss of "a third part of the hosts of heaven [who] turned he [i.e., Lucifer] away from me because of their agency."[71]

The Book of Abraham returned to this scene, presenting the contest between Jesus and Lucifer as an event that occurred during a heavenly council meeting of the noble and great ones. In the council, God asks, "Whom shall I send? And one answered like unto the Son of Man: Here am I, send me. And another answered and said: Here am I, send me. And the Lord said: I will send the first. And the second was angry, and kept not his first estate; and, at that day, many followed after him."[72] Abraham did not articulate what role it was that God sought to fill. The second figure was clearly Satan given his dividing heaven. Reading Abraham in connection with Moses in the Book of Mormon,

69. Revelation 12:3–9.
70. Moses 4:1–3.
71. D&C 29:36.
72. Abraham 3:27–38.

it is clear that the position in question is that of the world's future redeemer. Yet, without a familiarity with Moses, it would have been far from obvious that it was Jesus who opposed Lucifer. I'll return to this point momentarily.

Smith returned to the council again in the King Follet Discourse, where he described a premortal vote—in contrast to God's selection between two candidates—that had been conducted among the gathered assembly. "The contention in heaven was—Jesus said there would be certain souls that would not be saved; and the Devil said he could save them all, and laid his plans before the grand council, who gave their vote in favor of Jesus Christ. So the Devil rose up in rebellion against God, and was cast down, with all who put up their heads [hands?] for him."[73] Thompson's Enoch also depicted a premortal election in which a third cast their vote for the wrong individual. However, Thompson's one third did not debate over who would redeem the world but over which of deity's children would possess the first mortal body.

> Now it came to pass when Iame Organized the sons of God, He appointed the Elect One to receive the first Tabernacle because he was elected by the voice of two-thirds of all the sons of the Morning. But Lucifer who received one-third of the votes, disputed with Michael in reference to that matter, and wished to take the first Tabernacle: but Michael referred the matter to Iame who rebuked Lucifer, and appointed Michael to receive the first Tabernacle; so Michael entered into his Tabernacle, and Iame blew into his nostrils the breath of life, and thus man became a living soul. But Lucifer was angry, and he sought from that time forth to frustrate the plan of Iame.[74]

Thompson's depiction of the premortal council may have simply been a reading of Abraham that did not consider the Moses passage (or the King Follett Discourse) that clarified the identity of each character.

Thompson's Enoch frequently returned to the theme of embodied angels. In stark contrast to Smith's teachings of devils left eternally without bodies, Lucifer received his own tabernacle as Adam and Eve's son, Cain. Later, after receiving instruction from the archangel Raphael, Adam prayed for "one of

---

73. "Conference Minutes," *Times and Seasons*, August 15, 1844.
74. *Zion's Harbinger and Baneemy's Organ*, October 1852.

the holy angels, to be with me in this flesh, that I may council with him."[75] Raphael was then born as Adam and Eve's second son, Abel. This introductory narrative had no precedence in the Book of Enoch. By introducing angelic embodiment, Thompson was able to transform a major narrative component of the Book of Enoch into a condemnation of plural marriage.

In the same way that Thompson's Enoch expanded and altered the Book of Enoch, the Book of Enoch was already an extension and explanation of a story found only briefly in the sixth chapter of Genesis. According to the biblical account,

> And it came to pass, when men began to multiply on the face of the earth, and daughters were born unto them, That the sons of God saw the daughters of men that they were fair; and they took them wives of all which they chose. . . . There were giants in the earth in those days; and also after that, when the sons of God came in unto the daughters of men, and they bare children to them, the same became mighty men which were of old, men of renown.[76]

The Book of Enoch detailed how 200 angels, called *watchers*, made an agreement to marry mortal women. Their interspecies union produced a race of giants, which were responsible for the greatest evils among mankind.[77]

Based on the concept of embodiment, Thompson's Enoch portrayed the watchers as men who held the priesthood—angels, but angels in a state of mortality. This group made a covenant to practice plural marriage, despite a rule that "the Sons of God, shall not take to themselves wives of the daughters of men, for the Lord will give them each a wife of the seed of his chosen race."[78] The result of such marriages was an offspring of cruel giants mirroring Ethiopian Enoch.

75. Ibid.

76. Genesis 6:1–2, 4.

77. This interpretation of Genesis 6 appeared in other texts as well. According to one source, Joseph Smith was familiar with this idea that the "sons of God" were angels through the writings of Josephus. Early Latter-day Saint George Laub quoted Smith as saying, "Now the history of Josephus on speaking of angels came down and took themselves wives of the daughters of men (see Genesis 6:1–2). These were resurrected bodies [who] violated their laws." George Laub, Autobiography of George Laub, L. Tom Perry Special Collections, Brigham Young University.

78. *Zion's Harbinger and Baneemy's Organ*, August 1853.

In the Book of Enoch, the prophetic author relayed a divine message to the fallen angels condemning them for their rebellion. The text outlined a list of severe punishments for them and their seed. Thompson's Enoch built on this passage but applied the castigation to the polygamists and their descendants. Keeping in mind Orson Pratt's defense of plural marriage as a means to bring forth righteous seed, Thompson's Enoch suggested that God prohibited righteous Saints from entering plural marriage. The argument was that the Saints did not need numerous offspring because they knew that life continued after death. Thompson's Enoch implied that the desire for plural marriage was a faithless quest to preserve one's own legacy and immortality. There was no condemnation for unbelievers—likely the 80 percent of the world population that Pratt suggested accepted polygamy—who could "take as many wives as they choose, that sons might be born unto them, and that they may continue their seed upon the earth."[79] Yet the cursed giants born of polygamous unions were not the celestial spirits of Pratt's polygamous unions but "terrestrial spirits who have been born in carnal blood."[80] Certainly, to be born the product of a polygamous marriage was no favored status. Interestingly, the use of the word "terrestrial" was in the original Laurence translation, intended to mean "earthly." However, in its context of decrying celestial marriage it served to undercut these unions in a particularly Mormon way.

Point-by-point, Thompson's Enoch responded to Pratt's arguments. Pratt said that plural marriage would allow for the births of more children; Thompson's Enoch admitted this was so but regarded it as unnecessary for those who understood eternal life. What is the point of a numerous offspring if one's offspring would be cursed to die and become evil spirits, as Enoch portrayed? Pratt argued that, cross-culturally, polygamy was the norm. Enoch agreed, but clarified that these practitioners were unbelievers, not the faithful Saints. Finally, Pratt cited Smith's revelation that portrayed plural marriage as a law of the Holy Priesthood. Enoch declared the exact opposite. There was a law of the Holy Priesthood—monogamy.[81]

The Brighamites justified their practice of polygamy through scriptural precedence, namely the polygamy of Abraham and the 1843 revelation of

79. Ibid.
80. Ibid.
81. *Zion's Harbinger and Baneemy's Organ*, February 1853.

Joseph Smith. Thompson found utility for the Book of Enoch in delegitimizing these same concepts. If the Brighamites could turn to Abraham for support, then why couldn't Thompson appeal to Enoch? Such a figure could potentially trump even Abraham.

CONCLUSION

The Book of Enoch "Revised, corrected, and the missing parts restored" is a particularly revealing instance of mid-nineteenth-century scripture. In addition to what the text might reveal about features of the Latter Day Saint scriptural tradition, it is particularly illustrative of how scripture served as a strategy of contest. Scripture may be written and read to bring emotional comfort or uplift. It might wrestle with the problem of evil or promise a future end to injustice. Thompson's Enoch provided its readers with explanations about creation and the order of the cosmos, but underlying these messages was an effort to make polytheism and polygamy heretical. Thompson's Enoch reminds us that while, on one hand, we should see the mass of scriptures that emerged after Smith's death as a collective body of literature, we must also remember that they were polemical texts leveraged against one another.

11

William Bickerton's Cooperative Views on Scripture and Revelation

Daniel P. Stone

William Bickerton, the founding prophet of the Church of Jesus Christ, broke revelatory boundaries set by his Latter Day Saint predecessors.[1] For example, Joseph Smith had prophesied in 1830, "No one shall be appointed to receive commandments and revelations in this church excepting my servant Joseph Smith, Jun.," or "another in his stead."[2] Yet Bickerton, who considered himself Smith's prophetic successor, could accept revelations from anyone in his church, male or female, black or white, to help lead. In Bickerton's mind, he and his Saints were picking up where Joseph Smith had left off, reverencing the deceased prophet's righteous words, while correcting his errors and rejecting his vainglory. Bickerton may have been the prophet and president of his church, but he believed that anyone could receive revelation to instruct the Saints. In 1858, Bickerton and his Saints chose to keep a revelation book, so that "our children, and those that shall arise after us, they shall so value these revelations" and "that where the Smiths, Joseph and Hyrum fell, we take or carry forwards the Kingdom and this Church—[which] is a continuation of the same foundation."[3] How did Bickerton attain such egal-

---

1. This chapter is an amalgamation of three of my prior publications: "The Rocky Road to Prophethood: William Bickerton's Emergence as an American Prophet," *Journal of Mormon History* 43, no. 1 (2017):1–29; "Opening the Windows of Heaven: The Bickertonite Spiritual Revival, 1856–1858," *Journal of Mormon History* 44, no. 1 (2018):1–19; and *William Bickerton: Forgotten Latter Day Prophet* (Salt Lake City, UT: Signature Books, 2018).

2. D&C 28:2–7.

3. Idris A. Martin and John E. Mancini, eds., "The History of the Church of Jesus Christ: May 25, 1851 Thru October 7, 1905 along with commentary by Idris A. Martin—Assistant General Church Historian," in The Church of Jesus Christ Historical Archive, Greensburg, Pennsylvania 20, hereafter referred to as Church Minutes.

itarian views? No doubt, they stemmed from his earlier tumultuous relationships with Sidney Rigdon and Brigham Young. After forsaking these two Mormon leaders, Bickerton found himself isolated and confused. Nevertheless, after much prayer and soul searching, he witnessed a powerful vision that led him on a prophetic journey. William Bickerton's past relationships with Rigdon and Young prompted him to have cooperative views on scripture and revelation and enabled him to form egalitarian principles that would serve as a foundation for his church.

Bickerton's early journey to prophethood was rocky. Not long after moving from Wheeling, Virginia, to West Elizabeth, Pennsylvania (a borough just outside Pittsburgh), between 1844 and 1845, he encountered galvanizing news reports about the Mormons. As a commercial hub west of the Allegheny Mountains, Pittsburgh provided residents with local and national news. In the newspapers were numerous stories reporting the murder of the prophet, Joseph Smith Jr., and the ensuing power struggle among the church's leaders. Journalists commented on the idiosyncrasies of Mormonism and the alleged consequences of religious fanaticism. When Sidney Rigdon, the last surviving member of Joseph Smith's church presidency, relocated to Pittsburgh in September 1844 and established another church, known as the Church of Christ, reporters tried to discern his intentions, drawing curious locals into the drama.[4]

When Bickerton heard Rigdon preach in Limetown, Pennsylvania, in 1845, he wanted a better life. As a thirty-year-old English emigrant with no formal education, his employment opportunities were limited. His first job in West Elizabeth was as coal foreman working in the rich carbon deposits along the Monongahela River. He labored in one of the most arduous sectors of the emerging steam-driven economy, earning a pittance to sustain his family, which consisted of wife, Dorothy, and infant son, James.[5]

4. Some of the local newspaper articles written about Sidney Rigdon and Mormonism were, "Elder Sidney Rigdon Arrived," *The People's Organ*, June 29, 1844; "Death of Joe Smith and Others," *Pittsburgh Morning Post*, July 8, 1844; "The Progress of Mob Law," *Pittsburgh Morning Post*, July 9, 1844; "Death of Joe and Hiram Smith," *Pittsburgh Christian Advocate*, July 10, 1844; "More Mormon Fanaticism," *Pittsburgh Daily Gazette and Advertiser*, May 7, 1845; "Pittsburgh Mormonism," *Pittsburgh Daily Gazette and Advertiser*, May 8, 1845.

5. William Bickerton, "Testimony, June 1903," 1, The Church of Jesus Christ Historical Archive, Greensburg, PA; United States Census (West Elizabeth, Allegheny County, PA, September 19, 1850).

In 1845, he had not yet received American citizenship, and in Jacksonian America he also encountered anti-British sentiments, a common characteristic of the age. His family's love and perhaps the support he received from a local Methodist church buttressed his otherwise burdensome existence.[6]

In contrast, the local reports about Rigdon and Mormonism presented exhilarating stories of miracles and revelations. These reports most likely compelled him to hear Rigdon preach. His first encounter with Rigdon forever changed his life. Recalling the event later in his life, Bickerton remarked, "Sidney Rigdon was the best orator I have ever heard in classing the scriptures together." After only one sermon, Bickerton professed that Rigdon "had the power of God."[7] As a result,

> I was convinced of the doctrine of Christ, viz, Faith, Repentance and Baptism by immersion for the remission of sins, and the laying on of hands for the gift of the Holy Ghost and its effects is according to St. Paul's writing. There is but one Holy Spirit, and whether Jew or Gentile, bond or free, we have been all made to drink of the same spirit, and Jesus says, "signs shall follow them that believe, in my name they shall cast out devils, they shall speak with new tongues, they shall take up serpents; and if they drink any deadly thing it shall not hurt them, they shall lay hands on the sick and they shall recover." And I was never taught such a Gospel.[8]

Sidney Rigdon's church offered Bickerton an apostolic Christianity that bestowed spiritual gifts to its followers. For an immigrant who received limited rights and privileges in the United States, the Lord's promises satisfied unmet needs.

6. Bickerton filed for American citizenship in 1848; see William Bickerton Naturalization Records, United States Western Judicial District of Pennsylvania, August 5, 1848; Ishmael Humphrey, "Biography of William Bickerton and His Brothers in the Organization of 1862, Greenoak, PA," The Church of Jesus Christ Historical Archive, Greensburg, PA.

7. "A Letter," *St. John Sun*, August 4, 1887; Bickerton, "Testimony, June 1903," 1.

8. William Bickerton, Charles Brown, George Barnes, William Cadman, and Joseph Astin, *The Ensign: or a Light to Lighten the Gentiles, in which the Doctrine of The Church of Jesus Christ of Latter-Day Saints, is Set Forth, and Scripture Evidence Adduced to Establish it. Also, a Brief Treatise upon the Most Important Prophecies Recorded in the Old and New Testaments, which relate to the Great Work of God of the Latter Days* (Pittsburgh, PA: Ferguson and Co., 1863), 5; typescript, in The Church of Jesus Christ Historical Archive, Greensburg, PA; hereafter referred to as *The Ensign*.

In June, Bickerton received baptism from John Frazier, one of Rigdon's High Councilors.[9] He later recalled, "I received the gift of the Holy Spirit at the laying on of hands, and the signs have followed me. I have spoken in new tongues, have had the interpretation, I have seen the sick healed and I have been healed myself, so that I [k]now that the Gospel is the power of God." Just months later, he "was called by the Holy Spirit to be an Elder." He felt "the power of God came down and sealed the office upon me." He soon received two more callings as evangelist and prophet, priest, and king.[10]

Sidney Rigdon, at least at first, did not curb others in his church from manifesting spiritual gifts. All could receive revelation. They could speak in tongues, have interpretations to tongues, see visions, and dream dreams. This egalitarian spirit even applied to ordinations. Bickerton, who had not received the same education as Rigdon or experienced a similar ecclesiastical background, could now receive high holy callings just like his church president. This is not to say that a hierarchy did not exist within the Church of Christ, but overall, Bickerton and his colleagues did view their participation in the church as a collaborative effort. Together, they helped bear the responsibilities of the church and equally received heavenly rewards.

With other members of the priesthood, Bickerton studied in Rigdon's School of the Prophets. A March editorial in the *Messenger and Advocate* explained the school ensured that its members "be perfected in their ministry for the salvation of Zion, and of the nations of Israel, and of the Gentiles, as many as will believe." Bickerton, who until this point had no formal education, learned with men of different trades, crafts, and skills. Within this cooperative atmosphere, they discussed the scriptures, studied subjects of the liberal arts, and discovered the workings of the Holy Spirit to perpetuate the kingdom of God.[11]

However, Bickerton's cooperative participation in the Church of Christ was short lived. Two months after his conversion, Rigdon began preparations for building the New Jerusalem in Pennsylvania. When Bickerton had joined the Church of Christ, he knew that Rigdon wanted to prepare for the Savior's return. However, he had never anticipated Rigdon's hasty plans to usher in Zion. While attending the School of the Prophets, Bickerton,

9. Bickerton, *The Ensign*, 5; "A Letter," *St. John Sun*, August 4, 1887.
10. Bickerton, *The Ensign*, 5; Bickerton, "Testimony, June 1903," 1.
11. D&C 90:8, cited in "For the Messenger and Advocate," *Messenger and Advocate*, March 1, 1845.

along with other members of the priesthood, claimed that "many things were revealed to us, showing things were going wrong. No one followed Sidney Rigdon from that Branch, because we knew by the spirit that he was going wrong. He sent two of his apostles to stop our assembly of the school of the prophets ... and many things were revealed that came to pass." The school's members foresaw the failure of Rigdon's New Jerusalem on Adventure Farm. As time elapsed, they would find that their predictions would come true, but their prophecies were not the only indication of impending Rigdon's downfall. Reminiscing over half a century later, John Wickliffe Rigdon remembered that some of his father's followers believed "he was so extreme in his ideas that they left him. He was at times so perfectly wild that he could not control himself."[12]

In contrast to his earlier egalitarian, receptive attitude, Rigdon began to loathe the objectors to his Zion plans. To wreak his vengeance, he waxed prophetic at the 1846 April conference, the last general meeting of the Church of Christ held in Pittsburgh. Bickerton, as a newly appointed member of Rigdon's Grand Council, attended.[13] During this spring conference, Bickerton, no doubt, listened closely to Rigdon's visions pertaining to all malcontents.

> While sitting in his [Rigdon's] own house, reflecting upon the peculiar circumstances with which he was surrounded, suddenly the vision opened to his view.—Thousands stood before him, and the Lord told him, that they were the honorable men of the city, and through them the means should come for the redemption of Zion. It passed, and another scene opened to his view—He beheld a company of the old Mormon church of this city, among whom he recognised the faces of several, with whom he had formed a slight acquaintance, the Lord had shown him that many of these men were not the materials with whom Zion shall be built.

12. Bickerton, "Testimony, June 1903," 1; Karl Keller, ed., "'I Never Knew a Time When I Did Not Know Joseph Smith': A Son's Record of the Life and Testimony of Sidney Rigdon," *Dialogue: A Journal of Mormon Thought* 1, no. 4 (1966):40.

13. Interestingly, in December 1845, Bickerton had replaced Apostle William McLellin in the Grand Council when McLellin abandoned Rigdon's church. Jan Shipps and John W. Welch, eds., *The Journals of William E. McLellin, 1831–1836* (Provo, UT: BYU Studies, 1994), 337–38.

Rigdon further proclaimed,

> There seemed to have been a struggle between the Lord and satan, between the powers of light and the powers of darkness. The devil had sought to overthrow this kingdom—some of those whom we once loved as brethren had left us, or fallen by transgression, and by circulating the most base and malicious slanders against us, had shown the corruption of their own hearts. In the midst of this conflict, interposition of providence had placed it beyond their reach to do us harm. There could be no doubt now in what relation we stand to the heavens, and by whose wisdom power we are guided—no man in this kingdom could rise up and say he had had no evidence for in the gloomiest hour of our history, when human wisdom was of no avail, the great God had clearly shown us that he was our guardian and protector. I feel as if we stand on "terra firma."[14]

Rigdon believed members of the Church of Christ who questioned his plans—along with Brigham Young's supporters—futilely attempted to impede God's will. He portrayed the dissenters as Satan's disciples. To the shock of Bickerton and the rest of the members of the School of the Prophets, Rigdon began to flex his prophetic muscles; and apparently, no one could stand in his way. Rigdon still allowed others to exhibit spiritual manifestations, but only when their revelations did not contradict or challenge his, Bickerton soon learned. Apparently abandoning his prior egalitarianism, Rigdon was now an infallible prophet. Those who received revelations that he was erring were merely apostates.

Even though Bickerton claimed to have received such revelations, he hesitated at first to openly oppose his church's president. Rigdon had spoken strong words, promising damnation for those who stood in his way. At the conference, Bickerton said "he had lately become a member of the church and kingdom of Christ. He knew what it meant by being baptised [*sic*] with the Holy Ghost, and felt the weight of the responsibilities resting upon him." But as a member of the School of the Prophets, Bickerton knew that revelations

---

14. "Minutes of a conference of the Church and Kingdom of Christ, held in Pittsburgh, commencing on the 6th and ending on the 8th of April, 1846," *Messenger and Advocate*, June 1846.

were indeed being received regarding Rigdon's errancy. It appears that Bickerton's recent appointment to the Grand Council could not smother his conscience. He soon became more determined that his revelations about the downfall of Rigdon's New Jerusalem were true and eventually supported the dissenters. Although Rigdon sent two of his apostles to permanently dismiss the School of the Prophets, they could not break the objectors' resolve.[15]

With his limited congregation and capital, Sidney Rigdon vastly overestimated his church's capabilities. On Adventure Farm, his followers could only afford to equip a barn as a meeting house. Just seven months after his arrival in the Cumberland Valley, Rigdon's prophecies turned on his own head. Adventure Farm, the Zion that never flourished, returned to its previous owner in August 1847 during a sheriff's auction, while Rigdon fled to Friendship, New York.[16]

The remaining Rigdonites had to find a way to make a living. Many returned to Pittsburgh where they found charity from the dissenters who had refused to travel to the Cumberland Valley. Bickerton, who was one of those dissenters, remembered this trying time: "After Rigdon went wrong all that followed him fell away, and I was left alone, seeking to know what course to pursue. My house was a resting place for many of those who had followed Sidney Rigdon."[17] It is difficult to comprehend how these shattered converts felt. Bickerton, who had moved to the outskirts of Pittsburgh as a poor, uneducated, English emigrant, eventually became a prophet, priest, and king under the Mormon spokesman. Rigdon promised Bickerton a crown in the Millennium, and the Book of Mormon introduced an apostolic Christianity that he had never known. Then, in 1846, he became disenchanted with Rigdon. He now found himself churchless, consoling those who had lost their finances in pursuit of Zion.

William Bickerton's feelings may have correlated with John Wickliffe Rigdon's views of his father: "I do not think the Church [of Jesus Christ of Latter-day Saints] made any mistake in placing the leadership on Brigham Young. . . .

15. Ibid.; Bickerton, "Testimony, June 1903," 1.

16. Richard S. Van Wagoner, *Sidney Rigdon: A Portrait of Religious Excess* (Salt Lake City, UT: Signature Books, 1994), 391–393; B. M. Nead, "The History of Mormonism with Particular Reference to the Founding of the New Jerusalem in Franklin County," in *Kittochtinny Historical Society Papers* (Chambersburgh, PA: Franklin Repository Press, 1923), 9:423; Rigdon to Stephen Post, January 23, 1856, Post Collection, cited in Van Wagoner, 392.

17. Bickerton, "Testimony, June 1903," 1.

Sidney Rigdon had no executive ability, was broken down with sickness, and could not have taken charge of the Church at that time.... I have no fault to find with the Church with doing what they did. It was the best thing they could have done under the circumstances." Bickerton had witnessed firsthand the liability of Rigdon's erratic behavior and felt obliged to aid those who lost their means in the Cumberland Valley. After the downfall of Rigdon's New Jerusalem, Bickerton's writings are almost nonextant from late 1847 to mid-1851. During that time, he maintained his convictions in the Restored Gospel, but he needed ecclesiastical stability to foster his congregation.

At that point, Brigham Young appeared as a viable partner to champion God's latter-day work. But Bickerton harbored some serious questions. Were Rigdon's claims against Young a ploy to garner support for his pride? Were his allegations really a hoax? Bickerton probably wondered whether Young had spared his followers from Rigdon's volatile conduct. After all, contrary to Rigdon's scandalous reports, Young and other church leaders publicly contended they did not practice polygamy. As the year 1850 approached, Bickerton's prejudice toward the Mormon Twelve Apostles started to soften. Rigdon appeared the traitor while Young emerged as a practical ally to prepare for the Millennium.

By then, Young was Utah's territorial governor. Thousands of beleaguered Saints had settled in Salt Lake City and the outlying region. The city had become a flourishing commercial center where westward travelers, gold seekers, and religious pioneers congregated. Religiously, politically, and economically, Young's Latter-day Saints prospered. Young had succeeded where Sidney Rigdon had failed. Bickerton stood at a crossroad and did not know which way to venture. The more he learned about Young's success in the Great Basin, his suspicions, like those of so many other Americans, began to subside.

Sometime in 1850, Bickerton sent an inquiry to Kanesville, Iowa requesting information about the LDS Church. John Murray and David James Ross, two itinerant Mormon elders, eventually received Bickerton's request. In 1851, the pair traveled to meet his small congregation of nine members in West Elizabeth, Pennsylvania. They held a meeting with Bickerton's group where both parties shared their beliefs, concerns, and questions.[18] This was

18. "News from the Elders," *Frontier Guardian*, July 25, 1851; "News from the Traveling Elders," *Frontier Guardian*, August 22, 1851; Victor Emanuel Bean and William W. Allen to William Moroni Palmer, December 14, 1885, typescript by John E. Mancini, Lamb Foundation Archive, Albuquerque, NM.

a cooperative atmosphere that Bickerton obviously preferred. Both parties shared important similarities. Ross and Murray sustained that the Mormons did not practice polygamy. The duo lied to Bickerton, but their confirmation refuted Rigdon's accusation that Smith had fallen into apostasy by introducing the practice. The admission must have pleased Bickerton and enabled him to support the notion that Joseph Smith had maintained his prophetic office until his death.[19] And paramount to both group's convictions, Bickerton and the Latter-day Saints believed that Jesus Christ's Second Coming was imminent. According to a sermon that Smith had delivered in 1835, Christ would probably return sometime in 1891.[20]

After discussing their similarities and differences, Ross and Murray decided that Bickerton and his congregation could become part of the Mormon Church. They assured him their few differences were reconcilable. Ross and Murray primarily needed Bickerton to accept the axiom that the priesthood authority had transferred from Joseph Smith to Brigham Young. When he affirmed that concept, they welcomed his admission.[21]

Then, sometime in late 1851 or early 1852, Brigham Young decided to publicly endorse plural marriage. He had already told the Utah Saints in early 1851 that he was practicing polygamy, but now he wanted to make the doctrine official. He planned to acknowledge as well as defend the tenet. By this time, accounts of plural marriage were widespread. In 1851, a Mormon named Frederick Cox received a court order in Kanesville Iowa (present-day Council Bluffs) to abandon his two youngest wives. In early 1852, an exposé written by an ex-Mormon appeared in the *Lehigh Register* of eastern Pennsylvania that spoke of "licentiousness run mad" in Utah. Brigham Young withheld his official announcement of plural marriage until a special conference in August 1852, but traveling Mormon officials publicized the doctrine earlier in the year.[22]

19. Victor Emanuel Bean and William W. Allen to William Moroni Palmer, December 14, 1885; William Bickerton, *St. John Weekly News*, August 16, 1889; William H. Cadman, *A History of the Church of Jesus Christ* (Monongahela, PA: The Church of Jesus Christ, 1945), 1:5–6; Gary R. Entz, "Zion Valley: The Mormon Origins of St. John, Kansas," *Kansas History* 24, no. 2 (Summer 2001):101.

20. Joseph Smith Jr., *History of the Church of Jesus Christ of Latter-day Saints* (Salt Lake City, UT: Desert News, 1902), 2:182.

21. Entz, "Zion Valley," 101; Victor Emanuel Bean and William W. Allen to William Moroni Palmer, December 14, 1885.

22. John G. Turner, *Brigham Young: Pioneer Prophet* (Cambridge, MA: Belknap Press of Harvard University Press, 2012), 204; Matthew Bowman, *The Mormon People: The Making of an*

Bickerton was attending a church meeting in Allegheny City when he heard the shocking news. To prepare the Saints in the East for Brigham Young's August announcement, church officials informed the assembly that if they promptly accepted the doctrine of plural marriage, they would receive God's approval. On the other hand, if they denounced the practice, they would accept damnation. For Bickerton, the news was disconcerting. After all, he had recently dealt with another Mormon prophet who cursed those who disagreed with his revelations. Hearing the announcement, Bickerton arose and stood among the congregation, many of whom knew him personally. He declared, "If the approval of God were to come to [me] by accepting the doctrine of polygamy, [I would] prefer the displeasure of God." He then walked out of the meeting. At that moment, he abandoned the Mormon Church. The man who had helped triple his Mormon congregation the prior year vowed to never return.[23]

Brigham Young's polygamy announcement led William Bickerton to question some of the Mormon Church's theology, which, in the end, paved the way for him to form more egalitarian principles. Bickerton did not give a clear explanation regarding his reevaluation of Mormon theology, but by correlating his conclusions with the Bible and the Book of Mormon, it is possible to see how he came to new understanding. Once he heard that the Twelve supported plural marriage, he felt he had to disregard the precept of eternal exaltation because it was inseparably linked to polygamy. According to his understanding, the Book of Mormon clearly forbade plural marriage. In his mind, this alone proved the church's hypocrisy.[24] Since polygamy

---

American Faith (New York: Random House, 2012), 125; "Mormonism Exposed, by a Mormon," *Lehigh Register*, March 25, 1852.

23. Cadman, *A History of the Church of Jesus Christ*, 1:6; David Jordan, *A History of the Church of Jesus Christ* (Monongahela, PA: The Church of Jesus Christ, 2002), 2:36. William H. Cadman did not learn about William Bickerton attending the Allegheny City meeting from a contemporary account. Rather, he remembered that his father, William Cadman Sr., had told the story about Bickerton, making William Jr.'s recount, at first glance, seem a little dubious. William Jr. even wrote, "I have not pretended to relate this incident in my Father's exact words, but the thought conveyed is the same." However, several primary documents demonstrate that Bickerton abhorred polygamy and that he was very vocal about his disgust. In addition, primary documents also confirm that the doctrine of polygamy was the reason why Bickerton abandoned Brigham Young. In the end, Bickerton's sarcastic declaration about preferring God's displeasure rather than accepting polygamy is likely accurate.

24. *The Ensign*, 3.

increased a man's exaltation, the concept of a plurality of gods could not hold validity. Therefore, the New Testament did not suggest that men could achieve godhood. Instead, men received the same heavenly reward as Christ. He now thought God assigned deceased men as joint heirs to His eternal kingdom rather than granting them His omnipotent power. Bickerton's doctrinal understanding about eternity thus retreated to Protestant tradition. He saw a similar relationship between baptism for the dead because it connected families together eternally and granted exaltation to those who practiced it. Bickerton now felt that the Mormon Church used earlier revelations to create new doctrines, and he saw flaws in Mormon theology.[25]

Given Bickerton's reevaluations, he wondered how he could continue to preach the Restored Gospel. Joining another Mormon sect probably seemed out of the question, since all the leaders who believed in the Book of Mormon either endorsed plural marriage, baptism for the dead, or godhood. Nor would it have been easy to find a Mormon sect that did not esteem Joseph Smith's later teachings. The predicament weighed heavily. "Here I was left to myself," he remembered. "I paused to know what course to follow. I know [m]y calling was from heaven, and I also know that a man cannot build up the Church of Christ without divin[e] command from the Lord, for it would only be sectarianism and man's authority." As he stood in contemplation, he received a revelation: "But the Lord did not leave me. No, he showed me a vision, and in the vision I was on the highest mountain on the earth: he told me if I did not preach the Gospel, I would fall into a dreadful chasm below, the sight there was awful."[26] The vision astounded Bickerton. Its symbolism strengthened his conviction in the Restored Gospel and his own calling as a prophet. Placement on the world's highest mountain indicated that God saw him as the last man willing to preach the Gospel in its purity. He stood by himself, overlooking the earth as the Lord gave him instructions. God gave Bickerton only two options. He could continue to preach the Gospel, using the Bible and the Book of Mormon as primary texts, or he could plummet into a dark chasm, presumably to join Brigham Young and others. For him, this was divine confirmation that all the other Mormon prophets had departed from the truth, and he was the only man left to build up God's

25. For more information about Bickerton's doctrinal beliefs, see *The Ensign*, 9–14.
26. Ibid., 5.

kingdom on earth. He needed to preach the Gospel, share the priesthood authority, and prepare the world for the Millennium. "I was left alone," he later remarked. Nevertheless, "I moved with fear, having the Holy Spirit with me."[27] There is no specific date for this vision of mountain and chasm, but it was most likely in 1852 after his departure from Young's church.

The vision was also a clear example to Bickerton that anyone could receive direct revelation from God. He was an English emigrant who had forsaken two Mormon leaders, yet he still found that the Lord could give him spiritual authority to continue proselytizing. All who sincerely sought God could receive revelation—not just leading prophets of a church. In addition, Bickerton also learned that even prophets could spiritually falter, especially if they let pride enter their hearts and minds. After all, it is clear he thought Joseph Smith, Sidney Rigdon, and Brigham Young had all allowed this to happen. Still, Bickerton believed that received revelation had to correlate with the Bible and Book of Mormon. Otherwise, the revelation could be considered false and could be disregarded. If it was not discarded, Bickerton well knew the dissent it could create within his church.

So, following God's command, Bickerton began his new prophetic journey. After long hours in the mines, Bickerton preached to his neighbors. On Sundays, his day off, "I held outdoor meetings sometimes in the market place, sometime[s] in public houses, on streets or any other available place."[28] The bustling wharfs on Market Street, located on the west and east banks of the Monongahela River, docked steamboats that connected Elizabeth Township to the outside world. Ferries brought goods for local stores, passengers, supplies for the town's industries, and daily newspapers from Pittsburgh. When a steamboat blew its whistle, residents congregated by the dock. Ferries arrived at noon and in the evening.[29] Along this busy strip, Bickerton declared his Gospel message. As he recalled, he held his first meeting "beside the ferry, at a store house door." During the service, a woman walking by stopped to hear him preach. As she listened, she "testified to the gospel" and later received baptism.[30]

27. Bickerton, "Testimony, June 1903," 2; *The Ensign*, 5. Presumably Bickerton referred to the "fear of God."
28. Bickerton, "Testimony, June 1903," 2.
29. Richard T. Wiley, *Elizabeth and Her Neighbors* (Butler, PA: Ziegler Company, 1936), 116.
30. Bickerton, "Testimony, June 1903," 2.

He held almost no apprehension about preaching in public. He taught about Jesus Christ in the way of the original apostles. He recalled, "I held these outdoor meetings and many were convinced, and several were baptized."[31] Unlike most ministers in the United States who earned their salaries and reputations by gathering congregants in an established church building, Bickerton walked the streets, talking directly to people as they conducted their daily lives. He did not take a salary for preaching, nor did he expect his converts to help support his family. Bickerton believed he was literally following Christ's egalitarian philosophy: "[F]reely ye have received, freely give."[32] "I then went to Allegheny City," he remembered, "had good meetings there," and later established a church branch in the town. And he continued to have success. "I baptized a family, on the hills opposite Pittsburgh," he stated, "[a]nd also baptized a good many at Six-Mile Ferry; and had a good many members at Pine Run." By the end of 1852, Bickerton had rebaptized his one-time Mormon congregation and started to develop a new church with members surrounding the Pittsburgh area.[33]

In his new church, known as the Church of Jesus Christ of Latter Day Saints (colloquially referred to as the Church of Jesus Christ), Bickerton and many others openly manifested spiritual gifts. This could occur several times during a meeting, making church services exhilarating events. As God continued talking to the church, a new question arose: What should they do with the revelations? In 1858, one woman believed she had the answer. One night, this unnamed woman had a dream where she saw a book of "great value" to the Saints. When she shared her experience, the Saints became elated. "This book is nothing more, nor less, than the revelations and other gifts received by us," a secretary recorded. The church needed to keep a record of all the revelations. If it did, members could study God's latter-day prophecies, correlate them with the Bible and the Book of Mormon, and better understand the unfolding last days. The Saints could hardly fathom the spiritual knowledge that would result from this work. "[S]uch is the power that shall come upon us," the secretary wrote, "that our children, and those that shall arise after us, they shall so value these revelations that they

31. Ibid., 2.
32. Matthew 10:8.
33. Bickerton, "Testimony, June 1903," 2; Victor Emanuel Bean, Journals, 1884–1889, 4:3–4, CHL.

will have them published and embellished by the lives of the founders, Joseph and Hyrum Smith."[34]

In 1833, Joseph Smith published a collection of his prophecies and revelations and titled it the Book of Commandments. In 1835, he expanded the collection and republished it as the Doctrine and Covenants. Smith believed these revelations would help guide his church to spiritual prosperity and knowledge. The texts were not intended to usurp the Bible and Book of Mormon but to complement them.[35]

Bickerton did not agree with all the revelations in the Doctrine and Covenants, though he sometimes referenced certain ones. Nevertheless, he understood why the book had such a powerful influence on the Mormons. For Brigham Young's Latter-day Saints, the text was another proof that God spoke directly to His people. It was an open scriptural canon that could document the Lord's words over time, a powerful symbol of prophetic power that the Mormons used to prove their church's spiritual authority. Yet Bickerton and his Saints believed their church had been consecrated with God's *true* power. Their recent revelations had only proved this point. Thus, a need to keep a record of God's words was paramount to their mission.

The secretary wrote, "And this is the mind of the Lord that we keep a record of these things and we ar[e] accepted by the Almighty and that where the Smiths, Joseph and Hyrum fell, we take or carry forwards the Kingdom and this Church—[which] is a continuation of the same foundation."[36] Where Joseph Smith and the patriarchs of the early Restoration had failed, Bickerton believed his church pressed forward, and he, along with all other church members, could receive meaningful revelations worthy of record. This book of revelations would always remind their church of their egalitarian and prophetic purpose, forever enriching their posterity with a history of God's interaction with His people.

Of course, such outpourings of manifestations were bound to breed skeptics. In the past, Bickerton had himself been skeptical of Joseph Smith's, Sidney Rigdon's, and Brigham Young's public revelations when he thought they contradicted sound doctrine. But he soon found that a similar skepticism

---

34. Church Minutes, 20.
35. Richard Lyman Bushman, *Joseph Smith: Rough Stone Rolling* (New York: Knopf, 2005), 282.
36. Church Minutes, 20.

spread throughout the ranks of his church against him, given such consistent revelations. This unbelief greatly disturbed Bickerton and his counselors, and they agreed it had to stop. On January 1, 1860, First Counselor Charles Brown stood up and spoke in tongues. William Bacon received the interpretation: "Hear ye the word of the Lord, for verily thus saith the Lord, I have said unto you my people that I would protect my church and suffer no evil to enter therein, And now I say unto all that have come here deceive not yourselves neither think to deceive this people or I will set you as a monument as Lots wife Amen."[37]

It appeared that God chastised those doubting members. The message compared them to Lot's wife.[38] According to Bacon's interpretation of tongues, those in the church who doubted the revelations were symbolically looking back to their intellect, relying on their own understanding rather than exercising faith. Bickerton and his church presidency believed that God had already proven the revelations were from Heaven. Evidences of the revelations were apparent, Bickerton thought. Over the years, people had repented and asked for their baptism, and others received marvelous healings. What more could God do to prove Himself?

It is not clear how the scoffers reacted to these remarks. Quite possibly some felt that the church's leaders were becoming prideful. After all, it was apparent what had happened to Joseph Smith, Sidney Rigdon, and Brigham Young. When pride set in, a feeling of infallibility seemed to follow. These church leaders, they understood, had been blinded by their power and eventually lost track of their moral compass. Was Bickerton succumbing to the same fate? The events of the next day, January 2, may have stunned the entire church.

After Bickerton opened the meeting, he decided to handle a serious matter with Jacob Stranger. For a short period and reasons now unclear, Stranger had been separated from the church. Stranger attended the January conference to plead his case before the elders. He felt that the separation was unjustified, although he may have admitted an error on his part. As the assembly discussed Stranger's position, Bickerton spoke the word of the Lord: "Verily

37. A Book of Record of the Revelations given unto the Church of Jesus Christ of Latter Day Saints, The Church of Jesus Christ Historical Archive, Greensburg, PA, 12; hereafter referred to as Revelation Book.

38. Genesis 19:1–26.

thus saith the Lord ye are all fallible, and ye may transgress therefore tremble and fear before me for I am God and this is my word ye are all fallible therefore hear O my people and watch and pray for ye may fall, Amen."[39] Surprisingly, the Lord admonished the entire conference. Jacob Stranger may have erred, but God apparently showed the church that He was no respecter of persons. Sin could enter anyone's heart, God asserted, leading them down a path of spiritual destruction. Only those who humbled themselves before the Lord remained on a righteous path. It was now apparent that no one, including Bickerton, was immune to failure. Then George Barnes, speaking the word of the Lord, addressed those who held doubts about the church's manifestations. The message may have also addressed the issue regarding Stranger's separation: "A man must first believe in the word of God before he can believe in the power of God."[40] God's words again instructed the Saints to have greater faith. Otherwise, they would not see the Lord's full power.

Along with acknowledging his own faults, Bickerton also recognized when God called others as prophets. Two years later, on January 5, 1862, Charles Brown spoke to the Saints, informing them that he felt inspired to acknowledge John Dixon as a prophet. John Dixon had the gift of dreams and visions, and in 1861 his revelations had instructed the Saints on how to handle dissenters within the church. Bickerton was the leading prophet of the church, but Bickerton and those under him understood that he did not hold a monopoly on the prophetic gift. In the Bible and the Book of Mormon, God's people often worked together to deliver the Lord's messages. Therefore, any member in Bickerton's church could prophesy. Yet this did not mean all were prophets. The Saints had to feel compelled by the Holy Spirit to officially acknowledge a person as a prophet. Dixon's revelations had helped guide the church, so it only seemed reasonable to Brown for the Saints to recognize Dixon as a prophet. In addition, the Saints had no reason to question Brown's request. Back in 1849, Brown had confirmed that Bickerton was a prophet who would lead a church. Indeed, this prophecy was fulfilled in their eyes. Along with Bickerton, Dixon could continue to help guide the church, receiving and interpreting revelations. But in this case, the elders chose not to ordain Dixon a prophet as they had done for Bickerton

39. Revelation Book, 12.
40. Ibid.

in 1859. Bickerton's ordination may have been merely ceremonial to show that he was the leading prophet of the church.[41]

William Bickerton's egalitarian views on scripture and revelation didn't stop there. He opened the priesthood to men of color and gave women an opportunity to hold an ordained office. If anyone, male or female, regardless of color, could receive revelation from God, then they also could hold ordained offices within the church, he reasoned. And true to his spiritual convictions, Bickerton maintained that all who received an ordained office had to be confirmed to the church by direct revelation or inspiration. Compared to other Latter Day Saint traditions, including Brigham Young's, Bickerton's beliefs about church offices were fairly progressive.

In his adult life, Bickerton objected to slavery. To contemporaries, he could have been considered an abolitionist. Although most Northerners abhorred slavery, they almost never considered blacks equal to whites— politically or racially. Blacks were genetically inferior, most Northerners claimed, and did not have the same intellectual capabilities as whites. Bickerton, therefore, was a rarity within the United States. He viewed them as equals and offered membership in his church with the possibility of holding priesthood offices.[42] Even among Utah Mormons, who also offered church membership to blacks, Bickerton was an anomaly. Under Brigham Young, Mormons did not allow them to hold priesthood positions.[43]

Bickerton did not explain in depth why he detested slavery. Yet examining his religious thoughts in context of his socioeconomic environment, it is possible to deduce his rationale. We can surmise three reasons for his sympathies. First, because the Bible and the Book of Mormon contain several instances where slavery is discouraged and equality is demanded. For example, in the Bible, God parted the Red Sea to free the enslaved Israelites from the Egyptians. Also, in the Book of Mormon, King Mosiah, in a tone like the Declaration of Independence, publicly declared to the Nephites, "Inequality should be no more in this land, especially among this my people,

41. Church Minutes, 24, 42; Bickerton, "Testimony, June 1903," 9.
42. Larry Watson, "The Church of Jesus Christ (Headquartered in Monongahela, Pennsylvania), Its History and Doctrine," in *Scattering of the Saints: Schism Within Mormonism*, edited by Newell G. Bringhurst and John C. Hamer (Independence, MO.: John Whitmer Books, 2007), 204.
43. Bushman, *Joseph Smith: Rough Stone Rolling*, 288.

FIGURE 11.1. William Bickerton the year he died, 1905. Photograph by W.R. Gray. Courtesy Gray Studio Glass Plate Negative Collection, Stafford County Museum and Forsyth Digital Library.

but I desire that this land be a land of liberty, and every man may enjoy his rights and privileges alike."[44] Second, Bickerton too was trapped in a form of economic slavery. Manual laborers received very low wages in the United States and were often left to fend for themselves. In most lower-class American households, fathers and mothers worked; children commonly had jobs too. Bickerton may not have thought his life worse or equal to African slaves, but he certainly could have related to their harsh realities. Finally, he probably witnessed the practice of slavery while living in Wheeling, Virginia.

On September 10, 1868, Bickerton ordained Charles Burgess, the first recorded black elder of his church.[45] But three years later, in January 1872, Bickerton was forced to address resurgent racism. Members of the Little Redstone, Pennsylvania, branch, which had been organized in March 1871, began to argue that black men and women were inferior to whites. The news alarmed church leaders, who encouraged the winter conference to ask Joseph Astin, conference secretary, to write a letter to the Little Redstone branch.[46] Astin fused scripture into a calm and logical argument,

> Copy of a Letter from Conference
> about Collerd People
>
> By order of the Conference
> An Epistle
> unto the Church of Jesus Christ at Little Redstone
> Beloved Brethern & Sisters in the Lord the Conference sends greeting.
>
> It having come to the attention of the conference that there is some feeling incisting in some parts of the Church, that would rather slight the [colored] people, therefore the Conference sought after the minds of the Lord upon the subject
> And it was felt by the Holy Spirit that the Lord looked upon Israel and blessed them yet they, themselves looked upon the Gentiles as unclean, Until God showed unto his Servant Peter that he had clensed the gentiles by his Spirit, by them obeying the Gospel, therefore

44. Exodus 14:1–31; Mosiah 29:32.
45. Church Minutes, 75; Cadman, *A History of the Church of Jesus Christ*, 1:54–55.
46. Church Minutes, 85; Cadman, *A History of the Church of Jesus Christ*, 1:61.

he was not to call them unclean in like manner have we also been led to look on the Colloured people as being beneath the Gentiles but the Gospel brings them up and makes them have Equal access unto the Supper of the Lord, and Equal Fellowship in the Church of Jesus Christ
Amen

Joseph Astin
Recording Secretary
of the Church
Given January 2, 1872
West Elizabeth[47]

Astin's words demonstrated the views of Bickerton's church and gently rebuked the racist exploits of some of its members.

Regarding women, on April 6, 1863, Apostle Joseph Knox and Elder Charles Cowan advised Bickerton and the church's ministry to ordain a new office within the church—the office of a deaconess.[48] Knox and Cowan had most likely arrived at this idea after reading the apostle Paul's words in the New Testament, where the office of a deaconess is suggested in a few places. In his epistle to the Romans, Paul had asked Christians within the city to welcome a group of women, some of whom he identified as servants and helpers. For example, Paul wrote, "I commend unto you Phebe our sister, which is a servant of the church which is at Cenchrea: That ye receive her in the Lord, as becometh saints, and that ye assist her in whatsoever business she hath need of you: for she hath been a succourer of many, and of myself also."[49] The Greek word that Paul had used for "servant" was *diakonia*. Therefore, the passage suggested that Phebe was a deaconess who had tended to the Christian church in the same manner as a male deacon.[50] In the

---

47. "Redstone Valley Branch, March 11, 1871, to October 25, 1873," 1:8–9, typescript by John E. Mancini, Lamb Foundation Archive, Albuquerque, NM.

48. Church Minutes, 51.

49. Romans 16:1–2. See also Romans 16:6, 16:12, and Titus 2:3–5.

50. James Strong, *The New Strong's Exhaustive Concordance of the Bible* (Nashville, TN: Thomas Nelson, 1990), 940. *Diakonia* found in "Greek Dictionary of the New Testament," 22, reference number 1248, https://www.academia.edu/7171196/GREEK_DICTIONARY_OF_THE_NEW _TESTAMENT_by_James_Strong.

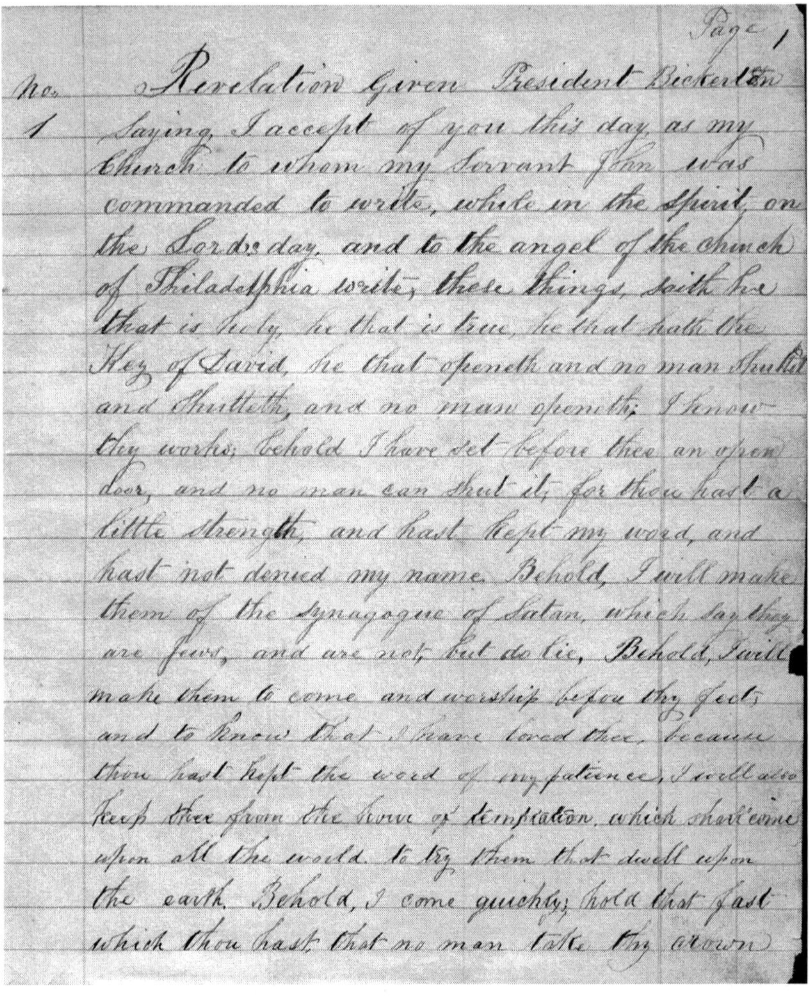

Page 1

No. 1 Revelation Given President Bickerton
Saying, I accept of you this day, as my
Church to whom my Servant John was
commanded to write, while in the Spirit, on
the Lords day, and to the angel of the church
of Philadelphia write, these things, saith he
that is holy, he that is true, he that hath the
Key of David, he that openeth and no man shutteth
and shutteth, and no man openeth; I know
thy works; Behold I have set before thee an open
door, and no man can shut it; for thou hast a
little strength, and hast kept my word, and
hast not denied my name, Behold, I will make
them of the synagogue of Satan, which say they
are Jews, and are not, but do lie, Behold, I will
make them to come and worship before thy feet,
and to know that I have loved thee, because
thou hast kept the word of my patience, I will also
keep thee from the hour of temptation, which shall come
upon all the world, to try them that dwell upon
the earth, Behold, I come quickly; hold that fast
which thou hast, that no man take thy crown

FIGURE 11.2. The first page of the revelation book begun by Bickerton's church in 1858. Courtesy Church of Jesus Christ Historical Archive.

early Christian movement, a deacon tended to the daily needs of the church, offered care for widows and orphans, and handled spiritual responsibilities that teachers or the ministry did not have time to manage. Paul explained the qualities of a deacon. They must "be grave, not double tongued, not given to much wine, not greedy of filthy lucre; Holding the mystery of the faith in a pure conscience." Deacons could also, by the power of the Holy

Spirit, perform "wonders and miracles."[51] In the same manner, Joseph Knox and Charles Cowan proposed to ordain deaconesses to accomplish the same tasks. After hearing their proposal, Bickerton and the ministry agreed to institute this new office, paving the way for women to hold an ancillary ministerial position.[52]

Sometime before his death, William Bickerton, with a simple reminiscence, reiterated his egalitarian spirit as a Latter Day Saint. "I was a miner all my life and never had any chance of learning or never was at school," he remembered. "During all this time I belonged to the Methodist church, up to 1845 when I went to Limetown, Washington county, Pa., to hear the Saints preach. As soon as I went in amongst them I found that they had more than I had, and I wanted to have all that the Gospel promised."[53]

Bickerton spent most of his life teaching his followers that they could receive the full power of the Holy Ghost. They could prophesy, speak in tongues, receive interpretations to tongues, and see visions and dreams. Anyone in his church, male or female, could receive revelation, and their revelations were taken seriously and were often recorded for future reference. In addition, Bickerton attempted to clarify and correct Mormon doctrine preaching mainly from the Bible, the Book of Mormon, and by occasionally referencing the Doctrine and Covenants. He declared his own prophecies and led his church with exceptional visionary power. Bickerton was a prophet among other Latter Day Saint prophets who, like him, attempted to propagate their own versions of the Restored Gospel and build up their own forms of Zion. But unlike those who monopolized the prophetic gift or barred blacks and women from church positions, Bickerton encouraged his people to manifest spiritual gifts and wanted all to have an opportunity to hold a holy office within his church.

---

51. 1 Timothy 3:8–9; Acts 6:8.

52. Church Minutes, 51. The Church of Jesus Christ entrusted deaconesses with rather progressive responsibilities. They could administer sacrament to sick women after the elders blessed the bread and wine, and they could anoint sick or afflicted women when an ordained male was not present. See Cadman, *A History of the Church of Jesus Christ*, 1:60; Church Minutes, 145.

53. "A Pioneer Gone," *St. John Weekly News*, February 24, 1905.

12

Scriptures for the Children of Zion
The Revelations of Sidney and Phebe Rigdon
Jay Burton

The Church of Jesus Christ of the Children of Zion was founded in Philadelphia, Pennsylvania, in 1863 and grew to approximately 200 members in
south-central Iowa.[1] It was unusual among Restoration churches because
Sidney and Phebe Rigdon—the church's respective prophet, seer, and revelator and prophetess—revealed God's will remotely from their home in New
York. Meanwhile, the church resided in Pennsylvania, then later Attica, Iowa,
and finally Manitoba, Ontario. Additionally, though a majority of the revelations written for the guidance of the new church came through Sidney Rigdon, Phebe's role as a second (and female!) authorized revealer of God's will
to the people was a unique innovation among the greater Latter Day Saint
movement. The day-to-day leader of the community, Stephen Post, led the
Children of Zion through the Rigdons' revelations he received by mail. Post
recorded the revelations in two ledger books with a title page labeling the
manuscript "Book of the Revelations of Jesus Christ to the Children of Zion
through Sidney Rigdon, Prophet, Seer, & Revelator."[2] Both volumes include

1. See Joseph Newton letter to Stephen Post, June 25, 1863, Joseph Newton letter to Stephen Post,
July 6, 1863, and newspaper clipping, October 28, [1863], Stephen Post papers, CHL. Stephen Post
papers hereafter cited as SPP. Also see Carol Freeman Braby, "Rigdonites in Manitoba, 1874–1884,"
John Whitmer Historical Association Journal 11 (1991):74.
2. Revelations Book A and Revelations Book B, SPP. Book A measures 20 × 25.5 cm and contains 124 ruled pages with marbled edges. The ruled pages are numbered by hand from 2 to 126
(skipping 1 and 3). Manuscript text fills each of the lined pages. Book A contains entries for sections
1–78. However, the texts of sections 9 and 34 were not copied into the book. Book B measures 20 ×
32.5 cm containing 240 lined pages with marbled edges. The lined pages in this volume are stamped
with numbers from 1 to 240. The writing is only found on 49 of the 240 lined pages. Book B contains Revelations 79–100 and a handful of other copied documents including a letter from Rigdon

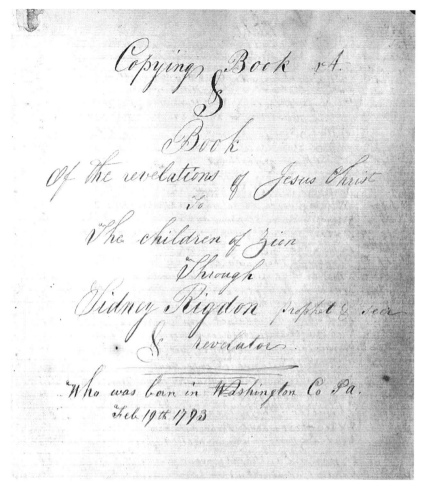

FIGURE 12.1. Revelations Book A title page. Courtesy of the Church History Library, the Church of Jesus Christ of Latter-day Saints.

a table of contents listing each of one hundred sections dictated between March 1856 and June 1876. Most sections are revelations dictated in the words of Deity, but the collection also includes letters and other statements.

---

to Post accompanying and explaining Section 38 on appointing Israel Huffaker as a Bishop in Zion; the mysterious Messenger & Advocate Extra containing the John C. Bennett fabricated 1841 revelation wherein Joseph Smith declares Sidney as his rightful successor; two sets of Children of Zion Conference minutes 1876 and 1877; and on the last page a copy of Stephen Post's 1836 Patriarchal blessing given under the hand of Joseph Smith Sen.

The Rigdons' Book of Revelations is a remarkable text—perhaps the most extravagant of the post-Smith Latter Day Saint scriptures.[3] It is reminiscent of Joseph Smith's Book of Commandments and Revelations, a manuscript that similarly collected his revelations before their publication in the Book of Commandments.[4] While it is not entirely clear that the Rigdons' Book of Revelations was intended for publication, it does seem clear that the revelations were intended as scripture for the Children of Zion.

In examining the Rigdons' revelations, we can see a path that many would-be successors to Joseph Smith's prophetic mantle had to navigate. Each had to grapple with a multitude of decisions regarding the expansive doctrines and institutions set up by Smith: accept and perpetuate them or reject aspects of his teachings and strike off in new directions. Since claimants to Smith's mantle were many, each sought to establish an unbreakable legitimizing link to him, while crafting a unique identity in contradistinction to the other claimants. This often involved selective adoption and rejection of Smith's teachings. With rejection came the task of justifying the decision and the complicated work of painting a new picture of Joseph's legacy.

This chapter examines three of the many themes that emerge from Sidney and Phebe Rigdon's revelatory writings: ecclesiology, the establishment of Zion, and expansions of Latter Day Saint scriptural narrative. In each case, the Rigdons demonstrate their ability to creatively build upon doctrines and institutions established under Joseph Smith. These and other topics addressed in the Book of Revelations were clearly built on the prophetic writings of Joseph Smith, though they also reverberated in new directions.

SIDNEY RIGDON, STEPHEN POST, AND THE CHILDREN OF ZION

Sidney Rigdon was a preacher among the millennialist and primitivist Disciples of Christ in 1830 as Mormonism dawned and its first missionaries were

---

3. The work of scriptural creation done by the Rigdons certainly rivals that of James Strang. See Christine Elyse Blythe and Christopher James Blythe "Strangite Scripture," chapter 9 herein.

4. See "Introduction: Manuscript Revelation Books," in *Manuscript Revelation Books, Facsimile Edition*, edited by Robin Scott Jensen, Robert J. Woodford, and Steven C. Harper, Revelations and Translations, vol. 1, Joseph Smith Papers, edited by Dean C. Jessee, Ronald K. Esplin, and Richard Lyman Bushman (Salt Lake City, UT: Church Historian's Press, 2009), xxv–xxx.

commissioned to gather the elect. Parley Pratt, one of the missionaries sent to preach among Native Americans, was formerly influenced by Rigdon and sought him out when the missionaries reached Ohio. In a short time, the Rigdons embraced the Book of Mormon and Joseph Smith's newly established Church of Christ.

After baptism, Sidney Rigdon soon set out to meet Joseph Smith himself. Smith quickly recognized what he had in his new convert from the western reserve. Rigdon's deep biblical knowledge and powerful preaching prowess rapidly drew him into Smith's inner circle. As Joseph Smith began his project to produce an inspired revision of the Bible, Rigdon served as scribe. Rigdon was called into the First Presidency to lead the new church alongside the Prophet. And in a defining moment for the young church, Rigdon joined Joseph Smith in experiencing "The Vision" of the glories of heavenly kingdoms.[5]

Sidney Rigdon enjoyed close companionship with the Prophet in good times and in bad. The two associates were dragged from their homes, beaten, and tarred and feathered by a mob in Kirtland. They were imprisoned in Missouri, and Rigdon's inflammatory rhetoric in response to mob oppression stoked the fires of persecution that eventually led to expulsion of the Saints from the state. Forced to begin again in Commerce-turned-Nauvoo, Illinois, the Rigdons established a new home for their family, and Sidney became postmaster, also continuing to serve alongside Joseph in the First Presidency. However, their once-strong bond began to dissolve as the crucible of Nauvoo polygamy tested and tried Joseph's closest disciples. Though their relationship was at times strained almost to breaking, Smith selected Rigdon as his running mate for the national election of 1844.[6]

In June 1844, Rigdon left Nauvoo for Pennsylvania to campaign. Smith was assassinated nine days later. When he learned of Smith's murder, a few days after arriving in Pittsburgh, he hurried back to Nauvoo. By August, Rigdon began to seek public recognition as "a Guardian appointed to build the

5. D&C 76. For more information on Rigdon's early biography and introduction to the Church of Christ, see Richard S. Van Wagoner, *Sidney Rigdon: A Portrait of Religious Excess* (Salt Lake City, UT: Signature Books, 1994), particularly chs. 1–6; For more information on Sidney Rigdon in Ohio, see Mark L. Staker, *Hearken O Ye People: The Historical Setting of Joseph Smith's Ohio Revelations* (Salt Lake City, UT: Greg Kofford Books, 2009).

6. For more information on Rigdon's association with Joseph Smith in the Nauvoo period, see Van Wagoner, *Sidney Rigdon*, particularly chs. 19–23.

Church up to Joseph as he had begun it."[7] Rigdon claimed to have had visions revealing he was the proper person to guide the church. Rigdon's claims and the apostles' response would leave the body of the church fractured. The majority of the Saints in Nauvoo sided with the apostles, who vowed to continue in Smith's footsteps. Rigdon retreated to Pennsylvania, where he still held influence among the Saints who had not gathered to Illinois.[8]

On April 6, 1845, Rigdon organized his supporters into the Church of Christ. This new organization attracted to its ranks some 400–500 Latter Day Saints in the northeastern United States. Seeking continuing prophetic leadership in the wake of Joseph Smith's untimely death, the converts were persuaded by arguments for Rigdon as proper successor to the prophetic office and convinced that the troubling reports of polygamy among the Saints in Nauvoo should be seen as the misguided actions of a fallen prophet. However, despite early successes, the movement crumbled after only two years. A poorly managed attempt to implement a communal system and a failed prophecy of the second advent of Jesus Christ resulted in almost total disaffection of church membership.[9] Rigdon lived the next decade in obscurity, until he received a letter in 1856 from a Latter Day Saint seeker, Stephen Post.

Post joined the Church of the Latter Day Saints in Pennsylvania in 1835. In 1836, he was ordained a Seventy and assigned to preach and "to gather the lost sheep of Israel."[10] After Smith's martyrdom, Post also had alternating sympathies when it came to which church and which prophet was Smith's rightful successor.[11] On July 19, 1846, after reading issues of the *Voree Her-*

7. William Clayton and George D. Smith, *An Intimate Chronicle: The Journals of William Clayton* (Salt Lake City, UT: Signature Books in Association with Smith Research Associates, 1995), 140.

8. For more information on Rigdon's views on succession and his conflict with the Quorum of the Twelve, see Ronald W. Walker, "Six Days in August: Brigham Young and the Succession," in *A Firm Foundation: Church Organization and Administration*, edited by David J. Whittaker and Arnold K. Garr (Provo, UT: Religious Studies Center, Brigham Young University; Salt Lake City, UT: Deseret Book, 2011), 161–196.

9. For more information on Rigdon's Church of Christ, see Van Wagoner, *Sidney Rigdon*, particularly chs. 25–26.

10. Stephen Post, Journal, February 13, 1836, SPP. Seventy is an office of priesthood designated in the revelations of Joseph Smith to preach the gospel under the direction of the twelve apostles. See Encyclopedia of Mormonism, https://eom.byu.edu/index.php/Seventy.

11. M. Guy Bishop, "Stephen Post: From Believer to Dissenter to Heretic," in *Differing Visions: Dissenters in Mormon History*, edited by Roger D. Launius and Linder Thatcher (Champaign: University of Illinois Press, 1994), 180–195; M. Guy Bishop, "A Tale of Two Mormons," *John Whitmer*

ald, a periodical published by the followers of James Strang in Wisconsin, he found "much good evidence that James Strang is appointed by the will of God to preside over his church as successor to Joseph Smith."[12] By 1850, Post had united with Strang's movement but had moved on by 1853, expressing doubts to his brother, Warren, one of Strang's apostles.[13] In 1855–1856, he participated in an effort by Martin Harris, one of the three witnesses of the Book of Mormon, and William Smith, one of the twelve apostles at the time of Joseph Smith's death, to form a church.[14] The Harris-Smith alliance did not last and Post was again unsure where to turn.

In 1856, Post contacted Sidney Rigdon to find out what had become of his aspirations to lead the Saints. Correspondence between Post and Rigdon, particularly those written in the early part of January 1856, became the impetus for Rigdon's revival. In March, Rigdon wrote to Post with a revelation calling him to "a great work in assisting my servant Sidney Rigdon in preparing the way before me . . ."[15] In time, Post responded to the call and became a dedicated follower who worked tirelessly until his death in 1879 to promote Rigdon's vision for the future of Latter Day Zion.

For over twenty years, Stephen Post acted as an intermediary between Sidney Rigdon and the church that accepted him as prophet, seer, and revelator. In response to direction from Rigdon, church leadership and a few families from the Attica, Iowa, branch moved to Manitoba, Canada, in 1874–1875 to establish their community. Within a year, Sidney Rigdon was dead and internal strife threatened the church. On December 18, 1879, Stephen Post—who had taken over leadership of the church—died. After Post's death, George M. Hinckle took lead of the Children of Zion in Manitoba. He would eventually be deposed after professing his support of Joseph Smith III and the Reorganization. Jane Post, Stephen's widow, would then lead the Children of Zion until her death. By 1884, the Manitoba branch had disintegrated, and the Children of Zion faded into history.[16]

Historical Association Journal 23 (2003):111–120; M. Guy Bishop, "'Simply Folly': Stephen Post and the Children of Zion," *John Whitmer Historical Association Journal* 16 (1996):79–90.

12. Stephen Post, Journal, July 26, 1846, SPP.

13. Stephen Post letter to Warren Post, October 2, 1853, Warren Post Papers, CHL.

14. Stephen Post, Journal, September 9–October 8, 1855, and April 4–11, 1856, SPP.

15. Sidney Rigdon letter to Stephen Post, March 1856, SPP. A portion of this letter was later recorded in the revelation books as Section 1 and is found in Revelations, Book A, SPP.

16. Braby, "Rigdonites in Manitoba," 71, 78–81.

ECCLESIOLOGY

Joseph Smith's revelations frequently described church government, detailing the responsibilities of councils and which priesthood offices could perform various ordinances. The Church of Jesus Christ of the Children of Zion was never large enough to require all the various councils and offices present in the Church of Jesus Christ of Latter-day Saints, but its structure mirrored the organization set up by Joseph Smith. This included parallels with local and general priesthood bodies as well as the church's hierarchy. This section considers the place of Sidney Rigdon as prophet, seer, and revelator, as well as two companion roles that had foundations in the early restoration: the spokesman, held by Stephen Post, and the prophetess of Zion, held by Phebe Rigdon.

Though Sidney Rigdon was an accomplished orator in the First Presidency of the Church of Jesus Christ of Latter Day Saints, it was not until the late 1850s and 1860s that his own prophetic voice flowered as head of the Children of Zion. Rigdon's revelations established a context for his last-days mission by framing his hardship and years in poverty following the collapse of the Church of Christ in 1846 as a necessary trial preparatory to fulfilling his role as a prophet and revelator. He alone had remained faithful to the restoration movement and would now fulfill a messianic responsibility. In 1863, Rigdon dictated a revelation explaining that God had "through much tribulations and some encouraging placed in the heart of my servant Sidney . . . the light that shall shine forth for the redemption of Zion."[17] Another revelation referred to Rigdon as the "organ through which I shall speak to you in all matters pertaining to Zion, and none other shall you receive; for him only have I proven before my face."[18]

Rigdon was encouraged to devote his energies to studying and receiving the word of the Lord. Echoing a July 1830 revelation to Joseph Smith, this revelation explained, "He who . . . is the head of Zion should not have power in temporal things, but should do my work." It continued: "No person can have power in temporal things unless he devotes his mind to it and no man can stand before the Lord and receive his word for Zion unless his whole mind

17. Revelation, October 1863, "Section 3d," Revelations, Book A, SPP.
18. Revelation, 25 January 1864, "Section 4th," Revelations, Book A, SPP.

is devoted to it. Hence it is that no man can attend to temporal things and be also a revelator in Zion."[19] The July 1830 revelation had similarly informed Joseph Smith that in "temporal labors thou shalt not have strength, for this is not thy calling."[20]

Therefore, to allow Rigdon to focus on his role as revelator, the revelation commanded recent convert Joseph Newton to "see that the temporal wants and necessities of my servant Sidney are supplied."[21] This emphasis on providing for their leader was repeated in later revelations that commanded all the Children of Zion to "relieve the temporal necessities of the priesthood through which their salvation comes."[22] Financial support for the Rigdons would be a demonstration that the Children of Zion recognized Sidney and Phebe Rigdon as the source of their salvation.

In addition to Rigdon's position as prophet, the Book of Revelations included several revelations establishing a role for Stephen Post. On March 17, 1856, in a letter addressed to Post, Rigdon included a revelation—which later became Section 1 of the Book of Revelations—explaining Post's call.

> Verily, verily thus saith the Lord unto my servant Stephen Post I have looked upon thee and seen thy works and thy desires to understand my revelations, and I have heard thy prayer. And now I the Lord say unto thee that I call [thee] to a great work in assisting my servant Sidney Rigdon in preparing the way before me, and Elijah which should come. . . . that my word might be brought forth to the children of men for their salvation and for the salvation of the house of Israel mine elect; So have I called thee to assist my servant Sidney Rigdon to send forth my word in deed, and in truth, and in power for the salvation of mine elect, and for the redemption of Zion.[23]

This passage explicitly mirrors language found in a December 1830 revelation dictated by Joseph Smith calling Sidney Rigdon to assist in the work. Compare it with the following:

19. Revelation, October 1863, "Section 3d," Revelations, Book A, SPP. See also D&C 26.
20. D&C 29:9
21. Revelation, October 1863, "Section 3d," Revelations, Book A, SPP.
22. Revelation, 25 January 1864, "Section 4th," Revelations, Book A, SPP.
23. Sidney Rigdon letter to Stephen Post, March 17, 1856, SPP.

Behold, verily, verily, I say unto my servant Sidney, I have looked upon thee and thy works. I have heard thy prayers, and prepared thee for a greater work. Thou art blessed, for thou shalt do great things. Behold thou wast sent forth, even as John, to prepare the way before me, and before Elijah which should come, and thou knewest it not. . . . Wherefore, watch over him that his faith fail not, and it shall be given by the Comforter, the Holy Ghost, that knoweth all things. And a commandment I give unto thee—that thou shalt write for him; and the scriptures shall be given, even as they are in mine own bosom, to the salvation of mine own elect.[24]

In a revelation dated March 27, 1866, Rigdon revealed that Post would serve as "a spokesman to my servant Sidney and to the children of Zion and my servant Sidney shall be revelator & expounder to him."[25] Once again, following the pattern set when Joseph Smith called him to be spokesman, Rigdon's revelation utilized similar phrasing.[26] With this step, Rigdon assumed the role vacated by Joseph Smith and the pairing of revelator and a spokesman was once more established.

Rigdon's revelations further amplified a biblical precedent for the prophet and his spokesman found in the relationship between Moses and Aaron.[27] Rigdon emphasized that he was not only following patterns established in the early years of the restoration under Joseph Smith, he was following an ancient system as well. The Lord declared through Rigdon that Stephen Post was rightly named, for "he is of the lineage of Stephen who was the first martyr for the truths sake" and that Post was chosen to be spokesman, "that the name of his progenitor 'Stephen' may be had in honorable remembrance in Zion forever." Not only were the two Stephens connected in name and revealed lineage, but Rigdon as seer revealed that the New Testament Stephen was "spokesman for the apostles though not one of them." In a

---

24. D&C 35:3–4, 19–20.

25. Sidney Rigdon letter to Stephen Post, March 27, 1866, SPP.

26. Compare D&C 100: 9–11: "And it is expedient in me that you, my servant Sidney, should be a spokesman unto this people; yea, verily, I will ordain you unto this calling, even to be a spokesman unto my servant Joseph. And I will give unto him power to be mighty in testimony. And I will give unto thee power to be mighty in expounding all scriptures, that thou mayest be a spokesman unto him, and he shall be a revelator unto thee . . ."

27. Revelation, 19 June 1864, "Section 6th," Revelations, Book A, SPP.

postscript to the foregoing revelation, Rigdon explained further that both Stephens traced a common lineage to Rigdon himself—that of the biblical prophet Samuel, who was of the lineage of Joseph of Egypt. Thus, Rigdon concluded, "It seems all the spokesmen the Lord appoints are of Joseph of Egypt from the days of Stephen the Martyr till the present time."[28]

Rigdon depended on Stephen Post to lead his church as spokesman, though it was subservient to Rigdon. However, Rigdon shared the responsibility of prophetic direction over the church with his wife, Phebe Rigdon, who would eventually dictate revelations like her husband. Her future prophetic role was foreshadowed in an 1864 revelation that referred to both Phebe and Sidney collectively as a "perfect priesthood." Rather than Sidney alone, it was to be "through them [Sidney and Phebe Rigdon] that the salvation of Zion comes. It is through them that deliverance comes to the house of Joseph. It is through them that the fullness of the gospel shall be preached to the ends of the earth, and Israel be gathered. For I the Lord have manifested myself to that priesthood, and I will continue to do it until Zion is filled with the light and knowledge of the Lord their God."[29]

The idea of a familial priesthood shared between spouses had a place in the theology of Joseph Smith that had been introduced toward the end of his life in Nauvoo.[30] Furthermore, Rigdon was at least partly inspired by Joseph Smith's July 1830 revelation addressed to his wife Emma Hale Smith that referred to her as "an elect lady" and stated, "Thou shalt be ordained under his hand to expound scriptures, and to exhort the church . . . and thy time shall be given to writing, and to learning much."[31] On March 17, 1842, at the organization of the Female Relief Society of Nauvoo, Smith referred to this revelation when Emma was recognized as the president of that society. He noted that she had been ordained at the time of the revelation "to expound the scriptures to all; and to teach the female part of community."[32]

28. Revelation, June 1867, "Section 28th," Revelations, Book A, SPP.

29. Revelation, 25 January 1864, "Section 4th," Revelations, Book A, SPP.

30. See Kathleen Flake, "The Emotional and Priestly Logic of Plural Marriage" (15th Annual Leonard J. Arrington Mormon History Lecture, Logan, Utah State University, October 1, 2009), p. 11–12.

31. D&C 25:4, 7–8.

32. "A Record of the Organization, and Proceedings of the Female Relief Society of Nauvoo," March 17, 1842, Relief Society minutebook, https://catalog.churchofjesuschrist.org/assets?id =3592a124-9532-4d6f-9fed-fd60215fea77&crate=0&index=30. Also see, Jill Mulvay Derr, Carol Cornwall Madsen, Kate Holbrook, and Mathew J. Grow, eds., *The First Fifty Years of Relief Society:*

In an 1872 revelation, Phebe was also given the responsibility to expound and teach as part of her role as "the first prophetess of Zion." Specifically, Phebe was charged with "the exposition of the Book of Mormon." Sidney Rigdon believed that the Saints' failure to emphasize the Book of Mormon's teachings was partly responsible for the corruption of the church under Joseph Smith. Phebe's exposition was a key to remedying this neglect. "All those who had professed to believe the Book of Mormon, their nominal faith will avail them nothing; it will tend to their condemnation unless they receive in their hearts and practice in their lives the righteousness of the kingdom of heaven as brought forth to you through the faith, patience diligence and perseverance of mine hand maiden [Phebe]."[33]

While Phebe's role as scriptural exegete had its basis in Emma Hale Smith's calling, Sidney's revelations amplified this position. Phebe assumed a role of preeminence as *the* expounder of scripture to the Children of Zion. "I the Lord speak to all the Children of Zion calling none such but those who learn righteousness through the instruction imparted through mine handmaiden Phebe.... and all who will be saved have to learn the law of my kingdom from the instruction which this mine handmaiden sends out among the Children of Zion."[34] The revelation went on to condemn those who rejected the teachings of the Book of Mormon as expounded by Phebe Rigdon. Phebe went on to produce twelve lessons that were distributed among the branches of the Children of Zion.[35]

The revelations resound with several more revealed titles given to Phebe Rigdon: handmaiden of the Lord; Mother of Zion; Lord's lamp in Zion; first born of woman; first born daughter of the holy Priesthood; beloved of the Lord; light of the world; first prophetess of Zion.[36] In her role as prophetess, Phebe Rigdon dictated at least six of the revelations recorded in the Book of

---

Key Documents in Latter-Day Saint Women's History (Salt Lake City, UT: Church Historians Press, 2016), 32.

33. Revelation, February 1, 1872, "Section 64th," Revelations, Book A, SPP.

34. Revelation, October 1871, "Section 63d," Revelations, Book A, SPP.

35. Phebe Rigdon, "Lessons from the Book of Mormon," SPP. The first lessons consist of Phebe's retelling of short Book of Mormon narratives followed by "thus we see" statements composed as exhortations to the Children of Zion to mirror the faithfulness of scriptural characters. Later lessons have fewer exhortations and many lengthy scriptural quotations.

36. Revelation, 25 January 1864, "Section 4th"; October 1871, "Section 63d"; 1 February 1872, "Section 64th"; October 1872, "Section 70th," Revelations, Book A; and Revelation, 1 November 1875, "Section 96th," Revelations, Book B, SPP.

FIGURE 12.2. Phebe Rigdon, ca. 1880. Courtesy of the Church History Library, the
Church of Jesus Christ of Latter-day Saints.

Revelations.[37] Further, in language reminiscent of the title given to Emma Smith, the Lord called and Sidney ordained Phebe to be the head of an "Elect Sisterhood," a quorum of female priesthood holders. [38]

Phebe was not destined to be alone in studying, exhorting, and expounding scriptures to all, "but others, [were to] attain to the same blessing."[39] Phebe's exposition of the Book of Mormon was to go to the Elect Sisterhood that, in turn, they would teach it to the Children of Zion.[40] Phebe exhorted these sisters commissioned to teach the lessons, "This is the beginning of a great duty that is to be continued from day to day and from year to year until all the holy principles contained in [the Book of Mormon] may be brought forth and laid before the priesthood of Zion. . . ."[41] The Children of Zion were urged to mine the Book of Mormon for precious truths and follow the righteous examples of their Nephite forbearers if they were to succeed in establishing latter-day Zion.

In the ecclesiastical structures built by the Rigdons, we can see recognizable patterns drawn from Joseph Smith's Latter Day Saint Church. This continuity would have offered the followers of Sidney Rigdon, most of whom were already a part of the Latter Day Saint movement, a sense of familiarity and a visible connection to the founding prophet. Yet Sidney Rigdon's revelations built in creative new ways on top of the structure Joseph had already established. Assuming the role of prophet, seer, and revelator demonstrated a continuity of prophetic gifts. Rigdon reestablished and reemphasized the

37. Revelation, 3 November 1873, "Section 82"; 6 November 1873 "Section 83"; 24 December 1874, "Section 91st"; 18 October 1875 "Section 94th"; 20 May 1876, "Section 99"; 15 June and 20 July 1876, "Section 100," Revelations, Book B, SPP. Also, Phebe is a cosignatory alongside Sidney for an additional seventeen revelations: Revelation, 13 December 1864 "Section 19th"; 1 March 1869, "Section 51st"; 1 April 1869 "Section 52nd"; 22 April 1869 "Section 53d"; 1 February 1872, "Section 64th"; April 1872, "Section 66th"; 6 April "1872 Section 67th"; October 1872, "Section 70th"; August 1873 "Section 74th"; 22 September 1873, "Section 76th"; 8 September 1873, "Section 78"; 4 October 1873, "Section 79th"; 5 December 1873, "Section 84th"; 1 January 1874, "Section 86th"; 23 September 1874, "Section 89th"; 30 March 1875, "Section 93d"; 26 October 1875, "Section 95th," Revelations, Books A and B, SPP.

38. Revelation, October 1864, "Section 17th"; 1 June 1868, "Section 35th"; October 1868, "Section 43d"; December 1868, "Section 49th"; October 1871, "Section 63d"; 1 February 1872, "Section 64th"; October 1872, "Section 70th," Revelations, Book A; and Revelation 24 December 1874, "Section 91st," Revelations, Book B, SPP.

39. "A Record of the Organization, and Proceedings of the Female Relief Society of Nauvoo," March 17, 1842, Relief Society minutebook., https://catalog.churchofjesuschrist.org/assets?id=3592a124-9532-4d6f-9fed-fd60215fea77&crate=0&index=30. Also see, Also, Derr, Madsen, Holbrook, and Grow, eds., The First Fifty Years of Relief Society, 32.

40. Revelation, 1 June 1868, "Section 35th," Revelations, Book A, SPP.

41. "First Preface to Lessons," Lessons from the Book of Mormon, SPP.

role of spokesman, which seems to have largely been abandoned during the last several years of Smith's life. But Rigdon also expanded Smith's concept of an "elect lady," first into the role given to his wife Phebe as prophetess in Zion and second in the creation of an elect sisterhood, with its own quorums. Unique among nineteenth-century Latter Day Saints, this sisterhood was organized under the direction of Phebe Rigdon into quorums of female priesthood holders ordained and commissioned to serve in a variety of church positions. Sidney Rigdon would come to see eschatological overtones for the emergence of female priests. They were key for the establishment of the last-days Zion in preparation for the Second Coming.[42]

ZION

Joseph Smith's conception of latter-day Zion developed within a cultural milieu saturated with Christian primitivist ideas of restorationism and imminent millennialism. Joseph Smith and several early converts had been influenced by the primitivist movement in early nineteenth-century America and brought many ideas with them into the Church of Christ. Zion as it appears in Joseph's earliest revelations was introduced with little context but quickly developed to incorporate the concept of gathering—both of God's chosen people as well as heavenly knowledge in a dispensation of fullness, preparatory to Christ's millennial reign on earth. The content of Smith's revelations then moved from theoretical gathering to geographic location, coupled with the idea of a city Zion. This was followed in December 1830 by his epic Vision of Enoch text, which anthropologist Steven Olsen has termed "the sacred charter for the quest of Zion." This vision, Olsen observes, "gave theological, cosmological, eschatological, social, and personal sanction to the quest for Zion. Strains of the ideas of the vision had been present in Mormonism, but the vision integrated and energized them in a powerful and unmistakable manner."[43] The three components of latter-day Zion—a Prophet, a people, and a gathering place—were given scriptural precedent.

42. Revelation, October 1864, "Section 15th"; February 1867, "Section 27th"; November 1868, "Section 46th"; October 1872, "Section 70th," Revelations, Book A; and Revelation, 5 December 1873, "Section 84th," Revelations, Book B, SPP. See also Ian G. Barber, "The Ecclesiastical Position of Women in Two Mormon Trajectories," *Journal of Mormon History* 14 (1988):63–79.

43. Steven L. Olsen, *The Mormon Ideology of Place: Cosmic Symbolism of the City of Zion, 1830–1846* (Provo, UT: Joseph Fielding Smith Institute for Latter-day Saint History, 2002), 26.

Echoes of many zionic concepts formulated in the revealed word to Joseph Smith reverberate in Sidney Rigdon's revelations to the Children of Zion in the 1860s and 1870s. What follows is a brief discussion of a few prominent motifs found in Rigdon's revelations as they relate to establishing earthly Zion: flee imminent destruction and gather to Zion; prepare the way for the priesthood (Sidney and Phebe) to settle in Zion; gather to a specific place (first in Iowa, later in Canada); and flee the jurisdiction of the United States to a place where Zion can flourish.[44]

In June 1864, Rigdon dictated a revelation prophesying imminent "desolations" on the "eastern lands," which consisted of "all the region of this country laying between what you call the Atlantic on the east and the Mississippi on the west. And between the Gulf of Mexico on the South and the great lakes on the North as it is named among you." "Famine sword and pestilence" would transform the eastern United States into a "howling wilderness." The Children of Zion could find safety "in the West where [their] lives or that of any others can be saved; for the decree of utter destruction ... as far as this country is concerned." The Children of Zion were counseled to finish their missionary work in the eastern United States, flee "Babylon," and "go as far west as the place known as Council Bluffs in Iowa."[45] Rigdon's revelations began to emphasize the importance of gathering.

Two months later, in August 1864, Rigdon dictated a revelation announcing that the missionaries had completed their work in the East to warn and call repentance. They were then called to turn their "whole attention to getting the priesthood [Phebe and Sidney Rigdon] settled in the place appointed for that purpose [Iowa]."[46] At this point, the Rigdons expected to join with the Children of Zion in the Midwest and pressed the leadership to prepare the way. Another revelation addressed to the general membership announced that God had "given to you the whole state of Iowa into which you will council all which believe my word through your testimony ... to go and take possession of the land I have chosen for them."

Having learned from previous attempts to gather the Saints and establish Zion in Missouri, which had resulted in widespread persecution and the Saints' eventual ejection from the state, Rigdon's revelation cautioned the

44. Ibid., chs. 1–2.
45. Revelation, 26 June 1864, "Section 7th" Revelations, Book A, SPP.
46. Revelation, 15 August 1864, "Section 10th," Revelations, Book A, SPP.

Saints to avoid attracting undue attention. They were counseled to "avoid as much as possible crowding together in large bodies. Let them go as other emigrants into the land being keepers of their own secret. Behold this is wisdom." God had promised the Children of Zion "the whole state of Iowa" as an inheritance but counseled that this pearl of knowledge was not to be cast before swine, that they should be keepers of their own secret. If the Saints were to "do in all these things as I the Lord direct," the result would be that "in process of time you should find Zion having possession of the whole state."[47]

By October 1864, Stephen Post and several families had relocated in and around the small south-central Iowa community of Attica in Marion County. As the Children of Zion began to settle themselves, Sidney Rigdon received further revelation commanding the Children of Zion to prepare a place for their prophetic head. In fact, they were warned that a mere immigration to Iowa was insufficient.

> Zion is not there neither can it ever be there till my holy priesthood [Sidney and Phebe] to which I have given Zion is taken there and established. . . . The Children of Zion must take it there and raise it up out of all its cares and afflictions or else it will be vain for them to go there. They may have houses and lands to live on; but Zion will not be in their midst.[48]

Sidney and Phebe Rigdon and their perfected priesthood were to be viewed as an embodiment of Zion. For the Lord had "made my priesthood [Sidney and Phebe Rigdon] to the Children of Zion what the ark of the covenant was to the children of Israel, and their salvation depends on having it with them."[49]

Seven years later, by October 1871, most of the Children of Zion had gathered to Iowa, yet the ark of the covenant remained in Friendship, New York. Stephen Post wrote to ask when the Rigdons would join them. In reply, he received a new revelation.

47. Revelation, 19 September 1864, "Section 11th," Revelations, Book A, SPP.
48. Revelation, October 1864, "Section 17th," Revelations, Book A, SPP.
49. Ibid.

Behold saith the Lord your God concerning my servant Sidney. It is not my will that he should go there at present on his own account that he may escape persecution which will fall on him if he goes there at present certainly.... Therefore I the Lord your God have kept him, and must keep him away until the storm is passed. Again I say concerning him he can do all that is necessary to enable you to move the cause of Zion as at present and be here and thus escape persecution.[50]

The revelation softened the earlier revelatory stance on the necessity of the Rigdons' presence in Iowa as a prerequisite for establishing Zion. By 1872, the revealed word of the Lord declared that Zion was established despite the absence of the Rigdons, who remained in the accursed eastern United States. Dire predictions and urgent warnings continued to highlight the revelations. The Children of Zion were continually called upon to flee from impending destruction in the East and to gather to the safety of Zion across the Mississippi, in Iowa.

But in September 1873, a revelation notified Stephen Post that Zion would be removed from Iowa.[51] On October 4, further word came: "The change of the location of Zion will be from under the rule of this government [the United States] to that of the British [in Canada].... Zion will be fixed there till the time spoken of when she shall become very great." The revelation promised that in Canada, "the Children of Zion can be perfectly safe while this side of the lakes [in the United States] the people shall be drinking their own blood as the old prophetic word has told us."[52]

The idea that the Saints had to abandon the United States was also a common argument among those who had gathered with Brigham Young to the Great Basin. Further, the Book of Mormon predicted that the descendants of Lehi would be crucial for the last-days building of Zion.[53] A November 3 revelation continued,

---

50. Revelation, October 1871, "Section 63d," Revelations, Book A, SPP.

51. Revelation, 22 September 1873, "Section 76th," Revelations, Book A, SPP.

52. Revelation, 4 October 1873, "Section 79th," Revelations, Book B, SPP. See also Braby, "Rigdonites in Manitoba."

53. Jared Hickman, "*The Book of Mormon* as Amerindian Apocalypse," *American Literature* 86, no. 3 (September 2014):429–461.

Zion will have to be situated in a country where access can be had to the Lamanites which cannot be had in this country.... There is but one place in the world from the midst of whom Zion can come forth. It is alone in the British possessions of this country where Zion can be established, no where else on the earth are Nephites found.[54]

We can see from the foregoing that Sidney Rigdon's concept of Zion followed many of the patterns already revealed by Joseph Smith. Under Rigdon, the geographic location shifted from Smith's Zion in Independence, Missouri, to Iowa and then to Canada, but the overarching structure of a prophet, a people, and a gathering place persisted.[55]

For the Children of Zion, there was a difficult tension between the concept of Zion as place versus Zion as embodied in the perfected priesthood of Sidney and Phebe Rigdon. Through most of the church's existence, the Children of Zion were required to sacrifice their means to prepare a place that in essence Zion may come to them. This would enable the Rigdons, the embodied ark of the covenant, the light and salvation of Zion, to rise, come forth, and bring Zion to her children. Several factors prevented the preparation of a place for the Rigdons among the Children of Zion, and, in the end, the infirmities of age caught up with Sidney, which made gathering with his followers impossible.

EXPANDING SCRIPTURAL MYTHOLOGY

While Joseph Smith was the translator of the Book of Mormon, Sidney and Phebe Rigdon were responsible for its interpretation and distribution. Sidney Rigdon was also responsible for illuminating the Bible. His revelations often consisted of scriptural exegesis focused on passages in the Bible or the Book of Mormon. He built on interpretations of the Saints' roles in the last days, the significance of the Americas as the promised land, and his own ministry in leading the Children of Zion. Rigdon's revelations placed current

54. Revelation, 3 November 1873, "Section 82d," Revelations, Book B, SPP.
55. It should be noted that though Zion as gathering place persisted, Sidney Rigdon does not appear to have incorporated Joseph Smith's revealed plan for the City of Zion with its prescribed features.

leadership in the context of scriptural figures, providing them with biblical progenitors or prophetic destinies. The female priesthood was represented as the woman in the wilderness from the Revelation of St. John.[56] What follows are three instances (among many) in which he expanded on established scriptural narratives.

First, Rigdon added to the narrative of Nephite civilization, building onto the Book of Mormon, Joseph Smith's introduction of an ancient Judeo-Christian, proto-American society descended from an Israelite community that left Jerusalem during the reign of King Zedekiah. Rigdon had already introduced this story on the origins of indigenous people in Canada four years before he commanded his flock to relocate to Manitoba, but it likely paved the way to help them see their new home as part of the sacred geography of their faith.[57] This was significant, given that Rigdon was moving his people away from the epicenter of Latter Day Saint mythology then in Missouri. Historian Christopher James Blythe has charted how post–1844 Nephite stories, including James J. Strang's translation of the Voree plates and Brigham Young's sermons on the spirits of the Gadianton Robbers in the Great Basin, transported the Saints' sacred mythology to new locations to inform colonization efforts.[58]

A February 1870 revelation designated "Section 58th" focused on the fulfillment of a promise made by Lehi to his youngest son, Joseph, that his "seed should not be destroyed." Lehi prophesied that from Joseph's posterity "shall rise up one mighty among them, who shall do much good, both in word and in deed, being an instrument in the hands of God, with exceeding faith, to work mighty wonders, and do that thing which is great in the sight of God, unto the bringing to pass much restoration unto the house of Israel, and unto the seed of thy brethren."[59] Rigdon's revelation explained how Joseph's posterity was able to survive the Nephite holocaust so that one could fulfill this prophecy in the future.

56. Revelation, October 1864, "Section 15th"; 10 October 1872, "Section 70th," Revelations, Book A, SPP.

57. Revelation, 23 September 1874, "Section 89th," Revelations, Book B, SPP.

58. Christopher James Blythe, *Terrible Revolution: Latter-day Saints and the American Apocalypse* (New York: Oxford University Press, 2020).

59. 2 Nephi 3:23–24.

When the time came for the entire overthrow of the Nephites there were three men all brothers, of the descendants of this Joseph, men who had made themselves well acquainted with all the writings and records of the Nephites, and in consequence of this were fully apprised of the fact that the days of the Nephites were numbered, and that their entire overthrow, and their abolishment drew near; and knowing of the promise made to their progenitor, came before me by whom the promise was given, and sought with mighty prayer & supplication that I the Lord would fulfil the promise made to their first father, and give an heir of the promise through them, & I their Savior heard and answered their prayers & intercessions. The name of the elder of the three was Joseph being called after his father. The name of the second was Abinadi, and that of the third Ammon. They were all righteous men and dwelt in the fear of the Lord their God. Also their women were full of faith & righteousness, very devout and given to much prayer. Thus the three with their companions formed a perfect priesthood & by the power of the priesthood which was established with them they obtained deliverance.

Rigdon added in a postscript that he had prayed about "the names of the women" and learned that "their names were Mehellonesse, Jesselonia, & Amaduthah & they were thus connected Joseph and Mehellonesse, Abinadi & Jesselonia, Ammon & Ammadutha." In one short sentence, Rigdon doubled the number of female names present in the Book of Mormon. He also invested these figures with the priesthood as he had women disciples in his own day. The revelation continued by describing the escape and subsequent journey of the three Nephite families.

Thus saith the Lord while the arrangement was making for their departure the Nephites and Lamanites were engaged in destroying each other, and they arose and fled from the midst of the scene of blood and carnage to the place of their deliverance. Of this departure none but themselves knew. It was with them as it was with Lehi when he left Jerusalem. Having made all preparations that could be made for their escape they and their families started they found game plenty after a few days journey, which they by their bows & arrows secured in abundance for themselves and families taking the opposite direction from the parties at war, for those pressed eastward while these went westward. A few days travel took them where they were out of all danger and where they could kindle fires at night for which they had made preparation before they started. I the Lord directed their course so as they might pass in the high lands which divided the waters of the north from those of the south, so that they escaped all large streams and in this way they reached the great waters of the west. There they pitched their tents and made their permanent home, there they lived raised their families, & there they died, and there are their Nephite children of the pure blood to this day. By the Gentiles they are known by the name of Esquimaux. . . . Verily saith the Lord these Nephite descendants of Joseph are a great people they stretch along the entire northern boundary of this continent from sea to sea, & it is from them that the great man promised to this Joseph shall come who is to bring forth much restoration to the house of Israel.[60]

Thus, Lehi's prophecy of the survival of Joseph's descendants was fulfilled. Rigdon's doctrine of priesthood shared by men and women was given a historical antecedent. Moreover, a specific North American indigenous population was identified as having direct Nephite (rather than Lamanite) ancestry, and its people were identified as those through whom the "great man," descended from the Book of Mormon Joseph, was to come. Of course, this extracanonical Book of Mormon narrative also demonstrated to Rigdon's followers his gift as seer.

Rigdon's expansions (such as this story on the origins of the Eskimo) did not restore ancient records as Joseph Smith or James Strang did. They might reveal ancient events without referring to an ancient record at all. In other cases, Rigdon's revelations merely discussed the content of ancient texts. This was the case with Rigdon's revelation on the contents of the "sealed plates" of the Book of Mormon. Since Joseph Smith translated and published the Book of Mormon in 1830, Latter Day Saints have looked forward to portions that were sealed and left untranslated. Smith promised that this greater record

60. Revelation, February 1870, "Section 58th," Revelations, Book A, SPP.

would eventually come forth. In October 1868, Sidney Rigdon dictated a revelation to address the Children of Zion's "anxiety to grasp after unrevealed things … and seeing their conjectures in relation to the character of those things and form opinions concerning them which are not correct." According to the revelation, there were already false ideas concerning the sealed portion that were entertained among the Children of Zion. Departing from what Latter Day Saints had typically expected, the revelation explained that "the record spoken of differs from the book of Mormon in its being historical instead of doctrinal."[61]

Continuing the revelation, Rigdon presented the sealed portion as an elaborate prophecy of what would occur in the last dispensation.

> The untranslated record deals in history, taking the history of Zion from the coming forth of the book of Mormon giving its history.... The sealed record begins with Zion as it existed from the commencement under the administration of Joseph Smith & gives not only the history of Zion but of Joseph Smith also under whose administration it first made its appearance, Shewing how it was that "he" was called to that work giving the history of his corrupting his way before the Lord and using the grace of God bestowed on him to gratify laciviousness [*sic*] & the prostitution of it to carnal & sensual purposes & gratifications. It gives his history until he was rejected & cut off from before the Lord & it continues his history to his final doom being cast out with hypocrites into outer darkness where there is weeping and wailing & gnashing of teeth.[62]

The language Rigdon employed here to condemn Joseph Smith to outer darkness represents a break with Joseph's teachings and made more specific in several other revelations. The carnality and lasciviousness referred to was Smith's practice of plural marriage, a polarizing practice rejected by many early Latter Day Saint groups. Rigdon's refusal to accept plural marriage in Nauvoo drove a wedge between him and Smith. Though many of Rigdon's revelations salute Smith as the first prophet of the restoration and the seer

61. Revelation, October 1868, "Section 42nd," Revelations, Book A, SPP.
62. Ibid.

who revealed the Book of Mormon, we see an utter rejection of plural marriage in other Rigdon revelations.[63]

The revelation continued, revealing that the sealed plates would also "give the history of the family to which Joseph Smith belonged, giving an account of their being lifted up in the pride of their hearts & in consequence of that fell into the condemnation of the devil and were rejected of God." The plates apparently also rejected Smith's descendants, then leading the Reorganized Church of Jesus Christ of Latter Day Saints. This direct condemnation of Joseph Smith and his family was "the reason why no part of this record could be made known until another revelator stood before the Lord through whom it could come & had there not another revelator rose up before the Lord no part of it could ever have come to light for it was not possible for any man to have brought to light his own fate as it is written in that record." The sealed plates also condemned Rigdon's other rivals, the twelve apostles of "the corrupted church." The sealed plates ended more optimistically with the success of Rigdon's church in building Zion. "It follows Zion as thus redeemed to her eternal glory." Rather than promise that he would one day reveal this record, Rigdon's revelation noted that "the rise & progress of Zion to her perfection are a practical translation of the sealed plates so that Zion as she passes along practically translates the sealed plates."[64]

Further, there were additional records in the sealed portion of the Book of Mormon, including "the prophecies of the former prophets such as Isaiah, Jeremiah, Ezekiel, Daniel & other prophets transferred onto the sealed plates." These revealed the history noted above. The revelation also mentions "the vision of Obadiah," noting that it "is of that number which is recorded on the sealed plates in full." That vision had already been revealed to the Children of Zion.[65]

It is to this vision of Obadiah, revealed in February of 1867, that we now turn. Rigdon's revelation rephrased and added context to the Old Testament book of Obadiah. This book had already become significant in Latter Day Saint theology after Joseph Smith declared that Obadiah's reference to

---

63. Ibid. For Rigdon's rejection of plural marriage see, Revelation, 27 March 1866, "Section 22nd"; October 1872, "Section 70th," Revelations, Book A; Revelation, 18 October 1873, "Section 81st," Revelations, Book B, SPP.

64. Ibid.

65. Ibid.

"saviors on Mount Zion" referred to the Saints of the last days who would build temples and perform baptisms for the dead and other vicarious ordinances for their progenitors.[66] Rigdon's revelation expounded on other passages of the text to relate the entire book of Obadiah to the Latter Day Saint experience.

> Among this number of prophets and righteous men was Obadiah who prophecied of your day and your times, for so great was his faith & his desire that nothing could be withheld from him. He beheld how entirely the Gentiles were given over to the works of darkness, and he looked till he saw the book of Mormon come forth, and he beheld that many of the Gentiles received it and gathered together to learn the things of God and he was glad: but he saw that after a season the devil began to get power over them also as well as other Gentiles. And he beheld that they began to be lifted up in the pride of their hearts and began to contend with one another, and he saw that they were overcome by the powers of darkness and were cast down as at this day.

Rigdon's revelation described Obadiah's reaction to the scene: "And when he saw it his heart sank within him and he fell upon his face and wept bitterly. Wailing before the Lord his God, fearing that all was lost forever. But I the Lord called unto him & said Obadiah look; and he arose and looked." The revelation proceeded to rephrase Obadiah's description of the saviors on Mount Zion. "Behold out of the midst of darkness & confusion which every where reigned over that people, he saw Saviors coming up and standing high up as though they were standing upon a mountain above the people and they looked to him as gold tried and purified in the fire: and he beheld that they had power through their faith and righteousness to judge this mountain of iniquity or of Esau as he called it, and to triumph over it, and his heart was glad unto exceeding joy."

Obadiah was moved by these saviors, "And so minutely did he mark the expression of countenance of each and their peculiar features that he will know them when he sees them in the eternal world." As Rigdon's revelation

66. "Discourse, 21 January 1844, as Reported by Wilford Woodruff," p. [182], JSP, https://www.josephsmithpapers.org/paper-summary/discourse-21-january-1844-as-reported-by-wilford-woodruff/2.

continued, the names of the Saviors were given in the voice of the Lord to the Children of Zion: Sidney, Phebe, Sarah and Joseph Newton, and Stephen Post. Each was a leader in Rigdon's new organization, and each was now given a place in scriptural mythology as having been seen and known by the prophet Obadiah thousands of years before their current ministry among the Children of Zion.[67]

In this expansion of the vision of Obadiah, we can see the confluence of Sidney Rigdon's ecclesiastical organization and his concept of Zion. The specifically named saviors on Mt. Zion are the same individuals commissioned in other revelations to fill the highest offices in the ecclesiastical structure of the Church of Jesus Christ of the Children of Zion. These saviors of Zion held fast "to the words of eternal life, and by these means were able to judge the mountain of Esaū ... [and] to try those who said they were apostles and prophets but were not." Because of their faithfulness, they were able to recognize that rival claimants to lead the Latter Day Saints were false prophets, and by this means they had "save[d] Zion from an entire overthrow."[68]

Sidney Rigdon's revelations routinely and creatively expanded on biblical narrative and themes to infuse his Zion project with sacred and scriptural precedent. He guided his followers to see fulfillment of ancient prophecy in the actions they were taking to establish latter-day Zion. Indeed, "All things written in books concerning the gathering of Israel, the salvation of Zion, & the redemption of the world belong to the priesthoods & to the Children of Zion."[69]

We have also seen how Sidney Rigdon rejected plural marriage and repositioned Joseph Smith as a fallen prophet to justify his move away from polygamy. By framing the rejection of Joseph's marriage doctrine as a rebuke from God, the Rigdons were empowered to stake out a position distinct from the followers of Brigham Young and James Strang.

CONCLUSION

Sidney Rigdon's numerical influence never reached its former heights when he worked closely with Joseph Smith in Ohio and Missouri. However, his

67. Revelation, February 1867, "Section 27th," Revelations, Book A, SPP.

68. Ibid.

69. Ibid.

prophetic voice blossomed while he expanded and shared that mantle with his wife Phebe. Together they produced one hundred revelations read as scripture. In the Rigdons, we see a second generation of prophetic gifts and remarkable continuity with those exhibited by Joseph Smith, as well as the continuation of a church guided by living oracles. At the same time, Sidney and Phebe Rigdon found in Joseph Smith's doctrine of plural marriage a bothersome thorn that had to be removed. While maintaining a deliberate connection to the Book of Mormon and earlier principles and practices revealed by Smith, the Rigdons removed the offending barb and became free to walk their own path.

Echoes of the word of the Lord through Joseph Smith resound: the ecclesiastical structures, vision of earthly Zion, and patterns of scriptural expansion developed under Smith were foundational for the Rigdons' later developments. Though certainly creative and sometimes unexpected, the Rigdons' innovations were variations on a theme, as in a complex fugue, more than they were new compositions. Sidney and Phebe Rigdon take their places in the ranks of second-generation restoration prophets who adeptly rejected certain teachings of Joseph Smith while embracing and mirroring his charismatic gifts.

PART IV

Case Studies in New Scripture

Twentieth and Twenty-First Centuries

13

Harry Edgar Baker and
The Word of the Lord

Thomas G. Evans and Christopher James Blythe

*And in a vision of the night, the Father came to me and laid
before me a tablet of a manuscript; and another said to me that
I should write; and the Spirit of the Lord came upon me that I
should write, even the word of the Lord.*

—Harry Edgar Baker, The Word of the Lord

On April 6, 1916, Harry Edgar Baker dictated the first of two apocalyptic "messages," which he titled collectively The Word of the Lord to His church in the wilderness: and to all the nations of the Gentiles. He financed the printing of the First Message in December 1917 himself, after failing to find an interested publisher. The next year, he dictated and published the Second Message. In both cases, his booklets were organized like "scripture" in section and verse. They were written in the voice of God, who had a warning for a modern world that had rejected the prophets, oppressed the poor, and initiated "the greatest of all the wars of history."[1] The messages detailed society's sins, lambasted Christianity's theological errors, and promised the imminent apocalypse culminating at the return of Christ.

The Word of the Lord was dictated during what has been called the period of transition (1890–1930) in the history of The Church of Jesus Christ of Latter-day Saints.[2] This period was characterized by the Saints' transition

---

1. The Word of the Lord to His Church in the Wilderness; and to All the Nations of the Gentiles, Message 1, 15. Subsequently cited as Message 1.
2. Thomas Alexander, *Mormonism in Transition: A History of the Latter-day Saints, 1890–1930*, 3rd ed. (Salt Lake City, UT: Grag Kofford Books, 2012 [1986].

from a polygamous, theocratic sect residing in the western territories of the United States to a monogamous, democratic denomination headquartered in the state of Utah. Visionaries and prophets emerged to condemn the church's Americanization. Baker's apocalyptic messages seem to speak to these concerns. What sets The Word of the Lord apart from typical Latter Day Saint prophecy literature is its emphasis on the errors of the LDS Church and the calling of a prophet outside of the standard church hierarchy.

In addition to examining the content of The Word of the Lord, we argue here that while the messages never led to the formation of a new community, as was usually the goal for similar prophetic works, they have been adopted by individuals and small groups within Mormon Fundamentalism. These disenfranchised Mormons were and continue to be attracted to the messages' condemnation of the LDS Church and their corresponding promises of a renewal of the tradition.

HARRY EDGAR BAKER AND THE WORD OF THE LORD

Harry Edgar Baker was born to Rose Lucia Thurston and James Heaton Baker on August 31, 1854, in Chillicothe, Ohio. His grandfather had been a well-known Methodist minister. His father, James Baker, graduated from Ohio Wesleyan University and had purchased a local newspaper, *Scioto Gazette*. A year after his son's birth, James became the Secretary of State of Ohio, the first of several state and federal appointments he would hold through his life. In 1858, the family relocated to Minnesota, where James continued to be active in Republican politics and again served as Secretary of State. He would go on to serve in the military in the Civil War and achieved the rank of Brigadier General. When James died in 1913, his obituary was published throughout the eastern United States.[3]

We know little about Harry Edgar Baker's upbringing or early life. He attended the University of Michigan and, at some point, followed in his father's footsteps working with newspapers. Baker's daughter recalled that he "worked for a time as a newspaper man, doing some cartooning and was an

---

3. "General James H. Baker Who Has Held Many Offices of Trust, Dies in Minnesota," *Cincinnati Enquirer*, May 27, 1913; "General James H. Baker Dies," *The [Chicago] Inter Ocean*, May 27, 1913; "Gen. J. H. Baker Dies; His Career Notable," *[Minneapolis] Star Tribune*, May 27, 1913.

excellent speaker."[4] As part of a prominent family, it is not surprising that he would later be described as "a gentleman, well-bred, educated, and refined."[5]

Baker married Lillaetta Warner in 1882 while still residing in Minnesota. Their son, Harry Warner Baker, was born two years later. On June 23, 1888, Harry Edgar Baker was baptized and confirmed a member of the Church of Jesus Christ of Latter-day Saints and moved west, leaving Lillaetta and his child in Minnesota.[6] In July of the following year, Baker was inducted or "set apart" as a missionary to the Northwestern States, residing in Baker City, Oregon.[7] He was a bachelor for only a short time after leaving Lillaetta, marrying Sarah Jane Mills on August 26, 1890. In 1900, he married two other women: Sarah's sister, Charlotte Ann Mills, and, later the same year, Rebecca Gertrude Lorden. The church had formally abandoned the practice of plural marriage in 1890 with the issuing of a statement known as "the Manifesto." But select church leaders continued to privately encourage members to practice plural marriage until 1904, when then-president of the church Joseph F. Smith announced that future polygamists would be excommunicated.[8] According to family histories, Baker had been invited by apostles James Talmage and Matthias Cowley "to participate in the institution of polygamy and persuaded him it was the desire of the entire First Presidency."[9] Talmage's involvement in such a request seems unlikely. While Baker was acquainted with Talmage as a neighbor in Salt Lake City, Talmage was a monogamist and would not be called as an apostle until 1911. However, it is possible that Cowley may have extended such an invitation. He had offered similar encouragement to others.[10] Grace Gertrude, a daughter born to Baker's third wife, recalled that her father had assured her mother that the Manifesto was not designed to end plural marriage but to have Latter-day Saints continue the practice on their own responsibility rather than turn to

4. Family History. Thomas G. Evans collected family histories from Baker descendants who wished to remain anonymous through email correspondence and interviews conducted from July 2009 to December 2013.

5. "Sherri's Account of H. E. Baker," familysearch.org.

6. Handwritten genealogical records from the descendants of Baker and his fourth wife, Rebecca Gertrude Lorden, note a "civil divorce" between Lillaetta and Harry with no date given.

7. See https://history.lds.org/missionary/individual/harry-edgar-baker-1854.

8. "Official Statement," *Conference Report*, April 1904, 75.

9. Family History.

10. B. Carmon Hardy, *Solemn Covenant: The Mormon Polygamous Passage* (Urbana: University of Illinois Press, 1992), 209, 316.

church leaders for permission. Her father had "erroneously explained that the authorities of the church did not want to know." Grace had also been informed that "Aunt Sarah had received a letter authorizing them to marry, from Apostle Cowley."[11]

We know only scant details about Baker's life in the twentieth century. In 1908, he became a high councilor in the North Weber Stake in Utah. When he resigned in 1912, he announced that "he would be absent in the east for six or eight months and was not certain he would remain in the stake when he returned."[12] He relocated to Chicago and did not return as expected. Rebecca Gertrude Lorden recalled that her youngest daughter, who was born in December 1909, was "about two when Mr. Baker left us."[13] According to the memoirs of his daughter, Grace Gertrude, "When it was known that our father was married in polygamy, to avoid the law and the shame of excommunication, he took his first wife and family and moved to Chicago."[14] Baker apparently desired to bring his eleven-year-old daughter, Lael, his eldest child with Rebecca Gertrude Lorden as well, but Lorden refused. Like many other fathers in polygamous families, Baker did not regularly see all the members of his family and did not support them financially. According to Lorden, "He hadn't cared for us ever as he should have."[15] Decades later, daughter Lael incorrectly recorded the date of her father's death believing that he had died years before he was actually deceased because she "did not remember seeing him after she was ten [sic—eleven] years old."[16]

According to family stories, Baker had visions leading up to his conversion to the Church of Jesus Christ of Latter-day Saints.[17] These same stories do not mention whether such events were common for Baker in subsequent years. Fortunately, Baker left his own account of the series of powerful experiences that began his prophetic ministry at the age of sixty-two. Around the first of the year in 1916, he was troubled by global events: "so very many afflictions overtaking the nations of the earth in recent years, so many disasters

11. "Introduction from Journal of Grace G. Baker Dimter started in 1966," Familysearch.org.

12. North Weber Stake Record, May 31, 1912, Beinecke Library, Yale University.

13. Rebecca Gertrude Lorden, untitled memoir, Familysearch.org.

14. "Introduction from Journal of Grace G. Baker Dimter started in 1966," Familysearch.org.

15. Rebecca Gertrude Lorden, untitled memoir, Familysearch.org.

16. Lael's Book, 9.

17. "Sheri's Account of H. E. Baker," Familysearch.org.

by sea and upon land, of appalling magnitude, and now this greatest of all the wars of history."[18]

He spent the next year "seek[ing] the word of the Lord" through long stretches of prayer and fasting, believing that "supplications became effective most frequently when accompanied with fasting." He would fast for a week and then would eat as usual for a week; then he would fast again for a week—repeating this process seven times. After his seventh round—sometime in late March—Baker had a frightening vision. "I saw in a vision of the night, a great and ferocious bull that was terrible to look upon, for he was exceedingly angry. A dreadful power was in his flanks, and he strode the earth up and down looking and waiting."[19]

After this experience, Baker suspended his fast for three days and then resumed it for a final three. On this night, presumably April 5, 1916, he was shown the vision described in this chapter's epigraph. Like revelators Ezekiel and Isaiah in the Old Testament, John the Revelator in the New Testament, and even Lehi in the Book of Mormon, Baker was presented with a book. In this case, it was apparently blank: "The Spirit of the Lord came upon me that I should write, even the Word of the Lord."[20] He quickly completed the seventeen sections contained in the First Message and began seeking a publisher.

Over the next several months, Baker submitted copies to the *Chicago Tribune*, the *Chicago Examiner*, and the *Chicago Daily News*. With three rejections in hand, he decided "to let the coming events of the great war, which was then but fairly commenced, speak out more fully before making a further attempt to bring it to the attention of the public."[21] Baker tried again in late 1917 and sent the manuscript to "nineteen of the leading American monthly magazines." Rejected once more, he resorted to personally financing the printing of the First Message.[22]

In March 1918, Baker dictated the Second Message, consisting of sixteen sections. While the First Message is largely in reference to prophecies of the last days, the Second Message is an explanation of various theological

18. Word of the Lord, 15.
19. Ibid.
20. Ibid., 16.
21. Ibid., 10.
22. Ibid.

concepts. Baker knew he would be self-publishing this work, which he did in October. But preparing the manuscript for the printer, he was "suddenly struck to the floor with some sort of a malady. I know not what, which totally incapacitated me to proceed any further with the publication. For months now, it has held me in its clutch, with sometimes a stronger and sometimes a weaker grip, beclouding my mind and shattering my memory so that it became, at times, next to impossible to carry on the simplest conversation. And now after six months, I am just able to revise the MS. and proofread it."[23] He now understood that the "angry bull" of his vision two years previous had represented the "powers of darkness" that would seek to prevent him from bringing forward the messages. Yet Baker completed the task, believing he was obligated to "publish it to this present generation; and if I do not, I know that I will be damned." In the preface of the Second Message, he noted his belief that in his diminished state, he would not have been able to finish the work without divine assistance.[24] Perhaps Baker never recovered from whatever ailment he first faced in 1918. We know nothing about his life or health over the next eighteen months, but on May 23, 1920, he passed away after a heart attack.

THE WORD OF THE LORD
AS LATTER DAY SAINT SCRIPTURE

The Word of the Lord built onto the established Latter Day Saint scriptural tradition. Like other American religious traditions that produced new scriptures, Mormonism had "borrowed cultural authority from the Bible to stake [its] own claim to religious value, and to convince a biblically literate reading public of [its] importance."[25] Thus, in the same way that Smith's revelations echoed Judeo-Christian scripture, Baker's revelations echoed both biblical and Latter Day Saint scriptural traditions. These echoes in the form of allusions and quotations from Smith's revelations keyed select readers into the book's position in the Mormon revelatory tradition, even while *The Word*

23. The Word of the Lord: Being the Words of Jesus Christ, the Son Of God, to the Scattered Sheep of all the House of Israel in all the World, Message 2, 10–11. Subsequently cited as Message 2.
    24. Message 2, 11.
    25. Laurie Maffly-Kipp, *American Scriptures: An Anthology of Sacred Writings* (New York: Penguin, 2010), xvi.

of the Lord concealed its place in that tradition by never overtly speaking of Mormonism or Mormon scripture.[26]

Even the date that Baker received his first revelation after so many weeks of fasting, April 6, 1916, was a date of great significance to Mormons: seventy-six years from the day that Joseph Smith legally established his church in New York. In 1915, the Latter-day Saint apostle James Talmage had published his highly esteemed *Jesus the Christ: A Study of the Messiah and His Mission According to the Holy Scriptures Both Ancient and Modern*, which made the claim that April 6 was even Jesus's birthday.[27] It was also true that many Latter-Day Saint sects officially organized their movements on April 6. The date was a sign to Latter Day Saints that the publication of The Word of the Lord was a momentous event.

A large portion of The Word of the Lord is devoted to explaining Latter Day Saint theological concepts. For instance, it refutes traditional Christian notions of Deity, invoking the Westminster Confession as a heretical proposition: "And yet in a creed, which reflects the general conception of the world, you declare Him to be, a being without body, parts, or passions."[28] Mainstream Christianity had proclaimed God a spirit, "as the Scriptures truly declare; but you have supposed also, that being a spirit, He could not be a man."[29] Joseph Smith had revealed that God the Father was a personal being with a glorified body.[30] The Word of the Lord echoes this position, referring to mankind as "him whom I have made in the image of God, both in similitude of the body, and in the attributes of the soul."[31] It argues that the scriptures taught "that the father of Jesus Christ was in the form of man, like unto the Son."[32]

The Word of the Lord places particular emphasis on correcting the traditional Christian doctrine of the virgin birth, which it incorrectly calls the

26. For a discussion of intertextuality and its impact on readers, see Grant Hardy, "The Book of Mormon and the Bible," in *Americanist Approaches to the Book of Mormon*, edited by Elizabeth Fenton and Jared Hickman (New York: Oxford University Press, 2019), 107–135.

27. James Talmage, *Jesus the Christ: A Study of the Messiah and His Mission According to the Holy Scriptures Both Ancient and Modern* (Salt Lake City, UT: Deseret News Press, 1915), 104.

28. Message 2, 6:7.

29. Message 2, 7:2.

30. Terryl Givens, *Wrestling the Angel: The Foundations of Mormon Thought: Cosmos, God, Humanity* (New York: Oxford University Press, 2014), 89–95.

31. Message 1, 12:22.

32. Message 2, 5:16.

"immaculate conception." Latter-day Saints emphasized that the fatherhood of God to Jesus was literal, with the implication that there was a physical sex act between God the Father and Mary. This was present in the Church of Jesus Christ of Latter-day Saints by the mid-nineteenth century and remained so in Mormon thought when Baker dictated his messages.[33] In 1915, President Joseph F. Smith explained, "Now, we are told in scriptures that Jesus Christ is the only begotten Son of God in the flesh. Well, now for the benefit of the older ones, how are children begotten? I answer just as Jesus Christ was begotten of his father. The Christian denominations believe that Christ was begotten not of God but of the spirit that overshadowed his mother. This is nonsense."[34] Similarly, The Word of the Lord criticizes modern Christianity for referring to Christ as "the Only Begotten of the Father" yet refusing to "believe that He is begotten at all."[35] The concluding section of the Second Message reiterates, "The Father provide[d] a Redeemer, of His own body begotten."[36]

There were numerous other characteristically Latter-day Saint doctrines throughout The Word of the Lord, including the promotion of a modified universalism. The afterlife will not consist of a bipartite model of heaven and hell, but, as in Joseph Smith's revelations, the ultimate destiny of the living consists of a tiered heaven. "For it is written that in my Father's house there are many mansions; and this meaneth that there are many kingdoms and degrees of glory; and also there are kingdoms which are without honor unto them that dwell therein."[37] The Word of the Lord also shares the skepticism that Smith's revelations held toward traditional notions of hell. A verse in Message 2 seems to specifically address a well-known revelation that explains scriptural phrases such as "endless torment" and "eternal damnation" do not mean one would be punished forever. Rather, "The punishment which is given from my hand is endless punishment, for Endless is my name."[38] The Word of the Lord similarly declares, "It is true that God's punishments are eternal; for He is eternal and His institutions likewise endure forever;

33. John G. Turner, *Mormon Jesus: A Biography* (Cambridge, MA: Harvard University Press, 2016), 168–169.

34. Messages of the First Presidency, vol. 4. "President Jos. F. Smith's Address Sunday Morning," *The Box Elder News*, January 28, 1915.

35. Message 2, 5:20.

36. Message 2, 14:4.

37. Message 1, 7:11.

38. D&C 19:6–7; 10.

even as the institution of heaven, so is the institution of hell. Nevertheless, I said not at any time, neither the Prophets or Apostles, that the spirits of men should go down into hell forever without hope."[39] Those suffering in hell could escape their torment through repentance.

The Word of the Lord echoes familiar Mormon narratives of a Great Apostasy sometime in Christianity's distant past. At this time, the "Gentile nations"—a reference to non-Jews—had "shed the blood of mine Apostles, and others of my servants from time to time, whom I ordained and sent forth to teach them, and to keep them in the unity of faith."[40] The result was that the Gentiles "received my Gospel only in fragments, and my Scriptures with numerous interpolations and omissions."[41] Following similar language as a Book of Mormon prophecy about biblical corruption, Baker's message states, "The plainness of the Scriptures was taken away, with many essential doctrines of my Gospel."[42] The Word of the Lord also criticizes Christian denominations for having feigned to have apostolic authority based on Christ's calling of the original apostles. "If ye be Apostles by whom were ye ordained, as they were ordained? And if ye be not ordained, then why take this honor unto yourselves?"[43] Apostolic authority was necessary to "expound the doctrines of mine Everlasting Gospel and to officiate in the holy ordinances thereof."[44] The authority could only be established by the "ordination of heaven," perhaps a reference to the angelic ordination through which Latter-day Saints traced their own apostolic authority.[45] The text refers to this apostasy as a curse that Deity would now lift.

> I will have mercy upon the children of men, and extend unto them the help of the Lord at this time, even unto this generation; for I have sent forth again the Spirit of Truth, and cause some to understand as they did of old. And they greatly rejoice because they have found the pearl of great price, even the kingdom of God.[46]

39. Message 2, 12:2.
40. Message 1, 5:2.
41. Message 1, 5:5.
42. Message 1, 5:7.
43. Message 2, 3:8.
44. Message 2, 3:6.
45. Message 2, 3:6.
46. Message 1, 5:11.

276 THOMAS G. EVANS AND CHRISTOPHER JAMES BLYTHE

Thus, there were some who had already found the Kingdom of God.

Because Baker's messages never let on that it was through the Church of Jesus Christ of Latter-day Saints that these promises could be fulfilled, it leaves the possibility that he was merely appropriating Mormon theology for a new movement. This does not seem to be the case based on Section XV, which addresses a segment of Christians referred to as "thou greatly favored."[47] Following the consistent reader interpretation of this passage, we have presumed this was a reference to the LDS Church. The opening verse reads:

> And unto thee, thou greatly favored, unto thee, I the Lord, at this time, have a word of warning and a word of sharp rebuke. The ear of the Almighty hath heard your slandering, and your back-biting, and your lying; and they are of that blackness which cometh from the depths of hell; yea, they are of the spirit of that Wicked One, who maketh war upon me; and who hath gendered strife, and bitterness, and hatred, in the hearts of my people from the first; for which cause, Zion was lost unto them. Take heed, therefore, for I will rebuke my people suddenly with the shaft of death. I will make bare my arm in the midst of them, and they shall know that I am God.[48]

This passage is potentially ambiguous, but it fits early Fundamentalist discourse leveled against church leaders. Fundamentalists often presented the Manifesto as a lie—a lie of such consequence that it had been prophesied by the prophet Isaiah. According to Isaiah 28, Israel's rulers would enact a "covenant with death" and "an agreement with hell."[49] Baker's mention of Zion being "lost unto them" sometime in the past is likely a reference to the Saints' expulsion from Jackson County in 1833. The promise that God would "rebuke my people suddenly with the shaft of death" invoked a well-known prophecy among those critical of the church's leadership. The phrase "shaft of death" appears only once in the standard Latter-day Saint canon: in a revelation Joseph Smith dictated on November 27, 1832, that was later canonized in the Doctrine and Covenants. The relevant passage reads:

47. Message 1, 15:1.
48. Message 1, 15:1.
49. Isaiah 28:15.

And it shall come to pass that I, the Lord God, will send one mighty and strong, holding the scepter of power in his hand, clothed with light for a covering, whose mouth shall utter words, eternal words; while his bowels shall be a fountain of truth, to set in order the house of God.... While that man, who was called of God and appointed, that putteth forth his hand to steady the ark of God, shall fall by the shaft of death, like as a tree that is smitten by the vivid shaft of lightning.[50]

This revelation caused an uproar in 1905 when John T. Clark of Provo wrote and circulated a statement claiming that it predicted a prophet would be called from outside of the church hierarchy to replace the current apostate leadership. Clark and other Fundamentalist interpreters identified Joseph F. Smith as the "man ... called of God" who would "fall by the shaft of death," making way for the messianic One Mighty and Strong.[51] In response, the church issued a statement condemning this interpretation.[52] Another reference in Section XV of The Word of the Lord seems to reference Smith's November 1832 revelation. The relevant portion reads: "With a man will I rebuke a great nation, and with my rod will I punish a holy people. For a rod, indeed, have I brought forth of the stem of Jesse."[53] The "stem of Jesse" references another passage in Isaiah that Latter-day Saints interpreted as a prophecy of a last-days figure descended from the biblical Jesse, father David. The Word of the Lord may have been drawing a connection between "the rod" and "the scepter" of the 1832 revelation, as frequently occurred in other prophetic literature of the era.

Regardless, the point was the same: a messianic figure would emerge. To the church, the message declared: "Behold, ye know that my coming is at the door, and ye look for a prophet." Yet, "At the door of the tabernacle of Zion have I laid a stone of stumbling and a rock of offense."[54] The same language occurs in 1 Peter—"a stone of stumbling, and a rock of offense"—to describe

50. D&C 85:7–8.

51. Christopher James Blythe, *Terrible Revolution: Latter-day Saints and the American Apocalypse* (New York: Oxford University Press, 2020), 198–203.

52. Joseph F. Smith, John R. Winder, and Anthon H. Lund, "The One Mighty and Strong," *Deseret Evening News,* November 11, 1905.

53. Message 1, 15:4–5.

54. Message 1, 15:6.

the obstacle Jesus presented to many Jews who were unable to recognize him as the Messiah.[55] By drawing on this verse, The Word of the Lord seems to warn the Saints that they might also fail to recognize the coming prophet who would emerge unexpectedly.

It is reasonable to suppose that Baker believed he was this messianic prophet, though there is no record that he ever made this claim directly. Yet Message 2 seems to state that he is the fulfillment of a prophesy first articulated in Deuteronomy 18, that there would be a prophet like Moses: "and I will put my words in his mouth and he will speak unto them all that I shall command him and it shall come to pass, that whoever will not harken unto my words which he shall speak in my name, I will require it of him."[56] After quoting this passage, Message 2 asks "Now, therefore, I say unto you again, how shall you answer unto God? ... I say unto you, that this is that one, which, if you will receive it, was promised of old. How, then, shall you answer unto God?"[57]

A final feature of Section XV is its declaration that God had ceased to extend revelation to the church. "Lo, these many years you have lied. Yet, I would not speak. I did not answer. I would not suffer my silence to be broken; that my people might fill up their cup to the full; that I might deal with them, saith the Lord; and that after that, I might once again renew unto them the word of the Lord, and bless them, saith the Lord of Hosts."[58] Again, this placed The Word of the Lord into the larger discourse of early Mormon Fundamentalism. LDS prophets had not presented a recorded revelation since the issuing of the Manifesto. It was with this betrayal that God had stopped speaking to them. A later commentator returned to Isaiah 28, quoting the verses believed to reference the Manifesto, and then continued with a passage from Micah, "Therefore, night shall be unto you, that ye shall not have a vision; and it shall be dark unto you, that ye shall not divine; and the sun shall go down over the prophets, and the day shall be dark over them. Then shall the seers be ashamed, and the diviners confounded: yea they shall all cover their lips; for there is no answer of God."[59]

---

55. 1 Peter 2:8.
56. Message 2, 9:4; cf. Deuteronomy 18:18–19.
57. Message 2, 9:4, 6.
58. Message 2, 15:7–8.
59. Micah 3:6–7.

Section XV ends with a promise that after the church is punished, "I might once again renew unto them the word of the Lord."[60] A reading of the Messages themselves suggests that it was Baker, the prophet like unto Moses, through whom these promises would be fulfilled. After all, he titled the messages The Word of the Lord. Yet, as we will see, this is not how most readers would approach the text.

MODERNITY, APOCALYPTIC, AND THE GREAT WAR

The Word of the Lord is deeply critical of modernity with its emphasis on scientific and technological advancements. New developments in communication, transportation, and medicine had made twentieth-century man increasingly secular, self-centered, and violent. Worse, these new technologies had mobilized the nations to war and increased their savagery. New weaponry consisted of submarines, aircraft, explosives, and poison gases. The Word of the Lord underscored God's disgust with the Great War.

> You have devised the murder of innocence [*sic*] under the sea, that sharks may devour the tender child, and the great deep swallow up a host. Your inventors have perverted the gift of God [i.e., scientific progress], to build your crafts of war, even for the very clouds of heaven; that you might rain your thunder-bolts of death upon the heads of the innocent, to take away the life which has given no offense; that you might horrify the world with cruelty, and thus constrain the nations to give you victory.[61]

Baker's message warns against militarization altogether. "He that buildeth for war, seeketh war, and sueth for the spirit of war, shall he not have war?"[62] Global leaders had paved the way for the conflict. One particularly graphic passage addresses those elites who served to benefit from nations at war.

> Wherefore, you sounded the trump of war, and it summoned the vultures to feed on the flesh of your sons. And now they circle the

---

60. Message 2, 15:8.
61. Message 1, 12:3.
62. Message 2, 12:13.

heavens over the heaps of your dead, that they may glut themselves on the carcasses of the slain. And the rivers of the valleys you have turned into blood.[63]

If there is one directing point in The Word of the Lord's treatment of the Great War, it is that God was not pleased with any of the nations involved. He chastises those nations that professed to have divine approval based on their comparative military prowess. "Ye are hypocrites. Ye speak boastfully and deceitfully, saying, Look at the progress of our arms, and our mighty strength in battle; can you not see that God is with us? Yet you know that it is not might that makes right."[64]

Latter-day Saints expected that the last days would contain a series of key events that they could check off one at a time as the Second Coming of Jesus Christ approached. The Word of the Lord presents the Great War as a key moment in this apocalyptic timeline. Recall that Baker hoped the war would compel an interest in the messages. According to his messages, the war, global disasters, and society's increase in knowledge were collectively undeniable signs of the times.

You discern that all things upon the face of the earth are in commotion, both in the wars of the elements and in the wars of men, wherefore the signs are plainly manifest unto you. For you know that it was to be in a day of wars and rumors of wars. Wherefore, you know that the time is at hand. Yea, it was to come when many should run to and fro and knowledge should be increased. Wherefore, you know that the time is at hand.[65]

Following the Book of Mormon, The Word of the Lord suggests that during the millennium there will be two centers of global government—a revived Jerusalem in Palestine and the New Jerusalem in the Americas—both of which will emerge prior to the Second Coming. Section IV, addressed to the "children of Judah," promises, "I will bring them into their own country, even into the land of Judea; for I will gather a host of them, saith the Lord, to the

63. Message 1, 12:2.
64. Message 1, 12:16.
65. Message 2, 9:7.

land of their fathers; and there will I plant them, and make of them a strong nation as in days of old."[66] An expectation for Jews to return to Palestine had been present since the Joseph Smith era.[67] Also, in keeping with Book of Mormon prophecy, The Word of the Lord states that the New Jerusalem will be established in the United States, a "country that is select and beautiful, a land that I have set my seal upon," where the Lord will "build my tabernacle."[68]

When the New Jerusalem is founded, another city—the City of Enoch, also called Zion—will make its appearance. According to the Book of Moses, this utopian city "was taken up into heaven."[69] The Book of Moses describes a joyous meeting when these two cities are united. Those of the heavenly city will "receive them into our bosom, and they shall see us; and we will fall upon their necks, and they shall fall upon our necks, and we will kiss each other."[70] The Word of the Lord picks up on these ideas, stating, "And then will the Zion of my bosom return, to fill the vacant place; and the New Jerusalem shall arise ... and together will they sing the praises of their redeeming Lord, and hosannas to their triumphant King."[71]

While The Word of the Lord introduced specific verses condemning the modern world and addressing events in Europe, it fit well with a Mormon Fundamentalist reading of the traditional Latter Day Saint apocalyptic narrative. Many Latter-day Saints subscribed to the fact that the Great War was key to last days prophecy, and they would have all recognized the other key events such as the return of the Jews to Israel before the Second Coming, the establishment of the New Jerusalem in the United States, as well as the spectacular return of the City of Enoch.

THE WORD OF THE LORD AND ITS READERS

We know little about how Baker circulated his volume once it was published. He had already begun gifting copies of the First Message to prominent

66. Message 1, 4:6.

67. Minutes and Discourse, April 6, 1840, in *JSP*, D7:245.

68. Message 1, 8:1; 14:1.

69. Moses 7:21.

70. Moses 7:63.

71. Message 1, 14:1. The reference to the "vacant place" refers to the location where the City of Enoch once was. Some Latter-day Saints had suggested this was the Gulf of Mexico. See Wilford Woodruff Journal, June 20, 1869, CHL.

individuals in Chicago while still seeking a publisher. It is reasonable to assume he would have sought to spread his work among LDS Church members. At least two apostles, James Talmage and George Albert Smith, had copies of the published prophecy in their personal libraries.[72] Talmage's copy was inscribed with his name, city of residence (Salt Lake City), and a date (August 20, 1918), presumably the date on which he received the book.[73] According to Talmage's journal, he was in Chicago on church business in mid-August 1918. On the evening of August 20, he preached to a packed meetinghouse. Talmage did not mention The Word of the Lord in his journal, but based on the date scrawled in the front, it is reasonable to suppose Baker attended and gave this copy to him then.[74] Talmage appears to have read the First Message, making tick marks throughout the whole prophecy and occasionally circling a word.

Yet even if Talmage found the time to read The Word of the Lord, his allegiances were with the Church of Jesus Christ of Latter-day Saints and his fellow general authorities. At the next general conference of the church, he warned the Saints that there was only one prophet appointed to lead the church.

> I do not think that you have found any of the general authorities of the church, of the Council of the Twelve or others, who have independently undertaken to give out to the people any new revelation involving vital principles of doctrine or practice; and no one of them would think of doing it until it had been submitted to the one man who holds the keys of that power and priesthood here upon the earth at this time.[75]

The Word of the Lord was a prime example of a "new revelation" that transgressed the proper channel of church government. And there were other

72. Both Smith's and Talmage's libraries eventually became part of the BYU libraries, and The Word of the Lord was listed in Flake's comprehensive LDS bibliography. See Chad J. Flake, ed., *A Mormon Bibliography: 1830–1930* (University of Utah Press, Salt Lake City, 1978), 23.

73. This edition of the First Message that belonged to James E. Talmage is in the Harold B. Lee Library, Brigham Young University, Provo, UT.

74. James E. Talmage Collection, 1876–1933, MSS 229, box 25, L. Tom Perry Special Collections, 19th Century Western and Mormon Americana, Harold B. Lee Library, Brigham Young University, Provo, UT.

75. Church of Jesus Christ of Latter-Day Saints, *Eighty-Ninth Semi-Annual Conference of The Church of Jesus Christ of Latter-Day Saints* (Salt Lake City, UT: Deseret News Press, 1918), 63.

revelations that did not come with the sanction of church leaders. Before
Talmage's discourse, President Joseph F. Smith had spoken out against "spurious revelations." In this case, he specifically referred to the famed White
Horse Prophecy and another apocalyptic prophecy that had been attributed
to himself. He assured the Saints, "When the Lord reveals something to
me, I will consider the matter with my brethren, and when it becomes
proper, I will let it be known to the people, and not otherwise.... Now, these
stories of revelations that are being circulated around are of no consequence
except for rumor and silly talk by persons that have no authority."[76] His point
was clear: revelation would not originate outside of the church's leadership.

Neither Talmage's nor Smith's comments were unusual for the era. The
period of transition had more than a few prophets who sought to guide the
Saints back to the nineteenth-century ideals of the faith.[77] In turn, church
leaders regularly condemned "spurious revelations" and would-be messiahs.
It would have been difficult for orthodox Latter-day Saints to have embraced
Baker's message. Their first question would be why God had revealed
The Word of the Lord through anyone other than Joseph F. Smith. This
alone may have been reason enough that Baker had no enduring supporters
in the immediate wake of the publications. His sickness in 1918 and subsequent death in 1920 curtailed any chance for a following if that had been
his intention. Yet his printed prophecies would find a receptive audience in
subsequent years and decades among individuals on the fringe of Utah's religious establishment, particularly those dubbed Mormon Fundamentalists.

The Word of the Lord has what Laurie Maffly-Kipp has called an "afterlife" where meanings can change, use can increase or decrease, and—most
importantly for Baker's prophecies—scriptures can be "picked up by new
groups and rediscovered as authoritative writings in entirely different settings."[78] Decades after Baker first dictated his messages, copies began circulating in Utah among some Mormon Fundamentalists who saw in The Word of
the Lord a prophetic voice that they believed had been missing in the church
for some time. It is not obvious how this took place or who first rediscovered
the book and began promoting it. We know some church authorities in Utah

76. Ibid., 57.

77. See Christopher James Blythe, *Terrible Revolution: Latter-day Saints and the American
Apocalypse* (New York: Oxford University Press, 2020), ch. 6.

78. Maffly-Kipp, *American Scriptures*, xvi.

owned copies by 1918, but it seems unlikely they would have been eager to share them with interested parties. Presumably, others owned The Word of the Lord. However, the earliest copy (before 1956) we have been able to track was owned by Salt Lake City barber, James Wardle, known for his vast collection of Mormon literature. A prominent member of the Reorganized Church of Jesus Christ of Latter Day Saints, Wardle was acquainted with Latter-day Saints from a variety of different communities as well as former Mormons. He was an important source of traded and copied manuscripts. It is entirely possible that some of The Word of the Lord's future supporters discovered Baker's messages through him.[79]

By the late 1950s, there was a group of Fundamentalists known alternately as the L.D.S. Scripture Researchers or the Angel Elias Study Class who considered it their communal mission to champion The Word of the Lord.[80] The Researchers presented themselves as a study group for the standard twentieth-century canon of Latter-day Saint scripture—the Bible, the Book of Mormon, the Doctrine and Covenants, and the Pearl of Great Price— as well as Maurice Glendenning's Book of Elias and The Word of the Lord. Sherman Russell Lloyd, their organizer, had discovered the Book of Elias through earlier ties with the Aaronic Order/House of Aaron.[81] The Researchers published a variety of tracts and a larger book, *This Is That Day*, which argued that the current LDS Church was in apostasy and had been since 1890, presumably since the issuing of the Manifesto (although none of the tracts explicitly promote plural marriage). Many of the writings focus on the coming of a future prophet, a reincarnation of Joseph Smith.

The Word of the Lord was held with such reverence by the community that when it was extensively quoted in *This Is That Day*, the author apologized for doing so.

> The writings of Jesus Christ through Baker, are written in continuity.
> They are written in great plainness and simplicity. They reason with

79. A photocopy of this manuscript is in the L. Tom Perry Special Collections, Brigham Young University.

80. Hans A. Baer, *Recreating Utopia in the Desert: A Sectarian Challenge to Modern Mormonism* (Albany: State University of New York Press, 1988), 88.

81. For a discussion of the House of Aaron and the Book of Elias, see Casey Griffiths, "The Levitical Writings of the House of Aaron," chapter 14 herein.

us, just like one man reasons with another, and God the Almighty not only tells us what He is now doing, but He tells us why. When we quote excerpts from these writings, we feel that they are being transfigured and desecrated. They are sublime, when left alone, building up, word after word, sentence after sentence.[82]

The writer hoped that readers would seek out the book for themselves, because "no one can know what is about to take place, or why without searching these words ... carefully."[83] They declared their willingness to help others find copies of The Word of the Lord and suggested that they "have been given to understand that there is now, in the library at B.Y.U., an original copy of the Writings of Jesus Christ through Baker."[84] Indeed, in 1956, the BYU Library had arranged for someone to make a typescript of the published copies of The Word of the Lord.[85]

By the early 1960s, other copies were circulating in Utah. In 1963, on two different occasions, Salt Lake City resident Lloyd Lamoreaux encountered The Word of the Lord and was so impressed with the prophecies that he decided to print additional copies to make it available to a wider audience. A note in his printing reads, "It is felt by the publisher that this document is precious and in it's [*sic*] time it will find a demand among those who recognize the word of the Lord and love it."[86] Lamoreaux printed 100 copies of Baker's prophecy on letter-size, one-sided pages bound by staples in a twenty-three-page booklet. One of those who received copies from this printing was Robert Eaby, an independent Mormon Fundamentalist involved with various early Fundamentalist groups.[87] When the authors of this chapter met Eaby in 2008, he remained fiercely devoted to the text and once declared that it surpassed the Book of Mormon in importance. Eaby had come to believe that the LDS Church had somehow obtained the copyright to The Word of the Lord to ensure that it could not again be published. This is incorrect, but

82. *This is "that day": for the promised return of Joseph Smith "in the flesh" or the raising up of the man like Moses* (Salt Lake City, UT: LDS Scripture Researchers, 1958), 76.

83. Ibid., 77.

84. Ibid, 1.

85. Harry Edgar Baker, The Word of the Lord, typescript, BYU Special Collections.

86. Harry Edgar Baker, The Word of the Lord (Salt Lake City, UT: L. D. Lamoreaux Printing, 1963), 23. Copy in author's possession.

87. Personal interview, July 18, 2008.

it reflects stories common among Mormon Fundamentalists regarding LDS Church efforts to prevent circulation of key documents from the Mormon past. Fundamentalists often saw it as their responsibility to keep nineteenth-century sources in circulation.

In fact, contra Eaby, The Word of the Lord had continued to be printed by its advocates. For instance, in 1980, Fred Collier, then a member of the Fundamentalist Church of the Firstborn and later a professed prophet himself, included Section XV from the First Message of The Word of the Lord in a book, *Branch Prophet*.[88] Two recent printings of The Word of the Lord show that there is still interest in Baker's messages approaching a century after their dictation. The first is printed on letter-sized paper and includes no publishing details. The second was published by the R and B Reed Estate Trust, Mesa, Arizona. Whether either of these printings were intended for use by a religious community is unknown, although perhaps unlikely.

As society entered the digital age, so did The Word of the Lord, largely owing to websites developed by Fundamentalist-leaning Spencer Kimball (not the LDS Prophet). Kimball has been Baker's most vocal supporter in the twenty-first century. At this writing, his website, newrevelations.com, includes the entire Word of the Lord in English and Spanish with various pages of commentary. One such commentary begins by asking whether there are prophets today like those of old.

> If the measure of greatness were the contributions left behind, could any man provide evidence of greatness as did the prophets of the scriptures? We look for great men and spokesmen for the Lord. At this point the field considerably narrows. Such a man would be foreign to the teachings of today's Church, most likely hated by current LDS, but a man who would love the Mormon religion and Church at any cost no matter how it's [sic] people treated him in return. The term spokesman implies one who will carry out and represent the Lord's will. Therefore, we look for a man who will produce words representative of the Lord's approval.[89]

---

88. A copy of this publication is in the L. Tom Perry Special Collections, Brigham Young University.

89. A version of this website appears at newrevelations.net, but the quotations here are available on the Internet Time Machine.

Kimball's search for such a man was not in vain. He continues,

> The Lord chose one such man to receive His word close to a century
> ago, and as far as it is known, in the twentieth century, there had been
> no greater words of wisdom produced the entire world over during
> this time than the Word of the Lord received by Harry Edgar Baker
> of Chicago. Harry Edgar Baker is the only known man to have been
> chosen to deliver a series of revelations from the mouth of God from
> the entire twentieth century, words that are unparalleled in intelligent
> thought.[90]

Kimball was not aware of Baker's biography except for what he had read in
The Word of the Lord. In his words, "we do not know exactly who Harry
Edgar Baker was." Yet he believed Baker had met with persecution from
the LDS Church. He saw the messages as unprecedented. As with others
who found The Word of the Lord, Kimball praised the messages for being a
rare—"the only known"—instance that a prophet recorded the word of the
Lord in the twentieth century.[91]

In 2001, Kimball compiled a series of responses from those who had
visited his digital posting of The Word of the Lord. Many of these emails
warned that only the head of the LDS Church could properly receive revelation for the church. An example reads: "The Lord doesn't work that way.
In 1916 the Lord's Prophet wasn't Harry Edgar. The Lord only talks to his
Prophet, if the word is for the whole church, he could talk to me if it was for
my family." Kimball refuted this response, arguing that the church was in
a state of apostasy, and in such situations God historically called prophets
from outside the church hierarchy.[92]

Kimball also included a handful of supportive emails. These mainly consisted of individuals who agreed with Baker's messages because they questioned the current incarnation of the Church of Jesus Christ of Latter-day
Saints and individuals who had already embraced Baker's messages. One
anonymous person wrote Kimball with the hopes of finding other believers
in The Word of the Lord. The writer had grown up in an LDS household

90. Newrevelations.com.
91. Ibid.
92. Ibid.

where The Word of the Lord was treated as scripture. The parents had found and duplicated a copy from the library at Brigham Young University. The writer concluded on a note of disappointment: "I have always felt sad and puzzled that it seemed to have come to nothing, but God has his own purposes and ways, and we will all answer for what we accept or reject in the long run."[93]

CONCLUSION

The Word of the Lord never became scripture in an enduring denomination. Instead, a series of individual Latter-day Saints have discovered it over the century and often have individually sought to preserve and distribute it. For its supporters, it is a symbol of revelation from outside the church's hierarchy. Kimball's web publication emphasized The Word of the Lord's Sections XIII and XV, its apocalyptic warning to the United States, and its messianic promises for the Church of Jesus Christ of Latter-day Saints. While many of the messages held warnings to a previous generation and theological teachings that were available elsewhere, these points remained attractive to a new generation.

The Word of the Lord has been a mysterious volume with a small but devoted following. It is significant not only because it documents how one Latter-day Saint revelator responded to global trauma during the second decade of the twentieth century. Its history also demonstrates both the resistance of Latter-day Saints to revelation that originate outside of the Church of Jesus Christ of Latter-day Saints as well as a persistent hope for dictated revelation, particularly among Fundamentalist Latter-day Saints.

93. Ibid.

14

The Levitical Writings
of the House of Aaron

Casey Paul Griffiths

In an arid valley near the Utah-Nevada border lies a community that upholds the ideals of consecration cherished by the early Latter-day Saints.[1] Eskdale, a small cluster of houses and trees, lies just a few miles to the north of U.S. Route 50, a road that *Time* magazine once dubbed the "loneliest highway in America."[2] Eskdale is the largest community in a series of settlements established in the mid-twentieth century by the House of Aaron,[3] a revitalization sect that broke off from the Church of Jesus Christ of Latter-day Saints in the 1940s. The community is nestled in the Snake Valley, just a few miles from Garrison, Utah—a Latter-day Saint settlement—and Baker, Nevada, an old mining town with no religious roots.

When the nearby Great Basin National Park opened in 1986, it brought more tourism to the region. But the community still enjoys relative isolation. Members of the House of Aaron, also known as Aaronites, and their neighbors interact at school and cultural events, but old misunderstandings sometimes persist. Many locals confuse the House of Aaron with the large number of polygamous groups rooted in the West Desert of Utah. The

---

1. Portions of this chapter previously appeared in Casey Paul Griffiths, "A Sojourn among the Children of Aaron," *Journal of Mormon History* 44, no. 1 (January 2018):95–118.

2. Nancy Gibbs, "The Backbone of America," *Time*, July 7, 1997, https://www.nationalgeographic.com/travel/destinations/north-america/united-states/nevada/pictures-loneliest-road-america-route-50/.

3. The name of the faith as given on their official website is "The House of Aaron." See "About," House of Aaron, http://www.houseofaaron.org/about.html. During my visits to Eskdale, members of the House of Aaron referred to themselves at different times as "Levites," "Aaronites," the "Aaronic Order," and the "Levitical Order." These terms will be used interchangeably throughout this article.

Aaronites, however, hold to a unique belief system and spiritual heritage, and they come from a more eclectic background of religious traditions than their polygamous neighbors do.

Over the course of more than eighty years, the House of Aaron has evolved from a Latter-day Saint sect to a unique fusion of several faith traditions, incorporating religious traits of Evangelical Christianity, Judaism, and even Hutterite teachings. Aaronites worship on Saturday, which they consider the true Sabbath. They also praise the Bible in language mirroring Protestant sermons and practice a form of consecration not unlike the attempts made by Joseph Smith, Brigham Young, and the early members of the Latter-day Saint tradition. The Aaronites even possess their own scripture, a collection of revelations entitled Levitical Writings.[4] These are the revelations of Maurice Glendenning, and they are the foundation of the Aaronite communal experiment. Like any religious movement, the House of Aaron has teachings and ideals that have been redefined over the course of its existence, and the role of Levitical Writings is still developing today.

A BRIEF HISTORY OF THE HOUSE OF AARON

The House of Aaron dates to the early 1930s, when a small group of dissident Latter-day Saints formed a new movement centered on the leadership and revelations of Maurice Glendenning. The House of Aaron defines itself today as "a Christ-centered ministry in the Body of Christ," declaring that its "mission is to prepare the Body of Christ for His Second Coming; to restore the Biblical, Levitical ministry to its prophesied fullness in Jesus Christ and reconcile individuals, families, and fellowships to their places in the Body of Christ."[5] Because they consider themselves to be literal descendants of the biblical tribe of Levi, members of the faith commonly refer to themselves as Levites or Aaronites.[6]

4. Maurice Glendenning, Levitical Writings (Eskdale, UT: The Aaronic Order, 1978).

5. "About," House of Aaron, http://www.houseofaaron.org/about.html.

6. I observed this during my stay with the House of Aaron in April 2015. One of the theological works published by the group refers to its members as the sons of Aaron, Zadock, and Levi. See Blanche W. Beeston, The Way of the Levites, (West New Haven, IN: ALEF BET Communications, 1989), 48–49.

Maurice Glendenning was born in 1891 in Randolph, Kansas, and was raised in the midwestern United States. He began to receive revelations at a young age and formed the habit of writing them down. Glendenning was somewhat of a wanderer throughout his life, but his spiritual quest eventually led him and his family to Utah, where he affiliated with the Latter-day Saints. In the years following that association, he received revelations and gathered a group of devoted followers.[7]

Glendenning's ability to receive revelations and his physical appearance made him a compelling figure to the people within his sphere of influence. One disciple described his physical appearance as "striking," writing further, "He is short, reaching the height of five feet seven and one-half inches; but when standing among tall men, who are his usual companions, he dominates the assembly by his towering spiritual strength and knowledge which are inherently present."[8] Glendenning also possessed a curious mind and had a wide range of interests. In a 1966 interview, he claimed to hold doctoral degrees in chiropractic, electric therapeutics, and divinity.[9] He was known to speak often on a diverse set of subjects ranging from geology to religion.[10]

Glendenning's knowledge of religion stemmed from the wide array of religious influences in his early life. His Midwestern upbringing exposed him to the Hutterite communes of the central states. While his parents worked as photographers, his father also served as an itinerant preacher who followed "the practice of preaching the Gospel wherever he went."[11] Glendenning's later association with the Church of Jesus Christ of Latter-day Saints was only part of his religious makeup, even though most of his early followers came from Latter-day Saint backgrounds.[12]

---

7. In the 1950s, Blanche W. Beeston, a member of the House of Aaron, wrote an extensive biography of Glendenning, entitled *Now My Servant: A Brief Biography of a Firstborn Son of Aaron* (Pullman, WA: privately published, 1957).

8. Blanche W. Beeston, *Now My Servant*, (Caldwell, ID: Caxton Printers, 1957), 12.

9. Ralph D. Erickson, "History and Doctrinal Development of the Order of Aaron," (master's thesis, Brigham Young University, 1969), 35.

10. Hans Baer, *Recreating Utopia in the Desert: A Sectarian Challenge to Modern Mormonism* (Albany: State University of New York Press, 1988), 48–49.

11. Beeston, *Now My Servant*, 34.

12. Douglas and Karma Childs, interview by author, April 3, 2015; John Conrad, interview by author, April 3, 2015; notes in author's possession.

LEVITICAL WRITINGS

Levitical Writings is a collection of revelations received by Maurice Glendenning from 1923 to 1966. The current edition of Levitical Writings was published in 1978 and is a compilation of earlier collections of Glendenning's writings found in The Book of Elias (published in 1944), The Book of New Revelations or the Record of John (1948), The Disciple Book (1955), and other previously unpublished sources.[13] The collection is 263 pages long and consists of 189 revelations and utterances. Each revelation or instruction is labeled as a chapter, beginning with Chapter 137, and continuing to Chapter 326. This curious numbering system may demonstrate a link to the Doctrine and Covenants, which consisted of 136 sections at the time Glendenning was affiliated with the Latter-day Saints. Some of the contents of Levitical Writings are sermons or instruction by Glendenning, but most of the writings consist of revelations that resemble the language and tone of those given to Joseph Smith in the Doctrine and Covenants. Still, they are also unique. The preface states their purpose as affirming "that the House of Aaron is a house unto all the tribes of Jacob and that there was not a son of Jacob in the beginning who was without the house of Levi; and as it was in the beginning, so also shall it be in the days of the restoration that all things, whatsoever they were that were of God, may be restored." The book also states that it "is published with a prayer that it may boldly and convincingly testify that Jesus Christ, the Redeemer, is the very Son of God and that the time of His second advent is nigh."[14]

Hans Baer categorizes Levitical Writings as follows: "(1) those outlining the politico-religious organization of the Aaronic Order; (2) those establishing various rituals and ordinances; (3) those prescribing various rules and regulations (such as tithing, dietary proscriptions, etc.); (4) those defining specific theological or cosmological points; (5) those defining the lineage and work of Glendenning and the Levites; (6) those urging the Levites to gather and work together; (7) those warning of internal opposition to the world of the Levites; and (8) those describing visions which Glendenning had."[15] Many of these categories overlap within individual revelations. Though some

---

13. Baer, *Recreating Utopia*, 195; Erickson, "History and Doctrinal Development," 104.
14. Levitical Writings, i–ii.
15. Baer, *Recreating Utopia*, 49.

of the contents of Levitical Writings are epistles written from Glendenning to his followers, most are transcriptions of communications from an angel he called Elias.

Describing the history of his revelations, Glendenning recalls that as early as age seven he began hearing music, which continued through his teenage years and gradually evolved into poems consisting of written texts that he began to write down. His father encouraged Glendenning to seek further revelations, telling him that the family descended from Aaron and were set apart from the rest of the world. After he married Helen Ruth Meeker in 1915, Glendenning showed her one of his revelations and gained her support of his prophetic gifts.[16] The voice that spoke to Glendenning eventually identified himself as "Elias," an angel designated to provide guidance from God to the House of Aaron.[17] Glendenning was usually alone when he received revelations, though they could come at any time or place. Sometimes he received them while driving his car, which forced him to pull over and record them on the spot. One was given while he was studying in the Salt Lake City library. He usually carried a pencil and paper with him to record the voice of inspiration when it came.[18]

Levitical Writings opens with a "disobedience curse" placed on Glendenning "because of your disobedience and because you have offended me by giving no heed unto my sayings." He was told, "You shall become poor and hungry, and your house shall suffer, and for seven years shall poverty reign over you and your house."[19] Glendenning received further revelation about the curse in 1923, when he was working as a chiropractor in Yankton, South Dakota. During the ensuing years, Glendenning did indeed struggle to find employment and provide for his family. He wandered from Kansas to Colorado, eventually settling in Provo, Utah. While living there, the Glendennings began their affiliation with the Church of Jesus Christ of Latter-day Saints. Their daughter, Myrth Lucile, was baptized on August 12, 1928, and Glendenning and his wife were baptized the following year on April 14, 1929.[20] Even while he was in the process of joining the church,

16. Beeston, *Now My Servant*, 32–36.
17. Levitical Writings, 214:7; Erickson, "History and Doctrinal Development," 10.
18. Baer, *Utopia in the Desert*, 49.
19. Levitical Writings, 137:3–4, p. 1.
20. Erickson, "History and Doctrinal Development," 10–11.

Glendenning continued to receive revelations, and his revelations began to reflect the theological nomenclature of the Latter-day Saints. A revelation from August 1929 declares, "As my people do dwell upon the lands of Zion, they shall not be disturbed. They shall give unto the Lord that which is the Lord's and unto Zion that which is Zion's."[21]

The year 1930 was the most prolific for Glendenning's revelations. He recorded forty-two communications, more than in any other year of his life by a wide margin. His revelations during this period seemed to concern all Latter-day Saints and emphasized the care of the poor. With time, the revelations took on a darker tone as they addressed concerns within the church. A January 1930 revelation warns, "My shepherds have fallen asleep. The wolves have entered my fold, and my sheep have gone astray. The wicked, the vile, the thief, and all manner of defiled beings have entered my fold; and the demons of hell do dwell there. The wolves do tear my Flesh and drink of my Blood in the house of the Lord. They do defile my tabernacle and boldly eat of my Flesh. They do read my commandments today and crucify me on the morrow."[22]

Over the next few years, the revelations became even more severe, carrying direct warnings about not remembering the poor. Glendenning's words capture a particular poignancy when placed in the context of the worsening national depression occurring at the time. For example, a revelation titled "Unto the Church of Utah" served as a harsh condemnation of the members of the Church of Jesus Christ of Latter-day Saints, declaring, "The ten talents they do hold in their hands, and the labors of one having the one do they do." It continues, "The Lord shall remove their fine things, and their money boxes shall be made empty.... The flesh of the old shall wither, and their houses shall be made empty, for among them do the widows and orphans suffer, and they come not at all to their rescue but do sit with the rulers to speak of their gold."[23]

CONFLICT WITH THE LATTER-DAY SAINTS

Glendenning and most of his followers remained formally affiliated with the Latter-day Saints during the 1930s, even as he continued to receive new

21. Levitical Writings, 144:4, p. 13.
22. Levitical Writings, 152:3–4, p. 23.
23. Levitical Writings, 167:1–5, p. 42.

revelations and to form his own religious tradition. Acting on the encouragement of several followers, Glendenning presented his revelations to members
of the church hierarchy but felt ignored by church leaders such as David O.
McKay and Heber J. Grant. He also spoke of a meeting with B. H. Roberts,
who responded positively to the revelations by declaring, "It is most wonderful."[24] In another account of the meeting, Glendenning said that Roberts
"encouraged me in receiving the Writings and stated that he possibly did not
understand them, but they were no doubt for my personal edification and
that if I were he [I] would not publicize them too much." Glendenning then
relates that Roberts introduced him to an unnamed church leader who was
"very kind in his reception; but upon learning of my mission, he became very
disgruntled and insulting in his remarks to me . . . after learning I had these
revelations, he condemned them completely as being of Satan without ever
having looked at or read a single one of them." The hostile church official
was possibly Joseph Fielding Smith—Glendenning did not specify anyone
in his account but left three blank underlined spaces to suggest the name.[25]

In 1931, Joseph Fielding Smith gave an address in the church's general
conference, declaring, "When we find people secretly distributing what are
said to be revelations, or visions, or manifestations, that have not come from
nor received the approval of the Authorities of the Church, we may put it
down that such things are not of God."[26] It is unclear whether Smith was
talking specifically about Glendenning or addressing breakoff groups generally, but Glendenning took the speech as a direct attack on his work and
writings. He received a revelation that stated, "Now that my works have been
declared to be of Satan, and that they of the house of the Lord have fulfilled
these things, and do not attempt to limit the Lord in the things which are
pleasing unto Himself, I say unto you prepare the works which have not
been sealed."[27] After this incident, however, fewer revelations were recorded.
Glendenning received them at a rate of only one or two a year, with none
recorded in 1935 and 1937.

24. Maurice Lerrie Glendenning, interview by Ralph D. Erickson, June 22, 1968, quoted in
Erickson, "History and Doctrinal Development," 12.

25. Beeston, *Now My Servant*, 57. The timing of this visit is likely incorrect, since Beeston says
the visits took place "in the summer of 1931." Joseph Fielding Smith's remarks, which she says are
about the House of Aaron, were given in the April 1931 general conference.

26. Conference Report of The Church of Jesus Christ of Latter-day Saints, April 5, 1931, 70–71.

27. Levitical Writings, 194:1.

A NEW PRIESTLY LINE

During this period of conflict, the Glendennings continued to associate with the Latter-day Saints. Helen even served in the church's Sunday school and Primary programs. At the same time, the family experienced persecution at the hands of other church members and suspected that their fellow Saints withheld financial assistance because of their peculiar beliefs.[28] As their estrangement grew, Glendenning sought to establish a new identity for himself and his followers.

Even before he left the Church of Jesus Christ of Latter-day Saints, Glendenning had experiences that convinced him that he possessed a direct link to the ancient Levitical priesthood, outside of Latter-day Saint lines of authority. One of the most important experiences occurred in 1938 on a remote Nevada mountaintop. According to Glendenning, after he ascended to the mountain's peak, he felt a light pressure on his head as if unseen hands were being laid there, and he heard a voice declare, "Unto you, my fellow servant, in the name of Elias, we come holding all of the keys and authority vested in the Priesthood of Aaron." He was instructed "to act in this authority with all of the keys of the Priesthood of Aaron as the First High Priest of the Order of Aaron."[29] After the experience ended, Glendenning ran his fingers through his hair and felt oil on his scalp.[30] The House of Aaron later placed a bronze plaque on the site and renamed the peak "Mount Aaron" to commemorate the occasion (Figure 14.1).[31]

The ordination on Mount Aaron holds many parallels with Latter-day Saint belief about the restoration of priestly authority in modern times through angels. Church teachings declare that Joseph Smith was ordained to the Aaronic and Melchizedek Priesthoods under the hands of ancient prophets, specifically John the Baptist and Peter, James, and John.[32] Later, Smith revealed the office of Church Patriarch, a position whose primary responsibility was to provide revelatory blessings to members. These blessings

---

28. Erickson, "History and Doctrinal Development," 18–19.

29. Blanche W. Beeston, *Purified as Gold and Silver* (Caldwell, ID: Caxton Printers, 1966), 55–57; Erikson, "History and Doctrinal Development," 19–20; Levitical Writings 207:1, 3.

30. "Historical Record of the Holy Pilgrimage to Mount Aaron," *Aaron's Star*, 1954, 2.

31. Douglas and Karma Childs, interview by author, April 3, 2015.

32. "History of Joseph Smith," *Times and Seasons*, August 1, 1842.

FIGURE 14.1. Maurice Glendenning on Mount Aaron, Nevada, with bronze plaque, unknown date. Courtesy Gerry Childs.

also designated members' tribal lineage in the House of Israel.[33] Glendenning's ordination on Mount Aaron served a similar function. It provided the Aaronites with an independent line of priesthood authority outside the Church of Jesus Christ of Latter-day Saints as well as their own tribal identity among the House of Israel, furthering the distance between the two organizations. Tribal identity remains an important part of membership in House of Aaron, and Aaronites still make yearly pilgrimages to Mount Aaron, just as Latter-day Saints visit the sites where Joseph Smith interacted with angels.

The ordination on Mount Aaron also marked a period of renewed revelation for Glendenning. Some of these revelations sought to redefine the relationship between the Latter-day Saints (referred to as Ephraim) and the House of Aaron. They show an attempt to reconcile Glendenning's continued membership in the church with his growing collection of revelations. One revelation from this period explains, "Ephraim has been restored first that Levi may receive of Ephraim according to the words of the prophets. For verily I say unto you that Levi shall first receive from the hand of Ephraim,

33. Gary Shepherd and Gordon Shepherd, *Binding Earth and Heaven: Patriarchal Blessings in the Prophetic Development of Early Mormonism* (University Park, PA: Pennsylvania State University, 2012).

but not through another; for behold, those of the house of Jacob shall come first through Levi, save it be a few chosen with Ephraim." Here, Elias, Glendenning's revealing angel, also refers to Moroni, the angel associated with the Book of Mormon, as a fellow messenger. He exhorts the Aaronites to "be comforted in Moroni, for verily did he write of this day; for behold, he abided in me and I in him, that we may be one with our Lord Jesus."[34] The revelation asserts a complex view of God's message in the last days. Both Elias and Moroni are presented as true messengers from God, depicting the work of the last days as involving multiple groups of people. This view is still held by the House of Aaron.

Glendenning's continuing revelations often put him at odds with the church, increasing the rift between him and his fellow Latter-day Saints. In 1942, another revelation instructed him to establish the Aaronic Order as a church under Utah state law.[35] A March 1943 revelation gave the new movement a name: "Now my servant, I command thee to rebuild unto me the Order of Aaron; and there shall be of it an House of Aaron." The same revelation instructed Glendenning to call a Chief High Priest to lead in spiritual matters and a First High Priest who would be assisted by a Council of Twelve to oversee the temporal affairs of the House of Aaron. Now that he headed his own ecclesiastical organization, the conflict between Glendenning and his Latter-day Saint leaders came to a breaking point. He was excommunicated on January 15, 1945, along with several followers.[36]

THE BLOOD OF AARON

Cut off from the Latter-day Saints, Glendenning began searching for other connections to the family of Israel and continued to establish the House of Aaron's theological identity. He traveled throughout the United States for most of his life, often seeking links to his Aaronic lineage. Glendenning made another discovery confirming ties to the family of Aaron on July 4, 1945, just a few months after his formal excommunication. While visiting a cabin once owned by his grandfather in Gentry County, Missouri, Glendenning discovered a stone tablet with a blessing written on it. The

---

34. Levitical Writings, 212:2, 6–7, p. 102.
35. Levitical Writings, i.
36. Erickson, "History and Doctrinal Development," 35.

writing on the tablet is in a smooth cursive script in a V-shaped form, as if a stylus had written in soft wax, though the tablet is made of marble. This blessing, written to Glendenning's father, dates to February 15, 1863. It reads in part, "Thou art of Aaron, the first born of our Lord in the flesh, and God shall give unto you a first born through whom the restoration of the keys of the priesthood of Aaron shall be made unto man in the flesh" (Figure 14.2). The text of the Marble Tablet in Levitical Writings is followed by an affidavit with the signature of Glendenning's father, signed by a notary public attesting to the legitimacy of the discovery of the tablet.[37] Glendenning presented the tablet for examination to Lee Van Vickle, the owner of a monument store in St. Joseph, Missouri. Van Vickle offered his professional opinion, noting, "The lettering was done by a novice but shows genius." He added, "I have been handling granite and marble for over one quarter century, but I am mystified as to the way the pebble grain polished effect was attained."[38]

During a trip to the eastern states in the spring of 1946, another experience further confirmed Glendenning's ties to the lineage of Aaron. He was led to an elderly, unidentified man who showed him a parchment written on an animal skin that he had guarded for nearly seventy years. The parchment (commonly known as the "Catskin Blessing" among the Aaronites) contains a blessing that was given in 1799 and designates one of Glendenning's ancestors as a literal descendant of Aaron. The Catskin Blessing reads in part, "Though wayward in thy youth I give this blessing unto you, my son John Glendenning, in whose seed shall continue the Priesthood of our lineage . . . for thou art of Aaron" (Figure 14.3).[39] Both the Catskin Blessing and the Marble Tablet are kept at Eskdale today, watched over by a trusted member of the faith.

37. Levitical Writings, 325, pp. 256–257. Erickson gives the date of the discovery of the Marble Tablet as July 4, 1945; Erickson, "History and Doctrinal Development," 26. The Marble Tablet was also shown to the author and photographed during visits to Eskdale in 2015, 2016, and 2019.

38. Lee Van Vickle, private letter, July 13, 1945, photograph in author's possession. It is traditional to show the letter along with the Marble Tablet to visitors of Eskdale. As of this writing, there is still a business named Van Vickle Monuments in St. Joseph, Missouri; see "Home," Van Vickle Monuments, https://www.vanvicklemonuments.com/.

39. Erickson gives the timing of this event as the spring of 1946, after Glendenning excommunication; Erickson, "History and Doctrinal Development," 23. Blanche W. Beeston, *Now My Servant*, 146–147; Levitical Writings, 324. The Catskin Blessing was shown to the author and allowed to be photographed during visits to Eskdale in 2015, 2016, and 2019.

FIGURE 14.2. Marble Tablet
Document, February 15, 1863.
Photograph courtesy of Casey
Paul Griffiths, 2019.

Glendenning's interest in his Scottish heritage played a role (along with
his discoveries related to his Israelite lineage) in developing the Aaronites'
distinct theological identity. One visitor to the Aaronite communities noted,
"They appear to combine Christian, Mormon, and Jewish tradition with
what might be termed as a streak of 'Scottish Romanticism.'"[40] The names of

40. Frederick S. Buchanan, "A Refuge in the Desert," *Sunstone* (January-February 1979):34.

FIGURE 14.3. Catskin Document, February 15, 1799. Photograph by Casey Paul
Griffiths, 2019.

two of the Levite communities, Partoun and Eskdale, are derived from Scottish terms. This came from the connection Glendenning felt toward his Scottish forebears, whom he believed were descendants of the house of Levi. In the sanctuary building of the settlement, a Jewish menorah stands next to a cross derived from the Glendenning family's Scottish coat of arms. The same cross is also featured on the cover of Levitical Writings, while the coat of arms is shown on the second page of the book, and the end of the sacred writings touches on the "Symbols of the Ensign of the Order of Aaron."[41]

While the revelations in Levitical Writings, along with Glendenning's blend of Christian symbolism and Old Testament typology, allowed the Aaronites to construct a theological identity outside of the Latter-day Saint tradition, the movement is still like its parent religion in many ways. Like the Latter-day Saints, the House of Aaron possesses its own sacred writings, its own sacred relics, its own founding prophet, and its own role in the grand restorative saga of Israel. Upon this system of divine lineage and prophetic

41. Levitical Writings, 258–259; Buchanan, "A Refuge in the Desert," 34.

guidance, the Aaronites launched an ambitious project: a community based upon the principles of consecration.

THE COMMUNAL EXPERIMENT AT ESKDALE

Communal living became a vital tenet of the Aaronite movement as members formed their unique faith identity. A 1945 revelation instructed followers, "They shall possess no lands nor sheep nor cattle; nor shall they possess any good thing of the fields nor of the forests nor of the mountains nor of the deserts nor of the seas, save it be unto them for a stewardship only." Further, "In the priesthood shall they labor to bring themselves for their many consecrations unto the Lord."[42] The most lasting and tangible effect of Levitical Writings lies in the Eskdale community itself, created in 1955 after several earlier failed attempts by members of the House of Aaron to establish settlements based on consecrated principles.[43] Glendenning, encouraged by his followers, had attempted to launch consecrated communities near Zion National Park, first in 1932 at Alton, Utah, and later near Springville, Utah, where a cluster of disciples lived. During these first attempts in the 1930s, Glendenning lived in extreme poverty, often living in a tent. His willingness to work hard and endure privations endeared him to his followers, who themselves were struggling during the Great Depression. Both early communal experiments endured for several years until Aaronites moved to newer and larger settlements in western Utah.

An undated revelation about 1944 instructs, "Go ye into the lands of the earth and search there for possessions where there can be had the necessities of life such as may be gathered from thy labors in the earth."[44] The Aaronites founded their first desert community, Partoun, in 1949. Located in the western reaches of Juab County, Utah, Partoun laid down many of the patterns followed when Eskdale was established a few years later. For example, the homes were arranged in a semicircle. Adherents, who had been scattered across the area, began to gather to the new settlement, but because of the soil's alkalinity, scarcity of water, and a lack of agricultural experience

42. Levitical Writings, 243:5, 7, p. 143.

43. Baer, *Recreating Utopia*, 52–56.

44. Levitical Writings, 241:1, p. 139. Levitical Writings places this revelation between two others given in 1944.

among the Aaronites, the community dwindled quickly. Although a small community remains in Partoun today, most residents emigrated to Eskdale when it was established.[45] The land for the Eskdale commune was selected by members of the House of Aaron after considering different locations in the United States, Mexico, and Canada. Eventually, they established the community in the Snake Valley on the Utah-Nevada border. The valley is a dry and inhospitable environment, but it was free under the Federal Desert Land Act (1877), an amendment to the Homestead Act (1862).

Demonstrating tremendous sacrifice, members of the House of Aaron drilled wells and cultivated land; through their efforts, the small community began to form. "We started with two little cabins and a hand well," Douglas Childs, an original member, recalled. After a while, the community was able to start a dairy. Profits from the dairy and other agricultural ventures provided for the Eskdale members.[46] Over the years, the settlement was arranged into a half circle of homes surrounding a sanctuary for worship services and a central community center where meals were served.

There are several small satellite communities near Eskdale, two of which are named Bethel and Petra. Partoun, the first community, is about fifty miles north. In contrast with several other religious settlements in the area, the House of Aaron has never allowed its members to practice any form of plural marriage and are quick to correct visitors who might assume otherwise. Reasoning for this comes from a revelation in Levitical Writings, which commands, "A Levite shall be the husband of one wife in the flesh."[47]

The canon of scripture accepted by the Levites continued to evolve over Glendenning's lifetime. Near the end of his life, he listed the scriptures of the House of Aaron as, "1. Holy Bible, Old and New Testament, 2. Book of Elias, 3. Book of New Revelations, 4. Book of Mormon, some parts as a secondary source, 5. Doctrine and Covenants, certain sections, 6. Dead Sea Scriptures, found by Qumran in 1947 near the Dead Sea, written on scrolls in Hebrew and Greek."[48] When asked about his acceptance of portions of the Latter-day

45. Baer, *Recreating Utopia*, 123–125.
46. Douglas and Karma Childs, interview by author, April 3, 2015, copy in author's possession.
47. Levitical Writings, 220:8, p. 112.
48. Erickson, "History and Doctrinal Development," 111. This information was taken directly from an interview with Glendenning on June 22, 1968. The Book of Elias and the Book of New Revelations both eventually became part of Levitical Writings. Glendenning did not specify which

Saint canon as scripture, Glendenning replied, "God has never pointed me to judge and I don't have the right to dispute what God has given another," though he did add that he felt Latter-day Saints were not living the teachings set forth in their own standard works.[49]

The inclusion of the Dead Sea Scrolls is a curious late addition to Glendenning's canon of scripture. The effect of Glendenning's study of the scrolls is difficult to quantify, though some Eskdale residents recalled that the habit of eating meals in silence came from practices described there.[50] Late in his life, Glendenning became increasingly concerned with ancient Jewish practices, including the Feast of Tabernacles. One Levite writer saw the renewal of these ancient feasts among the House of Aaron as a part of the modern restoration of all things, writing, "Those things given to be done 'perpetually' we found were to be continued and are being restored to us. The need for the light of the word to be kindled in the sons of God is a perpetual need, and among those of Israel this charge was given to Aaron."[51] The same writer also tied the feast to a passage in Levitical Writings, admonishing the faithful: "May our lamps be burning brightly with the oil of our salvation that when He cometh, He may find us and lift us from among the foolish things of the world."[52] This tendency to Judaize the community became more pronounced under Glendenning's successor, Robert Conrad.

THE SECOND GENERATION—
SCHISM OVER LEVITICAL WRITINGS

Over time, facets of life in Eskdale have evolved and have been reinterpreted by succeeding generations. For instance, when the community was first founded, members wore standardized clothing and ate all meals together and in silence as much as possible.[53] Women's clothing in the first few decades consisted of blue denim jumpers and white hats with "Levi" embroidered on them. Men's attire was less formal, usually blue denim shirts

---

parts of the Book of Mormon and Doctrine and Covenants were considered scripture by the Levites or whether he accepted all or part of the Dead Sea Scrolls.

49. Erickson, "History and Doctrinal Development," 111.
50. Joie Conrad, interview by author, April 3, 2015.
51. Beeston, *The Way of the Levites*, 110–111.
52. Levitical Writings, 272:12, p. 182.
53. John Conrad, Gerry Childs, and Douglas Childs, interviews by author, April 3, 2015.

and functional work clothes. Children lived in a separate dormitory for several decades, with a rotating series of couples operating as dorm parents.

The group underwent several dramatic changes after Glendenning's death in 1969. Robert Conrad, still affectionately known to community members as "Brother Bob," took over leadership as the Chief High Priest of the Aaronites. Conrad, raised as a Latter-day Saint, was initially hesitant about the House of Aaron. He joined the movement after his wife, Aileen, converted to Glendenning's teachings and was excommunicated from the Church of Jesus Christ of Latter-day Saints in 1948. Writing about her departure from the faith of her childhood, Aileen recalled, "I felt that everyone that was near and dear to me had been separated from me and I was full of grief ... then it was that Bob quietly touching me said, 'No one can cut you off from the Lord but yourself.'"[54] The Conrads moved their family to Eskdale in the 1950s. After Glendenning's death, Robert chose to leave his position at the University of Utah to lead the sect full time.

Shortly after Conrad became Chief High Priest, the House of Aaron underwent the most serious schism in its history. Maurice Glendenning had been open to evangelical preachers visiting Eskdale throughout the 1960s. After his death, some of the younger members of the faith began building relationships with a Pentecostal movement known as the Order of the Lamb, an offshoot of the Jesus People movement. The Order of the Lamb began visiting Eskdale in 1973, holding meetings that introduced the Aaronites to glossolalia and other spiritual gifts. In the beginning, even older members of the House of Aaron saw this as a welcome revitalization of the enthusiasm surrounding the movement's origins. Revivals held during this early period often went on into the early hours of the morning.[55]

However, a disagreement eventually developed between some of the older members of the faith and several of the younger members who had become enamored of the evangelical teachings and eschewed the House of Aaron's earlier connections to the Latter-day Saints. One older member of the community felt isolated by the charismatic enthusiasm of one of the younger members. She wrote, "I stood in the doorway, hearing her outcry; but something apart from the praying sisters pushed all else from my

---

54. Aileen S. Conrad, "My Testimony," personal account written July 12, 1987, Eskdale, UT.

55. Hans Baer, *Recreating Utopia*, 172–173.

thoughts. 'I can't pray in tongues! How could I join them?'" She continued her lament, "For many years we all knew the peaceful beauty of the Lord's Spirit. It had burned within our souls in the first place to bring us to settle in this place in the desert."[56] The schism was exacerbated by the fact that one of the leaders of the charismatic evangelical group married Robert Conrad's oldest daughter.

According to a community member living in Eskdale at the time, the heart of the split was a disagreement over the legitimacy of Glendenning's prophetic writings.[57] Excommunication does not exist among the Aaronites. Instead, they prefer to work out their differences without implementing ecclesiastical trials.[58] However, in this case, the leader of the schism was eventually asked to leave Eskdale, and many members of the younger generation followed him. A number of those who departed were Robert Conrad's children, making the split even more painful.[59] The current High Priest of the House of Aaron, who was a young man at the time, recalled, "There have been splits over authority. The last one was this battle over the Levitical Writings. A lot of people that we know and love decided that it was the Bible only, even though we have always looked at the Bible and still do as the foundation of our belief. But we believe that God didn't quit talking."[60] Those who left Eskdale during 1975 and 1976 failed to coalesce into a new movement, but the pain of the schism is still felt in the community decades later.

Despite this early crisis under his leadership, Robert Conrad's tenure as leader demonstrated a marked openness toward other faiths. Many evangelical phrases were incorporated into Aaronite terminology during this period, and the language heard at Eskdale today more closely mirrors the speech of evangelical Christians, rather than that of Latter-day Saints. "Brother Bob" also continued Glendenning's work to incorporate a number of Jewish festivals into the Aaronite faith, including Passover, Shavuot, Yom

56. Beeston, *Purified as Gold and Silver*, 1.

57. Gerry Childs and Joie Conrad, interview by author, April 3, 2015.

58. John Conrad, interview by author, April 3, 2015.

59. Notes by author from a conversation with John Conrad, January 27, 2015. John Conrad, interview by author, April 3, 2015. Hans A. Baer provides a few details of a dramatic schism in 1975–1976 over the younger members of the sect who were disillusioned with Glendenning's teachings and influenced by several Pentecostal groups that introduced dramatic spiritual gifts into the Eskdale community. Baer, *Recreating Utopia in the Desert*, 171–177.

60. John Conrad, interview by author, April 3, 2015.

Teruah (Rosh Hashanah), Yom Kippur, and Sukkoth, which all are observed at Eskdale today. This was perhaps a natural outgrowth of the Aaronite proclivity toward Judaic practices. A revelation given to Glendenning in 1958 established the Saturday as the Sabbath.[61] The festivals became an important part of community outreach, and members began to regularly invite their neighbors in the other Snake Valley communities to attend.[62]

Robert Conrad also oversaw the gradual alteration of some of the more monastic elements of life at Eskdale, making gradual changes to the order's expectation for families living at the settlement. At the same time, he felt a natural anxiety over the lifestyle changes the small community was experiencing. When he was interviewed by a reporter from the *Los Angeles Times* in 1993, he lamented, "It's the world seeping in . . . the culture around us now is very permissive and seductive. The older people feel the fear of being washed away."[63] Blanche W. Beeston, the semiofficial historian of the community, wrote *The Way of the Levites* during this time. The short text places a strong emphasis on the unique aspects of the faith, with many liberal quotes from Levitical Writings. Beeston extolls the virtues of remaining a part of the communal experiment, writing, "Those who have lived in a community relationship will tell you that nothing—literally no other way of living—will bring you into [a] true family relationship like community living. . . . If the family is filled with love, the blessings of community relationships are boundless."[64]

THE THIRD GENERATION AND
THE HOUSE OF AARON TODAY

Changes continued during the 1990s while John Conrad, the son of Robert Conrad, served as High Priest of the House of Aaron. About eighty-five members currently live communally in Eskdale. Exact membership figures are not available (in part because of a provision in the book of Numbers that

---

61. Levitical Writings, 278, 189; Erickson, "History and Doctrinal Development," 106.

62. Each of these Jewish festivals has a prominent place on the official website of the House of Aaron. Aaronites often send out email reminders to those who might be interested in attending. See "Home," House of Aaron, http://www.houseofaaron.org/.

63. James G. Wright, "To Survive, Children of Aaron Coming of Age: Isolationist Sect Finds It Must Let a Little of the World Seep into Its Commune to Keep It Alive," *Los Angeles Times*, September 6, 1993, https://www.latimes.com/archives/la-xpm-1993-09-06-mn-32223-story.html.

64. Beeston, *The Way of the Levites*, 182.

the Levites were not numbered), but Conrad estimates a total membership of 200 in several different locations.[65] John Conrad and his wife, Joie, moved to the community with their families as young children in the late 1950s.[66] Since then, the community and its members have modified many of the practices found in Levitical Writings and the teachings of Glendenning, but some tenets have remained.

Continuing revelation still plays an important role in the life of the Aaronites, though its function and practice have changed. Aaronites teach that revelations like those given to their founding leader ceased at Glendenning's death, but they believe that their current leaders may still receive revelations through the Spirit. When asked about revelation, John Conrad explained, "Our concept of present-day revelation would be one of inspiration through the Holy Spirit. Often the revelation will be offered to other trusted leaders so it can be confirmed by the prophets (plural) ... We are in the minority of those who believe God still speaks to men and that revelation has not ceased. We just believe it must agree with what God has said before or it is in error."[67] The members of the House of Aaron who knew Glendenning still speak of him affectionately, often referring to him simply as "the Bishop."[68] But fondness for their founder has not prevented the Aaronites from following the patterns of other religions in examining, deconstructing, and remaking their community and ways of worship. In some ways, they have stayed close to the original designs laid down by the first generation, but in other ways, they have continued to change.

For example, the Aaronites have stayed true to the principle of consecration. A revelation in Levitical Writings declares, "All Levites shall live for one and one for all, that there shall be none among you who shall suffer."[69] In regard to a consecrated life, there exist today different types of membership among the Aaronites. Those who live at Eskdale and its satellite communities are considered consecrated members: they live communally, sharing goods and means, though they retain individual stewardships over property.

---

65. John Conrad, interview by author, April 3, 2015; Numbers 1:47.

66. Robert Conrad passed away a few months after my visit to Eskdale in 2015. See "Robert James Conrad," Nickle Mortuary, http://nicklemortuary.com/obituaries/item/170-robert-james -conrad.

67. John Conrad, email to author, May 13, 2015, copy in author's possession.

68. Gerry Childs and Joie Conrad, interview by author, April 3, 2015.

69. Levitical Writings, 220:15, p. 113.

Other members believe in the teachings of the House of Aaron but do not live communally. They may be found in a variety of other locations, such as Murray, Utah, which is the home of the largest branch of the faith outside the Snake Valley.

All members living in Eskdale contribute to the work needed to provide for the community. Most are descendants of former members of the Church of Jesus Christ of Latter-day Saints, many of whom left their churches for a chance to participate in one of the longest-lived experiments in consecration. During one of my visits to Eskdale, one senior member of the community remarked, "A lot of people, like my dad and my wife's dad, got uncomfortable because they heard statements [in our Latter-day Saint congregation] like 'Consecration is wonderful but it's impractical, and we're never going to live it until Jesus comes.'"[70]

To join the Eskdale community, one must commit to fully participating in consecration. New members have a one-year probationary period before they are completely integrated into the economic life of the commune, and their assets are comingled with those of the community. "The last thing we want to do is force somebody to do something they don't want to do," Conrad explains. The community is considered an elite circle within the House of Aaron, and Conrad's leadership of the faith does not translate into automatic leadership of the community. Instead, it is governed by a council consisting of different members chosen from the men and women in the community. Women do not hold priesthood offices, but they are influential in the life of the commune.[71]

During conversations with people in Eskdale, one of the themes that emerged was the relationship between control and choice in a community where the prosperity depends on a joint effort of contributing. "Healthy organizations let the sunlight in," John Conrad commented. "It's scary, it's risky, but if you build a community and tell people that their family is no longer their family—I have seen it be successful, but it doesn't look like God, it doesn't look like love. Consecration is about sharing; it is about giving your life to others and not allowing needy people to suffer. Here we have a socially conscious gospel, but you have to be careful to allow freedom.... When you

70. John Conrad, interview by author, April 3, 2015; notes from observations of the Eskdale community, April 2015, in author's possession.

71. Douglas Childs, phone interview by author, September 13, 2016.

look at [the] community and what we have tried to do, [we've tried] to create a community where people take care of each other."[72]

AN EVOLVING MOVEMENT

The enduring nature of the Eskdale commune makes it unique among the communal efforts linked to the Church of Jesus Christ of Latter-day Saints. The arid desert in which Eskdale was planted has produced a small but amiable band of believers who have evolved over time. The remote setting suggests an attempt to withdraw from the bustle of the outside world, though the community has grown more cosmopolitan in recent years. When the community first began, Glendenning and other leaders taught that formal athletics, dancing, movies, and other recreational activities should be replaced with more constructive endeavors such as music, reading, and scripture study.[73] One communication from church leadership in 1968 stated, "Any person, or persons, guilty of bringing into Shiloah (Eskdale) a television in any form, or for any purpose, without the proper consent of the Office of the First or Chief High Priest of the Order of Aaron shall be guilty of a misdemeanor, and said television shall be subject to seizure and sale to the benefit of the school and the violator shall be subject to excommunication from Shiloah (Eskdale)."[74] Today, however, members of the community participate fully in the bustling conversation of the outside world. Homes in Eskdale feature internet access and flat-screen televisions; cell phones are ubiquitous. John Conrad regularly posts on Facebook, and he allowed members of the community to speak up and offer corrections to this study.

Without criticizing the methods the commune used prior to his leadership, John Conrad explains that he and his generation's leadership recognize that practices among the Levites needed more updating while staying true to the founding principles of the order. "When we look back, we had some issues where we had too much control," he reflects. He also openly acknowledges the importance of input from the women in the community, especially that of his wife, Joie. Speaking of the alterations, Joie Conrad remarks, "When our generation started making decisions, we made changes." John

72. John Conrad, interview by author, April 3, 2015.
73. Erickson, "History and Doctrinal Development," 88.
74. "Notice," *Aaron's Star*, September 1968, 11.

and Joie never lived with their parents after they came to Eskdale; instead, they grew up living in the dormitories designed for the children. This experience influenced their decision to reintegrate children into their parents' homes. They also ended the use of standardized uniforms, though members still wear them during holidays and special occasions. Joie Conrad notes the end of the traditional dress as a direct effort to be more sensitive to the needs of younger members of the House of Aaron: "We were having trouble with our own daughter because she didn't want to go on family trips with us because she had to wear the uniform." Many of the other young women of the community secretly changed into contemporary clothes whenever they left Eskdale. Under Conrad's direction, the women of the community took counsel, deciding first to make the uniform only a requirement for school, and then to end the practice outright as a requirement of community life.[75]

Another practice that changed was the silence required at main meals. Members eat together, but silence is no longer required. In fact, community members engage in lively conversation. This change also reflects the importance of women's influence on the practices of the House of Aaron. Joie points out the difficulty in having silent meals with small children. "I never liked [the silent meals] as a mother. The idea for silent meals came from a study of the Essenes," she explains, "but the Essenes were priests and they didn't have little kids!"[76]

Though the commune has survived for over sixty years, the slowly dwindling number of Aaronites living in Eskdale has become a concern. An article in the *Los Angeles Times* in the early 1990s stated that only one in ten college students choose to return home.[77] In the course of our conversations, John and Joie Conrad mentioned that out of ten siblings, John was the only one who chose to remain at Eskdale. John spoke wistfully about the departure of several of his siblings, most of whom aren't affiliated with any faith. Other members have left because of the difficulty of the lifestyle. Joie notes, "One of the things you find out in talking with people who have left is that you have to constantly be reevaluating. Is this action producing good fruit? If it's not producing good fruit, then why are we doing it?"[78]

75. Joie Conrad, interview by author, April 3, 2015.
76. Joie Conrad, interview by author, April 3, 2015.
77. Wright, "Children of Aaron Coming of Age."
78. Baer, *Recreating Utopia in the Desert*, 171–177.

John Conrad and many of the Levites still speak warmly of the movement's Latter-day Saint roots, though they are quick to point out that their
faith has evolved into a new creation born of Latter-day Saint, Judaic, Pentecostal, Hutterite, and other traditions. Services at Eskdale can feature a sermon from an Old Testament text, a minister blowing a shofar, a recounting
of the sacrifices made by the early founders of the community, the Lord's
supper featuring both bread and wine, and testimonies about the blessings
of a close community and family harmony. Every spring, members of the
House of Aaron enjoy a traditional Passover feast featuring all the trappings
of an authentic Jewish observance. Members end the feast with the triumphant cry, "Next year in Israel!" Justification comes from a mixture of ancient
and modern influences. "Our founder, Bishop Glendenning, he told us that
if something says 'forever' you should take a look at it."[79] Passover is just one
of the "forever" beliefs of the Aaronites. Their website notes, "We believe
God ordained the sons of Levi and Aaron to be priests and teachers in Israel
for all time. The present-day House of Aaron is a portion of the promised
restoration of that priesthood body."[80]

John Conrad notes the continuing eclecticism of religious influences:
"We have been impacted by our Mormon roots and our exposure and fellowship with the Hutterites. In the last twenty to thirty years we have become
much more aware of Messianic beliefs and also Judaism."[81] Asked about this
variety, Conrad cheerfully jokes that the Levites are "Mormons, Evangelicals,
and Messianic Jews all rolled up into one."[82]

While the observance of Glendenning's teachings and revelations have
undergone changes in the years following his death, he and Levitical Writings still influence the community and its beliefs. In June 2015, members of
the Mormon History Association (MHA) visited Eskdale as part of a post-
conference tour. The Aaronites were hospitable to this group of over eighty
visitors. MHA members walked freely around the settlement and received
a summary of their religious beliefs. The visitors also enjoyed a question-
and-answer session with John Conrad and other community elders in which

79. John Conrad, interview by author, April 3, 2015.
80. "What We Believe," House of Aaron, http://www.houseofaaron.org/what-we-believe.html.
81. John Conrad, email to author, May 13, 2015.
82. Notes from a presentation given by John Conrad to Mormon History Association, Eskdale,
Utah, June 8, 2015, in author's possession.

Conrad mentioned that once a year the youth of the community are still taken to "Mount Aaron" where Glendenning received the priesthood from the Angel Elias.[83] In the sanctuary where the meeting was held, the walls were adorned with flags representing the tribes of Israel. Conrad demonstrated his musical training by playing the trumpet and blowing the shofar, and a younger member of the community favored the visitors with an impressive classical piano piece. Members of the faith proudly displayed the Catskin Blessing and the Marble Tablet and permitted photographs.

THE FUTURE OF THE HOUSE OF AARON

While Maurice Glendenning is still viewed as a father figure in the Eskdale community, the influence of Levitical Writings is less potent among the current generation of Aaronites than among their forebears. This is less a rejection than a statement regarding the primacy of the Bible. But, when the legitimacy of Levitical Writings and Glendenning's prophetic call have been questioned, members of the House of Aaron have demonstrated a willingness to defend both. In 2013, a minister from another faith launched a savage attack on the House of Aaron, writing, "[Its] entire claim to have 'been restored and reactivated beginning with a special calling of Maurice Glendenning, a first-born son of Aaron' is based entirely on revelations Glendenning is supposed to have received from Elias. These revelations are steeped in Mormon doctrine and presuppose the truth of both the Book of Mormon and the prophecies of Joseph Smith and Brigham Young as found in the Doctrine and Covenants of the LDS (Mormon) Church." The author called upon the House of Aaron to repudiate Glendenning and revoke its claims of restored priesthood.[84]

A few days later, John Conrad offered a defense of Levitical Writings, citing it as "a major factor in the formation of the House of Aaron in 1942. Its primary impact was to move the adherents to a more Biblically based worship of Yeshua and a return to the covenants of Israel—clean and unclean

---

83. Ibid.

84. James Trimm, "The Plain Truth About MIA/ARI's House of Aaron," http://nazarenespace .ning.com/profiles/blogs/update-the-plain-truth-about-mia-ari-s-house-of-aaron. MIA/ARI refers to Alliance of Redeemed Israel, a Messianic group the House of Aaron belongs to at the time of this writing. See http://www.redeemedisrael.com/who-we-are-2/.

foods, 7th day Sabbath, and eventually to celebration of the Feasts." He added, "Our understanding is that God continues to speak but his Word will never disagree with itself. We do not make this an issue with other Believers and do not bring up the LW to those who are offended by it. Furthermore, it is a step on our path to full restoration but not something everyone needs to embrace." Outlining the relationship of Levitical Writings to the Bible, Conrad continued, "I would never say that I understand all things written in the [Levitical Writings]. But I can say that either it agrees with the Bible or it is wrong. This was also Maurice Glendenning's position. The 'evidence' that Maurice Glendenning is a false prophet springs from a superficial understanding of the writings and complete ignorance of Maurice's life." Addressing the connection of the House of Aaron to the Latter-day Saints, Conrad explained, "Our many-years-old former link with Mormonism is a fact of our history. And it is just that, 'history.' We simply are not Mormons today. Many of us, including me, have never been Mormons . . . the vast majority of early House of Aaron members were formerly LDS. However, while we bear no bitterness toward the LDS church it is not our work. We do believe that many of returning Ephraim are within the various groups who trace their origin back to Joseph Smith."[85] When Conrad was asked about the canonical works of the Aaronites in 2015, he commented, "We consider the Bible to be supremely authoritative. Our Levitical Writings are seen as commentary and supplementation to scripture." Concerning modern revelation, he added, "We have no problem with those who believe God continues to reveal his Word and his will."[86]

Nearly half a century after Maurice Glendenning's passing, the most potent influence of Levitical Writings on the Levites seems to be its role in documenting the priesthood line of authority and special lineage of the faith. At the same time, the House of Aaron's current position on priesthood authority has become more nuanced. Asked about the line of priesthood authority, John Conrad stated, "We do trace the authority of the Aaronic priesthood to Bishop Glendenning's experience on Mt. Aaron." He then added, "We do recognize a priesthood mantle on all believers but believe that the Aaronic

85. John Conrad, "A Statement from John M. Conrad," June 18, 2013, https://myemail.constantcontact.com/A-STATEMENT-FROM-JOHN-M--CONRAD.html?soid=1102838631876&aid=dZVNHpkrmak (emphasis in original).

86. John Conrad, email to author, May 13, 2015.

priesthood is a special case."[87] When I spoke with members at Eskdale, they often commented on their belief that they are literal descendants of Aaron, but they also felt comfortable discussing the patriarchal blessings of their Latter-day Saint friends as genuine revelations. One community member expressed belief that the descendants of Ephraim and Levi would eventually all come together. Conrad stated on another occasion, "We see all believers coming into some tribal identity in Israel—no one is necessarily excluded, just identified."[88] The lineage of Aaron is a vital part of the group's identity—even today, the sign welcoming visitors to Eskdale displays a menorah, and the foundations of a new temple are located within the settlement. Community members have even begun building the sacred furnishings of the new sanctuary, including an altar of incense, a replica of the ancient altar of sacrifice, and a large menorah, flanked on both sides by large, gold-colored crosses of the type presented on the Glendenning family coat of arms and discussed in Levitical Writings.[89]

Though it is difficult to predict the future of any religious text, especially one as recent as Levitical Writings, its influence is clearly demonstrated throughout the House of Aaron's history. Members at Eskdale and other locations are still working to carefully balance the expectations of newer generations with a reverence for the traditions and beliefs of older generations. But the continued existence of Eskdale itself is a testament to the power of Glendenning's revelations. At the heart of Levitical Writings is the idea of a Christian community built on earth in anticipation of heaven, and nearly seventy years later a small but devoted band of disciples still make their home in the desert as an expression of their belief in a God of continuing revelation.

---

87. John Conrad, email to author, May 13, 2015.
88. John Conrad, email to author, May 13, 2015.
89. Notes and photographs from a visit to Eskdale, Utah, April 5, 2019, copies in author's possession.

15

The Hidden Records of Central Utah and the Struggle for Religious Authority

Christopher C. Smith

In September 1823, an angel named Moroni—the resurrected military leader of an ancient Hebrew people called the Nephites—appeared to a New York farm boy named Joseph Smith and told him of a golden record buried in a nearby hill. On Moroni's instructions, Smith unearthed the record in 1827 and translated from it the Book of Mormon, a tome of Christian scripture that within a few years gave rise to the Church of Christ.[1] After Smith's 1844 martyrdom and a succession crisis rent the fledgling church, senior apostle Brigham Young led the largest and most viable faction west to the valley of the Great Salt Lake.

Moroni and the sacred geography of the Book of Mormon followed the pioneers west. Young taught his followers that the Jaredite, Nephite, and Gadianton peoples of the Book of Mormon had anciently inhabited central Utah and buried treasures there.[2] Furthermore, during his mortal life the Nephite general Moroni had traveled through Utah and personally consecrated the site of the Manti Temple before proceeding to New York to bury the golden plates.[3]

1. Moroni's visits are narrated in Joseph Smith—History 1:27–54.

2. James H. Gardner, *Historical Pamphlet*, May 1943, and Bryant Manning Jolley, *The Jolley Family Book* (Provo, UT: BYU Press, 1966), 429, cited in John Heinerman, *Hidden Treasures of Ancient American Cultures* (Springville, UT: Bonneville Books, 2001), 91–95; Scott G. Kenney, ed., *Wilford Woodruff's Journal*, 10 vols. (Midvale, UT: Signature Books, 1983–1991), 4:26, 6:338; G. D. Watt, et al., *Journal of Discourses Delivered by President Brigham Young, His Two Counsellors, the Twelve Apostles, and Others*, 26 vols. (Liverpool: George Q. Cannon, 1854–1886), 8:344; 12:128.

3. Orson F. Whitney, *Life of Heber C. Kimball* (Salt Lake City, UT: Kimball Family, 1888), 447; H. Donl Peterson, "Moroni, the Last of the Nephite Prophets," in *The Book of Mormon: Fourth Nephi Through Moroni, from Zion to Destruction*, edited by Monte S. Nyman and Charles D. Tate (Provo,

Such statements inspired legions of Utah treasure hunters, including Bishop John Koyle of the Koyle Dream Mine. In 1894, the angel Moroni appeared to Koyle and showed him a vision of the remnants of an ancient Nephite mine in the mountains near Salem, Utah. Koyle saw nine vast caverns heaped with golden relics and records, plus a rich vein of ore yet to be mined. Moroni revealed that the Lord intended this vast mineral wealth to sustain the church through the coming tribulation of the last days. Koyle and colleagues staked claims at the site he had seen in the dream, and devotees have intermittently worked the mine to the present day.[4]

Koyle's mine has monopolized the attention of academics, but other treasure hunters' activities are no less interesting. One of the more spectacular examples is the story of Earl John Brewer, who claimed to discover two eight-foot-tall Jaredite mummies and hundreds of inscribed tablets and plates. Until now, no study has chronicled his activities in the 1960s or the ensuing struggle to control his legacy.

Brewer viewed himself as an amateur archaeologist but also modeled his enterprise on the Joseph Smith story and the LDS prophetic tradition. He set out to prove the Book of Mormon's veracity and to fulfill its prophecies that additional sacred records would be brought forth in the last days.[5] He related his experiences in language reminiscent of Smith's discovery narrative, freely blending prayer and revelation with archaeological technique. As Smith had materialized and parochialized the Christian faith by transporting biblical narrative onto American gold plates, so Brewer parochialized the Mormon faith by transporting Book of Mormon narrative onto Utah stones and metal plates. His activities expressed his sense of Mormonism as a scientific religion and his own backyard as sacred space.

Brewer's discoveries, like Smith's, were immediately contested by rivals and skeptics. He sought and initially received acceptance by church authorities and Mormon academics but found himself pushed to the margins as his artifacts attracted scientific critique. Claims and counterclaims took aim at

---

UT: Religious Studies Center, 1995), 235–249. Historian Ardis E. Parshall questions the attribution of this story to Brigham Young: Parshall, "Moroni's Purported Rambles," *Keepepitchinin* (blog), November 18, 2010, http://www.keepapitchinin.org/2010/11/18/moronis-purported-rambles/.

   4. Ian Barber, "Dream Mines and Religious Identity in Twentieth-Century Utah: Insights from the Norman C. Pierce Papers," *Princeton University Library Chronicle* 70, no. 3 (2009):433–469.

   5. Monte S. Nyman, "Other Ancient American Records Yet to Come Forth," *Journal of Book of Mormon Studies* 10, no. 1 (2001):52–61.

the artifacts' authenticity and at personal reputations. After Brewer's death, an array of self-proclaimed successors struggled to control his artifacts and their legacy.

Brewer and his successors inherited from the Mormon tradition a deep sense of the religious potency of physical artifacts. His story illustrates that long after Joseph Smith's nineteenth-century translation of the Book of Mormon inscribed metal plates still exert a powerful pull on the religious imagination. At stake is nothing less than scientific proof of the supernatural and visible fulfillment of ancient prophecies of the last days.[6] Likewise, the struggle to control the artifacts illustrates the authority to be gained by controlling physical relics, records, and sacred spaces. Sacred objects don't just *symbolize* religious authority; they *mediate* and *confer* it in a very real way.

Brewer's plates accomplish all of this by virtue of their physical existence, not by virtue of any records they contain. English translations of their inscriptions are treated as either curiosities or esoteric secrets to be revealed at a future date. This highlights a deep tension in the Mormon concept of scripture. Joseph Smith insisted that his real treasure was not the golden Book of Mormon plates but the records they contained. Yet historians point out that early Mormons, including Smith himself, made little use of the Book of Mormon text. The Book of Mormon functioned for its first readers more as sign than scripture.[7] The similar use of Brewer's plates shows that not much has changed. We moderns crave empirical proof of religion more than we crave its teachings. The tantalizing promise of Mormon metal scriptures is to offer that proof.

EARL JOHN BREWER

Born February 11, 1933, in Moroni, Utah, Earl John Brewer lived most of his life near his childhood home and made a modest living as a laborer, most

---

6. Asked what drew him to the treasure-hunting movement, interviewee Adam Rodgers replied that he had wanted to prove the Book of Mormon true. Christopher C. Smith, interview with Adam Rodgers, March 14, 2017.

7. Grant Underwood, "Book of Mormon Usage in Early LDS Theology," *Dialogue: A Journal of Mormon Thought* 17, no. 3 (1984):35–74; A. Bruce Lindgren, "Sign or Scripture: Approaches to the Book of Mormon," in *The Word of God: Essays on Mormon Scripture*, edited by Dan Vogel (Salt Lake City, UT: Signature Books, 1990), 55–62; Terryl Givens, *By the Hand of Mormon: The American Scripture That Launched a New World Religion* (New York: Oxford University Press, 2002), 62–88.

notably at the Moroni Wastewater Treatment Plant. According to his one-time associate John Heinerman, whose stories may be more dramatic than factual, Brewer was an inactive "jack" Mormon. Although he had a testimony of Joseph Smith and the LDS Church, he never attended church meetings and cursed like a sailor, "smoked like a chimney, and drank coffee like it was going out of style." In 1953, he married Doris Jean Luetta Keisel, and together they raised five children. Heinerman suggests that treasure-hunting "made something of John Brewer,"—perhaps imparting some significance to a dissatisfying life.[8]

Unemployed at age 30 in 1963, Brewer made his treasure-hunting debut along with Carl Paulsen, another unemployed laborer.[9] In early November of that year, the "two men excitedly reported to Mrs. [Leona] Winch that while prospecting in the mountains west of Manti, they had discovered what appeared to be a sizable cache of engraved stone tablets. These stone tablets, according to their discoverers, had been buried in a large overhang not far from Manti." Winch persuaded the men to let her borrow a few of the tablets. She then contacted her nephew George Tripp, president of the Utah State Archaeological Society, who in turn contacted Dr. Jesse Jennings of the University of Utah Department of Anthropology. Jennings agreed to come to Manti and examine the tablets.[10]

According to Tripp, the tablets Jennings examined were of three different types. One set bore finely engraved Greek, Roman, Runic, Deseret Alphabet, and shorthand symbols. Another set bore an angular form of writing. A final artifact bore a single pictograph showing human figures with clubs or swords raised for combat. The largest piece in the collection was a roughly rectangular limestone tablet about 10 × 15 × ½ inches, engraved with several hundred characters in twenty-nine rows. It was formatted like a modern business

---

8. "Earl John Brewer," Family Search, https://www.familysearch.org/tree/person/details/KWZS-VX7; Christopher C. Smith, interview with John Heinerman, April 15, 2017. Brewer also worked as a turkey farmer. See [J. Golden Barton], "Manti Enigma," 1974–1990, MSS 2049, box 7, fd. 3, Paul R. Cheesman (1921–1991) Papers, L. Tom Perry Special Collections, Harold B. Lee Library, Brigham Young University (hereafter, Cheesman Papers).

9. John Brewer journal typescript, June 16, 1960, MSS 2049, box 65, fd. 4a, Cheesman Papers.

10. George Tripp, "Manti Mystery," *Utah Archaeology* 9, no. 4, (December 1963):1; letter from Jesse Jennings to Lambrose D. Callinahos, January 28, 1969, Anthropology Departmental Records, University of Utah Archives. Special thanks to archivist Kirk Baddley for finding and providing these documents.

FIGURE 15.1. Inscribed metal plates photographed in connection with a 1972 linguistic study of the John Brewer artifacts by BYU anthropologists Ray T. Matheny and William J. Adams. MSS 2049, box 65, fd. 4a, Paul R. Cheesman (1921–1991) Papers, L. Tom Perry Special Collections, Harold B. Lee Library, Brigham Young University.

letter, with three short lines in the upper right margin and a "signature" in the lower right corner. Mud stained the tablet, giving it an archaic appearance.[11]

Upon examining the tablets, Jennings noted that the mud that stained them was black, with a high humus content, unlike the soil in the cave where Brewer and Paulsen claimed to have found them. When the mud was washed off, "the engravings emerged sharp and clean," as if fresh and recently carved. Under a microscope, Jennings noted "microscopic shining bits of metal in the grooves of the characters," apparently "from the nail or other stylus with which the characters were inscribed." He concluded that the tablets were a hoax, created "with the notion that they could sell the slab to Mr. Tripp's aunt who is not only a collector of American Indian artifacts, but a devout

11. Tripp, "Manti Mystery," 1–2.

Mormon on the lookout for things which will 'prove' the Book of Mormon story about the origin of the American Indians. She was so embarrassed ... that she gave me the entire collection of slabs and they are now in our archaeological collections. Probably, she paid the fellows something, but she would not say so."[12] For his part, Brewer regarded Wintch's donation of his tablets to the university as a kind of theft.[13]

Disillusioned by Jennings's findings, Carl Paulsen and his wife, Louise, ransacked Brewer's bedroom. According to an affidavit they later signed, "We witnessed under Brewer's mattress several pieces of stone partly inscribed plus a pocketknife. When confronted with the accusation that he had frauded the ones under the mattress and the ones I, Carl Paulsen, had found with him west of Manti, he, John Earl Brewer, had no comment and shrugged off the accusation."[14]

Brewer's discoveries did not end with the limestone tablet. Over the next decade, he amassed a collection of hundreds of artifacts, including stone boxes and inscribed plates of copper, brass, and lead. Periodically, he displayed the collection to school children and gatherings of the curious.[15] In these settings he refined his telling of the story of his excavations.

Several written or recorded versions of Brewer's story are extant; most are reported secondhand and date no earlier than the mid-1970s.[16] One intriguing version, found among the papers of Brewer's friend Dr. Paul R. Cheesman of BYU, purports to be a typescript of Brewer's 1955–1960 diary.[17] However, the document misdates the Leona Wintch incident to July 1960, rather than November 1963, and it refers to plates rather than limestone tablets as the subject of Jennings's investigation. When I asked Brewer's one-time associate John Heinerman about these discrepancies, he explained that Brewer had written the document after the fact to get his memories in order

12. Tripp, "Manti Mystery," 1; letter from Jesse Jennings to Mrs. J. Wallace Wintch, November 27, 1963, Anthropology Departmental Records, University of Utah Archives; Jennings to Callinahos, January 28, 1969. Special thanks to archivist Kirk Baddley for finding and providing these documents.

13. John Brewer journal typescript, June 23, 1960.

14. Carl and Louise A. Paulsen affidavit, April 13, 1973, MSS 2049, box 65, fd. 4a, Cheesman Papers.

15. "John Brewer Has a Cave, but He's Not Giving Tours," *Deseret News*, November 26, 1975, B10.

16. Ibid.; Jared G. Barton, "Secret Chambers in the Rockies," *The Ancient American* 4, no. 28 (June/July 1998):3–4, 6; Christopher C. Smith, interview with Gail Porritt, January 19, 2013; Smith, interview with Heinerman, April 15, 2017.

17. John Brewer journal typescript.

and make sure he had his story straight.[18] It is also possible that someone other than Brewer wrote the diary. When an interviewer in the 1990s asked Brewer about Heinerman's publication of excerpts from the diary, Brewer replied, "He's never seen my diary."[19] But Brewer's trusted friend Paul Cheesman owned a copy of the diary, which supports its authenticity.[20] Heinerman may have obtained a copy from Cheesman.[21] Whether it was Brewer's work or not, the mysterious diary clearly draws on his stories and memories.

Brewer's story began with an art project in 1955, when he was twenty-two years old. He had always enjoyed hunting for arrowheads and had amassed a large collection, which he intended to arrange for display at the county fair. During this project, he became acquainted with an African American ranch hand named George Keller. Keller had been adopted as a baby by a local rancher and named for his adopted father. Never fully accepted by the white children of the community, he spent much of his boyhood playing with Indian children, who showed him their secret places.

Keller offered to tell Brewer where to find more arrowheads in exchange for a jug of wine. Brewer obliged, and Keller told him where to look. Brewer could find no arrowheads following Keller's directions, so he returned and asked Keller to show him in person. Keller said he would—for another jug of wine! And so, an inebriated Keller took Brewer to a hill behind the Manti Temple and showed him a place under an overhang where arrowheads lay on the surface of the soil. Keller told Brewer to dig because Indians had made arrowheads here for centuries.[22]

---

18. Smith, interview with Heinerman, April 15, 2017.

19. Gail Porritt, interview with Earl John Brewer, n.d. [ca. 1997], tape recording provided by Gail Porritt. Porritt asked Brewer about Heinerman's quotation from the diary in an unspecified article that he had sent Brewer. I could not locate the article, but Heinerman also quotes the diary in Heinerman, *Hidden Treasures of Ancient American Cultures*, 119–123.

20. The journal also discusses Brewer's relationship with Gail Edward McCaffery, a Manti neighbor who died in 1964 and was unknown to likely forgers of the diary whom Brewer met later. "Gail Edward McCaffery, 1932–1964," Family Search, https://www.familysearch.org/tree/person /details/KWJG-41G.

21. Linda Petty alleges that Heinerman once broke into Cheesman's office. Linda Karen Petty, "Linda Karen Petty's Personal History," 2016, https://www.familysearch.org/service/records/storage /das-mem/patron/v2/TH-904-67010-319-35/dist.txt?ctx=ArtCtxPublic.

22. Sources disagree as to the setting of Brewer's conversation with Keller—variously a ranch, cafe, or bar. They also disagree as to how the two men met each other, who initiated the conversation, and the number of jugs of wine. Smith, interview with Porritt, January 19, 2013; Barton, "Secret Chambers in the Rockies," 3–4; "John Brewer Has a Cave"; John Brewer journal typescript, entries for

Brewer dug. He did find many arrowheads, as well as a few pottery shards, but he also discovered something more remarkable: the records and treasures of ancient peoples. Here the story told by Brewer's friends departs significantly from the story told in his diary. The secondhand accounts report a sudden, spectacular discovery, whereas the diary tells a story of gradual excavation and tortured introspection spanning several years.

According to the more spectacular version, a few feet below the surface Brewer's shovel broke into an open stairwell with seven descending steps opening into a large chamber. On the left-hand side was a table, and beyond that lay two ten-foot-long stone crypts along each wall.

When Brewer later returned with tools and pried open the stone lids of the crypts, he found two eight-foot-tall mummies—one a redheaded male in full armor with sword and shield, and the other a blonde-haired woman, also in full armor. (Their hair colors signal white racial identity, a sign of righteousness in 1960s Mormon doctrine.) Brewer portrayed the mummies in some hand-drawn sketches, apparently unable or unwilling to photograph them.[23] There were also shelves cut into the walls. On these shelves lay "bundles," which when cut open proved to be stone and wooden boxes wrapped in juniper bark and covered with pitch to preserve them. Brewer broke some of the boxes open with reckless abandon. Inside lay metal plates inscribed with strange characters and illustrations of ancient people.

March 30, May 10, and May 19, 1955. For biographical details on Keller, see "George Keller Observes 86," *Manti Messenger*, February 3, 1966, 3.

23. Barton, "Secret Chambers in the Rockies," 3–4, 6; "John Brewer Has a Cave"; Smith, interview with Porritt, January 19, 2013; Smith, interview with Heinerman, April 15, 2017; [Barton], "Manti Enigma." The sketches of the mummies are reproduced in Heinerman, *Hidden Treasures of Ancient American Cultures*, 147–148, and Stephen B. Shaffer, *Treasures of the Ancients* (Springville, UT: Plain Sight Publishing, 1996), 31–32. Gail Porritt claims that Brewer made the sketches for Porritt's benefit. John Heinerman claims that Brewer made the sketches only after Brewer and Heinerman tried and failed to get a good photograph of the mummies, concluding that "the powers that be don't want them photographed." According to Utahna Jessop, it was John Brewer's son Johnnie who sketched the mummies. There also exists a diagram of the cave, recently rediscovered by Terry Carter. Carter's hints as to how he came by it suggest he got it from Ross LeBaron, who had obtained photocopies under false pretenses from John Brewer's photographer. See Terry Carter and Utahna Jessop, "Nephilim Giants found in Utah, Brewers Cave the untold story," YouTube, January 18, 2017, https://www.youtube.com/watch?v=1ab2jZYFeGY; Terry Carter and David Tomlinson, "Ancient Nephilim Giants Tomb, death trap found inside Brewers Cave," YouTube, September 24, 2017, https://www.youtube.com/watch?v=AcaRDTGwcgk.

FIGURE 15.2. An inscribed stone box containing copper plates and wrapped in juniper bark, photographed with a pen for scale. Date unknown. MSS 2049, box 65, fd. 5j, Paul Cheesman Papers.

Brewer also, to his great astonishment, encountered a tall glowing angel. He then described an out-of-body experience, during which the angel identified himself as the Book of Mormon prophet Ether. The angel said that the artifacts in the cave had belonged to ancient Jaredites and that Brewer was not to sell anything from the cave for gain.

Amid the thick dust on the cave floor, Brewer also discovered inscribed slate tablets that, when joined like pieces of a jigsaw puzzle, formed a map of the Manti area. The map identified other nearby hills that also contained Jaredite treasures. Some of these Brewer was able to locate; others he could not.

In subsequent years, Brewer treated the cave as his private workspace. He spent long hours there, widening the cave and excavating its floor. To protect his discoveries, he also booby-trapped it and carefully disguised the entrance, so that one could stand within three feet of it and not know it was there.[24]

The version of this story in the diary differs in important respects. Here, Brewer did not suddenly break into an underground chamber but instead slowly excavated the cave. When digging for arrowheads, Brewer encountered first a small rock with strange writing on it and then an old, muddy metal book. For the next several years, he dug out and virtually lived in this cave, often skipping work, and worrying his wife by spending all his earnings on the project. In the course of his digging, Brewer uncovered many more inscribed objects of stone, lead, copper, and gold.

The journal portrays Brewer as deeply introspective, blending the methods of science and religious devotion. From the outset, Brewer read books on archaeology and carefully documented his excavations. He also continually prayed for guidance and sought information from the leaders in his local LDS ward. The ward was unhelpful; nobody there seemed to take the Book of Mormon very seriously as a historical document, for no one could tell him anything useful about the ancient Book of Mormon peoples. As for prayer, Brewer concluded that God was guiding him but that God also wanted him to work things out in his own mind rather than rely on revelation.

An important subtext in the journal is Brewer's sense of identification with Joseph Smith. Brewer felt that God had chosen him for the work of bringing forth these records, but he struggled with a profound sense of inadequacy and moral unworthiness. In his struggle to obtain divine guidance, Brewer concluded that God would not answer him unless his motives were pure. He fought a long and difficult struggle against his own avarice before finally achieving a breakthrough. It was the contents of the records that were important, he realized, not their monetary value. This internal struggle mirrored Smith's initial conflicted feelings about the golden plates of the Book of Mormon. Brewer also mirrored Smith's anxiety about the threat of

24. Barton, "Secret Chambers in the Rockies," 4, 6; "John Brewer Has a Cave"; Smith, interview with Porritt, January 19, 2013; Smith, interview with Heinerman, April 15, 2017.

greedy persons who would like to obtain the artifacts. Like Smith, Brewer carefully guarded the locations of his caves, showing them only to a select few whom he felt God had appointed to assist him.[25]

The conflicting versions of Brewer's discovery narrative reveal perhaps less about the truth of his story than about the competition to tell it, each narrator for his own reasons and in his own distinctive way. Brewer's discoveries attracted a different kind of narration from skeptical academics. In 1965, BYU anthropology professor Ray Matheny took up the Brewer case, determined "to expose the people involved for what they are."[26] Matheny and his BYU colleague Hugh Nibley visited Brewer, examined his artifacts, and pronounced them fakes.[27] Matheny found that the inscriptions on Brewer's stone tablets were "lighter in color and fresh looking" and had probably been made with a stainless steel tool. Some of the tablets were also coated with pine pitch that showed no evidence of long-term exposure to the elements and had modern bleached cotton fibers embedded in it. As for Brewer's metal plates, their composition reflected modern alloying techniques. Furthermore, "The inscriptions in the copper and brass plates had been made with a modern chisel, and the plates were cut with scissors from the same metal sheet."[28] Nibley drew his own conclusion from a simpler datum: "Brewer's wife told somebody he knew that Brewer had made the plates himself."[29]

BYU linguist William James Adams also got into the act. He examined the inscriptions on Brewer's artifacts, and "found so very few clusterings that from

25. John Brewer journal typescript.

26. Letter from Ray T. Matheny to C. Melvin Aikens, March 17, 1965, Anthropology Departmental Records, University of Utah Archives. Special thanks to archivist Kirk Baddley for finding and providing this document. According to Dee F. Green, Matheny was "the first active Church member who can really be called an archaeologist with a Ph.D. degree [awarded 1968] and professional standing." Green, "Book of Mormon Archaeology: The Myths and the Alternatives," *Dialogue: A Journal of Mormon Thought* 4, no. 2 (Summer 1969):72.

27. Barton, "Secret Chambers in the Rockies," 6.

28. Ray T. Matheny and William James Adams Jr., "An Archaeological and Linguistic Analysis of the Manti Tablets," typescript of a paper presented at Symposium on the Archaeology of the Scriptures, Provo, Utah, October 28, 1972, MSS 2049, box 65, fd. 4a, Cheesman Papers. John Heinerman argues that the cotton fibers came from a cloth that Brewer, untrained in archaeological technique, had used to clean the artifacts. Smith, interview with Heinerman, April 15, 2017.

29. Post by bobhenstra, April 3, 2011, in "We're surely in it now: Hel/3 Nephi, Revelation D&C 29, 45," LDS Freedom Forum, http://www.ldsfreedomforum.com/viewtopic.php?f=14&t=6041&start =540. Brewer's erstwhile associate John Heinerman confirmed to me in an interview that Brewer's wife had not believed in the authenticity of his artifacts. Smith, interview with Heinerman, April 15, 2017.

a language point of view I am forced to conclude that instead of a meaningful script, the work was the haphazard scratchings of a forger." Sometime later, he ate at a restaurant and happened to look down at his napkin, emblazoned with the slogan "eat more beef" and a series of local cattle brands. He immediately noticed a similarity between the brands and the characters on some of Brewer's artifacts. Upon further investigation, he found that "nearly one-fifth of the signs on the tablets apparently were inspired by registered Utah cattle brands."[30] Matheny and Adams coauthored a report denouncing Brewer's artifacts as forgeries, and the *Deseret News* in 1975 ran an exposé of Brewer.[31]

Matheny's BYU colleague Paul Cheesman also took an interest in the case. But unlike Matheny, Cheesman befriended Brewer and earned his trust. Brewer gave Cheesman many inscribed stones and metal plates and promised to show him the location of his treasure cave. Cheesman's papers, now archived in the L. Tom Perry Special Collections at BYU, contain many photographs of artifacts discovered by Brewer during his excavations.

For a while, at least, Cheesman found Brewer persuasive. He put one of Brewer's tablets on display in the Joseph Smith Building at BYU. In 1971, he met with Church President Spencer W. Kimball and Apostle Mark E. Petersen to solicit $1,000 to study the plates along with BYU colleague Hugh Nibley. Kimball authorized the funding and offered additional First Presidency money if necessary.[32] Nibley came away from the trip convinced the plates were fake, but Cheesman remained a believer.[33] On March 5, 1974, he made another trip to Sanpete County, this time with Apostle Petersen.[34]

Also accompanying him on this trip were his wife, Millie Cheesman, his student aide, Wayne Hamby, and his friend J. Golden Barton. According

30. John Nelson interview, cited in Alice J. Mueller, "Old Graves, Gold Plates and Gadianton Robbers (A Study on the Lore of Nephites in Utah)," 65, FA 1 File 322, Folklore Archive, L. Tom Perry Special Collections, Brigham Young University; "John Brewer Has a Cave." The napkin is preserved in MSS 2049, box 65, fd. 4a, Cheesman Papers.

31. Ray T. Matheny and William James Adams, Jr., "An Archaeological and Linguistic Analysis of the Manti Tablets," typescript of a paper presented at the Symposium on the Archaeology of the Scriptures, Provo, Utah, October 28, 1972, in MSS 2049, box 65, fd. 4a, Cheesman Papers; "John Brewer Has a Cave."

32. Letter from Paul R. Cheesman to Gary B. Doxey, May 3, 1971, MSS 2049, Box 1, fd. 5, Cheesman Papers.

33. Cheesman noted Nibley's opinion in a handwritten note, MSS 2049, box 65, fd. 4a, Cheesman Papers. Nibley's view is also mentioned in [Barton], "Manti Enigma."

34. [Barton], "Manti Enigma."

to Barton's firsthand account of the trip, the group met Brewer at the home of Moroni, Utah, bishop Merlin Nielson. Brewer recounted his discoveries and displayed about sixty inscribed plates, including some that were gold and framed under glass. He said that he normally kept them in a safe deposit box at a bank and that he had used them as "security for a loan with a private party." "Brewer then said he had a set of plates that no one had seen before and he wanted to show them for the first time to Elder Petersen. He then produced a set of small [copper] plates with a metal band around them some five inches square." Petersen was impressed, but he suggested the seal should only be broken in the presence of scientific experts. Cheesman asked Brewer to show him the cave and allow him to photograph the mummies. Brewer "seemed reluctant to commit himself to an immediate excursion," but he promised Cheesman that once the snow cleared he could enlarge the cave entrance to accommodate Cheesman's height. He also agreed to show BYU archaeologists the cave after showing it to Cheesman.[35]

According to one possibly embellished account of this interview, Apostle Petersen asked Brewer, "Are you willing to testify this day before your Heavenly Father, that these things are genuine and not—repeat not—of your own manufacture?" Brewer "blinked in disbelief at what he had just heard and gave them a disgusted look. Getting out of his chair, he reached into his shirt pocket and pulled out a half-used pack of cigarettes and casually slipped one into his mouth. 'I don't know what it takes to convince you fellows I'm telling the truth,' he said. 'I know what I found and I don't give a f--- who believes me or not. Now, if you gentlemen will excuse me, I'm going outside for a smoke.'"[36]

During the drive home, Cheesman asked each of his companions to express their opinions the meeting. "Elder Peterson was the first to respond with his view 'that the farmer was telling the truth and most likely did not have the capacity to perpetuate such an elaborate hoax.'" The rest of the group agreed.[37] "We are very interested in this, as you know," Petersen wrote

---

35. [Barton], "Manti Enigma"; Christopher C. Smith, interview with Millie Cheesman, May 17, 2012. Barton's account seems to be the source of the narrative in Shaffer, *Treasures of the Ancients*, 29–33. Some of Barton's friends feel that Shaffer plagiarized Barton. Christopher C. Smith, interview with Utahna Jessop, October 27, 2018; Petty, "Linda Karen Petty's Personal History."

36. Heinerman, *Hidden Treasures of Ancient American Cultures*, 22.

37. [Barton], "Manti Enigma"; Jared G. Barton, "Secret Chambers in the Rockies," *The Ancient American* 4, no. 28 (June/July 1998):6.

to Cheesman a few months later. "President Kimball has inquired of Brother [Milton R.] Hunter [of the First Council of the Seventy] and myself on two different occasions as to what the status of the matter is."[38] He also mentioned, "Our brethren here are very interested and it will not surprise me at all if they should authorize purchase of the land involved so that we may get full control."[39]

According to Barton, "Spring came and went in the Manti valley and John Brewer [m]ade no effort to contact Dr. Cheesman and fulfill the agreement that he had made in early March. We received information that Brewer was experiencing some marital difficulties and so we chose not to pressure this man as he sought to solve his personal problems." Bishop Merlin Nielsen did report some additional intelligence, however. Brewer had shown him pieces of the mummies' cloth wrappings and had also reported the discovery of a second cave with additional boxes of plates. Barton also heard from Cheesman about Petersen's plan to purchase the land on which Brewer's tomb was located. "A follow up visit to the recorders office in Manti showed that the Corporation of the L.D.S. Church had in fact been deeded a parcel of ground directly east of the [Temple]."[40]

In the 1970s and 1980s, Brewer also met several other people who gained his trust. In 1974, an unidentified "Canadian Indian" produced a partial translation of some of the plates, supposedly drawing on ancient tribal knowledge. The translation shows signs of employing Joseph Smith's Egyptian Alphabet and Grammar, an 1835 text in which the Mormon founder gave instructions for translating Egyptian hieroglyphics. The completed translation suggested that Brewer's artifacts had been produced by a group of Jaredites who had traveled to America about 2500 BC under the leadership of a man named Piron. This group settled in the southwestern United States and thrived there because the desert landscape required hard work and faithfulness to make a living. The translation indicated, among other things, that the Jaredites had concealed more than 5 million inscribed golden plates throughout the modern-day United States and Mexico. It also revealed

38. Letter from Mark E. Petersen to Paul R. Cheesman, June 27, 1974, MSS 2049, box 1, fd. 6, Cheesman Papers.

39. Letter from Mark E. Petersen to Paul R. Cheesman, April 10, 1974, MSS 2049, box 65, fd. 5j, Cheesman Papers.

40. [Barton], "Manti Enigma."

technical information about Jaredite numerals, chemistry, and funeral rites.[41] In gratitude for the translator's work, Brewer gave him some artifacts.[42]

Around the same time, Brewer met Gail Porritt. In the mid-1970s, Porritt heard about him from a friend and visited Brewer at the Moroni Wastewater Treatment Plant, where he still worked. "He showed me some round lead plates with inscriptions on them with a hole in the middle," Porritt remembers. "I showed them to Hugh Nibley, and he said they were Jaredite things, and he said ... the reason they were made that shape with a hole in the middle was that when they went to move them they strung them on a pole, and two guys could carry them from place to place." Porritt befriended Brewer, who entrusted him with a cache of artifacts including stone boxes and plates. Brewer also showed him the location of a hill that had a cache of records in it. "How do you know?" Porritt asked. Brewer replied, "because the map in my cave says there is.... According to my map, the largest and the most important repository of records is up here on this hill.... I've looked for it for a long time, ... [and] it's finally occurred to me that I'm not the one that's supposed to find it.... They're up there; good luck to you if you can find them."[43]

Cheesman's friend David Tomlinson also earned Brewer's trust. In the late 1970s, Brewer concluded that God had chosen Cheesman, Porritt, and Tomlinson to see the cave and to aid in the work of bringing forth the records.[44] By this time, Brewer had been stalling Cheesman since 1971, but the arrival of two more trustworthy helpers did not end the delays. "Whenever I don't understand anything, I stall," Brewer told a *Deseret News* reporter in 1975.[45]

Indeed, Brewer always seemed full of excuses. The biggest concerned site ownership. "For years, there was a snag," reported the *News*. "The cave

41. Gail Porritt, "Report and Interpretation by a Canadian Man on Very Ancient Inhabitants of Utah," n.d., MSS 2049, box 24, fd. 3, Cheesman Papers; miscellaneous translations, June–December 1974, MSS 2049, box 24, fd. 3, Cheesman Papers.

42. Porritt, interview with Brewer, n.d. [ca. 1997].

43. Smith, interview with Porritt, January 19, 2013. Diarist Linda Petty's extensive notes on Porritt's stories from the 1990s add evocative details. The male mummy, Porritt told her, had an eight-foot sword that "was taken into Manti and used to split a radiator in two as a demonstration of its capability." To get to the cave that Brewer had pointed out to Porritt, "there is a 200 foot drop. At the 30 foot level it [is] necessary to swing onto a ledge and take steps down from there"; Petty, "Linda Karen Petty's Personal History."

44. Letter from Gail B. Porritt to Paul R. Cheesman, n.d., MSS 2049, box 24, fd. 4, Cheesman Papers.

45. "John Brewer Has a Cave."

was on private property. But the 'old man' who refused to sell died, and his son now has sold Brewer 10 acres, including the cave site, Brewer claims."[46] Still, the situation was not resolved. Brewer's letters and interviews alluded to continued legal battles over ownership well into the 1990s.[47]

Brewer also gave many other reasons for delaying. In a 1974 letter to Apostle Mark E. Petersen, Paul Cheesman listed two: "1. John Brewer's wife left him with all the children to care for, therefore a delay in our plans. 2. Brewer lost his job and is in the midst of changing to another job—further delay."[48] In 1975, Brewer listed three more for the *Deseret News* reporter: he valued his privacy, he worried that he wouldn't get credit for the discovery, and he wanted to leave an inheritance for his three boys.[49]

In the 1980s, Paul Cheesman continued to badger Brewer for access to the cave.[50] But according to Millie Cheesman, by this time "all kinds of people were stalking [Brewer] and made it very difficult for him to take anybody to the cave."[51] Instead, he directed inquirers' attention to the search for additional caves. In 1987, Dave Tomlinson hiked with Brewer in the mountains west of Manti and Ephraim, Utah, searching for a deposit of treasures marked on the "map rock" from Brewer's cave. Brewer told Tomlinson that the map identified Jaredite burial sites as far afield as Colorado and Idaho, "with little footprints going from one to the other." The "main" site on the map, however, seemed to be west of Manti. The map suggested the site was marked by a totem pole-shaped petroglyph. Brewer and Tomlinson searched for this "trail marker" without success.[52] In 1988, Cheesman loaned Tomlinson his stone box in case the map-like markings on its side could aid the search.[53] After

46. Ibid.

47. Letter from Earl John Brewer to Paul R. Cheesman, November 6, 1989, MSS 2049, box 24, fd. 2, Cheesman Papers; letter from Paul R. Cheesman to Earl John Brewer, December 4, 1989, MSS 2049, box 24, fd. 2, Cheesman Papers; Porritt, interview with Brewer, n.d. [ca. 1997].

48. Letter from Paul R. Cheesman to Mark E. Petersen, June 24, 1974, MSS 2049, box 1, fd. 6, Cheesman Papers.

49. "John Brewer Has a Cave."

50. Letter from Paul R. Cheesman to John Brewer, July 22, 1983, and Letter from Paul R. Cheesman to Earl John Brewer, January 15, 1986, MSS 2049, box 12, fd. 3, Cheesman Papers.

51. Christopher C. Smith, interview with Millie Cheesman, May 17, 2012.

52. Carter and Tomlinson, "Ancient Nephilim Giants Tomb"; Letter from David L. Tomlinson to Paul R. Cheesman and Millie Cheesman, November 25, 1987, MSS 2049, box 30, fd. 1, Cheesman Papers.

53. Letter from David L. Tomlinson to Marshall Payn, January 22, 1988, MSS 2049, box 30, fd. 1, Cheesman Papers.

Cheesman's death in 1991, Tomlinson returned the box to Cheesman's widow, Millie.[54]

Brewer continued to stall in an undated interview with Gail Porritt, which occurred sometime between 1998 and 2001. Observing that "everything is on hold in this program right now, because it's not time yet," Porritt asked Brewer, "Do you have any feelings at all about how close the time is that this stuff is supposed to come forth?" Brewer replied, "Mm hmm, I got a pretty good idea. It's gonna be within the next two years, anyway." However, Brewer felt strongly that the Lord had to send two more people—archaeologists—to help with the work before it could go forward.[55]

In 2013, Porritt explained that Brewer always "thought there was gonna be three people that would be involved [in bringing forth the records,] and he was waiting for some sort of sign to know who they were. . . . He was gonna turn everything over to them."[56] According to Linda Petty, Porritt told her in January 1997 that Brewer sought not three, but five people to turn the project over to before his death.[57]

But two years did not end the delay. When Brewer died in 2007, he still had not shown anyone the cave. "I've made a map and a video of how to get to [the cave]," an aging Brewer reassured Porritt in the late 1980s. "They're in escrow at a Provo bank, . . . in Paul Cheesman's name." Brewer, however, survived Cheesman. According to Porritt, "When Paul died, I went to [Brewer] and I said, 'you've got to put that in somebody else's name, because Paul just died.' And he was very shook up because he trusted Paul. And I don't know that he put all this stuff in somebody else's name or not. I haven't heard that anybody's got it. So maybe it's still in the bank waiting for somebody to pick it up, I don't know. I don't even know which bank it is, in Provo."[58] Even after his death, Brewer still delays.

---

54. Petty, "Linda Karen Petty's Personal History."

55. In an aside, Brewer suggested another reason for delaying: "I don't want to be like John Heinerman." He didn't clarify what he meant, but throughout the interview Brewer portrayed Heinerman as a "con man" and liar. Porritt, interview with Brewer, n.d. [ca. 1997].

56. Smith, interview with Porritt, January 19, 2013.

57. Petty, "Linda Karen Petty's Personal History."

58. Smith, interview with Porritt, January 19, 2013. Around 2002 or 2003, "a friend of the Brewer family" contacted Paul Cheesman's widow and asked that the Brewer artifacts in his collection be returned to the Brewer family. Millie Cheesman complied with this request and received "a lovely note from one of John Brewer's sisters" thanking her for the gesture. The returned artifacts included a "cement box" and some copper plates. Smith, interview with Cheesman, May 17, 2012.

CONTESTED LEGACIES

John Brewer's memory is kept alive today by a bewildering array of Mormon Fundamentalists, Book of Mormon archaeologists, treasure hunting enthusiasts, and skeptics, all with their own agendas. Brewer fell in with some of these colorful characters near the end of his life, and to a great extent they have controlled his legacy. Although Brewer himself adamantly denied that he ever took anyone into his treasure cave except his deceased son Johnnie, three men have claimed otherwise. John Heinerman, Jerry Mower, and Gerald Peterson Sr. have all claimed to have been in it.

Heinerman, an unconventional member of the LDS Church who calls himself a "Joseph Smith Mormon," met Brewer in the late 1970s. Heinerman lived in Manti with his father and brother at the time. On a trip to Salt Lake City, he heard about Brewer from a friend named Rodney Turner. Heinerman sought Brewer out at the Wastewater Treatment Plant and quickly gained his friendship and trust. In Heinerman's telling, he came onto Brewer's project as a sort of senior partner, instructing the naive Brewer on how to fend off predatory journalists and how to observe proper scientific protocol in his excavations. Brewer accepted the arrangement, and together the two men even dabbled in translation (though Heinerman emphasizes that the effort was not serious and that he is not a prophet).[59]

According to Heinerman, Brewer finally decided on his own initiative to show Heinerman the cave. One day Brewer "showed up unannounced and was surprised to see that I was already dressed and ready to go, the Holy Spirit having impressed me beforehand of his coming and the purpose of it," Heinerman wrote. "It was the night my testimony of this sacred record became granite-hardened and gold-enriched by the things I saw and touched and handled for myself." Heinerman encountered many wonders in Brewer's cave, including the two eight-foot-tall Jaredite mummies, the head of a unicorn, an ancient Jaredite dry-cell battery, and many colorfully painted stone boxes full of inscribed metal plates. "My own witness of where this man took me and what he showed me, has never once changed.... I have still always maintained that the two caves and their respective contents ... are genuine and DO EXIST!"[60]

59. Smith, interview with John Heinerman, April 15, 2017.

60. Heinerman speculated that the treasure was worth "billions." Heinerman, *Hidden Treasures of Ancient American Cultures*, 22–23, 28, 119.

After a short period of friendship, however, Brewer and Heinerman had a spectacular falling-out. Heinerman had gotten engaged to a Canadian woman named Louise, who had moved into an adjoining house. In Brewer's interpretation of events, Heinerman had proposed to her under false pretenses, convincing her to quit a prestigious job and to sell her beautiful house. "He got $34,000 out of that woman," Brewer asserted. "He ruined that woman.... And when she told me what he'd done, boy—'course I helped her, as much as I could, which wasn't that much. I just more or less helped her move her furniture, and store it, kinda looked after it till she got straightened around, and I haven't heard from her since." When Heinerman confronted Brewer about his role in ending the engagement, Brewer broke off their friendship and called him a "devil." He also provided evidence to a church court, which disfellowshipped Heinerman for one year for "fraud and misconduct with a woman."[61] According to a thirdhand report of Brewer's testimony, he also testified that Heinerman had sold fake copper plates to church members from Utah and Idaho and that he himself had manufactured the plates and "been a party to the fraud."[62] Regardless, Heinerman took all this as a personal betrayal. Together with his father and brother, he pronounced a priesthood curse on Brewer, consigning him and his progeny to eternal hell.[63]

Despite their falling-out, Heinerman remains the most successful promoter and popularizer of the Brewer treasure story. In the late 1990s, Gail Porritt interviewed Brewer about Heinerman's claims.

"Has he ever been in your cave?"

"No."

"Okay. Has anybody ever been in besides you and your son?"

"Not to my knowledge.... He's got 37 of my plates.... I entrusted him in that respect, but I never did get 'em back."[64]

61. Porritt, interview with Brewer, n.d. [ca. 1997]; Shaffer, *Treasures of the Ancients*, 38. Smith, interview with Porritt, January 19, 2013.

62. [Barton], "Manti Enigma"; Smith, interview with Porritt, January 19, 2013; Carter and Tomlinson, "Ancient Nephilim Giants Tomb." I did not ask John Heinerman about this, but he volunteered an anecdote in which Brewer's brother-in-law Jerry Mower enticed Brewer to manufacture and sell fake plates, and "they had to go and repay." Smith, interview with John Heinerman, April 15, 2017.

63. Smith, interview with John Heinerman, April 15, 2017.

64. Porritt, interview with Brewer, n.d. [ca. 1997].

Heinerman says he would have returned Brewer's plates if Brewer had ever asked, but Brewer never did.[65] Ancient knowledge, he claims, was the true treasure all along.[66]

Another set of claims about Brewer's cave arises out of the polygamist subculture in Manti, Utah. In 1990, Jim Harmston—who within four years would found his own polygamous sect—led a party to search near the Manti Temple for signs of Brewer's cave. A member of the search party found a rock inscribed with esoteric glyphs. This sparked a flurry of activity, and soon a Manti elder's quorum president announced that he had found the location of Brewer's cave directly west of the Manti temple. Manti bishop Lyman Willardson reported this to Dave Tomlinson, who relayed the news to Gail Porritt. Porritt and Tomlinson called Brewer, who told them not to concern themselves with it; his tomb was east of the temple, not west. Nevertheless, Bishop Willardson reported that "there was an excavation going on the West side of the Manti valley" and artifacts had been discovered there. He told J. Golden Barton that he feared the excavation might be illegal and that some of his parishioners were engaged in activities that might embarrass the church.[67]

I have not learned the full story of this excavation, but the upshot is that Brewer's brother-in-law Jerry Mower—leader of a small polygamous sect—claims to have discovered the secret of Brewer's cave. Historians H. Michael Marquardt and Gerald John Kloss visited Mower's home in 2001, and "Jerry showed us many artifacts he claims he found in the valley of Manti, including gold plates, boxes carved out of rock to place the plates in, ... and various other artifacts. Jerry told us that he has found many caves in the Valley of Manti and mummies, including he claims, the mummies of Adam and Eve—since he believes this was the Garden of Eden site and the site where Noah built the Ark. He feels the second coming will take place in The Valley of Manti. He also showed us [a] translation of the gold plates with symbols for God the Father, Jesus the son, and The Holy Spirit, who is Joseph Smith."[68]

65. Smith, interview with Heinerman, April 15, 2017.

66. Heinerman, *Hidden Treasures of Ancient American Cultures*, 123.

67. [Barton], "Manti Enigma."

68. Gerald John Kloss, "My Visit to Utah: A Personal Reflection," in *Latter Day Saint History* 13 (2001):18–19; additional details provided by H. Michael Marquardt on August 8, 2011. Wayne

Mower took Brewer's project to a sectarian extreme, occasionally bordering on science fiction. According to an informant who attended a Mower presentation in 2008, Mower showed his audience pictures of a disc-shaped rock, "which he said was an ancient CD, and that he could play it if he could figure out how to build a compatible player." Mower also showed the audience photos of a hill that he said contained an ancient record vault. The vault was guarded by a secret society, which, however, allowed him to borrow things from time to time. Mower described an outdoor temple with three altars—telestial, terrestrial, and celestial: "He said for the celestial altar, you had to take a leap of faith—and he totally ripped that off of Indiana Jones. He said you had to walk off a cliff on an invisible ledge to get to the altar. And he said it was booby-trapped and if you didn't know what you were doing, you would get killed." Mower also said that the ancient Nephite general Moroni had used a portal network to teleport between Mexico, Utah, and New York.[69]

A less flamboyant player in the Brewer story was fundamentalist prophet Gerald Peterson Sr., who in 1978 split from the Apostolic United Brethren to establish the Righteous Branch of the Church of Jesus Christ of Latter-day Saints, also known as Christ's Church. According to his soft-spoken grandson, Peterson met with Brewer in the late 1970s or early 1980s and was shown the cave. Supposedly Peterson took photographs of the mummies, now lost. He also borrowed some of the plates, which he translated and returned to Brewer. The translation, however, is sacred. On one occasion, Peterson read it aloud to his apostles, but afterward they couldn't remember anything they'd heard. When Peterson died, he passed the translation on to his son, who held onto it for thirty-eight years and never read it because it was sacred. Peterson's son left it to his grandson, who also hasn't read it. The translation is about a hundred pages long and written on yellow legal paper. "We don't use it as a way to kind of lure anybody, or anything weird like that," says the grandson. He does, however, consider it part of his mission in life to find out more about it.[70]

May has published photographs of stone boxes, foundations, and archways apparently found by Mower, although May calls him "John" to preserve his anonymity. (Compare these photographs to the photograph published by Kloss.) May, "Utah's City in the Clouds," *Ancient American* 27 (April/May 1999):3–4, 37–39.

69. Smith, interview with Rodgers, March 14, 2017.

70. Christopher C. Smith, interview with Michael Peterson, November 5, 2018.

Another fundamentalist circle that took a strong interest in Brewer's activities was the LeBaron family. According to John Heinerman, during his brief association with John Brewer the two men began receiving threatening phone calls from followers of Ervil LeBaron (who famously ordered the assassinations of many rivals, including his brother Joel). LeBaron demanded to know the locations of Brewer's treasure caves. One day, an armed member of LeBaron's group followed Brewer and Heinerman up a mountain. Heinerman pushed a boulder down the mountainside, and it struck and injured the pursuer, who then had to be evacuated by helicopter.

Later, after Heinerman's association with Brewer ended, he heard that the LeBaron group had tortured Brewer with a blowtorch and staged his oldest son Johnnie's death by drug overdose in a desperate attempt to extort the caves' locations.[71] Gail Porritt agrees that Brewer claimed to have been tortured and his son murdered but asserts that Brewer blamed the LDS Church, not the LeBarons.[72]

Ervil's nephew Ross LeBaron Jr. also showed an interest in Brewer. According to Porritt, "Johnny Brewer took a lot of these plates and tablets to a photographer in Manti and had 'em photographed. And Ross LeBaron found out about that and went up to that photographer and had him making photocopies of that. And Johnny Brewer got all pissed off about that."[73] A treasure-hunting enthusiast in his own right, LeBaron taught that nearly every important event in Gospel history had occurred in Utah. For instance, after being kicked out of the Garden of Eden, Adam and Eve had lived in a Utah "treasure cave."[74] LeBaron thus emerged as the ultimate parochializer, making his own home region the very epicenter of all biblical narrative.

In contrast to the likes of Heinerman and Mower, Gail Porritt seems humble for a man who proclaimed himself the "One Mighty and Strong"— a messianic figure prophesied in Doctrine and Covenants. God told Porritt

---

71. Heinerman, *Hidden Treasures*, 203–208; Branton, "Dreamland in the Rockies," August 10, 1995, http://www.v-j-enterprises.com/branton.html; post by Terry L. Carter, October 5, 2006, in "9' tall mummies . . . cool!" on the Ancient Lost Treasures Message Board, http://ancientlosttreasures .yuku.com/topic/4744; Smith, interview with Heinerman, April 15, 2017.

72. Smith, interview with Porritt, January 19, 2013.

73. Ibid. Terry Carter identifies the photographer as Lucian Bound. Carter and Tomlinson, "Ancient Nephilim Giants Tomb."

74. Gail Porritt, report on an interview with Ross LeBaron, n.d., 4, 11, MSS 2049, box 24, fd. 4, Cheesman Papers.

"that there would be great apostasy in the Church, but that it was not his con-cern"; his task was to "keep the records" until the Lord purifies the church. Rather than start his own church, Porritt has accumulated a loose network of charismatic white and Native American Mormons on the edges of official LDS fellowship. on August 13, 1992, three Porritt associates—Linda Petty, Karen Petty, and Joanna Posey—performed proxy temple rituals (baptisms and endowments for the dead) for Brewer's mummies, whom they called "King Orihah and his wife." "They are the first two Jaredites to be blessed with the ordinances of the temple in this dispensation that we are aware of," Linda Petty wrote in her diary. The mummies appeared to her in a dream to thank her for her work.[75]

Brewer's legacy is also kept alive by a few scholars at the margins of the discipline of Book of Mormon archaeology. In the 1960s and 1970s, BYU and church-owned Deseret Book published most of Paul Cheesman's work on disputed archaeological finds. In the 1980s, he increasingly published through a private press called Horizon Publishers.[76] BYU's University Archaeological Society went private in 1967 and changed its name to the Society for Early Historic Archaeology. In the early 1990s, it merged with the Foundation for Ancient and Historic Studies and took the name Ancient America Foundation at Cheesman's suggestion. Meanwhile, BYU adopted a different organization, the Foundation for Ancient Research and Mormon Studies, with stricter stan-dards for the sort of artifacts and evidence it was willing to entertain.

Scholars associated with the church increasingly deprecated the study of Brewer's plates, which became the province of private foundations.[77] For

75. Petty, "Linda Karen Petty's Personal History"; Smith, interview with Porritt, January 19, 2013. See also Bill Shepard, "'To Set in Order the House of God': The Search for the Elusive 'One Mighty and Strong,'" *Dialogue: A Journal of Mormon Thought* 39, no. 3 (Fall 2006):18–45.

76. Cheesman's gradual marginalization is evident from his letters. In the early 1970s, General Authorities praised his work on Book of Mormon archaeology. Letters from Thomas S. Monson to Paul R. Cheesman, March 17, 1972; Milton R. Hunter to Paul R. Cheesman, May 3, 1972; Spencer W. Kimball to Paul R. Cheesman, September 29, 1975; and Mark E. Petersen to Paul R. Cheesman, December 30, 1976, MSS 2049, Box 1, fds. 5 and 7, Cheesman Papers, transcribed by Bryan Cottle. But by 1983 Cheesman was citing endorsements of his work from deceased apostles and meeting routine rejection by church and university committees. Letters from Paul R. Cheesman to Vaughn J. Featherstone, October 5, 1983; Paul R. Cheesman to Howard W. Hunter, February 13, 1984; Paul R. Cheesman to Wendell Tolman, May 31, 1984; and Paul R. Cheesman to Jeffrey R. Holland, March 7, 1986, MSS 2049, Box 12, fd. 3, Cheesman Papers, transcribed by Bryan Cottle.

77. *Ancient America Foundation Newsletter* 63 (November 1995), http://www.ancientamerica .org/library/media/HTML/mf4ca25l/Aaf63.htm. For instance, BYU anthropologist John L. Sorenson

instance, Jerry L. Ainsworth, author of *Lives and Travels of Mormon and Moroni* and founder of the Foundation for Ancient American Studies, cites Brewer's plates as evidence that the ancient Nephite general Moroni passed through Manti, Utah, on his way from Book of Mormon lands in Mexico to the burying-place of the Book of Mormon plates in New York.[78]

One group that still explicitly takes Brewer seriously is the Ancient Historical Research Foundation (AHRF), founded by Terry Carter, June Balaich, and Shawn Davies. Advisors for the group in 2011 included Rodney Meldrum (controversial champion of a Great Lakes setting for the Book of Mormon), David Tomlinson (one of those whom John Brewer promised but ultimately failed to show his cave), Wayne May (publisher of *Ancient American* magazine), and Stephen E. Jones (a former BYU physics professor whose eccentric interests include scientific defense of Book of Mormon historicity).[79] As recently as 2005, the group carbon-dated a piece of bark from Brewer's cave (obtained from Paul Cheesman's widow, Millie), finding it to be approximately 2161 ± 70 years old.[80]

AHRF's website lampoons "Many of the 'Scientific Community' or 'Scholars,'" who not only ridicule but also steal and cover up the finds of honest amateur explorers. An individual member of the group has directed more pointed criticisms at Ray Matheny and Jesse Jennings, who are accused of

---

in 1976 and BYU art historian Martin Raish in 1981 classed Cheesman's work as "poor scholarship" using "fallacious methodologies" to meet "consumer demand for intellectual loot." John L. Sorenson, "Instant Expertise on Book of Mormon Archaeology," *BYU Studies* 16, no. 3 (Spring 1976):429; Martin Raish, "All That Glitters: Uncovering Fool's Gold in Book of Mormon Archaeology," *Sunstone* 6, no. 1 (January–February 1981):13–15. According to Dee F. Green, the church's effort to distance itself from dubious archaeology began in the 1960s. See Green, "Book of Mormon Archaeology," 76–77.

78. Jerry L. Ainsworth, *The Lives and Travels of Mormon and Moroni* (n.p.: Peace-Makers Publishing, 2000), 218.

79. "AHRF Bios," http://www.ancienthistoricalresearchfoundation.com/Pages/Bios/BioMain .htm; Terry Carter, "About my youtube channel, Treasure Hunting, Nephilim Giants, out of place archaeology, etc.," YouTube, December 8, 2017, https://www.youtube.com/watch?v=jaLTleZHCWs; Tad Walch, "BYU Places '9/11 Truth' Professor on Paid Leave," *Deseret News*, September 8, 2006, http://www.deseretnews.com/article/645199800/BYU-places-911-truth-professor-on-paid-leave .html.

80. Steven E. Jones, "Radiocarbon Dating of Bark Sample from Brewer's Cave, Manti Area," *Ancient American* 15, no. 90 (March 2011); Smith, interview with Cheesman, May 17, 2012; Smith, interview with Jessop, October 27, 2018. John Heinerman claims that scientists also have carbon dates for hair and fingernails from one of the mummies between 800 and 700 BCE, but I can find no evidence that such a test was performed. Heinerman, *Hidden Treasures of Ancient American Cultures*, 147–148.

"bullying" Brewer and reasoning like buffoons: "They . . . can't read the writing so it is obviously made up."[81] In a 2004 letter to U.S. President George W. Bush, one proponent of the Brewer plates accused academics of covering up the existence of ancient giants while selling their treasures to black market antiquities dealers.[82]

AHRF cofounder Terry Carter takes a particular interest in Brewer's cave. In a YouTube video, Carter admits that aspects of the Brewer tale are fishy. "John was an artist. I mean, I've interviewed a lot of people, and they say the things he could do with a piece of wood was just unbelievable. . . . He did, uh, forge some things, and he admitted it. . . . When he testified against [John] Heinerman in a bishop's court, he did admit to, uh, forging some stuff." However, Carter argues that the carbon-dated tree bark is undeniably ancient and "couldn't have been forged." Carter has located a cave near Manti, Utah, that matches the description of John Brewer's cave, though he found it empty except for a few items such as candles, blasting caps, and dynamite. He believes another underground cavern is nearby, waiting to be found.[83]

Closely tied to the AHRF is the "Morgan Pow-wow," an annual meeting of Mormon treasure hunters, Bigfoot hunters, ghost hunters, and UFO enthusiasts at a private campground in the mountains of Morgan County, Utah. Started by Kent Smith in 2000 as an informal gathering of six friends, the event now attracts hundreds of attendees. When I attended the Pow-wow on June 2, 2018, the event began with a half hour of stories about aliens, Bigfoot encounters, and Butch Cassidy's secret hideout in Canyonlands National Park. Then AHRF trustee Utahna Jessop delivered a two-and-a-half-hour presentation on Brewer's cave and the biblical Nephilim. Describing herself as a "born skeptic," Jessop presented Brewer's story and the carbon-dated

81. Post by DrJones, February 26, 2011, in "We're surely in it now: Hel/3 Nephi, Revelation D&C 29, 45," on the LDS Freedom Forum, http://www.ldsfreedomforum.com/viewtopic.php?f=14&t=6041&start=540.

82. Robert Shrewsbury, "An Open Letter to the President of the United States," Terra Firma Assayers, October 23, 2004, https://web.archive.org/web/20120729023110/http://www.terrafirmaassayers.com/bush.htm.

83. "Nephilim Giants found in Utah, Brewers Cave the untold story," YouTube, January 18, 2017, https://www.youtube.com/watch?v=1ab2jZYFeGY; Carter and Tomlinson, "Ancient Nephilim Giants Tomb."

bark as scientific evidence that the Book of Mormon is true. Her charisma has helped renew public interest in Brewer's story in recent years.[84]

Persons affiliated with the AHRF feel some ambivalence about their efforts to locate Brewer's cave. While supporting Terry Carter's efforts to locate the cave, David Tomlinson also warns of a "death trap" near the cave's entrance: a "bottomless pit" into which looters might fall. He also tells a story of someone who found Brewer's cave but was denied entry by guardian spirits.[85] Gary Taylor, another man to whom Brewer gave a box of plates, reported in 1998 that looters had mostly "cleaned out" one of Brewer's caves but that the last six stone boxes had mysteriously disappeared before the looters could take them and reappeared in another cave.[86] Such stories imply that the artifacts may not want to be found; that it may not yet be time.

The Brewer story has also made some impression outside Mormon circles. Loosely tied to the AHRF are the Epigraphic Society and the Midwestern Epigraphic Society, non-Mormon anthropological organizations that promote the controversial "diffusionist" model of Native American ancestry, positing a pre-columbian migration from Africa or Europe. Anthropologists associated with these organizations examined Brewer's plates at the request of Paul Cheesman and David Tomlinson. AHRF advisor Wayne May publishes *Ancient America* magazine, which covers diffusionist claims of all stripes, Mormon and non-Mormon.[87] One article in *Ancient American* suggested that Brewer's plates might be records of ancient migrants from the lost continent of Lemuria.[88]

84. Terry Carter and Kent Smith, "Brewers Cave come learn and share," YouTube, May 20, 2018, https://www.youtube.com/watch?v=5OuD5zof38g; Max Higbee, "Historian hopes there is truth to story of Book of Mormon-era artifacts found in Manti cave," *Sanpete Messenger*, October 6, 2017, https://sanpetemessenger.com/historian-hopes-there-is-truth-to-story-of-book-of-mormon-era -artifacts-found-in-manti-cave/.

85. Carter and Tomlinson, "Ancient Nephilim Giants Tomb." Perhaps Tomlinson heard the story of guardian spirits from a Navajo man called "Chief Badger," who told Linda Petty a similar story. Petty, "Linda Karen Petty's Personal History."

86. Petty, "Linda Karen Petty's Personal History." See also Dan Vogel's discussion of "slippery treasures" in Dan Vogel, *Joseph Smith: The Making of a Prophet* (Salt Lake City, UT: Signature Books, 2004), 35–52.

87. David L. Tomlinson to Marshall Payn, January 22, 1988, MSS 2049, box 30, fd. 1, Cheesman Papers; Cheesman to Doxey, May 3, 1971; Rick Osmon, "Midwestern Epigraphic Society and Ancient America," Ancient America [blog], April 10, 2014, https://ancientamerica.com/midwestern-epigraphic -society-and-ancient-america/; "AHRF Bios," http://www.ancienthistoricalresearchfoundation.com /Pages/Bios/BioMain.htm.

88. Barton, "Secret Chambers in the Rockies," 6.

Far stranger, the story of John Brewer's cave has also been incorporated into a popular UFO conspiracy theory involving a huge network of underground caverns concealed beneath the southwestern United States. These caverns are supposed to be the battleground for competing alien species clandestinely seeking to subjugate the earth. Bruce Alan Walton, a popular conspiracist who writes under the pseudonym "Branton," reported an informant's claim that Brewer broke into this underground cavernous network and found artifacts of alien manufacture. Walton's informant claimed that the LDS Church is cooperating with the U.S. government in a massive coverup. "[Brewer's] son was TORTURED AND KILLED by some unknown person or persons trying to force the secrets out of him," the informant wrote. "The church wanted the plates in the worst way—they still do."[89]

CONCLUSION

John Brewer and his successors inherited a Mormon fascination with hidden scripture and physical artifacts that traces back to Joseph Smith. Brewer, like Smith, understood the allure of physical objects. He cast himself in the mold of Mormonism's founding prophet, seeking and promising treasures beyond description. These treasures symbolized not material wealth but spiritual riches: proof of the ancient American setting of the Book of Mormon and fulfillment of end-times prophecies. In an age of science and special effects, to enchant the world requires a certain amount of evidence that we can see.

The intense competition for control of these treasures illustrates that others, too, have understood their evocative power and their potential to confer religious authority. This continuing competition has taken the form of struggle not only for ownership of artifacts but to control their meaning. Often it has taken the form of a running argument between skeptical elites, who seek to debunk the artifacts entirely and believers who view debunking as betrayal.

This is not to suggest that the quest for Brewer's caves is cynical. Nearly every believer in Brewer's treasures has a real sense of wonder and a deep sense of mission to help bring the records forth. They might prefer the word

---

89. Branton, "Dreamland in the Rockies," August 10, 1995, http://www.v-j-enterprises.com /branton.html.

"significance" rather than "authority" to describe what they seek. Theirs is a magical, enchanted world in which New York farm boys and central Utah sanitation workers can play central roles in saving the world and solving Gospel mysteries.

In an American religious context defined by Protestantism, the power of objects often goes unappreciated, even by scholars. Centuries of Protestant dominance in the Western academy have made artifacts and relics all but invisible—even as objects still profoundly shape Western religious lives. It may be time for scholars to revisit religious narratives with treasure hunters' eyes, in search of those luminous artifacts that drive conflict, confer authority, and enliven religious history.

And it could also be the case that scriptures matter to modern people more for what they signify than for what they say. Modern people seem more pre-occupied with whether (and which) religion is true than with the finer points of theology. Scripture is a resource mined for proof more than for religious messages. Like the Book of Mormon, Brewer's records perhaps derive religious power more from their physicality—their objectness—than from anything they teach.

16

Matthew Philip Gill, Joseph Smith, and the Dynamics of Mormon Schism

Matt Bowman

On a Friday night in 1990, Matthew Philip Gill, a twelve-year-old British member of the Church of Jesus Christ of Latter-day Saints (hereafter the LDS Church), finished reading the Book of Mormon.[1] Like thousands of LDS youth before him, Gill had determined to finish the book and test what contemporary Mormons call "Moroni's promise," the exhortation of the book's final prophet to "ask God, the Eternal Father, in the name of Jesus Christ, if these things are not true," coupled with the promise that a spiritual witness will be granted.[2] For many Saints, this rite of passage concludes with the religious experience they are taught to expect: "a burning in the bosom," an inner manifestation of the Holy Spirit confirming the book's divine provenance. Such an answer is also read as an endorsement of the prophetic claims of Joseph Smith and a sign of God's hand behind the church he organized. It is thus a form of what Thomas Alexander, following Max Weber, has described as the routinization of charisma in the LDS Church.[3]

---

1. The LDS Church, its members and institutions, are also commonly described with the adjective "Mormon." Here, that adjective will be reserved for what I call the "Mormon tradition," the multiple religious movements that claim Joseph Smith as their founder and who share a cultural and theological inheritance such as the Book of Mormon, the notion of modern prophets, and so forth. Members of the LDS Church will be referred to as Latter-day Saints or Saints and with the adjective LDS.

2. *Preach My Gospel: A Handbook for Missionary Service* (Salt Lake City, UT: The Church of Jesus Christ of Latter-day Saints, 2004); Moroni 10:4–5.

3. Thomas G. Alexander, *Mormonism in Transition: A History of the Latter-day Saints, 1890–1930* (Urbana: University of Illinois, 1985); Doctrine and Covenants 9:8–9; see also Boyd K. Packer, "That All May Be Edified," *Ensign* 24, no. 11 (November 1994):60. Citations to the Bible and Book of

Gill, however, reported a far more radical experience—one that broke LDS routine and summoned renewed charismatic experience. His prayer summoned a resurrected, angelic Moroni himself to witness for his book. Over the next decade and a half, this visitation was followed by a series of other dramatic spiritual experiences culminating in the summer of 2006 with a visitation of the angel Raphael, a Pentecost experience during a visit to Stonehenge, and, on July 12, an encounter with Jesus Christ and then a resurrected Joseph Smith. These experiences were not purposeless. In September 2006, Gill announced he had received a new book of scripture, and by November of that year he had founded the Latter Day Church of Christ in Derbyshire, England, claiming divine direction. As of 2017, the church had retitled itself the "Restored Branch of Jesus Christ," and Gill had ceded day-to-day leadership to his father, Philip.[4]

Gill's is only the latest of hundreds of churches born of the Mormon movement since Joseph Smith's death in June 1844. Most did not last long. Smith's peculiar combination of gifts and circumstance have been hard to match. He was a restorationist who appealed simultaneously to the Old and New Testaments, weaving their themes together in the new scripture he produced and the church he built. The first Mormons erected temples for ritual worship and a theocracy modeled upon ancient Israel in Utah while fervently testifying of Christian soteriology. The movement imitated the mixture of priestly and prophetic attributes in Smith himself, a prophet who claimed ecclesiological authority.[5]

The LDS Church, headquartered in Salt Lake City, Utah, and into which Gill was born, is by far the largest of the Mormon movements. It suffers from no shortage of competitors, however. Many of these are associated with polygamy, a practice Joseph Smith introduced in the LDS Church in the last years of his life but which that church renounced in 1890. Most famously,

---

Mormon will follow standard chapter-verse format. Citations to the Book of Jeraneck, which is not divided according to verse, will be parenthetical: (chapter, page number).

4. Matthew Philip Gill, Book of Prophecies and Revelations (Derbyshire, UK: Times and Seasons Press, 2008), 3–12, 33–39. This name change perhaps had to do with a legal contest with the LDS church. See https://therestoredbranchofchrist.blogspot.com/2019/11/our-prophet-is-not-ill-and-continues-to.html.

5. For many interpreters, this is a contradiction in terms, though it is a paradox that captures nicely the ongoing religious tensions of the Mormon movement. See, for example, the first two chapters of Walter Bruggeman, *The Prophetic Imagination* (Minneapolis, MN: Fortress Press, 2001); and Richard Bushman, *Joseph Smith: Rough Stone Rolling* (New York: Knopf, 2005).

the Fundamentalist Church of Jesus Christ of Latter Day Saints and several other groups that have appeared in the last half of the twentieth century—the True and Living Church of the Last Days (TLC), a small but sturdy organization led by the prophet Jim Harmston of Manti, Utah; the Church of the Firstborn of the Fullness of Times, headed by the charismatic LeBaron family of Mexico and Salt Lake City; and multiple other groups—either never rejected the practice or have picked it up again. However, the Community of Christ, formerly the Reorganized Church of Jesus Christ of Latter-day Saints, the largest of the LDS Church's competitors, has historically rejected polygamy, and Matthew Philip Gill denies that Joseph Smith ever practiced it. The luridness of polygamy tends to obscure other, deeper, dynamics that drive Mormon schism. Gill's movement is a useful test case, for it reveals that the tensions that produce schism have been in Mormonism's own DNA since its founding. They rest at levels far more profound than a single practice, deep in the ways in which Mormonism interacts with the culture around it.[6]

The course that young Matthew Gill attempted to follow was implemented in the church through the late nineteenth and early twentieth centuries. It is common for scholars to describe that trajectory using the terminology of Max Weber: a classic case of the routinization of charisma that overtakes religions as they age. According to this narrative, after the death of Joseph Smith, followers who had constructed a religious identity around his charismatic authority were forced, ultimately, to discard that sectarian impulse. They survived the traumas of Smith's death and integration into the American polity through reinventing themselves as a church, with a patriarchal bureaucratic hierarchy and a practical emphasis on cultural, social, and economic respectability rather than charismatic leadership. This interpretation reads schismatic groups as protests against the LDS Church's efforts to integrate with the society around it—with polygamy generally invoked as the leading example.

Examining the LDS Church more closely indicates that such a teleological reading of its past is insufficient, because, as some observers have noted, the sectarian tendency within the church itself remains potent. Some scholars call the church "strict"; it demands a great deal of its members, crowding

6. On the host of what one scholar calls restoration movements, see Steven Shields, *Divergent Paths of the Restoration* (Independence, MO: Herald House, 1990), as well as Newell Bringhurst and John Hamer, eds., *Scattering of the Saints: Schism within Mormonism* (Independence, MO: John Whitmer Books, 2007).

out competition from the culture around it. Other scholars, such as Armand Mauss and Jan Shipps, have suggested that it is more useful to understand these movements in terms of a continuum of tension, rising and falling with the surrounding culture rather than in terms of a church-sect polarity. They argue that the LDS Church is in a continuous state of negotiation with its surroundings, oscillating along a spectrum of resistance, tension, and accommodation, balancing the demands of the world (as Saints call it) with the impulse to preserve a distinct identity.

The revelation of Matthew Philip Gill, then, cannot be explained as simply another sectarian divergence from an institutional church grown comfortable with the culture in which it lives because that church itself is not so settled. Nor does Gill's vigorous rejection of polygamy and other embarrassing features of historical Mormonism the LDS church struggles with as it has sought assimilation mean his movement quite fits the parameters of the "church movement," the splinter group paring away the awkward distinctions of its parent in a bid for increased integration with the surrounding society. Gill reflects the paradoxes of his mother organization. He combines such gestures with an embrace of charismatic authority, spurning much of the LDS bureaucracy in favor of direct spiritual experience and calling for his followers to withdraw from mainline society.[7]

Gill's movement reveals the extent to which the dynamics of Mormon schism reflect the complicated cultural dynamics of the LDS Church itself and thus the ways in which all Mormon new religious movements draw upon the tradition. The Restored Branch is best understood as a practical attempt to reinvigorate what Gill perceives to be the increasingly strained methods of Mormon faith and practice, to adjust the balance of tension both within and without the church, and thus it tells us as much about these things in LDS Mormonism as it does about the new religious movement itself. Because Gill

7. On the church-sect typology, see S. N. Eisenstadt, ed., *Max Weber on Charisma and Institution Building* (Chicago: University of Chicago Press, 1968), 48–66; Ernst Troeltsch, *The Social Teachings of the Christian Churches*, trans. Olive Wyons ([1911] Louisville: Westminster/John Knox, 1992), 691–694; and the general argument of H. Richard Niebuhr, *The Social Sources of Denominationalism* (New York: Holt, 1929). In particular, I use Benton Johnson, "On Church and Sect," *American Sociological Review* 28, no. 4 (1963):539–549. On Mormonism's relationship to that typology, Jan Shipps, *Mormonism: The Story of a New Religious Tradition* (Urbana: University of Illinois Press, 1984); and Thomas Alexander, *Mormonism in Transition: A History of the Latter-day Saints, 1890–1930* (Urbana: University of Illinois Press, 1986).

is not merely adapting to a monolithic culture but also to the presence of the
LDS Church, his wrestling with the concept of tension should be seen as a
triangulation rather than two points on a pole: he watches the LDS Church
move, and reacts to it, seeking to resolve its contradictions and to create a
place for the sacred that appeals to him and his followers.

His balance of tension and accommodation with the culture around
him is sometimes contradictory and paradoxical, but these internal incon-
sistencies illustrate the specific issues and challenges that characterize one
moment in Mormon history: Gill grapples particularly with the challenges
that face the LDS Church in the late twentieth and early twenty-first centuries. Most obviously, his movement and his work of scripture reflect the
growing pains of an expanding movement. As Mormonism gains increasing
numbers of converts outside the United States, assimilating non-American
converts into a very American faith has created dissonance of culture, theology, and practice. Similarly, as Mormonism has increasingly participated
in the intellectual and communication revolutions of modern life, Mormons
have faced challenges from academic history and the problem of assimilating their patterns of worship in a technological age. Gill's scripture, which
sacralizes the British Isles just as the Book of Mormon does the American
continent—as well as his revisionist history of the founding of Mormonism—opens alternatives of sacred place and sacred time, which he hopes will
preserve traditionally Mormon patterns of piety against the unsatisfactory
solutions that he believes the LDS Church offers.

The Restored Branch remains small. Gill is reluctant to report precise
numbers, but a tally of people mentioned in the various media produced by
the church places its membership at around twenty, including a large contingent of his family. Indeed, Gill's first converts were his father Philip and
his friend David Smith, followed soon by the rest of his family. To this core,
Gill has begun to add other converts, some of whom have discovered his
movement through his website. Such small, self-selected organizations are
sociologically typical schismatic movements. Indeed, what one historian has
called the "family church" is the sort of sturdy foundation that has catapulted
many new religious movements to success, including Joseph Smith's.[8] Gill

8. Rodney Stark, *The Rise of Christianity: How the Obscure, Marginal Jesus Movement Became the Dominant Religious Force in the Western World in a Few Centuries* (New York: HarperCollins, 1997).

would find the comparison significant, because he sees his own church as the true inheritor of Smith's movement, and, as such, he seeks to preserve in his movement the Mormon religious narratives and practices with which he grew up.

THE LDS CHURCH AND CULTURAL TENSION

It has become a cliché among students of Mormonism to say the tradition does not have a theology but rather a history. That is, its claims to unique authority and religious truth are bound more deeply in the events of its own sacred past than in systematic theology or doctrine. As Jan Shipps has observed, Latter-day Saints depend primarily upon a specific type of narrative piety. Their devotional lives are centered around retelling and reenacting sacred stories through sacred narrative, and, in particular—drawing from the categories of Mircea Eliade—narratives that connect them into sacred time and sacred place, and hence, to the divine. Latter-day Saints are encouraged to think about their spiritual lives in terms of narrative archetype, and to imitate in their own lives a collection of sacred stories about Smith and scriptural figures in expectation of similar divine encounters. Collectively, the claims of the various branches of the LDS tradition rest upon a certain way of telling the history of Smith's life, visionary experiences and actions, as well as those of his successors.[9]

The business of maintaining healthy tension between the LDS faith and the world has therefore been that of modifying these sacred stories, revisiting and revising the sacred time and space that keep Mormonism vital. The most profound revision was that necessitated by the abandonment of polygamy. In the late twentieth century, the Saints revisited the life of Joseph Smith, now emphasizing—in historical novels, church-sponsored films and other

9. Shipps, *Mormonism*, 88–94; see also Mircea Eliade, *The Sacred and the Profane: The Nature of Religion*, trans. Willard Trask (New York: Harper, 1959); and Richard Bushman, "Joseph Smith and the Creation of the Sacred," in *Joseph Smith Jr.: Reappraisals after Two Centuries*, edited by Reid Neilson and Terryl Givens (New York: Oxford University Press, 2009). On this memetic piety, see, for instance, *True to the Faith: A Gospel Reference* (Salt Lake City UT: The Church of Jesus Christ of Latter-day Saints, 2004), 90. This is a small dictionary of theological and scriptural terms issued to the general membership of the church. "For your testimony of the restored gospel to be complete, it must include a testimony of Joseph Smith's divine mission. The truthfulness of The Church of Jesus Christ of Latter-day Saints rests on the truthfulness of the First Vision and the other revelations the Lord gave to the Prophet Joseph."

productions, Sunday school manuals, and the like—his romantic relation-ship with his first wife Emma, a revision coinciding with a public relations effort to deny the claims of polygamous groups like the FLDS to historical connection with the term "Mormon."[10]

The abandonment of polygamy also shattered old narratives of sacred space. Smith's church was founded upon the Book of Mormon, which derives much of its sacred power from replicating the key stories of the Bible, such as a chosen people guided by God to a promised land and the appearance of Jesus Christ on the American continent. Joseph Smith famously located the Garden of Eden in a Missouri valley and taught that the New Jerusalem would be built in North America. While early Mormons in the American West built an independent religious community, this sacralization of the United States allowed the LDS Church to embrace patriotism convincingly when it was forced to abandon the theocracy that supported polygamy in the Utah territory. Declarations that the United States was founded of divine inspiration are still common among the church's leadership, and Smith's Eden is a popular tourist site.[11]

In part because of this heritage, cultural adaptation to non-American settings can best be described as deliberate. By policy, Latter-day Saints in Angola, Argentina, and Armenia attend services in the suits and skirts of middle-class America, sing the same hymns as nineteenth-century Saints in Utah, and receive direction from Salt Lake City via satellite. Yet in some places, the LDS Church's strategies have begun creating dissonance within as well as outside the fold. These narratives, then, have become a source of both discord and strength. Outside the United States, the church struggles to retain converts. After all, Americans are now merely a plurality among the church's membership, whose numbers are growing most quickly in South America. The descendants of polygamy are now vastly outnumbered

10. Stephen Taysom, "A Uniform and Common Recollection: Joseph Smith's Legacy, Polygamy, and the Creation of Mormon Public Memory, 1852–2002," *Dialogue* 35, no. 3 (Fall 2002):113–144. For an example of the process in official church publications, see the Sunday school manual *Teachings of the Prophet Joseph Smith* (Salt Lake City, UT: The Church of Jesus Christ of Latter-day Saints, 2007).

11. Mauss, *The Angel and the Beehive*, 46–59. For Adam-ondi-Ahman, the name Smith gave to his Eden, and its present status among Latter-day Saints, see, generally, Michael Madsen, "The Sanctification of Mormonism's Historical Geography," *Journal of Mormon History* 34, no. 2 (Spring 2008):228–259; more particularly, LaMar C. Berrett, ed., *Sacred Places: A Comprehensive Guide to Early LDS Historical Sites*, vol. 4, *Missouri* (Salt Lake City, UT: Deseret Books, 2003), 380–388; and Robert J. Matthews, "Adam-ondi-Ahman," *BYU Studies* 13, no. 1 (Autumn 1972):27–35.

by first- and second-generation converts. The Mormon story is still largely told, even by historians, as a uniquely American heroic narrative of Smith himself, an uneducated young man who, inspired by faith, became perhaps the shining example of the egalitarian optimism of Jacksonian America. Matthew Gill feels these tensions acutely, and, even as he works to maintain what is unique about Mormonism, he seeks also to decenter the sacred space and sacred time that the LDS Church has created to preserve devotion in favor of his own strategies for attaining Mormon patterns of piety.[12]

MATTHEW PHILIP GILL AND CULTURAL TENSION

Even a cursory scan of the writings, practices, and rhetoric of the Restored Branch of Christ illustrates its deep commitment to traditional Mormon narratives. But this dependence serves a purpose. Rodney Stark and William Bainbridge have argued that leaders of new movements like Gill are religious "entrepreneurs." They reframe and modify existing theology and practice to fit historically particular needs, creating a synthesis that, as James Lewis has argued, appeals to converts precisely because of its association with authoritative figures. Gill's reliance upon the stories of Joseph Smith is more than mere calculation. Rather, his movement exists because of his hunger for the unique sort of spirituality that Mormon piety offers.[13]

In Gill's Book of Prophecies and Revelations, he pleads with his Latter-day Saint readers: "I'm not asking you to go apostate. I'm not asking you to deny the gospel is true, in fact all I have said reinforces the gospel position." He extends "an invitation to all those people who feel lost within the Mormon church that is out there.... We have a lot to offer you here.... Come and see us. We have people in our church who felt disenfranchised in the LDS Church." Gill's emphasis that joining his church is not to become "apostate" speaks to his desire to preserve continuity with Mormonism, but his

---

12. Philip Jenkins, "Letting Go: Understanding Mormon Growth in Africa," *Journal of Mormon History* 35, no. 2 (2009):1–27; Jehu Hanciles, "Would That All God's People Were Prophets: Mormonism and the New Shape of World Christianity," in *From the Outside Looking In: Essays on Mormon History, Theology, and Culture*, edited by Reid L. Neilson and Matthew J. Grow (New York: Oxford University Press, 2015), 353–383.

13. Rodney Stark and William Bainbridge, *A Theory of Religions* (New York: Peter Lang, 1987), 169; James Lewis, *Legitimating New Religions* (New Brunswick, NJ: Rutgers University Press, 2003), 73–87.

plea to those who feel "lost" makes clear that he knows his best targets are those Latter-day Saints for whom the LDS Church's balance of tension and accommodation ceases to be effective. He seeks to preserve, not destroy, and promises a renewal of Mormon spirituality rather than a departure.[14]

In the LDS Church, the stories of Smith's religious experiences are taught to children as models to follow, enshrined as evangelizing tools in missionary handbooks, and canonized in the selection of LDS scripture known as Joseph Smith—History. The history states that Smith's teenage First Vision of the Father and the Son, granted in response to his prayer about which church could save his soul, convinced him that a new faith must come forth to ensure human salvation. LDS converts and youths today are taught to seek their own spiritual confirmation in Smith's mission as a first step toward their own redemption (Joseph Smith—History 1:35). These are the models Gill himself emulates. Robert Alter, scholar of the Hebrew Bible, argues that the repetition of forms, stories, and phrases that appears in biblical narrative is not accidental but a strategy to make the mundane holy and typological. Alter's observations also reflect the ways Mormons seek the holy through echoing sacred narratives and scripture in their speech and thought patterns. Latter-day Saints pray, for example, in the archaic language and phrases of the King James Bible, which is also the language of the Book of Mormon. They bear testimony of their faith and spiritual experiences in formulaic phrases and patterns, often borrowing scriptural formulations. Such reiteration binds the religious experience of the average Saint into the historical experiences of Joseph Smith and into scripture itself through the covers of books and the reach of time into one great web of typology, allusion, and repetition. Thus, Gill's services, which he broadcasts on the internet, will seem familiar to LDS watchers. In a 2008 meeting, for instance, Gill's mother spoke of becoming emotional and, in a particularly Mormon idiom, "feeling the spirit" at the baptism of a convert videotaped for online broadcast. The prayers offered in meetings use traditional, if not quite scriptural, LDS rhetoric, such as the opening "Our Heavenly Father, we thank you for this day," and other standardized phrases.[15]

14. Gill, Book of Prophecies and Revelations, 26; Matthew Philip Gill, "Beliefs of the Latter day Church of Jesus Christ," http://thelatterdaychurchofchrist.blogspot.com.

15. Robert Alter, *The Art of Biblical Narrative* (New York: Basic Books, 1981), especially 47–63. Alter uses the term "type-scene" in which repetition of particular features in similar events reference

Gill's converts also follow Mormon patterns of devotional behavior. The early Mormon apostle Parley Pratt, for instance, converted after simply reading the Book of Mormon. He said, "As I read, the Spirit of the Lord was upon me, and I knew and comprehended that the book was true."[16] Gill believes that the Book of Jeraneck, the scripture he claims to have received through revelation, is intended to be a locus of this sort of personal devotion. "We encourage people to read and pray about it, because that's the only way you're going to get a testimony of it," he says. David Smith, who served as a scribe in the translation process, makes the comparison explicit. Reading the Book of Jeraneck, Smith says, "makes me feel not totally different compared to the Book of Mormon, but there's a stronger spiritual impression that comes from that than reading the Book of Mormon."[17]

While both works are acknowledged as scripture, Gill and his followers understand the Book of Jeraneck to be more relevant in their religious lives than any of the other standard works because of their proximity to its production. Smith's experiences reflect a particularly Mormon hermeneutical style like that of conservative evangelicals: reading with a sense of relevancy, a conviction that scripture was written particularly for contemporary believers, that its contents are uniquely applicable to their lives, and that those who read it will unavoidably feel that power. Indeed, the Book of Mormon claims its ancient authors were prophetically aware of their modern readers and wrote particularly for their benefit (e.g., Mormon 8:34, 2 Nephi 25:21). Latter-day Saints are taught to mine its verses for phrases taken as divine advice directed to them. When the redactor Jeraneck claims, "I have seen your day" (1,1), it signals that his scripture slips nicely into the Mormon hermeneutic to which Gill is heir. Thus, the "Testimony of Matthew Philip Gill" opens with a

each other and thus endow each with significance. On typology, which, strictly speaking, refers to scriptural events understood as prefiguring Christ, see Hans W. Frei, *The Eclipse of Biblical Narrative: A Study in Eighteenth and Nineteenth Century Hermeneutics* (New Haven, CT: Yale University Press, 1974); David Knowlton, "Belief, Practice, and Rhetoric: The Mormon Practice of Testimony Bearing," *Sunstone* 15, no. 1 (April 1991):20–27. Allyson Gill and Vicki Gill, "Testimony Meeting," http://thelatterdaychurchofchrist.blogspot.com, May 4, 2008. On LDS prayer, see also Caroline Gilkey, "Verbal Performance in Mormon Worship Services" (PhD diss., University of Pennsylvania, 1994), 33–37.

16. Parley Pratt, *The Autobiography of Parley P. Pratt* ([1874] Salt Lake City, UT: Deseret Books, 1995), 20.

17. Matthew Philip Gill, "Introduction to the Book of Jeraneck," February 6, 2008, http://thelatterdaychurchofchrist.blogspot.com; cf. *Preach My Gospel*, 111; David Smith, "Interview with the Apostle David Smith," May 31, 2008, http://thelatterdaychurchofchrist.blogspot.com.

paean to his parents, who "were the making of me for it was from them that I learnt how to commune with God."[18] Such sentiments are familiar to LDS ears, for children are taught to cultivate their own "testimonies" and to begin them with expressions of appreciation for families. But the structure runs deeper to what Mark Thomas calls "the autobiographical form," whose roots in Mormon narrative lie simultaneously in the canonized autobiography Joseph Smith—History—which begins with a description of Smith's childhood—and the opening sentence of the Book of Mormon: "I, Nephi, having been born of goodly parents, therefore I was taught somewhat in all the learning of my father" (1 Nephi 1:1). A Saint who hears the word "testimony" and a formulaic opening anticipates a familiar sacred narrative, one that echoes both scripture and Joseph Smith. Gill's narrative thus prepares the LDS reader to consider his story in the category of sacred narrative.[19]

The method of scripture study and prayer that Moroni's promise lays out is perhaps the most well known of LDS spiritual formulas, and it is no accident that Gill chooses to begin his own story with an enactment of this rite of passage. Like any other young Latter-day Saint, he asked God for quiet confirmation. But instead, he jumped the rails, shifting narratives to that of founder rather than follower, from type to archetype. Rather than a mere burning in the bosom, Gill received an angelic visitation, which he describes in phraseology and imagery that echo Smith's own boyhood visions: the sense of an evil force dispelled by "light gathering," a descending personage from an unclear space above.[20]

After this initial experience, the roster of Gill's divine visitors recapped those of Smith's own life: John the Baptist, Peter, James and John, Jesus Christ himself. In Smith's life, these visions extended further divine authority to him, culminating with a vision of Christ in the Kirtland, Ohio, temple, the first such building Smith erected. Gill experienced these visions in the same ascending order, though they culminated not in Christ but in a vision of Joseph Smith himself in August 2006. This addition makes Gill's story the

18. Matthew Philip Gill, "The Testimony of Matthew Philip Gill," preface to The Book of Jeraneck (Derbyshire, UK: Times and Seasons Press, 2004), i.

19. Brian Malley, How the Bible Works: A Study in Evangelical Biblicism (Lanham, MD: Altavista Press, 2004), 83–87; William Russell, "Beyond Literalism," in The Word of God, edited by Dan Vogel (Salt Lake City, UT: Signature Books, 1990), 43–54; Mark Thomas, Digging in Cumorah: Reclaiming Book of Mormon Narratives (Salt Lake City, UT: Signature Books, 2000), 17.

20. Gill, Book of Prophecies and Revelations, 4.

logical extension of Smith's. In contrast to the regularized succession pattern of LDS leadership, Gill claimed the immediate authority of Joseph Smith's charismatic religious experience. This, of course, is a classic invocation of charismatic authority of the sort Max Weber and other scholars have outlined. It is effective in Gill's case because it employs patterns of piety already firmly established within Mormonism.

Gill also emulates the LDS church's use of the internet and digital media. Increasingly, scholars have observed that—contrary to early suspicions—the internet can be an effective medium for religious conversion and experience, pointing to it as a venue for creative new religious expression and interaction. Mirroring this emerging scholarly consensus, the LDS Church started with a website, adding video, and most recently social media. As Brenda Weber argues, it is quite aware of what she calls "mediated Mormonism"—the associations, imagery, and semiotics surrounding the church in American culture—and has sought many paths of influence. Often, though, given the church's centralized authority, its efforts are closely managed, and "mediated Mormonism" is the product as much of individual church members or interested others as of the church itself.[21]

The Restored Branch might be seen as one of these eclectic interpretations of Mormonism online. The Branch's online presence has grown with the internet, developing from a blog (http://thelatterdaychurchofchrist .blogspot.com/) to a website (www.restoredbranch.com; the blog entries remain archives on the website). Far from a sense of impersonal institutional information, the Branch's site treats those who encounter it as fellow worshipers, not observers. On October 27, 2007, for example, the church's weblog announced a decision to broadcast video, stating, "If people want to join us live then they can do so by logging on at a certain time on Sunday morning and joining us for the meeting live in real time." Frequently, the speakers in such video services make references to those "attending online,"

21. On the transformation of religions' engagement with the Internet, see Lorne Dawson and Douglas Cowan, "Introduction," in *Religion Online: Finding Faith on the Internet*, edited by Lorne Dawson and Douglas Cowan (New York: Routledge, 2013), 1–17; J. F. Mayer, "Religious Movements and the Internet: The New Frontier of Religious Controversies," in *Religion on the Internet: Research Prospects and Promises*, edited by Jeffrey K. Hadden and Douglas E. Cowan (London: JAI Press, 2000), 249–276; see also Colleen McDannell, *Sister Saints: Mormon Women since the End of Polygamy* (New York: Oxford University Press, 2018), 173–195; Brenda Weber, *Latter-day Screens: Gender, Sexuality, and Mediated Mormonism* (Durham, NC: Duke University Press, 2019), 22–29.

addressing them directly, blurring the normal distinctions of worship space and the observer/participant divide that scholars have assumed the internet creates. Gill also posts video of himself or other church officials looking directly into the camera and answering questions received via email, using the internet to simulate conversations that turn all viewers into the sincere inquirers Gill presumes he is addressing. Unlike the leaders of the LDS church, who appear on the LDS website in carefully mediated and curated video and photographs, always dressed in dark suits and delivering scripted content, Gill frequently appears on his site unscripted and casual, wearing T-shirts with commercial logos, scribbling on a whiteboard, and answering viewers' questions.[22]

Gill believes the internet can be a successful medium of Mormon spiritual experience. Indeed, the church's first convert outside Gill's own circle of acquaintances, a man named Michael Clarke, says that reading the Book of Jeraneck online "helped me to understand that in times like Jeraneck's time and now that God will protect us." For Clarke, the online text of Gill's scripture reproduced the experience of Parley Pratt and countless other Mormons converted through reading. Clarke first learned of Gill's movement via the weblog. As he says, "I had a good feeling inside me, so I read and watched the videos on it and learnt about a new Prophet in our time." Clarke himself then sought out Gill, rather than the other way around, indicating the internet in his case was able to provide the sort of passionate engagement with religion that conversion requires. Gill's mother Allyson reported a similar experience, recalling a convert's baptism. "And for those who are listening on the web, you can see it on YouTube. And even seeing it on YouTube I started to cry." Gill relies upon this sort of user-driven missionary work. He consistently encourages curious web visitors to email, to call, to get in touch to request scripture. The Branch savvily uses social media, having attracted, as of August 2020, more than 3,000 followers on Facebook—numbers that far exceed the Branch's actual membership. Gill has great confidence in the possibilities of the internet, stating, "We hope that you are enjoying the video presentations and that you feel that you are gaining something form [*sic*] watching them." His use of the internet thus draws upon Weber's notion of

22. Matthew Philip Gill, "Questions and Answers," March 5, 2008, http://thelatterdaychurchofchrist .blogspot.com; Matthew Philip Gill, "Video Archive," August 9, 2020, www.restoredbranch.com.

"mediated Mormonism," seeking to create an image of itself in ways that encourage web surfers to become converts and reversing traditional models of proselytizing. Gill's strategy is the result of both theological and socio-logical reasoning, an impulse to adapt ineffable religious experience to the mediums of twenty-first-century communication.[23]

JERANECK AND MORMON

The Book of Jeraneck was originally produced in 2006. In 2015, it was com-bined with a smaller work, the Book of Rayaneck, and retitled the Chronicles of the Children of Araneck. I will use the earlier name throughout here. It is Gill's crowning prophetic accomplishment, not least because it exemplifies a very Mormon piety. Latter-day Saints of the early twenty-first century give scriptural priority to the Book of Mormon. They understand it to be a clari-fier, commentator, and interpreter to the Bible, the work that presents God's truth most clearly. However, it is also deeply dependent upon the Bible in a mimetic way. It quotes or paraphrases the Bible on more than 1,000 occa-sions, roots its plot in Biblical history, and echoes in types, that is, scenes, its most sacred events. It uses this relationship to justify both its existence and Joseph Smith's role as a prophet. The questions it asks and its claimed right to answer depends upon authority gained through its association with the powerful religious expressions of biblical Christianity. It reinvents, rather than manufactures, religion.[24]

The Book of Jeraneck functions in much the same way in relation to the Book of Mormon and is thus Matthew Gill's primary tool for reinventing Mormonism. Just as Gill presents himself as the culmination of Smith's pro-phetic mission, so is the book's existence proof. It weaves the multiplicity of Mormon sacred narratives, not only the forms and motifs and scenes of the ancient story of the Book of Mormon but also the sacred narrative of Joseph

---

23. Michael Clarke, "My Walk with Jesus," unpublished manuscript, 2008; Allyson Gill, "Testi-mony Meeting," May 4, 2008, http://thelatterdaychurchofchrist.blogspot.com; Matthew Philip Gill, untitled post, March 23, 2008, http://thelatterdaychurchofchrist.blogspot.com; www.facebook.com/restoredbranch, August 9, 2020.

24. Philip Barlow, *Mormons and the Bible: The Place of the Latter-day Saints in American Reli-gion* (New York: Oxford University Press, 1991), 224; Ezra Taft Benson, "The Book of Mormon Is the Word of God," *Ensign* 20, no. 1 (January 1988):2–5; Mark Thomas, *Digging in Cumorah: Reclaiming Book of Mormon Narratives* (Salt Lake City, UT: Signature Books, 2000), 17.

Smith's life. It thus legitimates Gill's attempts to emulate both in the present. The very fact of the Book of Jeraneck is a foundation upon which Gill can began to build his own Mormonism. But as Robert Alter notes, the key to finding meaning in types lies in the differences. Both the book and the prophet suffer from what literary critic Harold Bloom has called in poets "the anxiety of influence," the desire to replicate and yet separate oneself from predecessors. If the Book of Jeraneck were exactly like the Book of Mormon, it would serve little purpose to a prophetic reformer like Gill. While the forms, lessons, and typologies of the book revitalize the narratives of Mormon piety, they also give it the spiritual legitimacy Gill needs to confront those narratives and transform them.[25]

The Book of Jeraneck's emulation begins with its production. Joseph Smith claimed to have dictated the Book of Mormon to a set of scribes from plates delivered by the resurrected final author. The same is true for the Book of Jeraneck, delivered to Gill by Rayaneck, the final prophetic figure in the text. And like Joseph Smith, Matthew Gill presented his plates to witnesses who handled and testified of them. Gill claims to have used the Urim and Thummim, sacred devices mentioned in the Bible, to translate the book, devices that Smith also employed (Book of Jeraneck, ix–xi). Such parallels continue in the book's language. The Book of Jeraneck's language duplicates the stilted grammar of the Book of Mormon. It follows not the omniscient narration of the Bible but the personal, first-person voice of the Book of Mormon, a discourse deeply associated with Mormon spirituality. Its redacted structure, claiming to be the product of an ancient editor working many texts into a single prose narrative of exodus and civilization-building, models the Book of Mormon. Biblical and Book of Mormon characters, phrases, and type-scenes all make appearances in the pages of the Book of Jeraneck. It also emulates the Book of Mormon's structure. Both works claim to be a sacred narrative of a civilization produced by a godly redactor late in that civilization's history, writing in a nostalgic tone, for their civilizations are close to destruction because of wickedness. Both civilizations are established by the children of pilgrims, guided by God out of ancient Israel on the eve of a great

25. Alter, *The Art of Biblical Narrative*, 47; Harold Bloom, *The Anxiety of Influence: A Theory of Poetry* (New York: Oxford University Press, 1973), 5–19.

disaster, and brought to a new promised land, where they flourish and falter dependent upon their obedience to God, governed by prophet-kings.

In addition to imitating the Book of Mormon, the work also echoes the sacred history of Joseph Smith's life. The redactor Jeraneck opens his own story in the autobiographical form, writing, "I have been taught the Gospel of the Christ and the almighty God by my Father and Mother" (1,1). Jeraneck then tells us that in his youth, "I desired to know of many things." He went into "a great forest" to pray, and there "a great light gathered and I beheld in that light a personage and I became afraid and I was about to get to my feet and run when the personage spoke to me . . . and I stayed kneeling on the ground." We see in these words the shadowy images of both Nephi and Smith's First Vision, the stories so many Mormon children are raised on, but also that of the twelve-year-old Gill himself (Joseph Smith—History 1:14–17).

The blurring between the literary and the historical here is quite intentional. Gill marshals the imagery of Smith's scripture not only because he has absorbed its spiritual style but because it is Smith's prophetic legacy he seeks to fulfill. The origins of both books are tied inextricably to the supernatural experiences of the men who produced them, binding both prophets into the narratives they produce. The prophet's experience and the stories of the books are of a piece. The presence in their lives of heavenly messengers who are simultaneously characters in the texts—Moroni, Jeraneck—makes the two histories bleed into each other, become mutually reinforcing, and change the mundane history of the present age into an extension of a sacred, scriptural history. Reproducing Smith's accomplishment has been perhaps Gill's most important legitimating achievement, for it places him in Smith's prophetic mold and his movement in the providential iteration of history where Smith lived.

The book's ability to bridge the gap between sacred and secular history, to transform one into the other, is crucial because it means the stories of the Book of Jeraneck are legitimate grounds for reconceiving the relationship between Gill's version of the Mormon faith and the world around it. Indeed, Gill's attempts to re-vision the foundational narratives of Mormon sacred time and sacred space find their ultimate ground in that text, using its theological power to create revised stories of the Mormon past.

A NEW SACRED PLACE

The Book of Mormon provides Mormons a way to sacralize nationalistic rhetoric, but on a deeper level it presents the reader with a profoundly Christian American continent. Book of Mormon prophets from beginning to end are more unabashedly Christian than anyone in the Christian Bible. Christ's appearance to its people gives the New World a sacred Christian history to match the Old World's. Drawing upon this sacred history, American Latter-day Saints have understood their country to be blessed by God's favor—contingent upon righteousness (2 Nephi 1:6, 9). This is salvation translated from the merely spiritual into to the mundane worlds of politics and geography and has been extraordinarily effective among American members of the LDS Church, who have during a little more than a hundred years transformed themselves from theocratic separatists to some of the most patriotic of the citizens of the United States.

But as the LDS Church becomes increasingly international, the incongruity of such close identification of the faith with a particular place has become apparent. What meaning, scholar Laurie Maffly-Kipp asks, might the stories of the New York farm boy Joseph Smith about ancient Hebrew prophets in an American promised land have for Africans or Polynesians approached by Latter-day Saint missionaries?[26]

The LDS Church itself has pursued one possible solution. Since the 1950s, the principle of the "gathering," which urged converts to immigrate to the Salt Lake Valley, has been abandoned and the concept of Zion itself redefined: no longer is it a particular sacred ground but communion with other members in any location. All the world could thus be Zion, and sacred space expanded rather than contracted.[27]

Gill dismisses this as temporizing, a diffusion of the specific power of Mormon religiosity. The Book of Jeraneck revives particular sacred space in a way that both reproduces and, as Gill and his followers read it, contests the Book of Mormon. Its dominant theme, as in the Book of Mormon and even

26. Laurie Maffly-Kipp, "Tracking the Sincere Believer: Authentic Religion and the Enduring Legacy of Joseph Smith," in *Joseph Smith Jr.: Reappraisals after Two Centuries*, edited by Reid Neilson and Terryl Givens (New York: Oxford University Press, 2009), 175–201.

27. Gregory Prince and William Robert Wright, *David O. McKay and the Rise of Modern Mormonism* (Salt Lake City UT: University of Utah Press, 2005), 404.

the Bible, is God's rescue of a group of Israelites, whom he guides to a place all three texts describe as a "promised land" (1 Nephi 18:17; Exodus 12:25; Book of Jeraneck 4, 16). But as the Israelite's promised land was Canaan, and the Nephite's land in the Book of Mormon was the Americas, the People of Light in the Book of Jeraneck are brought from disaster—the collapse of the Tower of Babel—to the British Isles. Indeed, to underline the point of particularity and specificity, the leaders of the People of Light interact with figures in the Book of Mormon taken from the same disaster to a different continent. God has different plans for different peoples, it is implied, and Gill's iteration of Mormonism is British as Joseph Smith's was American.

The Restored Branch emphasizes this point. "Read the book of Jeraneck out in the open [in the British countryside]," Gill says, "because you do get a different perspective on the book."[28] Gill's rather pugnacious father, Philip, says similar.

> We also have the Book of Mormon, which tells of the dealings on the American continent of those people and their dealings with Jesus Christ. We also have the book of Jeraneck, which tells of another people, that left the plains of Shainar, which were in the Middle East, and which traveled through Europe, and eventually landed upon British shores, and set up cities and villages here in Britain at the time of Stonehenge, and that tells of those people's dealings with Jesus Christ. And don't be fooled. Christianity goes back a long long long way before mainstream Christian scholars will tell you that Christianity happened in Europe.[29]

The Book of Jeraneck, then, sacralizes the familiar and mundane world around the Restored Branch in the ways the Book of Mormon could for Joseph Smith's early church but is increasingly ineffective at achieving in a global church. Gill himself, for example, was confused and excited upon receiving the work, as he told his followers, "That never even crossed my mind that there would be a record from our own country, testifying of people's belief in Jesus Christ here." In the same meeting, his father Philip

28. Matthew Philip Gill, "Testimony Meeting."
29. Philip Gill, "Testimony Meeting."

FIGURE 16.1. The Book of Jeraneck explains that the monument known as Stonehenge is in fact the remnant of a central temple of an ancient Christian people in the British Isles, a teaching that mirrors the Book of Mormon's narrative of ancient Christian civilizations in the Americas. "What Once Was Holy," illustration by Mattew deWitte, the Book of Jeraneck. Courtesy Matthew Phillip Gill.

dismissed a point of LDS procedure, which demonstrated a similar awareness of regional differences: "Let others in the West do that. But for us, we're for the Lord, and we do it the Lord's way."[30]

Just as Joseph Smith could imagine the Book of Mormon prophets Moroni and Mormon walking in his backyard, Gill can imagine Jeraneck in his. The Book of Mormon explained many things to Joseph Smith in the Christian terms that shaped his world: the provenance of the Native Americans; the origins of the burial mounds that dotted his childhood landscapes; and the will of God for his new nation. Unlike the people in the Book of Mormon who still wandered Joseph Smith's America as Native Americans,

---

30. Matthew Philip Gill, "Zion's Camp Explained," February 15, 2008, http://thelatterday churchofchrist.blogspot.com; Philip Gill, "Testimony Meeting."

FIGURE 16.2. In the narrative of the Book of Jeraneck, as in the narrative of the Book of Mormon, an ancient Biblical people are led from destruction in the Near East to a new holy land by ship. This iteration of narratives is central to the Book of Jeraneck. The repetition implies not plagiarism but insight into the functioning of the divine. "Journey to the Sacred Island," illustration by Matthew de Witte, the Book of Jeraneck. Courtesy Matthew Phillip Gill.

the People of Light have not survived to populate the England of Matthew Philip Gill. The Book of Jeraneck, however, does offer its contemporary readers a visible sign, a signal of the sacred present in their landscapes. It is a remarkably consistent theme that runs throughout the book from the beginning, when God commands the people of Araneck, fleeing the Tower of Babel: "[M]ighty stone circles and monuments must be placed in all the lands they travel through" (2, 8). Throughout the Book of Jeraneck, these construction projects are a tangible symbol of the people's spiritual relationship to God, a means through which these two parties relate to each other. The narrator Jeraneck repeatedly invokes the construction of "monuments" to God as proof that the people seek his favor (6, 22), and the act of building "temples and places of worship" serves as a motif that indicates faithfulness (6, 25; 8, 31, 11, 50). The phrasing that describes the time of prosperity under the prophet Raynon is typical: "They farmed and built many beautiful buildings, and they made the land beautiful. And their children grew strong and became mighty men and women, true believers in the Almighty" (11, 50).

In this way, a sense of sacred location is even more pronounced in the Book of Jeraneck than in the Book of Mormon. The first structure the People of Light erect when they arrive in the British Isles is the "great temple" on the "plains of Shainnon" (6, 26). This is the central location of the history which follows. It is where all sacred ordinances were performed and serves as the locus of political power and the dramatic events of the narrative. Further, our narrator, Jeraneck, appears in the story right after the temple's construction to inform us, "It is the very same temple in which I, Jeraneck, do sit and compile the records of my father" (6, 26). That is, the great temple is not only the central location of the Book of Jeraneck but also the central location for us, as readers—the place where we are brought into the narrative. Such a sense of identification is only intensified when Matthew Philip Gill identifies the ruins of the great temple: the place today called Stonehenge. In this way, Gill inscribes Christianity into the prehistory of his own nation, just as Smith rewrote the history of the Native Americans. The solid stone evidence Gill can point to easily trumps the archaeologically elusive civilizations of the Book of Mormon. Like Smith before him, Gill has used his scripture to recenter God's focus in the world upon a single locale. As he teaches, reviving the principle of the gathering, "The Lord has ordained us to gather together in the British Isles."[31]

A NEW SACRED PAST

The narrative of the Book of Jeraneck follows closely that of the Book of Mormon. Though some might dismiss this as plagiarism, students of scripture might mark it with phrases such as "type-scene." The Book of Mormon follows the patterns of the Hebrew Bible, depicting a people falling into sin, war, and controversy, redeemed by prophets, and falling into sin again. So does the Book of Jeraneck. After the People of Light are guided to the British Isles, they begin worshipping God, only to find temptation in

---

31. Matthew Philip Gill, "Zion's Camp Explained," February 15, 2008, http://thelatterday churchofchrist.blogspot.com.

the worship of the pagan god Odinon, whose followers embrace cannibalism, destruction, and polygamy. The book is punctuated by three great wars with pagans and followers of Odinon. The last war sees the final destruction of the People of Light except for our scribe Jeraneck's son Rayaneck, who escapes with the record—just as Moroni, son of the Book of Mormon's compiler, Mormon, does in that text.

Members of the LDS church frequently quote the prophet Nephi from the Book of Mormon saying that he "did liken all scriptures unto us" (1 Nephi 19:23). Scripture in the Mormon tradition is taken as a model for one's life as well as for history. Likewise, Gill is no exception. He uses the Book of Jeraneck to retell the history of Mormonism itself.

Late in the Book of Jeraneck the fallen prophet Rendanoneck, a worshiper of Odinon, is said to have displeased God by taking multiple wives, defiling a temple by sleeping with them therein. Rendanoneck, we are told, "loved himself more than he loved God" (13, 59). He is eventually killed by righteous rebels. This contrasts with the somewhat more measured assessment of the practice in the Book of Mormon, which states that polygamy is forbidden unless God commands it (Jacob 2:24). Yet Gill argues that as scripture is normative for sacred history, Joseph Smith could never have embraced it.

Over the past several decades, the LDS Church has struggled to reconcile itself with the uncomfortable history of Joseph Smith's practice of plural marriage. For much of the twentieth century, polygamy was rarely discussed in official church venues and eliminated from devotional texts and manuals. But in the past twenty years, a number of church-sponsored historical projects—an edited collection of Joseph Smith's papers, a new official history of the church, and two official church statements on the practice—have sought to integrate Smith's marital history into official narratives of the past. This means the LDS Church has sacrificed some degree of control over its own past, upsetting older sacred narratives, causing some distress among members, and sparking a process of adaptation. At the same time, it has managed to decrease tension with academics and gain increased legitimacy.[32]

---

32. Taysom, "A Uniform and Common Recollection:," 140–144; Matthew Harris and Newell Bringhurst, eds., *The LDS Gospel Topics Series: A Scholarly Engagement* (Salt Lake City, UT: Signature Books, 2020).

Gill, however, turns the evidence on itself in service of a deeper religious narrative. He denies the difference between theology and history, emphasizing that by definition a prophet's life must follow what is described in scripture. Gill accepts that polygamy existed but argues that Joseph Smith died waging a losing battle against it. He declares, "There were a lot of things going on in the church that [Smith] could not control, that were out of his power, such as the spread of polygamy, which he fought all his life, and there's documented evidence to support that." Gill speaks the language of professional history, invoking "the evidence" and citing particular "sermons [Smith] gave and articles he wrote." Gill repeatedly makes much of a rather esoteric evidentiary fact: the number of surviving documents in which Smith denounces polygamy far outweigh in number the scattered primary sources that describe him engaging in it. Gill will stand with the Smith of his religious imagination, while on the other hand, he says, "the LDS Church backtracks."[33]

Despite this rhetoric, Gill is not marshalling all this evidence to make a historical argument, which would fail. Rather, Smith's inspired but ultimately unsuccessful war against polygamy is a sacred founding story of Gill's own, one with scriptural typology and one that can match the common Mormon narrative of the "Great Apostasy," in which the early Christian church, seeking to curry the favor of imperial Rome, lost priesthood authority and fell into ignorance. As he observes, after Smith's death, "The Lord did not want a successor appointed because the Saints had proven inadequate . . ." Gill thus has constructed an idealized Mormon past that many Latter-day Saints might secretly wish they could possess, one that follows a familiar sacred cycle of history: apostasy and restoration. In a similar fashion, to questions of gender Gill offers not historical analysis but a simple return to the authoritative sacred scriptural past.[34]

Gill's uncompromising stand on the issue reverses the LDS position. He raises the stakes and willingly sacrifices the accommodation the LDS

33. Matthew Philip Gill, "God Chooses Prophetic Leadership," unpublished manuscript, 2005; Matthew Philip Gill, "Beliefs and Practices of the Latter day Church of Jesus Christ," March 21, 2008, http://thelatterdaychurchofchrist.blogspot.com.

34. Gill, "Questions and Answers." On the LDS apostasy narrative, see Miranda Wilcox and John Young, eds., Standing Apart: Mormon Historical Consciousness and the Concept of Apostasy (New York: Oxford University Press, 2014).

Church has gained in pursuit of a sacred narrative of Joseph Smith's career unsullied by things that Mormons now find distasteful. At the same time, he adopts the authoritative modern veneer of footnotes. As with his sophisticated use of the internet, he uses his own religious imagination to revitalize traditional narratives of Mormon piety and propagates them through modern techniques.

CONCLUSION

Matthew Philip Gill moves fluidly in the sacred world Joseph Smith created. His great skill is his ability to focus the charismatic impulses of the nineteenth century upon the problems of the twenty-first. His revival of Smith's ideals— the gathering principle, abandoned by the LDS Church in the mid-twentieth century; the construction of a literal, millennial city of Zion in a real and physical sacred place; and the insistence upon a palpable sense of divinely ordained prophecy—all revive the tangible millennialism of early Mormonism, an impulse simultaneously urgent and optimistic, and an energy absent in the LDS Church today. Just as early Mormons expected an impending second coming of Christ, so does Philip Gill, his father, declare, "We want to gang together as a large group and prepare ourselves for the second coming of our Saviour, which is imminent, which is just around the corner."[35] Gill offers his followers a world in which the sacred is tangible, in both space and time, and to them, British children of contemporary Mormonism, more so than the LDS Church. Gill uses these strategies not only to assert prophetic authority but to work out his own religious experience, to solve the problems facing contemporary Mormonism with the tools that the tradition gave him. In this way, then, his new religious movement is really not very new at all.

35. Philip Gill, "The Personal Testimony of Elder Philip Gill," March 25, 2008, http://thelatterdaychurchofchrist.blogspot.com.

CONTRIBUTORS

Philip L. Barlow is associate director of the Neal A. Maxwell Institute for Religious Scholarship, Brigham Young University. He was previously the Leonard Arrington Chair of Mormon History and Culture at Utah State University. Barlow is the author of *Mormons and the Bible: The Place of Latter-day Saints in American Religion* (Oxford University Press, 1997) and coeditor of *The Oxford Handbook of Mormonism* (Oxford University Press, 2015). He received his ThD from Harvard University.

Christine Elyse Blythe is archives specialist, William A. Wilson Folklore Archives, L. Tom Perry Special Collections, Brigham Young University. She is president of the Folklore Society of Utah. Blythe received an MA in Folklore from Memorial University in Newfoundland.

Christopher James Blythe is assistant professor of English at Brigham Young University. He is the author of *Terrible Revolution: Latter-day Saints and the American Apocalypse* (Oxford University Press, 2020). Blythe received his PhD from Florida State University.

Matthew Bowman is the Howard W. Hunter Chair of Mormon Studies at Claremont Graduate University. He is the author of *The Mormon People: The Making of an American Faith* (Random House, 2012) and *Christian: The Politics of a Word in America* (Harvard University Press, 2018). He received his PhD from Georgetown University.

Jay Burton is an archivist for the Church History Library (The Church of Jesus Christ of Latter-day Saints), Salt Lake City, Utah. He holds an MLS from San Jose State University.

Thomas G. Evans is a scholar of religion. He received degrees from the University of Denver and Utah State University.

Kathleen Flake is the Richard Lyman Bushman Chair of Mormon Studies, University of Virginia. She is the author of *The Politics of Religious Identity: The Seating of Senator Reed Smoot, Mormon Apostle* (University of North Carolina Press, 2004). She received her PhD from the University of Chicago.

Casey Paul Griffiths is associate professor in Church History and Doctrine, Brigham Young University. He is the coauthor of *50 Relics of the Restoration* (Cedar Fort, 2020). Griffiths received his PhD from Brigham Young University.

Janiece Johnson is a Willes Center Research Associate, Neal A. Maxwell Institute for Religious Scholarship, Brigham Young University. She is the coauthor of *The Witness of Women: First-hand Experiences and Testimonies of the Restoration* (Deseret Book, 2016) and editor of *Mountain Meadows Massacre: Collected Legal Papers* (University of Oklahoma Press, 2017). Johnson received her PhD from the University of Leicester.

Laurie Maffly-Kipp is the Archer Alexander Distinguished Professor, John C. Danforth Center on Religion and Politics, Washington University in St. Louis. She is the author of *Religion and Society in Frontier California* (Yale University Press, 1994) and the editor of *American Scriptures* (Penguin, 2010). Maffly-Kipp received her PhD from Yale University.

Allen D. Roberts, FAIA, is a semiretired, award-winning architect, architectural historian, artist, and author in Salt Lake City, Utah. He is the coauthor of *Salamander: The Story of the Mormon Forgery Murders* (Signature Book, 1988).

Richard Saunders is an academic librarian, Gerald R. Sherrat Library, Southern Utah University. He is the author of *Printing in Deseret: Mormons, Economy, Politics, and Utah's Incunabula 1849–1851* (University of Utah Press, 2000) and editor of *Dale Morgan on the Mormons: Collected Works*, parts 1 and 2 (Arthur H. Clark Company, 2012 and 2013). Saunders received his PhD from the University of Memphis.

Christopher C. Smith is a scholar of religion. He has published in the *Journal of Mormon History, John Whitmer Historical Association Journal, Religion and Society*, and the *Claremont Journal of Mormon Studies*. He received his PhD from Claremont Graduate University.

Joseph M. Spencer is assistant professor of Ancient Scripture, Brigham Young University. He is the author of *An Other Testament: On Typology in the Book of Mormon* (Neal A. Maxwell Institute Press, 2016) and *The Vision of All: Twenty-five Lectures on Isaiah in Nephi's Record* (Greg Kofford Books, 2016). Spencer received his PhD from the University of New Mexico.

Daniel P. Stone is a researcher and archivist for a private archive. He is the author of *William Bickerton: Forgotten Latter Day Prophet* (Signature Books, 2018). Stone received his PhD from Manchester Metropolitan University.

Richard S. Van Wagoner was an award-winning historian. He was the author of *Sidney Rigdon: A Portrait of Religious Excess* (Signature Books, 1994) and *Mormon Polygamy: A History* (Signature Books, 1986).

Chrystal Vanel is a postdoctoral researcher, Groupe Sociétés, Religions, Laïcités, Paris. He has a PhD in Sociology (EPHE-Sorbonne), an MA in Religious Studies (EPHE-Sorbonne), and a BA in History (Paris 1-Sorbonne). His current research is on religious fissiparousness, Protestantisms, Mormonisms, and the margins of Protestantisms.

Steven C. Walker is Professor Emeritus of English, Brigham Young University. He is the coauthor of *A Book of Mormons* (Signature Books, 1982) and *Illuminating Humor in the Bible* (Cascade Books, 2013). He received his PhD from Harvard University.

INDEX

Universalism, 154, 274

Van Buren, Lewis, 178–79
Van Nostrand, James M., 174
visionary accounts (as category of LDS scripture), 9, 10–11

Walton, Bruce Alan ("Branton"), 342
Wardle, James, 284
Weber, Max, 114, 344, 346, 355–57
Welch, John (Jack), 88
Wentworth, John, 11
Wheaton, Clarence, 103–4
Wheelan, Jirah B., 174
Whitcomb, Edward, 174
White, Ellen, 21
whiteness (white), 8, 216, 232, 234, 322–23, 338
Whiting, Julian, 143
Whitmer, David, 16, 46, 53
Widtsoe, John A., 135
Willardson, Lyman, 335
Williams, Frederick G., 132
Wood, Samuel, 113–14
Woodruff, Wilford, 138, 187: Woodruff Manifesto, 139, 269, 276, 278, 284, 345
Word of Consolation to the Scattered Saints, A, 57

Word of the Lord, The (Baker): a call to repentance, 14; and modernity, 279–81; origins, 267, 271–79; reception, 281–88. *See also* Baker, Harry Edgar
Word of the Lord, The (Elijah Message), 14, 107–8
World War I (The Great War), 279–81

Young, Brigham: assigns Orson Pratt to update LDS canon, 119–21; and Bickerton, 217, 226–32; and the House of Aaron, 290, 313; and the Lectures on Faith, 142; and Lucy Mack Smith, 150; and Nephites, 256, 316; and the plurality of gods, 207, 209; and polygamy, 13, 32, 102, 224, 262; and succession debates, 43–45, 53–55, 100, 169, 221–25; western exodus, 28, 34, 48, 52, 254, 316

Zion: in Baker's thought, 277, 281; doctrine of gathering, 39, 45; in Gill's thought, 360; loss of, 124, 276; in Glendenning's thought, 294, 302; millennial, 122, 367; rebuilding of, 28, 57; in the Rigdons' thought, 14, 219, 222, 251–55; stake of, 171; Strang as King in, 184; in Thompson's Book of Enoch, 197
Zion's Camp, 203
Zion's Harbinger, 200, 203